The Image of Gender and Political Leadership

The Image of Gender and Political Leadership

A Multinational View of Women and Leadership

Edited by
MICHELLE M. TAYLOR-ROBINSON
AND NEHEMIA GEVA

OXFORD
UNIVERSITY PRESS

Oxford University Press is a department of the University of Oxford. It furthers
the University's objective of excellence in research, scholarship, and education
by publishing worldwide. Oxford is a registered trade mark of Oxford University
Press in the UK and certain other countries.

Published in the United States of America by Oxford University Press
198 Madison Avenue, New York, NY 10016, United States of America.

© Oxford University Press 2023

All rights reserved. No part of this publication may be reproduced, stored in
a retrieval system, or transmitted, in any form or by any means, without the
prior permission in writing of Oxford University Press, or as expressly permitted
by law, by license, or under terms agreed with the appropriate reproduction
rights organization. Inquiries concerning reproduction outside the scope of the
above should be sent to the Rights Department, Oxford University Press, at the
address above.

You must not circulate this work in any other form
and you must impose this same condition on any acquirer.

Library of Congress Cataloging-in-Publication Data
Names: Taylor-Robinson, Michelle M., editor. | Geva, Nehemia, 1946– editor.
Title: The image of gender and political leadership : a multinational view
of women and leadership / Michelle M. Taylor-Robinson and Nehemia Geva.
Description: New York, NY : Oxford University Press, 2023. |
Includes bibliographical references and index.
Identifiers: LCCN 2022054509 (print) | LCCN 2022054510 (ebook) |
ISBN 9780197642733 (paperback) | ISBN 9780197642726 (hardback) |
ISBN 9780197642757 (epub) | ISBN 9780197642764
Subjects: LCSH: Women political candidates—Cross-cultural studies. |
Women political candidates—Case studies. |
Political leadership—Cross-cultural studies. | Political leadership—Case studies. |
Young adults—Political activity—Cross-cultural studies. |
Young adults—Political activity—Case studies. |
Young adults—Attitudes—Cross-cultural studies. |
Young adults—Attitudes—Case studies.
Classification: LCC HQ1236.I45 2023 (print) | LCC HQ1236 (ebook) |
DDC 306.2082—dc23/eng/20230118
LC record available at https://lccn.loc.gov/2022054509
LC ebook record available at https://lccn.loc.gov/2022054510

DOI: 10.1093/oso/9780197642726.001.0001

Paperback printed by Marquis Book Printing, Canada
Hardback printed by Bridgeport National Bindery, Inc., United States of America

To Forest
To Anat

Contents

Acknowledgments	ix
Contributors	xi

PART I: MENTAL TEMPLATES OF LEADERS AND DESIGNING AN EXPERIMENT TO STUDY TEMPLATES

1. Mental Templates of Leaders   3
   Michelle M. Taylor-Robinson and Nehemia Geva

2. Research Protocol   22
   Nehemia Geva and Michelle M. Taylor-Robinson

PART II: FINDINGS IN INDIVIDUAL CASES

3. Costa Rica—Where Urban Young People View Women as Leaders   57
   Gerardo Hernández Naranjo and Michelle M. Taylor-Robinson

4. The Masculine Template in Perceived Competence of Women in
   Israeli Politics   77
   Ayala Yarkoney-Sorek and Nehemia Geva

5. Attitudes Toward Women in Government: Evidence from an
   Experiment in Canada's Alberta and Quebec Provinces   98
   Melanee Thomas, Valérie-Anne Mahéo, and Guillaume Bogiaris

6. Young Adults' Attitudes to Women Candidates in Uruguay:
   No Obstacle to Change   121
   Niki Johnson

7. England: Young People View Women as Leaders   141
   Claire Annesley, Beatriz Lacerda Ratton, and Jake Watts

8. Party over Gender: Young Adults' Evaluations of Political
   Leaders in California and Texas   162
   Kostanca Dhima and Jennifer M. Piscopo

9. A Generation Without Political Gender Biases?: The Case
   of Sweden   185
   Elin Bjarnegård, Josefina Erikson, and Pär Zetterberg

viii CONTENTS

10. Chile's Shift to the Left and the Rise of Women 205
    Alejandra Ramm, José Manuel Gaete, and Milena Morales Bonich

PART III: CROSS-NATIONAL FINDINGS AND CONCLUSIONS

11. Meta-Analysis Assessment of Candidate Gender as an
    Attribute of Young Adult Leadership Templates 229
    Michelle M. Taylor-Robinson and Nehemia Geva

12. Do Women Fit the Leadership Image? Yes! 252
    Michelle M. Taylor-Robinson and Nehemia Geva

References 261
Index 281

Acknowledgments

This project is an endeavor that has spanned several years, and it would not have been possible without the support of many, many people. The idea for the project came from Richard Matland's 1994 article in the *British Journal of Political Science* that presented the findings of an experiment that he conducted in Norway to study young people's attitudes about gender and leadership. Rick's experiment set a new standard for studying whether women are considered to be capable of political leadership because of the quantity and nuance of information provided to the study participants, and because he conducted his research outside of the United States in a country with a high level of women's representation. That experiment needed to be followed up with additional experiments in other countries. Pär Zetterberg and Taylor-Robinson in 2013 discussed that it would be interesting to conduct a similar study in Costa Rica and Sweden and began to pursue funding. Those conversations led to a Seed Grant from the College of Liberal Arts at Texas A&M University that funded the pilot study in Costa Rica and then the second pilot study in Israel. The success of the experiment in those two cases, with their contrasting results, enabled Taylor-Robinson and Geva to receive funding from the National Science Foundation to add six more countries (eight cases) to the study (NSF Grant # 1624370, "SBP: A Cross-National Experimental Study of Attitudes about Women in Government and Leadership"). We sincerely thank Brian Humes at NSF for his support for this complex project.

Funding was essential to conduct this multi-country experiment. However, the support of many people was equally essential. This volume would not have been possible without the participation of the 6,000+ young adults who took part in the experiment, along with the support of many university faculty and high-school teachers who allowed us to conduct the experiment with their classes. Equally essential is the hard work of the country collaborators who helped design the speeches for their case, obtained access to schools and classes where the study could be conducted, and found the assistants who worked in classrooms to implement the experiment. Without the many hours of work of the RAs in each country/location, it would not have been possible to collect the data for this project. We also must thank the country collaborators for continuing to support this project by taking part in a mini-conference in College Station to bring the volume together, preparing their chapters that interpret the experiment's findings within the context of their case, and for persisting with the project even with the delays the pandemic added to completing the volume.

X ACKNOWLEDGMENTS

Many scholars made this project better with their truly helpful comments at talks and conferences and in office conversations. At the project's inception we need to thank Kim Fridkin, Rick Matland, Catarina Thomson, and Rick Wilson for advice about the experiment's design, though of course any flaws in the design are purely our own. The project benefitted from insights offered by colleagues at the University of Costa Rica, the University of Salamanca in Spain, the University of Mannheim in Germany, and the University of Vermont. Beneficial and supportive feedback came from discussants and commentators at EGEN-Europe, and several APSA, MPSA, and ECPG conferences, including Amy Alexander, Michelle Dion, Jason Eichorst, Zachary Greene, Thomas Gschwend, Heather Hicks, Farida Jalalzai, Melody Valdini, and Catherine De Vries. Special thanks are due to Robin Devroe, Maria Escobar-Lemmon, Sarah Fulton, Diana O'Brien, Amy Pond, and Jane Sell for supportive feedback at the TAMU mini-conference on the volume, and for conversations whenever the project needed a new viewpoint. Brenna Armstrong, TAMU PhD candidate, also deserves our sincere thanks for her work taking detailed notes throughout the TAMU mini-conference, merging all ten datasets for the project (which was a huge task), and for providing support in many ways large and small throughout the writing and production of this volume. We also thank the anonymous readers of the manuscript for their many comments that truly improved the volume. In addition, we thank our editor, Angela Chnapko, at Oxford University Press, for her early advice on the volume and her continued support of the project throughout its development and production.

Thanks are also much needed for Elaine Tuttle—accountant extraordinaire. She navigated the complex process and competing bureaucracies of getting reimbursements to collaborators and salaries to research assistants in eight countries. She is amazing, and always smiled when we had requests—thank you Elaine.

We also thank our department at Texas A&M. It has been a big boon to this project to be able to work in such a supportive department, with its leadership, faculty, graduate students, and staff.

Finally, the support of our spouses was invaluable to our sanity while working on this lengthy project. Special thanks goes to Forest for not only providing emotional support, but also all types of project assistance, ranging from intellectual insights while we were writing the NSF grant, to logistical support and hard work to conduct the experiment in Costa Rica for a month, and support as we began the experiment and trained RAs in several of the other countries, to helping to input data, and making all the final figures and tables for the entire volume. Your support and help has made this volume possible.

College Station, Texas, November 2021

Contributors

Claire Annesley is Dean of Arts, Design and Architecture and Professor of Politics at the University of New South Wales.

Elin Bjarnegård is Associate Professor of Political Science at Uppsala University.

Guillaume Bogiaris is a strategic consultant in data management and governance for the Government of Quebec and Adjunct Professor of philosophy and humanities at Champlain Saint Lawrence College.

Kostanca Dhima is Assistant Professor of Political Science at Georgia State University.

Josefina Erikson is Associate Professor of Political Science at Uppsala University.

José Manuel Gaete is Profesor Adjunto in Sociology at the Universidad de Valparaíso Chile.

Nehemia Geva is Associate Professor of Political Science at Texas A&M University.

Gerardo Hernández Naranjo is Profesor Asociado of Political Science at the Universidad de Costa Rica.

Niki Johnson is Profesora Agregada of Political Science at the Universidad de la República, Uruguay.

Valérie-Anne Mahéo is Professeure adjointe of Political Science at the Université Laval.

Milena Morales Bonich is a Master's student in Social Sciences at the Universidad de Santiago de Chile.

Jennifer M. Piscopo is Associate Professor of Politics at Occidental College.

Alejandra Ramm is Profesora Adjunta in Sociology at the Universidad de Valparaíso Chile.

Beatriz Lacerda Ratton has a Masters in Migration Studies from the University of Sussex.

Michelle M. Taylor-Robinson is Professor of Political Science at Texas A&M University.

Melanee Thomas is Associate Professor of Political Science at the University of Calgary.

Jake Watts has a PhD in Politics from the University of Sussex and is studying law at the University of Law.

Ayala Yarkoney-Sorek is a Lecturer in the Government School at Reichman University.

Pär Zetterberg is Associate Professor of Political Science at Uppsala University.

PART I

MENTAL TEMPLATES OF LEADERS AND DESIGNING AN EXPERIMENT TO STUDY TEMPLATES

1

Mental Templates of Leaders

Michelle M. Taylor-Robinson and Nehemia Geva

Introduction

In recent years Germany's Chancellor Angela Merkel was called the de facto leader of the European Union.[1] Time Magazine named her "Person of the Year" in 2015. An essay for Carnegie Europe is titled "How Angela Merkel Has Redefined Leadership" (Ulrich 2017). Yet when Merkel began climbing the political ladder within the Christian Democratic Union, as Chancellor Kohl's minister of women and youth, the media called her *mein Mädchen* (Kohl's girl). When Merkel became Germany's first woman Chancellor in 2005, *Bild* newspaper ran a headline of "Miss Germany?" with Merkel's photograph, and she was expected to be a temporary leader, "holding that place until they could find a real CDU man to replace her" (Kottasová 2021 interview with Joyce Mushaben). In sum, the woman politician who in 2021 defined success as a global leader was initially not viewed as fitting the media's or her party hierarchy's ideas of a leader.

People have mental templates for common occupations, such as doctor, military officer, teacher, plumber. People also have mental templates for political leaders: legislator, cabinet minister, president/prime minister. A *New York Times* article titled "Picture a Leader: Is She a Woman?" (Murphy 2018) explained that when asked to "draw an effective leader," most people draw a man. So long as "male" is the common, even sub-conscious concept of leader, mental templates of leadership may help explain why women remain severely under-represented in most governments, even long established democracies.

Mental images of what the people who do certain jobs "look like" can be deeply embedded in society's past, and politics has a long history of male leaders. Just "Google" pictures of world leaders at an economic summit, or cabinet meetings—they will be overwhelmingly of men. Media images may shape voter expectations and help the political elites who nominate or appoint officials to justify keeping those offices filled with people like themselves.

---

[1] This research was funded by NSF Grant #1624370: "SBP: A Cross-National Experimental Study of Attitudes about Women in Government and Leadership" and by a Seed Grant from the College of Liberal Arts, Texas A&M University.

Michelle M. Taylor-Robinson and Nehemia Geva, *Mental Templates of Leaders* In: *The Image of Gender and Political Leadership*. Edited by: Michelle M. Taylor-Robinson and Nehemia Geva, Oxford University Press. © Oxford University Press 2023. DOI: 10.1093/oso/9780197642726.003.0001

4 MICHELLE M. TAYLOR-ROBINSON AND NEHEMIA GEVA

Yet templates can change. Change is predicted with increased exposure to more diverse kinds of people doing a job. If most doctors you encounter are women, why would your mental template of doctors be male? Similarly, if more politicians in the news these days are women, mental templates of political leaders may include women. With this project we examine mental templates of young adults because they are the group with the greatest proportion of their lives exposed to women in politics and in higher profile posts, be it in their own country or in influential countries.[2] A central expectation of the literature is that increased exposure to women in politics reduces gender bias regarding the perceived leadership potential of a candidate: both general ability of women to lead, and women's capacity to lead in diverse policy areas.

Social welfare policies are associated with home and family; the private domain that has traditionally been the domain of women, and social welfare government posts often provide an inroad for women into politics. However, the most powerful and prestigious policy areas within the public domain, such as defense and finance, are traditionally viewed as the domain of men. Accordingly, national policy context has much potential influence over whether gender is a central component of mental templates of leaders. Building on the literature's expectation that women are more accepted in gender-appropriate jobs, a national policy agenda focused on social welfare programs should be more conducive to leadership templates that do not emphasize gender than an agenda focused on defense.

In addition to country history and context, individuals within a country may have different views about who can lead. Individuals may identify in-groups, giving them increased affinity for a candidate, such as of their same sex or from their preferred party. As this study focuses on attitudes of young adults, home experience may influence their ideas about leaders. Observing one's mother operating outside the traditional norm that a woman's domain is the home could shape ideas about the capacity of women to be leaders. A son or daughter would be more likely to have a leadership template in which gender is not a central component if their mother has acquired resources that could translate into the political arena, such as extensive education or a high-status occupation. Individual "context may mediate the impact of institutional, structural, and cultural factors to promote or undermine the election of women" (Franceschet et al. 2012: 8).

We study leadership templates by conducting a randomized, factorial experiment between August 2014 and November 2018 with 6,324 young adults in eight strategically selected established democracies that vary with regard to type

---

[2] We thank Zachary Greene for the suggestion that young people's templates may be influenced by seeing women leaders in neighboring countries (also see Brooks 2013: 35, regarding US state governors).

and breadth of incorporation of women in government, national policy agenda, and institutional design. The countries are Canada, Chile, Costa Rica, England, Israel, Sweden, the United States, and Uruguay. The multi-national nature of this study is novel as most prior research has focused on one country, often the United States. Our multi-country design enables rigorous examination across countries of common assumptions that overcoming gender stereotypes about policy competence and broadening leadership templates to include women requires exposure to extensive incorporation of women in government.

In our experiment a man or a woman candidate (factor 1—Candidate Gender) gives a lengthy speech about positions of one of the two largest parties (factor 2—Party Platform), and the speech either states the name of the party or does not mention the party name (factor 3—Party Label). This design creates eight different speech types for each country, though the man and woman candidates from the same party have identical speeches. Participants are randomly assigned one speech and not told there are seven more types of speeches. After reading their speech they answer a questionnaire, including eighteen questions evaluating the candidate on ability in various posts, capacity to win votes, and to manage twelve policy areas. The party-specific effects measured (due to policy text from the party, or different exposure to the party name) serve as experimental controls against which the candidate gender effect is compared, allowing confirmation of the absence of an important gender effect when that is the case. The party effect also provides a baseline or context for cross-country analysis of data from parallel experiments conducted in diverse countries.

Mental Templates of Leadership

In psychology, leadership is often considered as a perceptual product or construct that represents an interface between our expectations and our observations (Lord and Dinh 2014). Prior to alluding to the interrelationship between the expectations (internal knowledge) and the reality (external), it is necessary to summarize the general components of the construct found in individuals or societies. Social science literature applies several concepts that can be used to describe and recognize our leadership construct and help us to identify the leaders around us: schema, prototype, cognitive categories, stereotype, template (Lord and Dinh 2014).[3] The common denominator of these concepts is that they

---

[3] Cognitive category or schema are employed across fields, while stereotype is used mainly as categorization of humans (see Brooks 2013: chapter 2, for a review of gender stereotypes literature). Horowitz and Turan (2008) use the concept prototype to address a knowledge structure employed commonly by a group, while denoting template as more individualistic expression of a knowledge structure.

express a cognitive structure (an element of personal knowledge) that contains or is linked with a set of features, characteristics, and elements that together provide us with the meaning of leadership. Furthermore, all these concepts suggest that the building blocks of that structure are interrelated and associated with the "title" (e.g., leader) of this particular structure. These characteristics may include attributes of a leader such as age, height, sex, patterns of behavior (talkative, extravert, humorous), or more abstract elements such as personality traits or ideology. Horowitz and Turan (2008: 1056) further explain that

> The elements of a prototype are not simply a list of features; they are an organized list . . . ordered (or graded) from the most prototypical to the least prototypical. Furthermore, highly prototypical features tend to be more strongly associated with one another than are less prototypical features and, therefore, have a greater capacity than other features to activate each other as well as the concept itself.

The elements and the links among them were considered as the specific Implicit Leadership Theory (ILT) that people have (Lord et al. 1984). Another way to look at the link between the characteristics and a template is to consider the hierarchy in the prototypicality of its attributes in terms of their relevance to the fit between the template and the target, or the weights given to the characteristics (Tavares et al. 2018) that determine whether a person fits the template of a political leader.

Three points are key. First, the structure of a template develops as a consequence of perceiving co-occurrence of perceived stimuli. Those perceptions affect the prototypicality of particular attributes or features of the template (as they appear more frequently) and enable a template to change. When individuals realize that a particular characteristic is no longer relevant, it becomes unbound from the template, and the composition of the template changes. For example, if you realize that leaders are both old and young, age is lost (or weakened) as a relevant component of a major prototype for the leadership template. The same logic may apply for gender. Second, regarding specificity of the template, leadership posts, varied in hierarchy or area of responsibility, may include different attributes. For example, leadership in education policy may entail different attributes than leadership in security policy. Third, major attributes of the template may act as heuristics allowing a person to "think fast" when the perceiver applies only part of the template to evaluate the fitness of the target as a leader (Kahneman 2011). Our study uses an experiment to measure whether a candidate's sex is a major attribute that is used for such "think fast" evaluations of the candidate.

Why Mental Templates of Leadership Matter

If a candidate's sex is a heuristic, it facilitates fast and low-information evaluation of the candidate's ability. Unless women fit mental templates of a leader, those templates will be a factor that makes it hard for women to win election or to be credible in appointed posts. Moving our knowledge forward about leadership templates is critical because women remain vastly under-represented in government in most countries, a damming situation considering the call from women's suffrage groups for women's representation began over a century ago. John Stuart Mill argued over 150 years ago that government benefits from diversity, and for that reason women should be enfranchised.

Society benefits from increased presence of women in government in many ways. Women bring different policy topics and solutions to the agenda. Karpowitz and Mendelberg (2014: 36) explain that "women's low numbers matter in part because they allow a less deliberative and democratic interaction style, which in turn depresses women's authority." Women's presence in government can increase women's political engagement (Reingold and Harrell 2010; Barnes and Burchard 2013; Fridkin and Kenney 2015; Franceschet 2018: 149; Schwindt-Bayer 2018: 4; Hinojosa and Kittilson 2020). Government institutions and decisions are viewed as more legitimate when women take part in the deliberation (Kittilson and Schwindt-Bayer 2012; Clayton et al. 2019).

Inclusion of women signals the true citizenship of a half of the population that has traditionally been excluded from the public domain (see Phillips 1995: 40; Mansbridge 1999; Young 2000: 134–37, 144; Karpowitz and Mendelberg 2014: conclusion chapter). It acknowledges that women are political people, with useful opinions and expertise (Escobar-Lemmon and Taylor-Robinson 2016: 16; Paxton et al. 2020: 3).

Mental templates of leaders strongly influence attitudes and biases of voters as any clash between being female and leadership templates erects hurdles women must clear to get into government. As Sanbonmatsu (2002: 20–22) explained, voters can hold "baseline gender preferences" (see also Mo [2015] about explicit and implicit gender attitudes). Moreover, expectations of voter bias can prompt party leaders to avoid nominating or appointing women, and to not finance women's campaigns (Bateson 2020). Yet in some countries women are entering government in increasing numbers and holding more diverse posts, sometimes even as head of government. Thus, investigation of factors that influence gendered attitudes and leadership templates, particularly among young adults, is timely.

Macro and Micro-Level Influences on Leadership Templates

We build from several literatures that create expectations about when mental templates of leadership will, or will not, include women. The literature points to both macro (national) and micro (individual) aspects of context.

One macro-level factor is *exposure to women in government*. Women holding diverse, more important government posts, and more visible women in government and candidates, are expected to help women appear capable of leadership (Carli 2001; Campbell and Wolbrecht 2006; Beaman et al. 2009; Koenig et al. 2011; Brooks 2013: 34 and 42). However, findings differ on the impact of women in the legislature or cabinet on voter confidence in women's ability to govern (e.g., Dolan 2010; Alexander 2012; Morgan and Buice 2013; Alexander and Jalalzai 2016; Barnes and Taylor-Robinson 2018). In addition, questions remain regarding the relative importance of, for example, a woman president or prime minister in your own country, or a woman leader holding an internationally prominent post who is not from your country.

The literature does predict that attitudes can change (Eagly and Karau 2002). In more recent experiments women are less commonly viewed as lacking leadership traits (Diekman et al. 2004; Sczesny et al. 2004; Beaman et al. 2009; Eagly and Sczesny 2009; Koenig et al. 2011: 632; Burden et al. 2017). Public opinion data reveals more positive attitudes among younger cohorts about women as politicians (Inglehart and Norris 2003; Alexander 2012; Morgan and Buice 2013). Yet it is unclear specifically how exposure to women leaders changes mental templates of leaders, for example, if women are viewed as equally capable in diverse as well as specific posts, or if election of a woman head of government produces an enduring change in attitudes about women's ability to govern (see Beaman et al. 2009; Kerevel and Atkeson 2015).

Change in leadership templates is predicted after participation by women in politics has increased (Duerst-Lahti 2005; Jennings 2006; Brooks 2013: chapter 9), especially "contemporaneous observations of women in leader roles" (Koenig et al. 2011: 619). But many factors remain uninvestigated, for example whether experience seeing more women candidates makes women less of a novelty (Dolan 2014: 25–26), if increased election of women to the legislature due to a gender quota law changes leadership templates (De Paola et al. 2010), whether a woman president, prime minister, or gender parity cabinet change mental templates of leaders. Leadership templates may not change, as people are often unaware of the percentage of women in their legislature (Dolan 2014; Verge et al. 2015: 10; Stauffer 2021), they may view "quota women" as unqualified (Franceschet et al. 2012), and women presidents are particularly harshly punished for corruption scandals (Reyes-Housholder 2019).

A second macro-level factor is the *government's policy agenda*. Leadership templates could be more likely to include women where the government agenda focuses on social welfare topics, often referred to as stereotypically feminine policy areas. Where the agenda is dominated by stereotypically masculine policy areas, especially defense, mental templates of leadership may remain traditional, favoring men.

Research shows that expectations about leadership vary with the "gender-typing" of the task (Carli 2001: 726). If the task is viewed as requiring social skills or is stereotypically feminine (e.g., social services), women are often selected as group leaders. For tasks in a male-dominated context, such as the military, men are preferred as leaders and are more likely to be viewed as effective (Eagly et al. 1992; Boldry et al. 2001; Ridgeway 2001: 647; Dolan 2010). Further, if a post is defined in masculine terms, men who hold those jobs are evaluated more favorably than women (Eagly et al. 1992, 1995; Brescoll et al. 2010). "Men are therefore seen as more similar to the leader stereotype than women are, producing disadvantage for women" (Koenig et al. 2011: 617).

Gendered personality traits are thought to map onto policy areas (Herrnson et al. 2003; Lammers et al. 2009), producing gender issue ownership. Women are viewed as best able to handle policy areas related to nurturing (e.g., health, education, child and elder care); men are seen as best at topics requiring hard-nosed negotiations (e.g., defense, terrorism, crime) (Lawless 2004; Lammers et al. 2009). Ramm (2020a: 18–19) writes, "The predominance of conventional gender roles also defines who can speak about certain issues, and motherhood and childcare constitute one [of] the few realms, if not the only one, in which women are considered legitimate actors."

Competence stereotypes are also shaped by the occupations where women are commonly observed (Lee and James 2007: 230). Women are still more likely to be appointed to social welfare cabinet posts and committees in legislatures (Heath et al. 2005; Luna et al. 2008; Borrelli 2010; Schwindt-Bayer 2010; Krook and O'Brien 2012; Kerevel and Atkenson 2013; Tremblay and Stockemer 2013; Jacob et al. 2014; Escobar-Lemmon and Taylor Robinson 2009, 2016; Barnes 2016). Consequently, women are not typically the "face" presenting policy related to stereotypically masculine policy areas, though this is changing as women become more broadly incorporated into government.

Experiments typically find that men are viewed more favorably than women in masculine policy areas, and women are only viewed more favorably in stereotypically feminine policy areas, especially when the policy topic is not discussed in the treatment text (Sapiro 1981–82; Rosenwasser et al. 1987; Leeper 1991; Fridkin Kahn 1992; Matland 1994; Herrick and Sapieva 1997; McDermott 1998; Chang and Hitchon 2004; Carli and Eagly 2007; Matland and Tezcür

2011; Holman et al. 2016; Ono and Yamada 2020). Furthermore, public opinion punishes women, particularly women presidents, for policy failures in "masculine" policy areas (Lawless 2004; Dolan 2010; Carlin et al. 2020).

US survey data indicates that women and men candidates are viewed as equally competent at handling corporate crime, reducing the deficit, and assisting the poor. Some studies find that women candidates are viewed as equal to men for handling the economy, though the economy is still "often considered the domain of male candidates . . ." (Hayes and Lawless 2015: 106). Men are still preferred in defense, while women politicians are viewed as more competent to improve children's welfare and healthcare (Lawless 2004; Bystrom 2006; Falk and Kenski 2006; Fridkin and Kenney 2009: 309, 313; Holman et al. 2016). Devroe and Wauters (2018) find similar attitudes in Belgium. Dolan found that party identification is more important to candidate evaluations in US House, Senate, and state governor elections than the sex of the candidate or abstract policy competency stereotypes (Dolan 2014: chapter 4; also Huddy and Capelos 2002; Hayes 2011; Bauer 2015; Hayes and Lawless 2015; Holman et al. 2016). However, in the Netherlands, Lammers et al. (2009: 192) express concern that decline in party ID and the increase in what they call floating voters suggest "that in the near future the importance of peripheral cues [such as gender] will most likely only increase."

These diverse literatures related to gender stereotypes and policy competence indicate important questions remain largely unanswered and need investigation in diverse settings. For example, do gender stereotypes play a greater role in evaluations of policy competence in low-information contexts, as has been found about partisanship (Brooks 2013: 40; Ditonto et al. 2014; Peterson 2017)? More information is needed about how macro-context is related to when attitudes about the policy aptitudes of women politicians change as more women serve in government, and when people come to view women as capable to hold the most high-ranking posts (Lawless 2004: 481; Hayes 2011: 134; Dolan 2014: 98; Devroe and Wauters 2018).

A third macro-level factor is *institutions*. Literature predicts that the design of institutions can focus attention on the individual candidate or else on the party, enhancing or diminishing the potential importance of candidate sex and gender stereotypes.

In presidential systems voters directly elect the leader, prompting voters to consider candidate traits, such as sex, when making their vote choice. In parliamentary systems people vote for a district candidate or a party's slate of MPs, and parliament selects the country's leader.[4] That more distanced role of voters

---

[4] The prime minister is generally the leader of the largest party in parliament, so becoming party leader is essential for women's opportunities to become prime minister. Women are most likely to obtain party leadership posts during bad times when the party is more willing to "select new types of leaders" (O'Brien 2015: 1026).

in national leader selection makes a potential prime minister's sex less important when voters cast their ballot for parliament, though party leaders are a major focus of attention during campaigns. Additionally, in parliamentary systems the leader can be removed by parliament or their party, making a woman leader seem less risky than in presidential systems where the president's fixed term means voters must commit to a woman leader for several years (Jalalzai and Krook 2010).

Rules for electing legislators that enable voters to focus on individual candidates (single member district [SMD], open-list proportional representation [PR], preference votes) allow voters to use their gender stereotypes when making their vote decision.[5] Rules that require voting for a party (closed-list PR) focus attention on the party platform and label, and invite voters to ignore attributes of individual candidates, so that individual candidates—men and women—get "lost in the pack" with co-partisans. Under these institutions, voters cannot use candidate gender as a heuristic to make their vote choice because they must vote for a party's list. Yet the impact on women fitting the leadership template for higher posts (e.g., cabinet, chief executive) is unclear.

At the micro-level, creating variance *within* countries, the first factor we examine is the influence of *in-groups* on mental templates of leadership. Social categorization theory holds that dimensions of shared identity can prompt a person from an out-group to become part of the in-group (Gaertner et al. 1989). Bias against the out-group can be reduced by sharing a common experience, allowing recategorization into the in-group (Dovidio et al. 1997; Chattopadhyay et al. 2004; Lee and James 2007; Zhu et al. 2014: 243–46; Zhang and Qu 2016).

In-group effects explain for example, how women, and ethnic/racial minorities, can become accepted as corporate board members and CEOs. Likewise, traits similarities should help a person to reclassify women politicians as acceptable leaders (Cutler 2002; Holman et al. 2011). Social categorization can lead women to respond more favorably to women candidates, and men to resist women's leadership even more (Eagly et al. 1992; Forsyth et al. 1997; Carli 2001: 727; Ono and Yamada 2020). In general, people will like women candidates more when they share traits, such as political party, which is borne out by US studies finding sex stereotypes to interact with party (McDermott 1997; Dolan 2010; Branton et al. 2018; Thomsen 2020). Because much of this literature is based on data from the United States, which has a highly candidate-centered electoral system, more studies in other contexts are needed.

---

[5] These electoral systems give candidates an incentive to seek a "personal vote." An extensive literature explores how personal vote systems impact women candidates (see, e.g., Matland 1993; Thames and Williams 2010; Ragauskas 2021). Valdini (2013: 80) shows they have "a conditional effect that depends on the level of bias against female leaders in a society."

A second micro-level factor producing variation *within* countries is *family background*, which may influence a person's mental leadership template, as socialization "ties support for gender equality to background factors like mother's work status and mother's education" (Bolzendahl and Myers 2004: 762). Ostensibly, family where the father works outside and the mother inside the home would promote traditional mental templates where leaders are men, whereas when the mother is a breadwinner and a role model of the professional woman, leadership templates might not include gender as a central attribute (Bolzendahl and Myers 2004: 778; Davis and Wills 2010: 583–84; Gidengil et al. 2010; Dotti Sani and Quaranta 2017: 32–33). However, it is also possible that a person's mother works, possibly as the sole breadwinner for the family, but she is not highly educated and does not work in a professional job. In that case the impact of family on leadership templates may be different.

The concept of *role congruity* generates predictions about the types of posts where women will "fit" (or not fit) mental templates about leaders. Stereotypes about feminine traits cause women to be seen as "not hav[ing] what it takes for important leadership roles" (Koenig et al. 2011: 616), with incongruity greatest "at the highest levels of leadership" (Eagly and Karau 2002: 577; also Sweet-Cushman 2022). "Maleness" and agentic traits are seen as necessary in particular to perform top ranking executive post jobs (Rosenwasser and Dean 1989; Huddy and Terkildsen 1993a; Watson et al. 2005: 55–56; Carroll and Fox 2006: 203; Eagly 2007; Rhode and Kellerman 2007: 6–7; Sweet-Cushman 2022).

Women are viewed as compassionate, sensitive, honest; men as aggressive, decisive, tough (Alexander and Andersen 1993; Huddy and Terkildsen 1993a, 1993b; Fridkin Kahn 1994; Heilman 2001; Sanbonmatsu 2002; Lawless 2004; Banwart 2010; Dolan 2010; Dittmar 2015a). Women *politicians*, however, are not seen as having the positive gender stereotypes normally attributed to women, or the masculine gender stereotypes that are expected for politicians (Schneider and Boss 2014). Chappell and Waylen (2013: 608) explain that a "gendered logic of appropriateness" for behavior within government institutions tells people what "acceptable" masculine and feminine behaviors are. Yet Brooks' "leaders-not-ladies" theory "postulates that women politicians will be evaluated by the public more as politicians than as women" (2013: 29), and her study of US voters finds support for her theory and indicates that women are not punished for being tough (Brooks 2013: chapter 6). Thus, while the literature contains rich theory, more extensive tests in additional contexts are needed to enhance understanding of when women are viewed as leaders, particularly in the most prestigious posts and diverse policy areas.

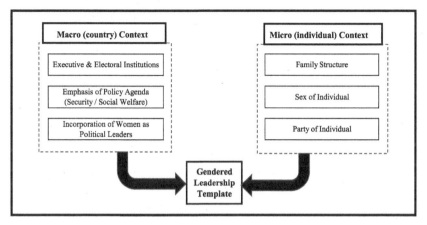

Figure 1.1 A multi-dimensional framework about context and leadership templates

The literatures reviewed above indicate macro- and micro-level factors that are predicted to favor "traditional" leadership templates where leaders are men, or templates where gender is not a central attribute of leadership. Synthesizing these literatures, we propose a multi-dimensional framework about how context molds mental templates of leadership (see Figure 1.1). Those factors may interact (e.g., the impact of representation of women in government tempered by the policy areas that are the focus of the national government), and we design our investigation to enable detection of such interactions. From the literature, we identify the following hypotheses as guidelines for our multi-country investigation:[6]

Macro-level factors that differ only across cases

Leadership templates will be less traditional (leaders are men)
 1: As representation of women in government increases.
 2: As the government policy agenda focuses more on social welfare policy and less on defense.
 3: In parliamentary compared to presidential democracies.
 4: Where electoral rules are party-centered instead of candidate-centered.

---

[6] The hypotheses were not pre-registered, however, #,1 5–6, and 8–11 were included in the NSF proposal filed for the January 2016 application deadline (though the hypothesis numbers were different).

Micro-level factors that differ within a country

In-group effects

5: Male participants will give men candidates more favorable evaluations; female participants will give women candidates more favorable evaluations.

6: Participants will evaluate the woman candidate more favorably if she is from their preferred party.

Socialization within home environment

7: Participants whose mother is highly educated or has a high-status job will not exhibit traditional leadership templates.

Factors testable within and across countries

Role congruity theory

8: Participants overall will more favorably evaluate the man candidate than the woman candidate in "general" evaluation questions.

9: A gender gap in evaluations will be larger the higher the level of the post.

Gender stereotypes and policy domains

10: Participants will more favorably evaluate the man candidate than the woman candidate in stereotypically masculine policy domains.

11: A gender gap in evaluations will be larger for policy areas not covered in the candidate's speech.

Case Selection

To test these hypotheses, we selected a broad range of countries that are established democracies. All eight countries (ten cases) have largely urban, educated populations and UN HDI scores in the "very high" or "high" categories. We limited the study to established democracies to remove regime type effects, as women's representation in government often is sidelined during early years of a new democratic regime (see, e.g., Waylen 2000; Baldez 2003; Franceschet 2005: 94). We selected countries with high levels of education for both women and men, and of women's participation in the workforce, since education and workforce participation influence the supply of women as potential politicians. These scope conditions, however, limit the countries to which we should extrapolate study findings.

Countries were selected for variance on the macro-level factors: extent of incorporation of women in government, national policy agenda, institutional design. Table 1.1 provides summary information for each country and

Table 1.1 Country Variation on Women in Government, Institutional Design, Women's Workforce Participation and Education

	Case countries							
	Canada	Chile	Costa Rica	England	Israel	Sweden	United States	Uruguay
Women head of government (most recent)	1993	2014–18	2010–14	2016–19	1969–74	2021	never	never
Women head of government (next most recent)	–	2006–10	–	1979–90	–	–	–	–
Women in cabinet in 2015 (%)	50	39*	38	33	12	50	20	39**
Women in legislature unicameral or lower chamber in 2015 (%)	26.0	15.3	33.3	29.4	22.5	43.6	19.4	16.2
Women in legislature upper chamber in 2015 (%)	37.3	15.3	–	24.6	–	–	20.0	29.0
Gender quota and year adopted (%)	some parties	2017 (40%)	2002 (40%) 2013 (50%)	some parties	some parties	some parties	never	2014 (30%)
Government type (parliamentary or presidential)	parliamentary	presidential	presidential	parliamentary	parliamentary	parliamentary	presidential	presidential
Ballot type (party or candidate-oriented)	SMD-P	open PR	closed PR	SMD-P	closed PR	PR with pref vote	SMD-P	closed PR**

(*continued*)

Table 1.1 Continued

	Case countries							
	Canada	Chile	Costa Rica	England	Israel	Sweden	United States	Uruguay
Average district magnitude (DM)	–	2*	8.1	–	120	10.7	–	5.2
Governing party during experiment	Liberal	Chile Vamos	PAC	Conservative	Likud	Social Dem.	Republican	Frente Amplio
Main opposition party during experiment	Conservative	Nueva Mayoria	PLN	Labour	Avoda	Moderate	Democrat	National
Female percent of labor force (year)	47.3 (2017)	42.2 (2018)	39.3 (2014)	46.8 (2017)	47.0 (2015)	47.7 (2018)	46.1 (2018)	45.4 (2017)
Firms w/female top manager (year)	no data	5% (2010)	15% (2010)	no data	10% (2013)	13% (2014)	no data	11% (2017)
Tertiary enrollment gender parity index (year)	1.34 (2017)	1.15 (2017)	1.24 (2014)	1.36 (2017)	1.38 (2015)	1.56 (2017)	1.36 (2017)	1.68 (2006)

* President Bachelet's initial cabinet in 2006 was a parity cabinet. As part of the electoral reform implemented in the 2017 election Chile implemented a national gender quota and decreased the number of electoral districts and increased DM.

** Before 2014 the cabinet in Uruguay never had more than 16.7% women. Members of the legislature are elected by closed-list PR, with multiple lists from the same party competing against each other in a double-simultaneous vote.

Sources: employment and education data from the World Bank https://data.worldbank.org/indicator/SE.ENR.TERT.FM.ZS, https://data.worldbank.org/indicator/IC.FRM.FEMM.ZS and https://data.worldbank.org/indicator/SL.TLF.TOTL.FE.ZS, accessed June 15, 2020

Table 1.1 Continued Sub-National Cases in Canada and the United States

	Canada		United States	
	Alberta	Quebec	California	Texas
Women head of government (most recent)	2015–19	2012–14	never	1991–95
Women head of government (next most recent)	–	–	–	1933–35
Women head of government (least recent)	–	–	–	1925–27
Women in cabinet (% in 2017)*	half	8 of 26	1 of 7	1 of 9
Women in legislature unicameral or lower chamber (% in 2017)	29.8	44.0	25.0	19.6
Women in legislature upper chamber (% in 2017)	–	–	22.5	25.8
Government type (parliamentary or presidential)	parliamentary	parliamentary	presidential	presidential
Title of head of government	premier	premier	governor	governor
Largest party (legislature)**	NDP	Liberal	Democrat	Republican
Female percent of labor force (year)	66.0% (2017)	60.9% (2017)	57.1% (2016)	57.9% (2016)

* Canadian provincial premiers appoint their cabinet. In California and Texas several of the posts that perform the function of cabinet members are elected.
** Party with the most seats in the provincial/state legislature when the experiment was conducted.
Sources: Status of Women in Alberta Annual Report 2018–2019, Women in Canada: A Gender-based Statistical Report 2016 Statistics Canada, Institut de la Statistique Quebec https://www.stat.gouv.qc.ca/statistiques/profils/profil06/societe/marche_trav/indicat/tra_sexe06_an.htm, Status of Women in the States https://statusofwomendata.org/state-data/, accessed June 16, 2020

MACRO-CONTEXT FACTORS

LOW ← Expectation of Strength of Gender Bias → HIGH

Executive Institutions	**Parliamentary**	**OR**	**Presidential**
	Alberta CA		Chile
	Quebec CA		California US
	England		Texas US
	Israel		Costa Rica
	Sweden		Uruguay

Electoral Institutions	**Party focused** ← – – – – – – – – – – – – – – – – – → **Candidate focused**				
	Israel	Uruguay	Chile	Alberta CA	California US
	Costa Rica	Sweden		Quebec CA	Texas US
				England	

Policy Agenda Emphasis	**More Social Welfare** ← – – – – – – – – – – – – → **Less Social Welfare**				
	Sweden	Alberta CA	Uruguay	England	California US
	Costa Rica	Quebec CA	Israel	Chile	Texas US
	Less Defense ← – – – – – – – – – – – – – – – – – → **More Defense**				
	Costa Rica	Alberta CA	Sweden	England	Israel
	Uruguay	Quebec CA	Chile	California US	Texas US

Incorporation of Women in Government	**Greatest** ← – → **Least**				
	Sweden	Chile	Alberta CA	Uruguay	Texas US
	Costa Rica	England	Quebec CA	California US	Israel

Figure 1.2 Position of cases on macro-context factors

Figure 1.2 shows how the ten cases often array differently on each macro-level factor, which we expect to dampen the ability of any single factor to influence whether gender is a major attribute in mental templates of leadership.

Women in Government

The literature predicts that seeing women in government will alter attitudes about the ability of women to be leaders. However, the literature does not predict the relative impacts of the quantity of women, or the types of posts women hold. We thus selected countries that vary in percentage of women in the national legislature and cabinet, women as head of government, gender quotas, and the length of time that women have been major players in a country's politics. This dimension of case selection is linked to H1.

Policy Agenda

Literature about gender stereotypes and "gender typing" of tasks predicts that women will be more accepted as leaders in some policy areas (i.e., feminine) than in others (i.e., masculine). From this we predict the national policy emphasis is part of the context establishing mental templates of leaders. Hence, we selected some countries that for decades have had a highly developed welfare state (e.g., Canada, Costa Rica, England, Israel, Sweden, Uruguay) and others with social welfare services that are largely privatized (Chile, United States). We also selected countries that range from long-time global powers in defense or that face major security threats (e.g., England, Israel, United States), to countries where military work is predominantly through participation in peacekeeping forces (Canada, Chile, Sweden, Uruguay), to a country with no military (Costa Rica). This dimension of case selection is linked to H2.

Institutions

The literature predicts the importance of gender varies between parliamentary and presidential systems, and party-focused versus personal-vote systems. We selected four parliamentary and four presidential systems, and different types of ballots for legislative elections. This dimension of case selection is linked to H3 and H4.

In the federal countries—Canada and the United States—we conducted the experiment in two geographically separated locations to incorporate some of the country's diversity. The study includes more unitary than federal countries to limit cost. Cost is also why we have England as a case rather than the United Kingdom.

Organization of the Book and Overview of Findings

Chapter 2 presents the experimental protocol, and statistical methods used to test the hypotheses. In Chapters 3–10 experts who coordinated the experiment in the country explain the country's macro-level context and provide in-depth interpretation of the experiment's findings about leadership templates in the context of their country. The chapters are presented in the chronological order in which the experiments were conducted because domestic and international incorporation of women into government is a dynamic process. Chapter 11 conducts a meta-analysis of the data for each of the eleven hypotheses across all cases. Chapter 12 summarizes the project's findings that women are viewed as leaders, discusses continuing challenges women face in politics, and offers suggestions for further research.

We find in most cases in this study that women candidates fit young adults' mental templates of leaders. In Sweden and Costa Rica, both cases with extensive inclusion of women in government, young people view women as capable to govern across levels of posts and all types of policy areas, which comports with the prediction in the literature that exposure to women in government will prompt people to no longer view gender as a relevant attribute for evaluating who a leader is. Young adults in Chile, England, Canada, Uruguay, and California also exhibited attitudes that women can govern, despite less extensive exposure to women in government. This calls into question the tacit assumption in the literature that extensive, *domestic* exposure to women in government is necessary for women candidates to fit mental templates of leaders.

The influence of micro-level factors on evaluations of women as leaders is more nuanced than expected in the literature. In most cases female participants give favorable evaluations to women candidates, as predicted based on in-group theory. But male participants also in many cases give favorable evaluations to women candidates. Meanwhile, in-group expectations are robustly supported in all our cases regarding party. Participants give more favorable evaluations when they receive a speech by a candidate from their preferred party, than when the candidate is from the opposition—regardless of whether the candidate is male or female. Overall, this study finds that in-group effects related to candidate and participant sex are miniscule compared to in-group effects of party. Party also matters for evaluations as participants gave higher scores to candidates in policy areas "owned" by the candidate's party. This finding about the strong impact of party compared to gender, found across diverse democracies with different executive and electoral institutions, is an important contribution to the literature. Micro-level context arising from family background has a less clear effect on leadership templates. We find that young adults often view women as potential leaders whether or not their mother is well educated or has a high-status job, and in some cases participants whose mother lacks those resources give more favorable evaluations of women candidates.

Contrary to expectations about gender stereotypes, we find that evaluations of women and men candidates are not often significantly different in stereotypically masculine policy areas, even when policy information is not provided in the speech. However, women candidates receive more favorable evaluations than men in some stereotypically feminine policy areas.

The government's policy agenda has explanatory power for maintenance of traditional leadership templates. In Israel, and in the Texas sample for the United States, both cases where citizens and government consider national defense (Israel) or self-defense (Texas) as a top priority, young people are more likely to exhibit traditional leadership templates. Though women candidates are viewed as capable in stereotypically feminine policy areas, men candidates receive higher evaluations in some masculine policy areas, and in Israel men are more favorably evaluated across all levels of posts.

Findings from this experiment in diverse established democracies indicate that for many young adults gender is not a central component of mental templates of leadership. Party affects evaluations more than candidate gender. Unless these attitudes change as these young adults age, party leaders may find that to win elections they should abandon the presumption that it is too risky to nominate and appoint women.

2

Research Protocol

Nehemia Geva and Michelle M. Taylor-Robinson

To study mental templates of leadership, we conducted an experiment in eight countries (ten cases) with 6,324 young adults. This is the first study to implement parallel experiments producing directly comparable data to study gender as a component of leadership templates across a large number of countries. In this chapter we explain the design of the experiment, and how it was implemented in the eight countries. We then provide an overview of the types of statistical measures that will be used to test the hypotheses.

An experiment offers advantages of providing 1) measures of attitudes that are relatively unbiased by the process of taking the measurement, and 2) an experimental control or baseline (here, a party effect) against which the primary treatment effect of interest (gender) is measured. The experiment was implemented with young adults in metropolitan areas in Canada (Alberta and Quebec), Chile, Costa Rica, England, Israel, Sweden, the United States (California and Texas), and Uruguay. Young adults are our target population because their generation has grown up with more women in government and women holding higher profile posts.

Origin and Overview of the Study

The experiment utilized a hypothetical political candidate's gender in the context of a partisan speech given by a candidate. The experiment parallels the experiment Richard Matland conducted in Norway in 1991 where participants who were the equivalent of high school seniors read a 500-word speech representing one of the two largest parties in parliament, with texts drawing on actual political speeches generating a partisan distinction across the two speeches (Matland 1994). Matland's experiment was novel for the extent of realistic information it gave participants, and for its focus on Norway, where inclusion of women in government was extensive. His purpose was to directly test whether increased incorporation of women in government leads to gender-neutral views of political leaders. He chose young adults as participants because they were socialized when "women were prominent on the political scene" (Matland 1994: 278). An

Nehemia Geva and Michelle M. Taylor-Robinson, *Research Protocol* In: *The Image of Gender and Political Leadership.* Edited by: Michelle M. Taylor-Robinson and Nehemia Geva, Oxford University Press. © Oxford University Press 2023. DOI: 10.1093/oso/9780197642726.003.0002

important finding of Matland's study was that even in Norway, gender influenced candidate evaluations, particularly in stereotypically masculine and feminine policy areas, even when the policy was discussed in the speech.

Earlier experiments, conducted in the United States, gave participants little information about the candidate, often a bio with minimal or no policy information (e.g., Sapiro 1981–82; Sigelman and Sigelman 1982; Rosenwasser et al. 1987; Rosenwasser and Seale 1988; Leeper 1991). Recently studies have been conducted in other countries, though still single cases with limited information about the candidates and issues, such as Aguilar et al. (2015) in Brazil; Devroe and Wauters (2018) in Flanders, Belgium; Clayton et al. (2020) in Malawi; and Ono and Yamada (2020) in Japan. Koenig et al's (2011) review shows the limited geographic breadth of research that overwhelmingly has been about the United States and northern European countries.

Our candidate speeches are based on actual speeches and party platforms, providing policy statements that represent the governing and the largest opposition parties for each country. The speech was followed by a questionnaire to evaluate the candidate for different levels of posts and policy areas and obtain information about participants' demographics. This format allows us to determine whether participants based their evaluations on speech content, or on gender schema facilitated by knowing the candidate's sex. Our study differs from Matland's in our random assignment of participants to a speech, rather than allowing them to select the party. We also included a short bio and manipulated the availability of the party name as described below.[1]

The great strength of this study is its multi-country research design that enhances the external validity of the findings. However, conducting a study in many countries creates challenges. We needed to implement an experiment with the same structure in countries with different party systems (two parties, several important parties) and electoral rules (SMD-P, different types of PR), so we needed a baseline control that resonates across diverse democracies. Party (measured as Platform and Label) serves as the control because political parties are key actors in all democracies. Dolan (2014), in her important study of the United States, measured the impact of gender stereotypes on candidate choice relative to party, incumbency, campaign spending, and candidate experience; all factors known to be important in US elections. In countries where voters select among closed party lists, incumbency or experience of individual candidates are not central factors in vote decisions (Chin and Taylor-Robinson 2005); parties are the focus. In open-list PR elections, attributes of individual candidates can attract votes (Carey and Shugart 1995) because voters can select a candidate on

---

[1] We thank Kim Fridkin, Rick Matland, Catarina Thomson, and Rick Wilson for their advice on the experimental protocol. Of course any errors are our own.

their party's list. Participants in our experiment evaluated the individual candidate whose speech they read; they do not compare two candidates. This allows us to study leadership templates across countries where voters do not choose between a pair of candidates, and instead select from more than two parties by voting for a party's list, or faction list, possibly with the option to vote for a particular candidate on a list.

The project began with a pilot test of our protocol with 696 young adults in Costa Rica in 2014. We obtained highly significant results in gender and party effects, with sufficient statistical power to test hypotheses about politically important gender effects and the factors influencing them. A similar level of statistical power was seen in a follow-up pilot study in 2015 with 564 young adults in Israel. We then conducted the study in six more countries (eight cases) in 2017 and 2018, yielding the ten cases presented in this volume.

Experimental Materials and Methods

The experiment included eight treatment combinations in a 2×2×2 factorial, randomized block design where the three factors (or independent variables) and their respective two levels were: *Candidate Gender* (woman or man), *Party Platform* (governing or major opposition), and *Party Label* (presence or absence—of the explicit party name). Each participant randomly and unknowingly received one of eight possible combinations of factor levels (for example, a governing party platform woman candidate providing no explicit mention of her party's name). Consequently, each participant scored the suitability of one candidate, but never directly compared two candidates or parties. Each treatment combination was embodied within text on a single sheet of paper starting with candidate information in the form of a circa 100-word bio followed by a circa 600-word speech given while running for the national legislature.[2] Thus there were eight distinct types of treatment sheets, randomly assigned to participants in sets of eight participants (Figure 2.1). We used a randomization table to separately randomize the eight speeches (conditions) within each block. During experiment implementation in a classroom, speeches are distributed in sets (randomized blocks) of eight speeches (conditions) per block at a time. This process results in random assignment of eight participants to eight factorial (2×2×2) experimental conditions, so that the students of the block are likely to be physically close to each other in the room, minimizing seating location effects on our results. Treatment

---

[2] We use the term legislature generically (i.e., Israeli Knesset, Swedish Riksdag, US House of Representatives).

RESEARCH PROTOCOL 25

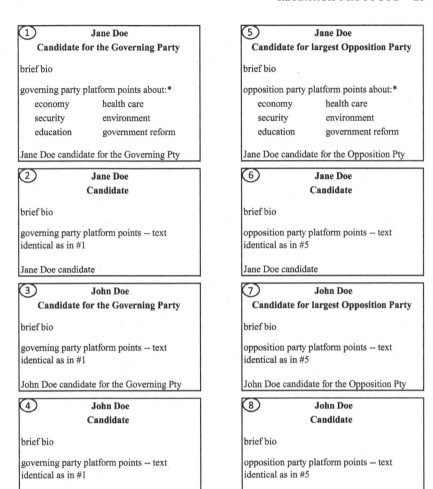

Figure 2.1 Description of speeches to produce the 2×2×2 factorial design

*Policy areas listed were included in the speech texts for all cases except Costa Rica and Israel. The Costa Rica speech covered economics, education, energy, environment, government reform, and security. The Israel speech covered defense, internal security, foreign policy, education, health, housing, and corruption.

sheets were coded for investigators' use but otherwise appeared so similar that participants normally were unaware they differed. The only differences in fact were the candidate's name (male or female) centered at the top of the page in bold print above the bio and again after the speech underneath the bio, gender-specific pronouns in the bio, the party name if included, and other party-specific content within both bio and speech that was identical across the four treatment sheets for each party.

Configuration and Incorporation of Independent Variables into Treatment Sheets

Candidate Gender

Candidate gender was identified by candidate names and reinforced by the pronouns in the bio. Otherwise within a party, the *speech text, bio, and surname were identical for the woman and man candidate*. Country coordinators were consulted to select ethnically, culturally, and politically neutral and common yet unmistakably gender-specific first and last names for the two hypothetical candidates in each country. We "Googled" names to ensure they were not famous or notorious, and that they were not the name of an employee of the institution of the country collaborator(s). The bio listed the candidate's major in school, type of employment before being elected,[3] how they became active in politics, prior posts, community activities, that he/she has two children,[4] and their pastimes. The descriptors were formulated from coding bios on the webpage of the legislature for all sitting members from the candidate's party to form a composite that was consistent with the most common background and lifestyle of a legislator from the party. The balance of male versus female bios used for this process varied across countries and parties, typically with a male majority. We intentionally did not mention a spouse (only the Israel bio says "married").

Our short bio describing women and men identically was intended to reinforce the sex of the candidate without gender bias. We must note relevant findings published after our project went into the field, concluding that women candidates in the United States face a "double bind" because voters prefer candidates with traits that are particularly difficult for women politicians to develop, especially being married with children (Teele et al. 2018: 526 and 534).[5] Teele et al's data come from conjoint experiments with hypothetical candidates running for an open seat in their party's primary, conducted with US citizens in 2014, and with public officials in 2014 and 2017. Their candidate bios varied characteristics "such as gender, occupation, age, marital status, political experience, and number of children" (p. 526). They underscore that in US politics "motherhood has become increasingly politicized" (p. 528) and call for

---

[3] Occupation and political experience have been found in US studies to serve as heuristics for candidate qualifications in low-information electoral environments and when a party name is not given (McDermott 2005; Kirkland and Coppock 2018). Men and women candidates of the same party have the same occupation and political experience.

[4] In all treatments the candidate had two children, even if many legislators, particularly men, had more children. This accommodation was made because of the empirical reality that women politicians are less likely than men to have children, or they wait until their children are grown to run for office (Rosenbluth et al. 2015: 18–20).

[5] Clayton et al. (2020) find evidence in an experiment in Malawi that people prefer married candidates with young children.

future work "to explore how the double bind operates in politics outside the U.S." (p. 537). Accordingly, our woman candidates could be argued to be atypically "feminine." We tested for and discounted participant confusion caused by children in women candidates bios by checking for, but not finding, a significantly higher incidence of candidate gender misidentification for women than for men candidates in the questionnaire's candidate gender manipulation check question.

Party as a Baseline Control

Party Platform and Party Label serve as a conceptual and experimental control to facilitate an empirical conclusion (at a known uncertainty level) of whether non-detection of the gender treatment is due to the absence of an effect stronger than a predefined critical magnitude, rather than to inadequate sensitivity of the detection instrument. They also enable comparison, at least roughly, of results from different cases against a common denominator (the control). As an additional measure of a party effect, we also examine if participants evaluate candidates differently if the candidate is (is not) from their preferred party.

Party Platform

Party Platform information was given to participants through the speech. Party-specific source language also provided a partisan flavor to bios. The two platforms utilized in each country arose from the governing party and the largest opposition party in the national legislature after the most recent election. Relative party positions were clear. The speech for each party was a composite of speeches given by members of that party in response to the opening speech for the new parliament or a major presidential address near the time the experiment was implemented, or the party platform for the most recent election. With guidance from country coordinators, text excerpts were selected and slightly edited to improve speech flow of topics covering the same policy areas that were stereotypically masculine, feminine, or neutral. Speeches were thus representative of issues as they were being discussed by each major party in each country, and the treatment of the issues varies across the speeches in ways that reflect party differences as well as the degree of consensus or polarization across the two largest parties on these issues. Following Kruglanski and Kroy's (1976) expansive approach to external validity, our experimental material is tailored to fit the context of each country. Conducting this study in eight countries (ten cases) enhances external validity, which "results primarily from *replication of*

28 NEHEMIA GEVA AND MICHELLE M. TAYLOR-ROBINSON

particular experiments across diverse populations and different settings . . ." (McDermott 2011: 34).

A short introduction was followed by six topics: economics, security, education, health, environment, and government reform. The policy topics in the speeches for the pilot studies were somewhat different. The Costa Rica speeches covered economics, education, energy, environment, government reform, and security. In Israel the speech covered defense, internal security, foreign policy, education, health, housing, and corruption.

Party Label

For half of the randomly assigned participants the party name associated with the policy positions in the speech was not mentioned, while for the rest the party name was printed in bold at the top and bottom of the speech.[6] There is an important utility of the party name deletion condition. While some democratic countries have only two relevant parties (e.g., the United States), many countries have several parties winning substantial representation in the legislature, and some commonly have coalition governments. Where many parties win seats, many voters identify with a party other than the governing party or the largest opposition party. In some countries large parties still win elections (for example, they can win the presidency) but have lost much of their vote share. No party name on the speech may diminish candidate rejection by participants so frustrated with both large parties that their mere mention evokes anger. For participants who like coalition partners of a large party, but not the large party, party name absence allows focus on issue stances in the speech that they like. Simply omitting party names from speeches then would, in a politically realistic manner, augment party effects without increasing the number of party treatments in the experiment. When speeches include the party name along with the candidate's name, some participants may feel ready to answer the questionnaire accurately and quickly after reading only the heading—using the party name as a heuristic. Since US-based research indicates that party often outweighs gender in candidate evaluations in elections, we conduct robustness tests for whether the effect of Candidate Gender differs for participants whose speech did/did not include the name of the candidate's party (Dolan 2014; Kirkland and Coppock 2018).

---

[6] For speeches that included the party name it was always at the top of the speech. This "ensures that any change in the use of partisanship . . . [is] not due to changes in the probability candidate partisanship received a prominent profile position" (Peterson 2017: 1194). Party name does not appear in the body of the speech. We did not include conditions where party name (label) is inconsistent with the positions in the speech.

Questionnaire

After reading the speech, participants answered a questionnaire that began with eighteen questions to assess gendered attitudes about capacity to govern: general effectiveness or approval of the candidate, and competence of the candidate in twelve policy areas. By design, six of the twelve policy areas were the same six policy areas discussed in the speech, and the other six were not discussed in the speech but include stereotypically feminine and masculine policy areas. Speeches and questionnaire from the US study are in the Chapter Appendix. Questionnaires and speeches used in each country, along with the full dataset, are available at the ICPSR (https://doi.org/10.3886/E179721V1). The questionnaire was essentially identical in all countries, except for Sweden that has preference votes, and Chile where ballots are open-list, questions 17b and 18b pertaining to voting were added to fit the country's electoral system.

The questionnaire included manipulation checks. Table 2.1 shows participants could identify the sex of the candidate and the party, indicating that they perceived the treatment. The questionnaire also included background questions about the participant: sex, age, occupation and education level of their mother and father, attention to the news, party preference, ideology self-placement, and a ten-question battery to assess gender role attitudes developed by Brown and Gladstone (2012).[7] The questionnaire ended with questions about the importance of members of the legislature, cabinet, and party leaders for the life of the participant's family (not included in Costa Rica and Israel). The US questionnaire included a final question about race/ethnicity.

The standard order of the policy area questions in the questionnaire strategically alternated masculine and feminine policies while simultaneously alternating policies discussed or not discussed in the speech. Consequently, the order of policy questions was never randomized, nor was the order of the questions regarding the suitability of the candidate for various posts, which were ordered strategically with the question about the post for which the candidate was running first. Non-randomization of questions, however, had no effect on the validity of the main treatment effect of interest (candidate gender) because questionnaires in speech packets for men and women candidates were always identical. Not randomizing questions was necessitated by experiment

---

[7] The ten gender role attitudes questions load on two factors: a workplace dimension and a chivalry dimension (Brown and Gladstone 2012). Consistent with Brown and Gladstone (2012: 156) and indicating the construct validity of this measure, the average score for female participants in each of our ten cases is more "liberated" than the average score for male participants (p-values for t-tests for participant sex =.000 in each sample). Scores also have a strong negative correlation with participant responses to the ideology self-placement question.

30 NEHEMIA GEVA AND MICHELLE M. TAYLOR-ROBINSON

Table 2.1 Answers to Manipulation Check Questions by Country and Case

	Candidate gender (% correct)	Party (% correct)		
		Overall	Labeled speech	Not labeled
Canada				
Alberta	93.3	85.8	93.4	78.6
Quebec	95.7	74.2	92.3	56.6
Chile	95.2	65.5	90.1	41.2
Costa Rica	NA*	NA**		
England	97.2	75.1	90.5	59.9
Israel	92.3	NA**		
Sweden	93.9	81.3	96.7	65.8
United States				
California	93.6	75.9	87.9	64.0
Texas	94.8	81.4	89.2	73.6
Uruguay	92.1	68.6	88.4	48.7

* In the Costa Rica pilot study the small number of participants who answered the candidate gender manipulation check incorrectly were dropped from the dataset.

** The Costa Rica and Israel pilot studies did not include a party manipulation check.

Notes: Among participants whose speech was not labeled, many selected the answer option "none of these," which could be interpreted as a correct answer since the candidate did not state their party affiliation. As explained in the Uruguay chapter, it was not possible to include party names on the speeches when conducting the experiment in high schools and technical colleges, so "center-left" and "center-right" party were substituted on the Labeled speeches.

implementation on paper in classrooms. This method enabled students from schools of widely differing resources and socioeconomic backgrounds to take part, because participation was not influenced by having access to the internet or a computer lab to participate in the study.

Study Participants

Participants are young adults. The target sample size per case was 800 (100 per treatment), and across cases the cumulative sample totaled 6,324 students from 212 classrooms. The large number of participants provides robust statistics for cross-national and within case comparisons facilitated by the factorial experimental design, and within country datasets it enables post hoc comparisons requiring partitioning of participants into groups based on participant attributes. Some countries' participants included primarily high school seniors and college students. Other countries' participants were all attending universities or technical schools. In all cases the average age was eighteen or older, accurately classifying participants as young adults—people with the opportunity to participate in the most recent national election, or who could anticipate voting in the next election. Table 2.2 provides a brief overview of the participants in each of the ten cases.

Selection of participants addresses basic issues of external validity, which are tricky in experimental designs (see Mook 1983; Morton and Williams 2010). Our use of young adults as the study participants follows Matland's (1994) research design (his Norway study was conducted with high school seniors most of whom would be eligible to vote in the next election). Young adults are the logical group to test how context is related to attitudes and leadership templates because in most countries increased incorporation of women in government is relatively recent, so young people are the subset of the population who grew up in a political world where women politicians are more common. Research on political socialization shows late adolescence and early adulthood to be politically formative years (Campbell and Wolbrecht 2006; Jennings et al. 2009; Amnå and Zetterberg 2010).[8] Voter turnout by young adults in the United States has been found to be higher when they experienced competitive campaigns while they were adolescents. Building from this Pacheco (2008: 416) concludes that "contexts experienced during political development are as important to understanding political behavior as contemporaneous political contexts." According to Jennings (2006: 195), "Period effects will fall more heavily on young people because they are presumably more impressionable than the more resistant old". In sum, young adults are likely to have already formulated party preferences. In addition, more gender egalitarian attitudes are generally found within younger cohorts (see Inglehart and Norris 2003; Morgan and Buice 2013; McDonald and Deckman 2021).

Pragmatically, including students in their final year of secondary school increases the diversity of participants, as Matland (1994) also noted for his study, because it allows the study to include people who do not or cannot continue their education beyond high school. The education and occupation background of participants' families indicate that participants come from diverse socioeconomic backgrounds, enhancing the generalizability of our findings (see Table 2.3).

---

[8] Fridkin and Kenney (2007), studying eighth graders in Arizona found that partisanship and gender gaps in partisanship, are established even younger than late adolescence. Lay et al. (2021) study how the magazine TIME for Kids, a common teaching tool in US elementary schools, presents women and men politicians (in the United States and globally) to very young children.

Table 2.2 Description of Datasets

	Costa Rica	Israel	Alberta	Quebec[†]	Uruguay	England	California	Texas	Sweden	Chile
Study dates	Jul–Aug 2014	Jun–Jul 2015	Mar–Apr 2017	Mar–Apr 2017	May–Oct 2017	Nov–Dec 2017*	Jan–Feb 2018	Jan–Feb 2018	Mar–Jul 2018	Sep–Nov 2018
Number of participants	696	564	253	419	707	531	734	1000	609	811
Percent female	49%	53%	60%	48%	54%	65%	60%	49%	62%	51%
Average age	18	23	22	20	20	18	20	19	21	22
Left(1)—Right(10) Scale	4.8	5.4	4.7	4.5	4.5	4.1	4.3	5.5	4.7	3.9
Preferred party:										
Governing party	57%	32%	41%	47%	34%	16%	10%	40%	21%	8%
2nd largest party	13%	33%	31%	4%	19%	54%	61%	31%	15%	3%
Number of schools	11	6	3	4	9	5	4	4	12	11
Number of classes	29	23	on-line	14	26	35	6	19	27	33
Average class size (range)	24 (14–56)	25 (4–63)	NA	29 (11–61)	27 (8–134)	15 (3–36)	122 (23–263)	53 (8–225)	23 (6–56)	25 (3–63)

† The Quebec dataset includes an additional 531 participants who received treatments with speeches from the two largest parties in the provincial government.

* Due to university strikes in England a few final classes were utilized for the experiment in May 2018 (n=33).

Table 2.3 Sampling of Occupation Backgrounds of Study Participants by Country

OCCUPATION:	Alberta (n=253)		Quebec (n=419)		Chile (n=811)		Costa Rica (n=696)		England (n=531)	
	Father	Mother	Father	Mother	Father	Mother	Father	Mother	Father	Mother
accountant	7	12	5	14	24	28	27	7	10	13
architect	1	0	4	3	10	2	11	2	4	2
business	53	16	52	26	78	85	109	53	73	43
engineer/scientist	45	7	45	3	64	9	35	7	24	0
lawyer/judge	7	2	7	4	18	6	11	13	10	7
manager	11	15	41	23	59	23	55	14	90	46
medicine	8	11	11	16	16	22	7	8	19	29
researcher	2	1	5	1	3	1	2	1	3	3
teacher/professor	10	22	11	35	50	77	18	54	24	63
assistant	10	29	3	17	11	20	29	16	9	37
construction	19	7	37	0	58	11	89	24	42	6
custodial	0	23	3	7	10	28	4	21	3	9
food service	3	2	13	12	15	18	13	26	7	10
hair dresser/barber	0	1	0	9	2	8	1	17	1	3

(continued)

Table 2.3 Continued

OCCUPATION:	Alberta (n=253)		Quebec (n=419)		Chile (n=811)		Costa Rica (n=696)		England (n=531)	
	Father	Mother	Father	Mother	Father	Mother	Father	Mother	Father	Mother
nurse	0	11	1	19	3	8	5	8	4	27
sales/clerk/cashier	7	23	15	16	18	44	40	41	13	19
seamstress/tailor	0	0	0	2	1	5	3	11	0	0
secretary/receptionist	0	3	0	18	0	66	2	48	0	14
security	4	3	12	2	35	3	31	1	11	4
social work/carer	0	7	2	14	0	23	0	4	7	44
transportation	11	2	9	0	54	8	48	2	24	1
worker	5	0	12	6	26	11	17	19	5	3
housewife		13		1		120		202		5
unknown	20	20	38	32	120	63	46	20	31	41
% of dataset*	88%	91%	79%	68%	83%	85%	87%	89%	78%	81%

OCCUPATION:	Israel (n=564)		Sweden (n=609)		California (n=734)		Texas (n=1000)		Uruguay (n=707)	
	Father	Mother	Father	Mother	Father	Mother	Father	Mother	Father	Mother
accountant	5	3	4	3	6	18	11	37	6	12
architect	4	4	4	3	5	3	6	1	7	6
business	34	9	63	21	79	53	137	51	96	49
engineer/scientist	61	28	57	11	35	9	87	18	25	5
lawyer/judge	12	9	16	6	13	1	19	6	12	7
manager	39	30	55	49	62	50	122	76	35	16
medicine	25	45	26	43	17	20	43	29	23	33
researcher	9	6	23	30	3	0	5	2	4	1
teacher/professor	31	115	39	110	27	62	36	119	11	74
assistant	13	9	14	35	16	29	9	45	2	8
construction	36	1	41	2	121	19	148	18	122	43
custodial	1	3	8	13	22	19	9	28	7	47
food service	10	8	9	3	19	21	6	21	21	19
hair dresser/barber	4	14	1	7	4	17	0	12	4	15
nurse	2	18	5	50	1	27	2	63	4	25
sales/clerk/cashier	11	14	11	14	26	39	51	51	20	28
seamstress/tailor	0	3	0	0	3	6	0	1	2	13
secretary/receptionist	0	26	0	7	0	11	0	24	4	38
security	32	3	7	3	26	4	34	7	35	11

(continued)

Table 2.3 Continued

OCCUPATION:	Israel (n=564)		Sweden (n=609)		California (n=734)		Texas (n=1000)		Uruguay (n=707)	
	Father	Mother	Father	Mother	Father	Mother	Father	Mother	Father	Mother
social work/carer	2	11	12	24	1	36	1	21	0	28
transportation	10	0	20	0	34	11	24	5	48	3
worker	10	3	4	3	18	18	19	5	28	15
housewife		53		4		54		40		46
unknown	41	37	40	35	120	129	134	164	111	95
% of dataset*	68%	79%	75%	78%	90%	89%	90%	84%	89%	90%

* Many additional occupations are included in the dataset.
Accountant includes actuary and auditor.
Business includes administrator, banker, CEO, director, entrepreneur, farmer/rancher, insurance broker, owner, self-employed, stock broker.
Engineer/scientist includes agronomy, biochemistry, environmental science, geology, geophysics, programmer, systems analyst.
Manager includes contractor, financial manager, foreman, supervisor.
Medicine includes chiropractor, dentist, doctor, head nurse, nutritionist, pharmacist, psychologist/psychiatrist, therapist, veterinarian.
Researcher includes economics, mathematician, sociologist, statistician.
Teacher/professor includes school principals.
Assistant includes dental, legal, medical, teacher.
Construction includes construction worker and specific trades (e.g., blacksmith, carpenter, electrician, mason, painter, plumber, roofer, welder) and repair trades (e.g., air conditioning, exterminator, handyman, machinist, mechanic).
Custodial includes bathroom attendant, gardener, maid, sanitation.
Food service includes baker, barista, bartender, butcher, chef, cook, waiter.
Hair dresser/barber includes beautician, manicurist, massage.
Sales/clerk includes cashier, customer service, gas station attendant, insurance sales.
Seamstress/tailor includes fashion design, upholstery, wardrobe.
Security includes doorman, fireman/woman, guard, police, soldier (except officers).
Social work/carer includes child and elder care, foster mother, helper.
Transportation includes bus, delivery, truck, and taxi drivers, courier, dispatcher, train conductor.
Worker includes dock and factory work, forklift driver, heavy equipment operator, laborer, machine operator, warehouseman, worker.

Schools were chosen to maximize this diversity. However, our study population is primarily urban, so we caution against extrapolation of findings to rural areas. Another advantage of conducting the experiment with university and high school students in classes is that it gave us a controlled environment for implementing the experiment and made it possible to conduct a debriefing.

The dataset descriptions show that young people tend to support left- more often than right-leaning parties even when the right was governing. We have no reason to believe that this is sampling bias. As the country chapters discuss, greater support for left parties by the young adult participants in our study resembles the age group breakdown of party support found in recent elections. Given that our study utilized the two largest parties, left bias among participants might alter the percentage of participants receiving speeches by their preferred party, but would unlikely decrease the utility of partisan effect size for assessing the political relevance of observed gender effects.

Experiment Implementation

We obtained ethics approval for the study for all countries from the Texas A&M University IRB (IRB2014-0327D). Signed consent was waived because the signatures would be the only way to identify participants. Outside the United States, approvals were also obtained from the relevant authorities: school ethics boards in Canada, the minister of education in Costa Rica, the regional ethics board in Sweden. In Chile approvals were obtained from school deans and teachers. In England and Israel ethics approval was obtained from a major university and from school directors and teachers. In Uruguay approvals were obtained from the regulating bodies for each level of education and from teachers.

The experiment was conducted in classrooms during normal class times,[9] and typically few students opted out of the study. As standard procedure, gender was not mentioned to potential participants. Administrators and teachers were cautioned in advance that any hint to students of a study on gender would contaminate the experiment. The experimenter introduced him or herself, explaining that he/she was conducting a study of candidate nomination procedures. Students received an Information Sheet explaining their rights. They received an instruction sheet, a randomly assigned candidate speech, and the questionnaire. Students who opted not to participate returned a blank questionnaire. Participants could leave specific questions unanswered.[10] After

---

[9] The Alberta, Canada, study was conducted on-line because local ethics boards would not permit the study to be conducted in classes.

[10] Due to this provision of the ethics approval, the N for analysis of different dependent variables in a case can differ.

participants in a classroom had returned their study packet to the researcher, the researcher gave a debriefing.

Benefits of implementing the experiment in classes with paper materials include: 1) usually, a high level of participation by diverse students, because while students could choose to not participate, most participated; 2) participation by students without internet access, or a school computer lab, advantageous in underfunded schools and increasing sample socioeconomic breadth; 3) tight control by researchers over study implementation, along with direct observation of participants, time spent on the study (usually ten to twenty minutes), distractions, notes made in speech margins.

The debrief allowed giving something in return to the students and teachers, namely, an explanation of the experimental method and its uses, using an example from agriculture, and then an explanation of this experiment. After explaining the experimental method, the researcher asked sequentially how many of you had speeches by a man, by a woman, by Party A, by Party B, by an unidentified party, with different sets of hands raised each time. Surprised participants looking around visually informed us that students did not know they were reading different speeches. Students were receptive to learning about the mechanics and power of the experimental method, and the explanation that they had just observed the comparison of an experimental treatment (gender) with a control (party). Responses by the class during the debrief confirmed participants' lack of awareness that gender was the subject of the experiment. This suggests that our method did not augment social desirability bias.

In some classrooms a male and in others a female researcher conducted the study, and when both were present, only one spoke. In the pilot studies the researcher was female. In the other cases researchers were graduate students of similar age. The PIs trained the country coordinators and graduate assistants on how to implement the experiment in classrooms. Information sheets, instructions, and experimental materials were given to students in their own first language.

In high schools, where potential participants were underaged, the Information Sheet and a questionnaire were sent home to parents/caregivers before the experiment.[11] The questionnaire was stamped "example" to prevent substitution in the classroom.

Participation was lower if faculty scheduled the experiment at the latter part of a multi-hour course after mandatory lecture ended and gave students the option to leave early, observed primarily in some university classes in Quebec

---

[11] In Sweden, people aged fifteen to eighteen are allowed to provide their own consent, so parents were not involved.

and Sweden. Some classes were quite small, not due to low participation rates but to low overall attendance.

Overview of Analytical Strategy for the Volume

The central question of this project is *not* whether candidate gender influences voting. Rather, the question is whether gender is important compared to factors related to political parties, and we answer that question by quantitatively comparing 1) response to gender against 2) response to party platform statements in the speech, and against 3) response to presence or absence of a party name. Thus, party is our experimental "control." We do assume though that factors related to political parties are likely to be strong drivers of voting behavior. We also understand that other candidate attributes can affect evaluations, for example, candidate communication skills, ethnicity, physical attractiveness, accent, voice tone. However, we do not vary those other candidate attributes and our central question concerns only the size of effects associated solely with gender when compared directly to effect sizes associated with party, and we are prepared to classify gender effects unimportant if, under identical circumstances, we observe marked party effects and detect no gender effects at all. On the other hand, if we find no party effects, the experiment is unsuccessful, and the results tell us nothing of interest.

We measure and present effects of treatments conventionally in terms of the mean arithmetic scores given by participants to treatments when statistically significant accompanied by the significance level, but most importantly also via partial eta squared values (η_p^2) as a more reliable measure of differences between effect sizes or magnitudes (Richardson 2011; Norouzian and Plonsky 2018). We initially do this gender effect size versus party effect size comparison in our experiment by means of 2×2×2 ANOVA factorial analysis of responses to the first question on the questionnaire: scores participants gave for the effectiveness of the candidate in the speech to be a legislator, that is, the post for which the speech says the candidate is running. We also strategically devise the questionnaire and case selection to enable similar quantitative comparison of gender and party effects under variable circumstances related to our hypotheses about when and where gender is and is not important compared to party (incorporation of women into government, emphasis of national policy on defense or social welfare, differing electoral rules, presidential vs. parliamentary systems, policy areas).

We further utilize participant attributes to partition participants post-hoc enabling statistical comparison of participant-candidate in-group effects (shared-sex, shared-party) as well as gendered effects related to participant parent employment and education. Additional post-hoc comparisons within our dataset but beyond the scope of this volume are available for future investigators.

Some of the above factors vary only across cases, while others vary within cases as well. They all relate to the testable hypotheses delineated in Chapter 1 based on literatures in psychology and political science, underpinning the study design.

The specific statistical analyses conducted (explained below) are identical across countries, that is, unlike the country-specific interpretations of the results, the statistical analyses themselves are intentionally not adapted to country context. Note, however, that as a rule only statistically significant effects are included, so that in countries where there simply are few significant effects for gender even though clear party effects are present, it is because the gender effects are absent or quite small, not because we did not have the ability to detect them.

That said, in our meta-analysis in Chapter 11, findings from the country-specific chapters are presented together fully to permit cross country comparisons, and the testing of corresponding hypotheses. The meta-analyses also compare sets of countries partitioned by meta-factors (incorporation of women in government, national policy emphasis on defense vs. social welfare, presidential vs. parliamentary system, type of electoral institutions).

For every case, a standard sequence of analytical steps was followed to interpret the results from that case. Results with statistical significance are presented and discussed by the country chapter authors, who in all cases are long-term residents of the country. Table A2.1 in the Chapter Appendix outlines the analyses used in the country chapters to test hypotheses 5–11 presented in Chapter 1. Meta-analyses that examine all hypotheses (1–11) are explained in Chapter 11. All statistical analyses were performed in SPSS version 27.

Appendix Sample Speeches and Questionnaire from the US Case

Speeches shown are for the woman candidate, but the name of the man candidate is listed here (in parentheses) to indicate what name was used. These speeches include the party label. Speeches without the party name listed were otherwise identical. The next pages show how the speech was formatted for the participants with the speech on one page. For a more readable version of all the speeches that were used in the different countries in English and the original language, please access the ICPSR webpage with the dataset. Note also that the questionnaire was formatted the same, with the same page breaks, for all countries.

Table A2.1 Statistical Analyses Utilized in All Country-Specific Chapters

Code	Hypothesis tested	Runs	Model	DV's (questions utilized)	Factors	Levels	Treatment combination description
A1	**H8** Man will score higher than woman in general questions.	49	2×2×2 ANOVA Run on each general dependent variable regarding candidate competence, i.e. questions 1,2,3,17,18 with #3 excluded from countries with presidential systems.	Candidate ability for: Legislator Cabinet Minister Party Leader* Support Winning Votes	I Candidate Gender II Party Platform III Party Label	1. Man Candidate 2. Woman Candidate 1. Governing Party 2. Opposition Party 1. Label Present 2. Label Absent	1. Man Candidate of Governing Party with Label Present 2. Woman Candidate of Governing Party with Label Present 3. Man Candidate of Opposition Party with Label Present 4. Woman Candidate of Opposition Party with Label Present 5. Man Candidate of Governing Party with Label Absent 6. Woman Candidate of Governing Party with Label Absent 7. Man Candidate of Opposition Party with Label Absent 8. Woman Candidate of Opposition Party with Label Absent
A2	**H9** The man's advantage is increased by post prestige.	10	2×3 repeated measures ANOVA Note: Prestige is highest for Party Leader in parliamentary systems, for Minister in presidential systems, and lowest for Legislator in both kinds of systems.	Candidate ability for: Legislator Cabinet Minister Party Leader*	I Candidate Gender II Gov-Post Prestige (as repeated measure)	1. Man Candidate 2. Woman Candidate 1. Legislator 2. Minister 3. Party Leader*	1. Man Candidate for Legislator 2. Woman Candidate for Legislator 3. Man Candidate for Minister 4. Woman Candidate for Minister 5. Man Candidate for Party Leader* 6. Woman Candidate for Party Leader*

(continued)

Table A2.1 Continued

Code	Hypothesis tested	Runs	Model	DV's (questions utilized)	Factors		Levels	Treatment combination description
A3	H5 Gender in-group effects will impact candidate evaluations.	49	2×2 post hoc ANOVA (between post hoc groups)	Candidate ability for: Legislator Cabinet Minister Party Leader* Support Winning Votes	I	Candidate Gender	1. Man Candidate 2. Woman Candidate	1. Man Candidate scored by Male Participants 2. Woman Candidate scored by Male Participants 3. Man Candidate scored by Female Participants 4. Woman Candidate scored by Female Participants
					II	Participant sex (post hoc groups)	1. Male Participant 2. Female Participant	
A4	H6 Party in-group effects will impact candidate evaluations.	49	2×2 (or 2×3) post hoc ANOVA (between post hoc groups)	Candidate ability for: Legislator Cabinet Minister Party Leader* Support Winning Votes	I	Candidate Gender	1. Man Candidate 2. Woman Candidate	1. Man Candidate scored by My Party Participants 2. Woman Candidate scored by My Party Participants 3. Man Candidate scored by Not My Party Participants 4. Woman Candidate scored by Not My Party Participants 5. Man Candidate scored by No Stated Party Participants 6. Woman Candidate scored by No Stated Party Participants
					II	My Party (post hoc groups)	1. My Party 2. Not My Party 3. No Stated Party	
A5	H6 (See above.)	49	A5 was the same as analysis A4 but restricted to the half of the participant pool receiving speeches with party name label present on the speech. The A5 analysis was performed only where so indicated within country chapters.					

A6	**H10, H11** 10: Masculine policy area favors man. 11: See below.	10	2×2×2 ANOVA Run on question responses to four policy areas selected by country experts for relevance to country context from among dependent variables (questions) 5–16 and meeting the criteria listed in the next column to the right on DV's.	Policy area partitions based on being IN or NOT in the speech: masc. area IN, fem. area IN, masc. area NOT in, fem. area NOT in. Policy areas depend on country.	I Candidate Gender II Party Platform III Party Label Factor effect sizes compared via η_p^2.	1. Man Candidate 2. Woman Candidate 1. Governing Party 2. Opposition Party 1. Label Present 2. Label Absent	1. Man Candidate of Governing Party with Label Present 2. Woman Candidate of Governing Party with Label Present 3. Man Candidate of Opposition Party with Label Present 4. Woman Candidate of Opposition Party with Label Present 5. Man Candidate of Governing Party with Label Absent 6. Woman Candidate of Governing Party with Label Absent 7. Man Candidate of Opposition Party with Label Absent 8. Woman Candidate of Opposition Party with Label Absent
A7	**H10, H11** 10: See above. 11: Lack of policy information will widen gender gap.	10	2×2 repeated measures ANOVA	Explained above.	I Candidate Gender II Policy area IN speech as repeated measure	1. Man Candidate 2. Woman Candidate 1. Masc. policy area IN speech 2. Fem. policy area IN speech	1. Man Candidate × masc. policy area IN speech 2. Woman Candidate × masc. policy area IN speech 3. Man Candidate × fem. policy area IN speech 4. Woman Candidate × fem. policy area IN speech
A8	**H10, H11** Explained above.	10	2×2 repeated measures ANOVA	Explained above.	I Candidate Gender II Policy area NOT in speech as repeated measure	1. Man Candidate 2. Woman Candidate 1. Masc. policy area NOT in speech 2. Fem. policy area NOT in speech	1. Man Candidate × masc. policy area NOT in speech 2. Woman Candidate × masc. policy area NOT in speech 3. Man Candidate × fem. policy area NOT in speech 4. Woman Candidate × fem. policy area NOT in speech

(*continued*)

Table A2.1 Continued

Code	Hypothesis tested	Runs	Model	DV's (questions utilized)	Factors	Levels	Treatment combination description
A9	H10, H11 Explained above.	34	Robustness checks for #7 and #8 above, re-running same analysis for #7 and for #8 but with other possible combinations of specific masculine and feminine domains.				
A10	H10, H11, H5 Explained above plus same-sex in-group.	10	2×2×2 between groups ANOVA with repeated measures	Questions on candidate competence in selected policy area categories	I Candidate Gender II Participant Sex (post hoc groups) III Policy area IN speech as repeated measure	1. Man Candidate 2. Woman Candidate 1. Male Participant 2. Female Participant 1. Masc. policy area IN speech 2. Fem. policy area IN speech	1. Man Cand. × Male Partic. × masc. policy area IN speech 2. Woman Cand. × Male Partic. × masc. policy area IN speech 3. Man Cand. × Female Partic. × masc. policy area IN speech 4. Woman Cand. × Female Partic. × masc. policy area IN speech 5. Man Cand. × Male Partic. × fem. policy area IN speech 6. Woman Cand. × Male Partic. × fem. policy area IN speech 7. Man Cand. × Female Partic. × fem. policy area IN speech 8. Woman Cand. × Female Partic. × fem. policy area IN speech

					Factors	Levels	Interactions
A11	H10, H11, H5 Explained above.	10	2×2×2 between groups ANOVA with repeated measures	Questions on candidate competence in selected policy area categories	I Candidate Gender II Participant Sex (post hoc groups) III Policy area NOT in speech as repeated measure	I 1. Man Candidate 2. Woman Candidate II 1. Male Participant 2. Female Participant III 1. Masc. policy area NOT in speech 2. Fem. policy area NOT in speech	1. Man Cand. × Male Partic. × masc. policy area NOT in speech 2. Woman Cand. × Male Partic. × masc. policy area NOT in speech 3. Man Cand. × Female Partic. × masc. policy area NOT in speech 4. Woman Cand. x Female Partic. × masc. policy area NOT in speech 5. Man Cand. × Male Partic. × fem. policy area NOT in speech 6. Woman Cand. × Male Partic. × fem. policy area NOT in speech 7. Man Cand. × Female Partic. × fem. policy area NOT in speech 8. Woman Cand. × Female Partic. × fem. policy area NOT in speech
A12	H10, H11, H6 Explained above plus same-party in-group.	10	2×2×2 between groups ANOVA with repeated measures	Questions on candidate competence in selected policy area categories	I Candidate Gender II My Party (post hoc groups) III Policy area IN speech as repeated measure	I 1. Man Candidate 2. Woman Candidate II 1. My Party 2. Not My Party III 1. Masc. policy area IN speech 2. Fem. policy area IN speech	1. Man Candidate × My Party × masc. policy area IN speech 2. Woman Candidate × My Party × masc. policy area IN speech 3. Man Candidate × Not My Party × masc. policy area IN speech 4. Woman Candidate × Not My Party × masc. policy area IN speech 5. Man Candidate × My Party × fem. policy area IN speech 6. Woman Candidate × My Party × fem. policy area IN speech 7. Man Candidate × Not My Party × fem. policy area IN speech 8. Woman Candidate × Not My Party × fem. policy area IN speech

(continued)

Table A2.1 Continued

Code	Hypothesis tested	Runs	Model	DV's (questions utilized)	Factors		Levels	Treatment combination description
A13	H10, H11, H6 Explained above.	10	2×2×2 between groups ANOVA with repeated measures	Questions on candidate competence in selected policy area categories	I II III	Candidate Gender My Party (post hoc groups) Policy area NOT in speech as repeated measure	1. Man Candidate 2. Woman Candidate 1. My Party 2. Not My Party 1. Masc. policy area NOT in speech 2. Fem. policy area NOT in speech	1. Man Candidate × My Party × masc. policy area NOT in speech 2. Woman Candidate × My Party × masc. policy area NOT in speech 3. Man Candidate × Not My Party × masc. policy area NOT in speech 4. Woman Candidate × Not My Party × masc. policy area NOT in speech 5. Man Candidate × My Party × fem. policy area NOT in speech 6. Woman Candidate × My Party × fem. policy area NOT in speech 7. Man Candidate × Not My Party × fem. policy area NOT in speech 8. Woman Candidate × Not My Party × fem. policy area NOT in speech
A14	H7 Participants with highly educated mother will exhibit non-traditional template.	89	2×2 between groups ANOVA	Candidate ability for: Legislator Cabinet Minister Party Leader* Support Win Votes Masc. & fem. policy areas both IN and NOT in speech	I II	Candidate Gender Mother Education	1. Man Candidate 2. Woman Candidate 1. High Education 2. Low Education	1. Man Candidate × High Education 2. Woman Candidate × High Education 3. Man Candidate × Low Education 4. Woman Candidate × Low Education

	Hypothesis	N	Test	DV	Factors / Levels	Post hoc groups
A15	H7 Participant with high status job mother will exhibit non-traditional template.	89	2×2 (or 2×3**) between groups ANOVA	Same DV's as A14	I Candidate Gender 1. Man Candidate 2. Woman Candidate II Mother Job Status (post hoc groups) 1. High Job Status 2. Low Job Status 3. Housewife**	1. Man Candidate × High Job Status 2. Woman Candidate × High Job Status 3. Man Candidate × Low Job Status 4. Woman Candidate × Low Job Status 5. Man Candidate × Housewife** 6. Woman Candidate × Housewife**
A16	H7 Explained above.	89	2×2×2 between groups ANOVA	Same DV's as A14	I Candidate Gender 1. Man Candidate 2. Woman Candidate II Mother Education (post hoc groups) 1. High Education 2. Low Education III Participant Sex (post hoc groups) 1. Male Participant 2. Female Participant	1. Man Candidate × High Education × Male Participant 2. Woman Candidate × High Education × Male Participant 3. Man Candidate × Low Education × Male Participant 4. Woman Candidate × Low Education × Male Participant 5. Man Candidate × High Education × Female Participant 6. Woman Candidate × High Education × Female Participant 7. Man Candidate × Low Education × Female Participant 8. Woman Candidate × Low Education × Female Participant

(continued)

Table A2.1 Continued

Code	Hypothesis tested	Runs	Model	DV's (questions utilized)	Factors	Levels	Treatment combination description
A17	H7 Explained above.	89	2×2×2 (or 2×3×2**) between groups ANOVA	Same DV's as A14	I Candidate Gender II Mother Job Status (post hoc groups) III Participant Sex (post hoc groups)	1. Man Candidate 2. Woman Candidate 1. High Job Status 2. Low Job Status 3. Housewife** 1. Male Participant 2. Female Participant	1. Man Candidate × High Job Status × Male Participant 2. Woman Candidate × High Job Status × Male Participant 3. Man Candidate × Low Job Status × Male Participant 4. Woman Candidate × Low Job Status × Male Participant 5. Man Candidate × Housewife × Male Participant** 6. Woman Candidate × Housewife × Male Participant** 7. Man Candidate × High Job Status × Female Participant 8. Woman Candidate × High Job Status × Female Participant 9. Man Candidate × Low Job Status × Female Participant 10. Woman Candidate × Low Job Status × Female Participant 11. Man Candidate × Housewife × Female Participant** 12. Woman Candidate × Housewife × Female Participant**

* Party Leader DV was used only in parliamentary cases.

** Treatment combinations including housewife not examined in cases with very small number of housewives.

Angela Smith (or David Smith)
Candidate for the U.S. House of Representatives for the Republican Party

Angela Smith is a candidate for the U.S. House of Representatives. She studied business in college and then earned a law degree. She worked in business consulting and then started her own company before being elected to Congress. She became active in the Republican Party in college and has held posts in local government and served in the state legislature. She is involved in her community, working with the American Cancer Society and Special Olympics. She is the mother of 2 children and in her free time enjoys sports and painting. Her speech follows:

Free enterprise is fundamental to our way of life, creating prosperity that enables people to be independent from government, raise their children by their own values, and build communities.

To aid our families the government needs to establish a pro-growth tax code, abolish the death tax, and balance the federal budget by cutting spending. High corporate taxes and regulatory burdens reduce the ability of American businesses to compete overseas and encourage companies to move abroad. We will cut corporate tax rates and negotiate better trade deals that put America first. We will promote first-class physical infrastructure, so business can grow and create wealth. We will also help small businesses gain affordable access to capital by relieving community banks of excessive regulations.

Peace comes through strength. We will rebuild the U.S. military into the world's strongest fighting force, prioritizing personnel readiness, not using the military to advance a political or social agenda. The U.S. participates in many international organizations which can, but sometimes do not, serve the cause of peace and prosperity. Our country must always reserve the right to go its own way. In a time of terrorism, drug cartels, and gangs, having millions of unidentified individuals in this country poses grave safety risks. To keep our people safe we must secure our borders and enforce our immigration laws. We oppose any form of amnesty and believe "sanctuary cities" shouldn't receive federal funding. We support everyone's right to keep and bear arms. Lawful gun ownership enables Americans to exercise their right of self-defense to protect the safety of their families and homes.

We support education savings accounts, vouchers, and tuition tax credits so parents can choose good, safe schools for their children. We should make use of teaching talent in the business community and among our returning veterans, and adopt a merit-based approach to attract the best teachers. The government should not be in the business of student loans. To bring down college costs and give students financing options, private sector participation in student financing should be restored. Admission to public colleges and universities should be based solely on merit.

We will save Medicare by modernizing it, giving states a free hand with block-grants, and setting a more realistic age for eligibility in light of today's longer life span. Consumer choice is the most powerful factor in healthcare reform. To achieve that choice we will repeal and replace the Affordable Care Act with a market-based, competitive, transparent health care system, including health savings accounts and small business insurance pools, which will result in more affordable healthcare and assist all patients, including those with pre-existing conditions, to obtain coverage in a robust consumer market.

Climate change is not our most pressing national security issue. We support common sense environmental regulations that allow for prosperity, using market based incentives when possible instead of regulation. Environmental regulations must be evaluated for the effects they have on the economy. Entrepreneurs, using innovation and incentives, are more likely to solve environmental problems than bureaucrats. Where regulation is necessary our modern approach to environmentalism will shift responsibility for regulation from the federal bureaucracy to the states, including control of public lands.

Voting must be secure, so we support requiring a photo ID to vote. Our constitutional order is threatened by unelected bureaucrats writing countless rules with the force of law. Decisions by federal agencies must be approved by Congress before taking effect. Non-essential federal functions should be returned to the states because governments closest to the people can best deliver public services

Please remember my name is Angela Smith and I am a candidate for the U.S. House of Representatives for the Republican Party. Thank you.

Angela Smith (or David Smith)
Candidate for the U.S. House of Representatives for the Democratic Party

Angela Smith is a candidate for the U.S. House of Representatives. She studied political science in college and then earned a law degree. She worked as a public interest lawyer before being elected to Congress. She became active in the Democratic Party in college and has held posts in local government and served in the state legislature. She is involved in her community, working with groups to empower local residents and Head Start. She is the mother of 2 children and in her free time enjoys running and watching sports. Her speech follows:

Unity is better than division, empowerment is better than resentment, bridges are better than walls. We are proud of our heritage as a nation of immigrants. We are stronger together.

Capitalism is essential to growth, but government must promote equal opportunity. Our economy should work for everyone, closing instead of widening the wealth gap. Every worker should be paid a living wage of at least $15/hour so that a full-time job can adequately care for a family. To strengthen Social Security we will ask those at the top to pay more. By asking the largest corporations to pay their fair share, we can pay for ambitious investments and rebuild our infrastructure without adding to the debt. The federal government should expand credit for small business because they create jobs.

We are stronger when we work with our allies. Our military must remain the best trained and equipped in the world, and welcome all Americans who want to serve. Our nation comes together to stand up to terror. We reject building walls, and instead will invest in regional partnerships. We can respect the rights of responsible gun owners while keeping our communities safe by strengthening background checks and keeping assault weapons off our streets. A community-based approach to crime fighting makes neighborhoods safer, with more officers on the streets in underserved areas, supported with technology and training to balance their dual role to serve and protect, and working to end racial profiling. We support comprehensive immigration reform, providing a path to citizenship.

We must provide every child quality education through college or career programs. We need to provide preschool and afterschool programs, and programs to promote school retention and graduation. Public charter schools should provide options for parents, without destabilizing traditional public schools. We believe that if you have the drive to pursue higher education you should be able to do so and money shouldn't stand in the way. We must make debt-free college a reality for all Americans.

Health care is a right, not a privilege for those who can afford it. We oppose privatizing Medicare, or cuts in Medicaid programs that would harm millions of Americans. We must expand government commitments to Community Health Centers and care for addiction, ensure that loss of employment does not cause a loss of health care, and address health care disparities. We must crack down on price gouging by drug companies and cap the amount Americans pay for prescription drugs. Seniors and people with disabilities want to live with dignity at home, so we must facilitate programs that promote independence and expand the home care workforce.

Climate change is a real threat, seen in brutal droughts in the West and flooding in the South. Science tells us that without immediate action to cut greenhouse gases its impacts will become worse. We cannot leave our children a damaged planet. We reject the notion that we must choose between protecting our planet and creating good-paying jobs. We will do both by making U.S. manufacturing the cleanest in the world, creating green collar jobs with incentives for environmentally friendly products, and a revenue neutral carbon tax. Clean air and water are basic rights, so we will work for environmental justice for all communities.

We must make it easier to vote, not harder, by repealing restrictive photo voter ID laws. Money should not determine who wins elections. We will reform campaign finance to limit spending and end the doctrine that money is speech, and create a system that can be trusted by voters.

Please remember my name is Angela Smith and I am a candidate for the U.S. House of Representatives for the Democratic Party. Thank you.

QUESTIONNAIRE

*Please answer the following questions and return the packet to the researcher. In each case, please put a circle around just **one** answer.*

In your opinion, **how effective** would this person be as a member of the **U.S. House of Representatives**?

1 = outstanding	5 = poor
2 = very good	6 = very poor
3 = good	XX = don't know
4 = fair	

In your opinion, **how effective** would this person be as a member of the **President's cabinet**?

1 = outstanding	5 = poor
2 = very good	6 = very poor
3 = good	XX = don't know
4 = fair	

In your opinion, **how effective** would this person be as a **party leader**?

1 = outstanding	5 = poor
2 = very good	6 = very poor
3 = good	XX = don't know
4 = fair	

What is your assessment of the **ability** of this candidate to **argue** for his/her **political views**?

1 = outstanding	5 = poor
2 = very good	6 = very poor
3 = good	XX = don't know
4 = fair	

Please evaluate the **ability** of the candidate to **deal with policy** in each of the following **areas**: (*Circle one evaluation of the candidate's ability for each policy area.*)

Agriculture	(very competent)	1 / 2 / 3 / 4 / 5	(incompetent)
Education	(very competent)	1 / 2 / 3 / 4 / 5	(incompetent)
Energy	(very competent)	1 / 2 / 3 / 4 / 5	(incompetent)
Security	(very competent)	1 / 2 / 3 / 4 / 5	(incompetent)
Government reform	(very competent)	1 / 2 / 3 / 4 / 5	(incompetent)
Child care	(very competent)	1 / 2 / 3 / 4 / 5	(incompetent)
Health care	(very competent)	1 / 2 / 3 / 4 / 5	(incompetent)
Environment	(very competent)	1 / 2 / 3 / 4 / 5	(incompetent)
Infrastructure	(very competent)	1 / 2 / 3 / 4 / 5	(incompetent)
National economy	(very competent)	1 / 2 / 3 / 4 / 5	(incompetent)
Unemployment	(very competent)	1 / 2 / 3 / 4 / 5	(incompetent)
Women's rights	(very competent)	1 / 2 / 3 / 4 / 5	(incompetent)

In each case below, please put a circle around just **one** answer.

Would you vote for this candidate for **the U.S. House of Representatives**?

1 = yes 2 = no

Do you think this **candidate** would be **good at winning votes**?

(very good) 1 / 2 / 3 / 4 / 5 (very poor)

Was the candidate whose speech you read a **woman** or a **man**?

1 = man 2 = woman XX = don't remember

Is the **mayor** of your city a **woman** or a **man**?

1 = man 2 = woman XX = don't remember

Are you **male** or **female**? 1 = male 2 = female XX = prefer not to respond

What is your **age**? _____

What **city or town** do you live in? _____

   How long (years) have you lived there? _____

How **much education** does your **mother** have?

   1 = incomplete elementary school   5 = technical school or junior college
   2 = complete elementary school   6 = incomplete university
   3 = incomplete high school   7 = complete university
   4 = complete high school   8 = post-graduate school
                               9 = don't know

How **much education** does your **father** have?

   1 = incomplete elementary school   5 = technical school or junior college
   2 = complete elementary school   6 = incomplete university
   3 = incomplete high school   7 = complete university
   4 = complete high school   8 = post-graduate school
                               9 = don't know

What **job** do **you** aspire to after you complete your education? _____

What is the **occupation** of your **father**? (If he is not currently working, what was his most recent job? _____

What is the **occupation** of your **mother**? (If she is not currently working, what was her most recent job? _____

How often do you follow **political issues** news in the **news**?

     1 = daily   4 = less frequently than once a week
     2 = 2 or 3 times a week   5 = never
     3 = once a week

Within national politics **what party do you identify with**: (please circle one answer)

    1 = Democratic Party   2 = Republican Party
    5 = none of these [skip next question]

How strong is your attachment to your **political party**? (please circle one answer)

    1 = very strong   2 = fairly strong   3 = not very strong

The speech you have read was given by a candidate of the following party: (please circle one answer)

    1 = Republican Party   2 = Democratic Party
    5 = none of these

In politics they normally talk about "**left**" and "**right**." In a scale where 1 is "left" (or **most liberal**) and 10 is "right" (or **most conservative**), where would you place yourself?

    (left) 1 / 2 / 3 / 4 / 5 / 6 / 7 / 8 / 9 / 10 (right)

Below, please rate **your degree** of **agreement / disagreement** with each of the **following statements** (on a scale from 1 to 7 where 1 = strongly agree, 4 = undecided, 7 = strongly disagree).

- It is disrespectful to swear in the presence of a lady.
  (strongly agree) 1 / 2 / 3 / 4 / 5 / 6 / 7 (strongly disagree)
- The initiative in dating should usually come from the man.
  (strongly agree) 1 / 2 / 3 / 4 / 5 / 6 / 7 (strongly disagree)
- Women should have as much sexual freedom as men.
  (strongly agree) 1 / 2 / 3 / 4 / 5 / 6 / 7 (strongly disagree)
- Women with children should not work outside the home if they don't have to financially.
  (strongly agree) 1 / 2 / 3 / 4 / 5 / 6 / 7 (strongly disagree)
- The husband should be regarded as the legal representative of the family group in all matters of law.
  (strongly agree) 1 / 2 / 3 / 4 / 5 / 6 / 7 (strongly disagree)
- Except perhaps in very special circumstances, a man should never allow a woman to pay the taxi, buy the tickets, or pay the bill.
  (strongly agree) 1 / 2 / 3 / 4 / 5 / 6 / 7 (strongly disagree)
- Men should continue to show courtesies to women such as holding the door open and helping them on with their coats.
  (strongly agree) 1 / 2 / 3 / 4 / 5 / 6 / 7 (strongly disagree)
- It is ridiculous for a woman to drive a truck and a man to sew clothes.
  (strongly agree) 1 / 2 / 3 / 4 / 5 / 6 / 7 (strongly disagree)
- Women should be concerned with their duties of childbearing and housekeeping, rather than with the desires for professional and business careers.
  (strongly agree) 1 / 2 / 3 / 4 / 5 / 6 / 7 (strongly disagree)
- Swearing and obscenity is more repulsive in the speech of a woman than a man.
  (strongly agree) 1 / 2 / 3 / 4 / 5 / 6 / 7 (strongly disagree)

When you consider members of the **U.S. House of Representatives** - how much impact do they have on the life of your family?

No impact 1 / 2 / 3 / 4 / 5 A lot of impact

When you consider members of **President's cabinet** - how much impact do they have on the life of your family?

No impact 1 / 2 / 3 / 4 / 5 A lot of impact

When you consider a **leader of a major national party** - how much impact does she or he have on the life of your family?

No impact 1 / 2 / 3 / 4 / 5 A lot of impact

Which categories describe you? (please circle all that apply)

1 = White	2 = Hispanic, Latino or Spanish Origin
3 = Black or African American	4 = Asian
5 = American Indian or Alaska Native	6 = Middle Eastern or North African
7 = Native Hawaiian or Other Pacific Islander	8 = Some other race, ethnicity or origin

When you are finished, please give your survey and the speech you read to the researcher. Thank you for taking part in this research.

PART II
FINDINGS IN
INDIVIDUAL CASES

3

Costa Rica—Where Urban Young People View Women as Leaders

Gerardo Hernández Naranjo and Michelle M. Taylor-Robinson

MACRO-CONTEXT FACTORS: COSTA RICA AND OTHER CASES				
LOW ← Expectation of Strength of Gender Bias → HIGH				

Executive Institutions	**Parliamentary**		**OR**	**Presidential**
	Alberta CA			Chile
	Quebec CA			California US
	England			Texas US
	Israel			Costa Rica
	Sweden			Uruguay

Electoral Institutions	**Party focused ← - - - - - - - - - - - - - - - → Candidate focused**				
	Israel	Uruguay	Chile	Alberta CA	California US
	Costa Rica	Sweden		Quebec CA	Texas US
				England	

Policy Agenda Emphasis	**More Social Welfare ← - - - - - - - - - → Less Social Welfare**				
	Sweden	Alberta CA	Uruguay	England	California US
	Costa Rica	Quebec CA	Israel	Chile	Texas US
	Less Defense ← - - - - - - - - - - - - - → More Defense				
	Costa Rica	Alberta CA	Sweden	England	Israel
	Uruguay	Quebec CA	Chile	California US	Texas US

Incorporation of Women in Government	**Greatest ← - → Least**				
	Sweden	Chile	Alberta CA	Uruguay	Texas US
	Costa Rica	England	Quebec CA	California US	Israel

Introduction

This study shows, with striking consistency, an absence of traditional gendered leadership templates, and that Costa Rican urban young adults view women as capable government leaders.[1] We expected that Costa Rica could be a favorable context for young people to move beyond traditional leadership templates

---

[1] We thank Bethany Shockley for assistance implementing the experiment.

Gerardo Hernández Naranjo and Michelle M. Taylor-Robinson, *Costa Rica—Where Urban Young People View Women as Leaders* In: *The Image of Gender and Political Leadership*. Edited by: Michelle M. Taylor-Robinson and Nehemia Geva, Oxford University Press. © Oxford University Press 2023. DOI: 10.1093/oso/9780197642726.003.0003

due to the combination of a lengthy history of women in government and a national policy agenda that emphasizes government provision of social services. Our study, conducted in July–August 2014 with 696 young adults, finds that evaluations of the man and woman candidate are equivalent, or when there is a significant effect of Candidate Gender, women are evaluated more favorably. Importantly, the baseline controls—Party Label and Party Platform—are significant, which indicates that participants read and understood the speeches, and reacted to the treatments, yet Candidate Gender was relatively unimportant to leadership templates.

The Context of Costa Rica Politics and Its Expected Effect on Gender Attitudes

Women in Government

Costa Rica is the oldest democracy in Latin America, with regime stability since the promulgation of the 1949 Constitution, after the 1948 civil war. Women received the right to vote and run for office in the 1949 Constitution, and in the 1953 election for the Legislative Assembly women won three of the forty-five seats (Gonzalez-Suarez 1994: 178).[2] The first woman cabinet minister was appointed in 1958. In 2010 the first woman was elected president, Laura Chinchilla of the National Liberation Party (PLN). Chinchilla won an impressive victory, winning election in the first round with 46.9 percent of the valid vote, including winning in eighty of the eighty-two cantons, while the candidate who came in second received 25.1 percent of the vote (Alfaro 2010). Being a woman was one of the factors that had a big influence on her victory (Florez-Estrada 2010; Raventos et al. 2012).

Women's participation in the executive branch expanded in recent decades. In the late 1970s, during the Carazo administration, 12 percent of cabinet posts were held by women. In the Chinchilla administration (2010–2014), 27 percent of cabinet ministers were women. The initial cabinet of the Solís administration (2014–2018 Citizen's Action Party [PAC]) contained 36 percent women.[3] Many women have held portfolios handling social policy. Women have also held stereotypically masculine posts: agriculture, economics, foreign trade, and security (Escobar-Lemmon and Taylor-Robinson 2016; Hernández Naranjo and Guzmán Castillo 2018). Several women have served as vice-president since the 1980s. Costa Rica has two VPs, and since 2010 the parity gender quota law

---

[2] See Piscopo (2018) for a detailed review of women's participation in Costa Rica.
[3] President Alvarado Quesada's (PAC, 2018–2022) initial cabinet had 52 percent women.

applies to presidential slates (*Tribunal Supremo de Elecciones (TSE)* resolution 3671-E8-2010).

Women's participation in the legislative branch has also been extensive by world standards and began to increase in the 1980s. During the years when this study's participants were growing up, the percentage of women in the Assembly varied between 19.3 percent (1998) and 38.6 percent (2010) (TSE 1998; Valitutti Chavarría et al. 2015). Women held nineteen of fifty-seven seats in the Assembly that took office in May 2014 (33.3 percent).[4] Numerous women have been Assembly vice-president; however, the Assembly presidency has been held by men, except in 2018–2019, 2001–2002, and 1986–1987.

Election Rules

Assembly and (first round) presidential elections are concurrent. Deputies in the Legislative Assembly are elected via party-presented closed and blocked lists, with the seven provinces as the electoral districts (magnitude range 4–19), which encourages voters to focus on party rather than personal attributes of candidates. There is no immediate reelection for deputies or presidents. The experiment was conducted in the capital and surrounding cities, so DM of the electoral districts of study participants ranged from six to nineteen. In 1996 Costa Rica adopted a 40 percent gender quota with a strong enforcement mechanism. In 2009 the quota increased to 50 percent with gender alternation on lists.[5] Despite the parity quota less than half of Assembly seats are held by women due to party system fragmentation. Nine parties held seats in the fifty-seven-member Assembly when the experiment was conducted, but several won just one seat, and party lists are typically led by a male candidate.[6]

When this experiment was fielded, Laura Chinchilla had just completed her term as president. There were many charges of corruption against members of her government, and clashes between Chinchilla and former president Oscar Arias, who was from her party (Frajman 2014: 62; Thomas 2014).[7] Consequently, by the end of her term public opinion of President Chinchilla was unfavorable. In the March–May 2014 LAPOP survey, 24.6 percent answered that she was doing

---

[4] Women held 45.6 percent of seats in the Assembly that took office in May 2018 (ipu.org).

[5] Costa Rican women began pushing for a quota in the 1980s (see Saint-Germain and Morgan 1991; Jones 2004; Sagot Rodríguez 2010).

[6] The PAC is the exception with three of the seven PAC lists in the 2014 elections headed by a woman (Valitutti Chavarría et al. 2015). Beginning with the 2018 elections the TSE ruled that party slates must comply with "horizontal parity," which was a rallying cry for female politicians during the 2014–2018 legislature (Vote of the Constitutional Court N° 2015-16070 and TSE Resolución N° 3603-E8-2016).

[7] Chinchilla was 1st vice-president during Arias' 2006–2010 administration, and Arias supported her in the PLN's selection of its presidential candidate.

her job badly, and 19.6 percent answered "very badly" (LAPOP 2014). Thus, even though Costa Rica is one of the few countries to have had a woman president, and she would have been the president most familiar to the participants in our study, it was unclear whether experience with a woman president would produce favorable attitudes toward women politicians.

Government Policy Agenda

Costa Rica has a unitary government. Cantonal governments administer some public services and make specific policies that apply to their local jurisdiction, but the principal public policies are made by the national government.

In the early 1940s the government developed a social security and health-care system. The government expanded public education from university through kindergarten, including technical schools, night, and distance education programs. The government also addressed housing needs, expanding that program in the late 1970s and 1980s. While social welfare policies are areas where women are typically viewed as "fitting" in government posts, and women have led the education, health, and housing ministries, and the Social Security Agency, historically these programs were developed and implemented by men politicians. Thus, while important parts of the government's long-term policy agenda are focused on stereotypically feminine policy areas, they cover policy topics that men still often direct, and posts men want to hold.

A second factor that makes the government policy agenda favorable for acceptance of women politicians is the absence of a military since 1948. Costa Rica has no army, or ministry of defense. However, security—fighting common crime, organized crime, and drug gangs—became an increasingly important problem, and concern of voters, starting in the 1990s.

Economic policy is also an important component of the government's agenda. Topics of labor market access, salary equity, and poor households headed by women bring women's interests into economics policy. While women have been under-represented in economics posts in the cabinet (Escobar-Lemmon and Taylor-Robinson 2016: 158), three women held economics posts in the Chinchilla administration (economics/industry/commerce, foreign trade, planning and economic policy).[8]

The 2014 LAPOP survey asked Costa Ricans what they viewed as the most important problem facing the country. The most frequent responses were corruption and unemployment (each 20 percent of responses), crime (19 percent), problems with the economy (17 percent).

---

[8] The first economic post held by a woman was Foreign Trade from 1986–1990.

Historically, the policy agenda of Costa Rica's government creates a setting that should be favorable for women politicians because long-time government programs line up with stereotypically feminine policy areas. However, in the young adult lives of our study participants, security concerns and economic challenges, including growing inequality, dominated political debates (Alfaro-Redondo and Gómez-Campos 2012, 2014). Thus, it is conceivable that study participants would want men politicians to handle stereotypically masculine policy areas.

Political Socialization, and Survey Data about Gender Attitudes

Schools have been a means for political socialization about democratic values. Along with civic education programs, the 1960s saw introduction of elections for student government in public schools, which have spread throughout the country. In 2008, new civic education programs were implemented that included topics of human rights and a gender perspective (MEP 2009), and in 2009 a new Regulation on the Organization and Operation of Student Government included gender parity and alternation on ballots for student body elections (TSE-IFED 2010). This has led to increased presence of girls and young women in student representative bodies, which is important for political socialization of the student participants in this experiment.

Survey data provide information about attitudes of the broader Costa Rican population. The 2008 and 2012 LAPOP surveys asked respondents the extent to which they agree or disagree with the statement that men make better political leaders than women. In 2008, 72.3 percent of respondents disagreed or strongly disagreed, increasing to 78.6 percent. in 2012. When asked in 2012 if a man or a woman would be better at handling the national economy, 70.2 percent said that both sexes were equal (21.5 percent preferred a woman, 8.3 percent a man). The 2012 survey also asked whether men or women are more corrupt politicians, and 72 percent said that the sexes are equal (25.2 percent men are more corrupt, 2.7 percent women are more corrupt). Yet even with these expressions of gender equal attitudes in LAPOP surveys, a 2013 survey conducted by Costa Rica's National Women's Institute (INAMU) found that 74.2 percent of respondents indicate there is discrimination against women (70 percent in the workforce, 62.3 percent in politics). Machismo is viewed as the biggest obstacle women face in politics (according to 68.3 percent of men, and 76.6 percent of women). Lack of economic resources was the second most listed obstacle. In addition, 33.7 percent of women and 34 percent of men said that politics is for men (Valitutti Chavarría et al. 2015: 250).

Education and Workforce

Data from 2015 indicate that almost 40 percent of Costa Ricans (age fifteen or older) have complete secondary school or more education. Slightly more women than men have completed secondary school or college or have post-graduate education (INEC 2015).

Workforce participation is lower for women than men. In 2014, the employment rate of men was 69.6 percent and for women 40.4 percent (Programa Estado de la Nación 2017). Women's work situation is more precarious than men's, with lower salaries and higher unemployment. Women are more likely to work in education and health, while men are more highly represented in agriculture and construction. The numbers of women employed in managerial, professional, and scientific positions is increasing, and their salaries come closer to those of men. However, women are underrepresented in top management especially in the private sector, with seven of ten positions held by men (Valitutti Chavarría et al. 2015: 89–96, 256).

Description of the Costa Rica Experiment and Dataset

The minister of education approved the study and selected the high schools to provide a socio-economically representative array of schools.[9] The experiment was conducted in classrooms, during regular class times at eleven schools (public *liceos*, technical high schools, private high schools, and public universities). All schools were in urban areas in the *Meseta Central*. High school classes were small, selected by the school principal or vice-principal, and included diverse topics (e.g., biology, math, machining, philosophy). University classes were introductory classes taken by students from diverse majors. The experiment was conducted by the female PI, and a female graduate student.

Study Participants

The Costa Rica dataset has 696 participants (49 percent female). Average age of participants is 17.9. Average ideology self-placement on a left-right scale (1=left,

---

[9] Costa Rica was the first pilot study that led to an eight-country project, and there are some minor differences in how this study was conducted compared to the later cases. In Costa Rica we dropped the small number of participants who incorrectly answered the manipulation check question about the sex of the candidate. To create only complete blocks in the final dataset, six "participants" were created via bootstrapping data from all the other participants, and when a participant did not answer a specific dependent variable question, answers were bootstrapped based on average answers for the dataset.

10=right) is 4.8.[10] Participants come from diverse socio-economic backgrounds as gauged from answers about the education and occupations of their parents. For example, 41 percent of mothers had less than complete secondary education, as did 37 percent of fathers.[11] Table 3.1 describes the dataset.

Relevant Aspects of the Time-Period When the Study Was Conducted

The experiment was conducted approximately two and a half months after President Solís took office. His predecessor was Costa Rica's first woman president. Solís was the first president from the PAC and his government followed two administrations from the country's oldest party, the PLN.

Party fragmentation in the Assembly was high after the 2014 election, with nine parties winning seats (Alfaro-Redondo and Gómez-Campos 2014).[12] Party system fragmentation is relevant to the experiment because, while the two parties presented in the speeches were the governing party (PAC) and the largest opposition party (PLN), they collectively won only 60.3 percent of the vote in the first-round presidential election and 54.4 percent of Assembly seats. Many voters preferred another party. For the urban young adult participants in this study support for the PLN was very low: only 13.2 percent listed the PLN as their preferred party.[13] While 51.8 percent of participants identified with the PAC, 13.0 percent identified with the left-leaning Frente Amplio (FA) and nine other parties were the preferred party for small numbers of participants. This is consistent with analysis of the 2014 election, where the PAC and FA both had greater support in urban areas. They are also the most progressive parties on women's rights (Alfaro-Redondo and Gómez-Campos 2014). Just 21.9 percent of participants said that they did not have a preferred party. Consequently, 52.5 percent of participants received a speech from a party that was not their preferred party, and 36.8 percent received a speech of their preferred party.

---

[10] While left-right scales are commonly used in multi-national studies, the terms "left" and "right" are not very common in ordinary political language or debates in Costa Rica.

[11] Nationally 62.2 percent of the population age fifteen or older has less than complete secondary school (INEC, ENAHO 2015).

[12] The effective number of parties increased from 2.6 in 1998 to 4.9 in 2014. Simultaneously voter identification with parties declined (Pignataro 2017; Pignataro and Cascante 2018).

[13] For the Costa Rica study we determined the participant's preferred party by answers to three open-ended questions: With which political party do you most closely identify, if there is one? If you could have voted in the presidential elections in February, for which party would you have voted? If you could have voted in the Assembly election in February, for which party would you have voted?

64 HERNÁNDEZ NARANJO AND TAYLOR-ROBINSON

Table 3.1 Description of Participants in Costa Rica

	Overall	Male only	Female only
Number of participants*	696	351	339
Percent of participants	100	50.9	49.1
Average age	17.9	18.1	17.8
Left (1) to Right (10) self-placement	4.83	4.67	5.00
Preferred party (%):			
Governing (PAC)	51.8	51.8	51.9
Largest opposition (PLN)	13.2	10.7	15.9
Frente Amplio	13.0	14.9	11.1
Other or no preference	21.9	22.7	21.1
Total	100	100	100
Parents' education** (% of participants):			
Fathers w/high level	27.2	31.6	22.7
Mothers w/high level	22.2	24.5	19.8
Fathers w/low level	49.4	48.1	50.7
Mothers w/low level	56.7	56.7	56.6
Parents' occupation (% of participants):			
Fathers w/high status job	45.5	49.2	41.5
Mothers w/high status job	26.3	25.8	26.8
Housewives, as % of participants	30.3	29.1	31.6
Housewives, as the actual number	203	98	105

* Six of the 696 were simulated from bootstrapping in order to create complete treatment blocks.

** Note: Education levels of participants' parents are divided into "high" (complete university or more) and "low" (complete secondary or less), and the remaining percentage (not shown) is defined as "intermediate" or "don't know."

Candidate Gender, Party, and General Evaluations of Candidates

The Costa Rica experiment, like all cases in this project, used a 2×2×2 factorial design with Candidate Gender, Party Platform, and Party Label as the three factors presented in a relatively long candidate speech for each of the two largest parties. Each speech discussed six policy areas. Party Platform was developed from reading the president's 2012 annual address to the Assembly (*Informe Presidencial*) and responses from deputies of the PAC and PLN. (Chapter 2 provides a detailed explanation of the experiment design and implementation.)

Each participant scored the suitability of one candidate with a specific gender (indicated by the candidate's name and gendered pronouns) and party (party name stated or implied). Participants did not directly compare candidates. We thus avoid terms like "preferred" or "preferable" because they suggest the same participant making a comparison across candidates. Instead, we present which candidates scored higher or lower when comparing average candidate evaluations across treatment conditions. The notation, H5 through H11, refers to hypotheses and statistical methods outlined in Chapters 1 and 2.

Role congruity theory expects people will evaluate a candidate unfavorably who does not "look like the norm." We ask then, given the Costa Rican context, do young people's evaluations indicate that women "look like the norm" for politicians? To begin, we examine four general evaluation questions: (1) How effective would this person be as a deputy in the Legislative Assembly?[14] or (2) as a cabinet minister?[14] (3) Would you support this candidate at your party's nominating convention?[15] (4) Do you think this candidate would be good at winning votes?[16] Factor analysis of the general questions is in the Chapter Appendix.

To test H8, for each general question we conduct a 2×2×2 ANOVA with Candidate Gender, Party Platform, and Party Label as factors to measure the strength of a gender effect against our baseline control: the party effect. For effectiveness as a *Deputy*, and ability to *Win Votes* the main-effect of Candidate Gender is not significant ($[F(1,682)=2.293, p=.130]$ and $[F(1,682)=1.007, p=.316]$ respectively), but the main-effects of Party Platform and Party Label are significant (p=.009 and p=.005 for *Deputy*, p=.001 and p=.053 for *Win Votes*). In both cases the PAC candidate is more favorably evaluated than the PLN candidate, which comports with the 2014 election results. Evaluations are also more favorable when a party name was not on the speech, which is consistent with the increasing percentage of Costa Ricans supporting parties other than the two largest parties, or who do not identify with any party (see Figure 3.1).[17] The significant effects for these two measures of party indicate that participants reacted to the treatments, and we can interpret with confidence that the lack of

---

[14] Scored 1 (excellent) to 6 (very bad). Answers have been inverted so that high scores are favorable.

[15] Scored 1=yes, 2=no, thus low scores are favorable.

[16] Scored 1 (very good) to 5 (very poor). Answers have been inverted so that high scores are favorable.

[17] Many Costa Ricans do not identify with a political party, as shown in LAPOP surveys. In 2010 47.7 percent said they did not identify with a party, 73.8 percent in 2012, and 32.6 percent in 2014.

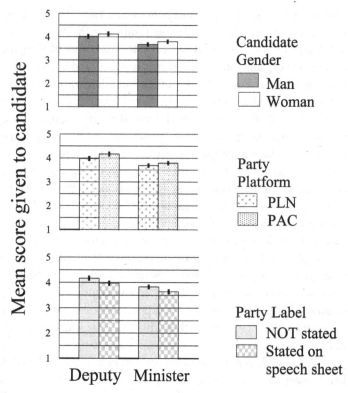

Figure 3.1 Main effects of treatment and baseline controls for *Deputy* and *Minister*
2×2×2 ANOVA (Candidate Gender, Party Platform, Party Label) 95 percent confidence intervals included.

significance of Candidate Gender is a sign that Costa Rican urban young adults do not have traditional leadership templates.

Regarding effectiveness to be a *Minister*, the woman candidate is evaluated more favorably (M=3.80) than the man (M=3.68), and the main effect of Candidate Gender approaches significance [F(1,682)=3.37, p=.067]. For cabinet ministers, gender appears relevant for leadership templates, but it favors women, so this is not a traditional "leaders are men" template. Party Label is also significant (p=.005) and has a greater impact than Candidate Gender on evaluations (η_p^2 for Party Label=.012, and .005 for Candidate Gender). For *Support* the candidate (here low scores are more favorable), the woman candidate is scored more favorably (M=1.26 woman, M=1.36 man, [F(1,682)=7.828, p=.005]). Party Platform (p=.019) and Party Label (p=.004) are also significant. The impact of Party Label (η_p^2=.012) is slightly greater than the impact of Candidate Gender

(η_p^2=.011), and both are greater than Party Platform (η_p^2=.008). In sum, women appear to "look like the norm" for candidates, and party has larger effects on candidate evaluations than gender.

Role congruity theory also indicates that women will be viewed as incongruent for high-ranking posts. Cabinet posts are more powerful than a seat in the Assembly, as ministers implement laws and make decisions about budgets, so the existing literature about role congruity leads to the expectation that women will be less favorably evaluated compared to men to be ministers than deputies (H9). Yet we find that the woman candidate is evaluated more favorably than the man candidate for both posts, and the difference in the evaluation for *Minister* is greater than the difference in the evaluation for *Deputy* (|man – woman candidate evaluation|=.121 for *Minister*, .109 for *Deputy*).[18]

But does support for women candidates come only from female participants? Literature about in-groups indicates that people will support candidates with whom they have a common group identity. Due to a shared sex in-group effect, male participants may give man candidates more favorable evaluations, and female participants more favorably evaluate woman candidates (H5). A shared party in-group effect may prompt both male and female participants to evaluate a woman candidate more favorably if she is from their preferred party (H6).

To test if shared gender identity is the source of favorable evaluations of women candidates (H5), we conduct 2×2 between groups ANOVAs with Candidate Gender and Participant Sex as factors. A significant interaction would indicate that male and female study participants evaluate candidates differently. We find that the interaction was not significant for any of the general questions, indicating no support for a shared sex in-group effect.[19] The analysis above showed that women candidates were evaluated more favorably for *Minister* and *Support*. This analysis indicates that both male and female participants give favorable evaluations to the woman candidate.

To examine if there is an in-group effect of shared partisan identity (H6), we conduct a 2×2 ANOVA with Candidate Gender and My Party (whether the candidate was from the participant's party or not) as factors. For all questions the main effect of My Party is highly significant,[20] and participants always give a more favorable mean evaluation to candidates when they are from their preferred party. However, the interaction Candidate Gender×My Party is not significant

---

[18] Repeated measures ANOVA with Post (*Deputy* and *Minister*) and Candidate Gender as factors shows that participants evaluate the posts differently [$F(1,688)$=104.0, p=.000], and that they more favorably evaluate women candidates (M=3.97) than men candidates (M=3.85) [$F(1,688)$=3.65, p=.056]. However, the interaction Post×Candidate Gender is not significant [$F(1,688)$=.036, p=.849].

[19] For the interaction Candidate Gender×Participant Sex p-values range from .348 to .583.

[20] For *Deputy* (p=.003), *Minister* (p=.002), *Support* (p=.000), *Win Votes* (p=.011).

(p-values range from .259 to .762).[21] In sum, a woman candidate does not need to be from the participant's preferred party (shared in-group) to fit their leadership template. These findings are not an artifact of combining speeches with and without party labels. If we limit our test to participants who got a speech that stated the party name on the speech, My Party is again always significant (p<.05), and the interaction Candidate Gender×My Party is not significant.

In summary, for general evaluation questions, leadership templates accept women. This acceptance does not appear to be limited to an in-group. Male participants do not evaluate men candidates more favorably than women candidates, and women are acceptable leaders even when they are not from the participant's party. Additionally, while women candidates are evaluated more favorably than men on two of four general questions, Party Platform or Party Label have a greater impact on candidate evaluations than Candidate Gender.

Candidate Gender, Party, and Competence in Specific Policy Areas

Costa Rica's policy agenda offers what we would expect to be a favorable situation for women candidates to fit templates of leaders. For decades, the government has provided a social welfare state that emphasizes policies in which women traditionally have credibility. But since the turn of the century, stereotypically masculine policies of security and economics have been a focus of the public's attention, and in 2014 Costa Ricans listed corruption, unemployment, crime, and economy as the most important problems (LAPOP 2014).

To explore whether and how Candidate Gender and Party influence candidate evaluations in stereotypically feminine and masculine policy areas, we examine one masculine and one feminine policy that was discussed in the candidate speeches, and one of each type of policy that was not discussed. Participants were asked to "evaluate the ability of the candidate to manage policy" in twelve policy areas, half of which were discussed in the speech.[22] The policy areas discussed in the Costa Rican speeches are education, energy, environment, government reform, national economy, and security.

Education is stereotypically feminine. Education gained attention right before the experiment was fielded as the national teachers' unions went on strike the day the Solís government took office. The new education minister, a woman, resolved the strike, though it caused the new school year to begin a few weeks late.

---

[21] When we conduct this analysis with three categories: my party, not my party, participant does not state a party, findings are substantively the same.

[22] Scored from 1 (very capable) to 5 (incapable). Scores have been inverted so that high scores are favorable.

WOMEN AS LEADERS IN COSTA RICA 69

Not only was the minister of education a woman at the time this experiment was conducted, but the first woman to hold a cabinet post (in 1958) was minister of education, and women have been education minister from 1978 to 1982, 2002 to 2003, and 2003 to 2004.[23] Discussion of education in the speeches focused on preparing students for work. The PAC speech emphasized expanding post-secondary technical education. The PLN speech pledged to expand computer and internet access at schools, and to promote technical education by working with the private sector to determine its employment needs.

We examine security as the stereotypically masculine policy area discussed in the speech because crime was a top problem facing the country. Recall, however, that Costa Rica does not have a military, so security means handling crime. A woman was minister of security from 1996 to 1998 and 2008 to 2010,[24] and president of the Council of Security (2002–2004).[25] The PAC speech emphasized combating narco-traffic, homicides, and corruption, with education as the best tool to promote social mobility and win the fight against poverty. The PLN speech stated that insecurity was due to organized crime, homicides, and narco-traffic, but also due to corruption and violence against the most vulnerable populations, and they pledged to fight crime by better training for the police. Thus, the presentation of security policy, taken from discussions of the topic by both parties, does not have a strongly masculine presentation.

Participants also evaluated the candidate on six policy areas not discussed in the speech: agriculture, childcare, foreign relations, health, unemployment, and women's rights. We examine childcare as the stereotypically feminine policy because expanding childcare programs was a major initiative of President Chinchilla, culminating in Law # 9220 of March 4, 2014, which set up the National Network for Childcare and Infant Development (Valitutti Chavarría et al. 2015: 86). For the stereotypically masculine policy area we examine unemployment, which was viewed as one of the top problems facing the country in 2014.

To test for an effect of gender stereotypes (H10) we use repeated measures ANOVA with Domain (two policy areas discussed in the speech: *security* and *education*) and Candidate Gender as factors. The analysis shows that these policy areas are viewed as different ($p=.000$). Importantly for our interest in gender stereotypes, the interaction Domain×Candidate Gender is significant [$F(1,688)=5.995$, $p=.015$], and the woman candidate is evaluated more favorably for *education* policy (M=3.833) than the man (M=3.712) (see Figure 3.2).[26]

---

[23] Source: https://guide2womenleaders.com/Costa_Rica.htm (accessed December 15, 2018).

[24] President Laura Chinchilla (PLN 2010-2014) was Minister of Security from 1996 to 1998.

[25] Source: https://guide2womenleaders.com/Costa_Rica.htm (accessed December 15, 2018).

[26] As a robustness check, we conduct repeated measures ANOVAs for the other masculine policies discussed in the speech. For *economy* and *education* the policy areas are viewed as different (p= .000) and Candidate Gender has a significant main-effect (p=.044) with more favorable evaluations

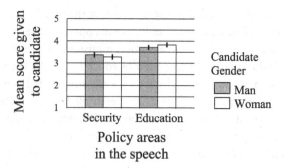

Figure 3.2 Candidate evaluations for masculine and feminine policy areas discussed in the speech
2×2 repeated measures ANOVA (Policy Domain, Candidate Gender) 95 percent confidence intervals included.

We conduct the same type of analysis for policy areas not discussed in the speech (*unemployment* and *childcare*). Again, the policy areas are viewed as different (p=.000), but here the interaction is not significant [F(1,688)=.687, p=.408]. While the literature indicates that gender stereotypes will be used as heuristics to evaluate candidates when policy information is not available (H11), we find that male candidates are not evaluated more favorably for the masculine policy area.[27] However, for *education* policy, which *was* discussed in the speech, and for which the man and woman candidate of the same party provided the exact same information, the woman candidate is evaluated more favorably.

To directly compare the effect of Candidate Gender to the effect of party, our baseline control, we conduct a 2×2×2 ANOVA (Candidate Gender, Party Platform, Party Label) for each policy area. We find a significant main effect for Candidate Gender only for *childcare* (p=.025) with a more favorable evaluation of the woman candidate (M=3.108) than the man (M=2.936). However, there

of the woman candidate (M=3.527) than the man (M=3.401), but the interaction is not significant [F(1,688)=.016, p=.900]. For *energy* and *education* the policy areas are viewed as different (p=.000), and the interaction Domain×Candidate Gender is significant [F(1,688)=4.307, p=.038]. The man and woman candidates are evaluated equivalently for *energy* policy, but the woman candidate is evaluated more favorably for *education*.

[27] As a robustness check we conduct repeated measures ANOVAs for the other masculine and feminine policy areas not discussed in the speech. For *agriculture* and *women's rights* the policy areas are viewed as different (p=.000), the interaction Domain×Candidate Gender is highly significant [F(1,688)=36.439, p=.000], and the main-effect of Candidate Gender is highly significant (p=.000). The men and women candidates are evaluated as equivalent on *agriculture*, but the woman candidate is favored on *women's rights*. For *foreign relations* and *health* the policy areas are different (p=.000), but the interaction is not significant [F(1,688)=.272, p=.602].

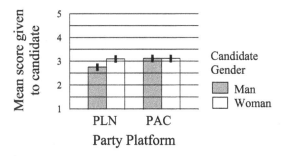

Figure 3.3 Interaction of Party Platform and Candidate Gender for *childcare* policy
2×2×2 ANOVA (Candidate Gender, Party Platform, Party Label) 95 percent confidence intervals included.

are significant party effects for each policy area. Party Label is highly significant for *security* (p=.008) and *education* policy (p=.007), in both cases with a more favorable evaluation when the party name is not on the speech. For both *unemployment* and *childcare* policies, Party Platform is significant (p=.001 and p=.013 respectively), and the candidate of the PAC is evaluated more favorably. For *childcare* policy, the effect of Party Platform (η_p^2=.009) is slightly larger than the effect of Candidate Gender (η_p^2=.007), and the interaction Candidate Gender×Party Platform is significant [$F(1,682)$=5.222, p=.023, η_p^2=.008]. The man and woman candidates are evaluated equally favorably if they are from the PAC, but for PLN candidates the woman candidate is evaluated more favorably (see Figure 3.3).

We again want to explore if a shared sex in-group effect determines when women candidates are viewed as capable leaders (H5). To do this we add Participant Sex as a factor in the above repeated measures ANOVAs. For policy areas discussed in the speech, and not discussed, we do not find a significant interaction of Domain×Candidate Gender×Participant Sex.[28] Both male and female participants evaluate the candidates equivalently, including for *education* policy, with both favoring the woman candidate.

To test if a shared party in-group effect explains candidate evaluations (H6), we redo the repeated measures analysis with Candidate Gender and My Party (my party, not my party) as factors. The interaction Domain×Candidate Gender×My Party is not significant.[29] Evaluations are more favorable for

---

[28] For policy areas discussed in the speech [$F(1,686)$=.113, p=.737]; policy areas not discussed [$F(1,686)$=.418, p=.518].

[29] For policy areas discussed in the speech [$F(1,612)$=.077, p=.782]; policy areas not discussed [$F(1,612)$=.996, p=.319].

Domain, both when the policy topics were discussed in the speech, and not discussed, if the candidate is from the participant's preferred party, which is another demonstration of the importance of party. However, it is not necessary for a woman candidate to be from the participant's preferred party for her to receive a favorable evaluation.[30]

There is some evidence that gender stereotypes influence evaluations of candidates, as the woman candidate is evaluated more favorably than the man in stereotypically feminine policy areas of *education* and *childcare*. However, we do not find evidence of gender stereotypes producing a significantly more favorable mean evaluation of the man candidate, even when policy information is not provided in the speech. Based on role congruity and schema theories we anticipated that the man candidate would be more favorably evaluated in stereotypically masculine policy domains, but that is not what we find. Even when the policy area is viewed as highly important (e.g., crime, unemployment) candidate gender does not appear to be a relevant component of leadership templates.

As a whole, the analysis of diverse policy areas indicates that women are accepted as leaders across both masculine and feminine policies, although women receive higher scores than men candidates in some stereotypically feminine policy areas. In addition, party effects are stronger than gender effects. These are strong indications that Costa Rican urban young people view women as possible political leaders in all policy areas. We also checked if Candidate Gender matters when the candidate's party is not clearly stated in the treatment. Dolan (2014) found significant gender effects in her US study when party information was not provided. We reran the analysis partitioning the dataset to only include participants whose speech did *not* state the name of the party (ANOVAs utilizing Candidate Gender and Party Platform factors), and we did not find evidence that Costa Rican participants use gender stereotypes in their candidate evaluations when the party name is *not* given on the speech, though for *Win Votes* and *education* policy the main effect of Candidate Gender is significant. For *Win Votes* Candidate Gender is weakly significant [$F(1,342)=3.212$, $p=.074$] with a more favorable mean evaluation of the woman candidate ($M=3.71$) than the man ($M=3.56$), which does not indicate prejudice against women as candidates. For *education* the main effect of Candidate Gender is significant [$F(1,342)=5.926$, $p=.015$] with a more favorable mean evaluation of the woman candidate ($M=4.00$) than of the man ($M=3.75$). While that finding is consistent

---

[30] We also conducted this analysis with three categories of My Party (my party, not my party, no preferred party stated), and the results are substantively the same.

WOMEN AS LEADERS IN COSTA RICA   73

with gendered policy domain stereotypes, it is not prejudicial against women as candidates.

Socialization within Home Environment

We have seen that Costa Rican urban young adults generally do not exhibit traditional leadership templates. But do women look like leaders to participants from families that might be anticipated to hold traditional values about gender roles? A mother with a high-status job or a high level of education can signal that women are capable actors in the public sphere (H7). Conversely, growing up in a family where the mother lacks these resources or does not work may render participants more likely to exhibit the traditional leadership template, that leaders are men. To test H7 we conduct post hoc tests to examine the effect of the mother's work (high status, low status, housewife) and mother's education on candidate evaluations.[31] These analyses compare experimental participant subgroups expected to be differentially affected by societal pressures constraining employment of women outside the home and competition with men for jobs (see Bolzendahl and Myers 2004; Morgan and Buice 2013).

To examine these micro-level factors, we conducted 2×2 ANOVAs with Candidate Gender and Mother Education, and 2×3 ANOVAs with Candidate Gender and Mother Job for each general question and policy areas examined above, and we repeated these analyses adding Participant Sex as a factor. Our principal interest is whether there is a significant interaction of Mother Job or Mother Education with Candidate Gender, which would indicate that the view that women are leaders is restricted to specific subgroups of participants. Only for *Minister* do we find that the interaction Mother Education×Candidate Gender is nearing significant [$F(1,540)=3.720$, $p=.054$],[32] and it is participants whose mothers have a lower level of education who give a more favorable evaluation to

---

[31] Mother Job Status is coded as high (N=176), low (N=290), or housewife (N=203) (see Chapter 2 for an explanation of job status coding). For Mother Education, high education is complete university or graduate school (N=153), low education is complete secondary or less (N=391).

[32] Concerns about possible insufficient sensitivity of the experiment are addressed by significant main-effects for Party Platform and Label in ANOVAs with Candidate Gender and Mother Education that also include Platform and Label. Party Platform is significant for six questions and Party Label is significant for five questions. Only in the model for *security* policy is neither measure of party significant. In addition, with Party Platform and Party Label included in the model for *Minister*, the interaction Candidate Gender×Mother Education meets conventional significance levels [$F(1,528)=4.012$, $p=.046$].

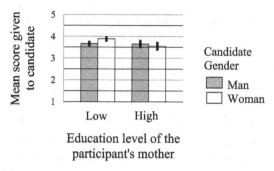

Figure 3.4 Effect of Mother's Education on evaluation to be a *Minister* 2×2 ANOVA (Candidate Gender, Mother's Education) 95 percent confidence intervals included.

the woman candidate (see Figure 3.4). Further, for none of our general or policy questions is the interaction Mother Job×Candidate Gender significant. These results underscore that incorporation of women into leadership templates for these urban Costa Rican young adults occurs broadly across family situations and social classes.

Discussion of Study Findings in the Costa Rican Context

Among Costa Rican urban young adults there appears to be a broad acceptance of women politicians and political candidates as effective across levels of post, able to win votes, and capable to manage diverse policy areas, whether the young adult is male or female, and regardless of whether they support the woman candidate's party. Party is significant to evaluations, but Candidate Gender is not generally a relevant component of leadership templates among these young people, and when there is a significant Candidate Gender effect, it favors the woman candidate.

This acceptance is notable given the National Women's Institute 2013 survey that indicated discrimination against women, in the workforce and in politics. That young adult men, along with young adult women, favorably evaluate women candidates is important since the same survey suggested that machismo is viewed as the biggest obstacle women face in politics. While we cannot know from this study that discrimination and machismo come from older generations, this study's findings indicate that young urban adults are not discriminating against women politicians. The broad inclusion of women into young adults' mental templates of leaders is consistent with our expectation stated in the chapter introduction that Costa Rica could be a favorable context for young people to move beyond traditional leadership templates due to the combination of a lengthy history of women in government and a national policy agenda that emphasizes government provision of social services. It also could be viewed as an indication that new civic education programs implemented since 2008 covering human rights and a gender perspective, and since 2009 requiring gender parity and alternation on ballots for student-body elections have had an impact on students, as those programs were in effect for many years of these participants' schooling. But still, the broad acceptance of women politicians is somewhat surprising given the negative evaluations of President Laura Chinchilla's job performance by the end of her term, and the dominance of masculinized policy areas (particularly crime) as major policy concerns at the time the experiment was conducted.

In light of these findings that women are viewed as viable leaders, we propose some ideas for reflection about possible explanations as topics for future investigation. Young people in Costa Rica have been exposed to new viewpoints about human rights and gender, through the education system, and in society in general. They have also grown up in a context in which, in practice, women have held many relevant posts in government (deputies, mayors, municipal councilors, judges, magistrates, cabinet ministers, and also president). Yet, despite the large number of government posts held by women (compared to most countries), politics and the majority of government posts remain occupied by men. Therefore, greater access by women remains a component of future social and political change, and that change may be viewed positively by young adults like the participants in the experiment. Noteworthy in this regard is the fact that Laura Chinchilla's gender was considered to have contributed heavily to her winning the presidency in 2010.

Yet politics and politicians have been going through a period of low esteem in Costa Rica. If political posts continue to be dominated by men, and at the same time politics and politicians continue to have a bad reputation, is it possible that greater participation by women will be viewed positively, under the assumption, for example, that female officials are less corrupt, or that women would be able to "clean the dirty face of politics"? Maybe the hope is that women might have new ideas for addressing society's problems? Could it be something similar to the interest by Costa Ricans in new political parties?

In sum, the Costa Rica study indicates that urban young adults view women as capable political leaders. Future research should explore how negative attitudes about politics, parties, and politicians affect leadership templates, and whether negative attitudes are applied with a gender-equal brush as well.

Table A3.1 Factor Analysis of General Evaluation Questions for Costa Rica

Component matrix component 1	
Q1 Deputy	.813
Q2 Cabinet Minister	.757
Q17 Support	−.735
Q18 Win Votes	.688
Variance explained:	56.20%

Extraction method: Principal component analysis.

4

The Masculine Template in Perceived Competence of Women in Israeli Politics

Ayala Yarkoney-Sorek and Nehemia Geva

MACRO-CONTEXT FACTORS: ISRAEL AND OTHER CASES

LOW ← Expectation of Strength of Gender Bias → HIGH

	Parliamentary	OR	**Presidential**
Executive Institutions	Alberta CA		Chile
	Quebec CA		California US
	England		Texas US
	Israel		Costa Rica
	Sweden		Uruguay

	Party focused ← - - - - - - - - - - - - - - → **Candidate focused**				
Electoral Institutions	Israel	Uruguay	Chile	Alberta CA	California US
	Costa Rica	Sweden		Quebec CA	Texas US
				England	

	More Social Welfare ← - - - - - - - - - - - → **Less Social Welfare**				
Policy Agenda Emphasis	Sweden	Alberta CA	Uruguay	England	California US
	Costa Rica	Quebec CA	Israel	Chile	Texas US
	Less Defense ← - - - - - - - - - - - - - - - → **More Defense**				
	Costa Rica	Alberta CA	Sweden	England	Israel
	Uruguay	Quebec CA	Chile	California US	Texas US

	Greatest ← - - - - - - - - - - - - - - - - - → **Least**				
Incorporation of Women in Government	Sweden	Chile	Alberta CA	Uruguay	Texas US
	Costa Rica	England	Quebec CA	California US	Israel

Introduction

This study, conducted with 564 young adults in Israel in June–July 2015, shows that Israeli young people are biased against women as political leaders. The constant security threats faced by Israel are a potential reason for why we find evidence for maintenance of traditional leadership templates. Mandatory military service for both men and women did not suppress the male-dominance orientation. Despite a parliamentary system with Knesset members (MKs) elected by closed-list proportional representation, institutions that are typically found to be

Ayala Yarkoney-Sorek and Nehemia Geva, *The Masculine Template in Perceived Competence of Women in Israeli Politics* In: *The Image of Gender and Political Leadership.* Edited by: Michelle M. Taylor-Robinson and Nehemia Geva, Oxford University Press. © Oxford University Press 2023. DOI: 10.1093/oso/9780197642726.003.0004

78   AYALA YARKONEY-SOREK AND NEHEMIA GEVA

favorable to women politicians—the exposure of the young generation to female political leadership in Israel is quite limited. To preview our findings, on multiple dimensions, men candidates are rated significantly more favorably than women candidates.

The Context of Israeli Politics

The State of Israel was founded on May 14, 1948. At that time equal voting rights for men and women were introduced.[1] Israel's Declaration of Independence was one of the earliest "constitutional" documents in the world to include sex as a group classification within a guarantee of equality in social and political rights. The message of the declaration spoke against discrimination, highlighted the issue of group discrimination, and emphasized the need for equal treatment of women. Still, the clear message of the declaration has not subsequently become a fundamental law of the country. This was due to opposition by the religious political parties in the Knesset claiming that such law would undermine the religious monopoly on marriage and divorce in which there are differences in the treatments of men and women. In 1951, the Women's Equal Rights Law was passed, but it was an ordinary statute and not part of the fundamental law. The constitutional tension reflects the Israeli context in which noble intentions to create equality have proven unrealizable without additional legal or cultural changes.

Women in Israeli Politics and Society

Women's representation in Israeli politics has been characterized by a slow increase over time. Women's share of the 120 seats in the Knesset only started to grow after the 1970's (5 percent), exhibiting a very moderate increase in the 1980s (8 percent) and 1990s (10–15 percent). In February 2012 an unprecedented three parties represented in the Knesset were headed by women: Labor, Kadima, and Meretz (Shapira et al. 2016: 15). The Knesset elections that took place in March 2015, three months before we began conducting this experiment, elected twenty-nine women (24 percent of MKs), a historical high (Inter-Parliamentary Union). These women were mostly associated with secular parties, with few

---

[1] Jewish women began campaigning for suffrage in Palestine in the early twentieth century. Before the State of Israel was established, women were elected to local committees and to the Constituent Assembly, though ultra-Orthodox parties were opposed to women voting (Hannah Safran, Jewish Women's Archive, "Suffrage in Palestine" https://jwa.org/encyclopedia/article/suffrage-in-palestine (accessed August 25, 2020).

from religious Jewish parties or Arab parties (Chazan 2018: 147). Interestingly, Shapira et al. (2016: 104–105) found in analysis of bills and of parliamentary questions that "overall, women are more involved in non-women's domain issues than in women's domain issues" though women's committee assignments are primarily on committees associated with stereotypically feminine policy topics. Thus, it is not completely clear based on that analysis of the work records of MKs whether the Israeli public would view women politicians as capable in policy domains outside of the stereotypically feminine sphere.

The share of women ministers serving in the Israeli government is gradually improving, but is still quite low (Shapira et al. 2016: 30). No women have held the coveted defense or finance posts, and only two women have held the important minister of foreign affairs post (Golda Meir 1956–1964 and Tzipi Livni 2006–2009). The only woman prime minister was Golda Meir (1969–1974). Despite the fact that Israel belongs to the minority of countries in which a woman has occupied the highest political position (Jalalzai 2013), all prime ministers appointed since 1974 (when Golda Meir resigned) have been men. In the governments immediately preceding and during the time when the experiment was implemented, women again held few cabinet posts, and mostly minor posts. In the 33rd government, led by PM Netanyahu (March 2013–May 2015), four of twenty-nine posts were assigned to women, though one resigned (minister of health) and one was dismissed (minister of justice), while the women ministers of Culture & Sport and of Immigrant Absorption held their portfolios until the 34th government was formed. In the initial cabinet of the 34th government, also led by PM Netanyahu (May 2015–2020), four of twenty-two posts were assigned to women: Culture & Sport, Justice, Senior Citizens, and Diaspora Affairs.

Regarding women's societal status in Israel the rate of women's participation in the labor market has been increasing consistently. In 1990, 41 percent of eligible women were in the workforce. In 2000, the number grew to 48 percent, by 2011 it increased to 53 percent, and by 2017 it was above 56.4 percent. One of the tensions is that despite Israel's high percentage of working women, especially in the Jewish sector, birth rates are significantly higher than in Europe. The trouble is that while economy policy presumes that both parents work, childcare policy has not yet been reconfigured to support women's employment (Agassi 1989). Publicly funded childcare was expanded after "the stroller protest" in 2011, such that all children aged three and older are entitled to free education, but care for younger children and after-school care are still unresolved problems (Hasson and Buzaglo 2019: 16). In addition, even with women participating in the labor force at increasing rates, women's representation in management is still low, and women's average wages are generally lower than men's wages (Swirski et al. 2001: 17–18; Chazan 2018: 146).

The Security Agenda

The major component that influences leadership templates in Israeli society is the centrality of the security agenda. Israel has been in a nearly constant state of war since it became an independent state in 1948. The national security threat places the Israeli military (IDF) in a central and salient position in the day-to-day life of the Israeli people (Levin 2011). Israel is the only "Western" nation that has mandatory military recruitment for both men and women, unlike in other Western armies, where women may choose to serve. Military service is a key developmental experience in the lives of most Israelis and is often regarded as tantamount to "good citizenship" (Sasson-Levy 2003). One could argue that this "joint" service of men and women provides an element of integration of women into the "male domain" of the armed forces (Yuval-Davis 1987). It would be reasonable to assume that the presence of women soldiers would somewhat change the masculine nature of the military and therefore the Israeli military will be less gendered. However, theories of gendered organizations make clear that in institutions such as the military just shifting the proportion of males and females does little to alter the masculine construction of the organization (Kanter 1977). Orlee Hauser (2010) in her study of Israeli women in combat units demonstrates that women, while working in dangerous areas, mostly fill secretarial or social work roles.[2] Even when we are exposed to cases where women occupy conventional male combat roles, it is publicized as an anecdote and often rejected by religious elements in Israel (Ahroneim 2019). It is accepted that women can occupy a limited range of jobs in the IDF, which blocks their advancement to the highest ranks that are considered the top military leadership. For example, only one woman, Orna Barbivai (2011–2014), has held the rank of major-general.[3] In 2014, not long before our study was carried out, there were a few "firsts" for women in the IDF. The IDF appointed Major Oshrat Bacher as Israel's first female combat battalion commander, and Dr. Shani became the first female combat doctor in an elite counterterror unit (Gidon 2014).

Golan (1997: 583) asserted that "the presumed superior qualities developed in the course of a military career, coupled with the status accorded the professional soldier in a country at war, provide privileged positions for the ex-military man upon his return to civilian life." In the IDF, combat roles are among the most

---

[2] We acknowledge that women's service in the military in Israel may bring a sense of self-worth to these women and may affect the perceptions of their male counterparts and yet it is not sufficient to change a traditional template of political leadership where leaders are men.

[3] Major-general is the second-highest rank in the IDF. Only the lieutenant general, who is chief of the general staff, has a higher rank.

COMPETENCE OF WOMEN IN ISRAELI POLITICS 81

esteemed positions and their prestige is transferable to civilian life. Until recently these combat leadership roles and their advantages were unavailable to women.[4] Klein (1999: 48) noted about the Israeli army: "the military has determined the boundaries of the collective. Military service defines who is 'in' and who is 'out' with respect to the collective and the informal system." Thus, the experience of being a chief of staff in the battlefield makes the person more suitable in the eyes of the public to hold leadership positions in government than a competent female candidate without such military experience.

From this discussion we draw our expectation regarding leadership templates in Israeli society. We expect the young adult Israelis in our sample to give higher ratings on average to the men candidates than to women candidates.

Given the Israeli context of security domination, many prestigious executive posts are considered masculine. For example, the defense minister is often reserved to former IDF chiefs of staff. The internal security and finance ministers are always men (The Knesset website). As explained above, the number of government posts that women in Israel have occupied is limited and generally of lower prestige. It is therefore clear that the Israeli public was not exposed to many women in key political positions.

This situation of limited women in top government posts, and the specification of the political leadership template to a defense policy domain (see Chapter 1) suggests that for certain policy areas the gender factor is more relevant. We therefore expect that men will receive higher scores on masculine policy domains, but that this effect will be attenuated for feminine policy domains.

Gender as a Partisan Issue

Like other cases around the world, gender in Israel is a partisan issue. Sanbonmatsu and Dolan (2009) tested how gender and party stereotypes operate simultaneously in the United States. They show that Democrats are more likely to hold gender stereotypes that benefit women in politics. Democrats are more likely than Republicans to see an advantage for women on the issue of education and are less likely than Republicans to see a male advantage on

---

[4] For much of the IDF's history women could "not hold a field command—which is the prerequisite for advancement to all but one of the highest positions in the army" (Golan 1997: 582). In 2000 the Military Service Law was amended to include the Equality amendment allowing women to serve in any role in the IDF ("Statistics: Women's Service in the IDF for 2010, 25 Aug 2010" Israel Defense Forces, https://idfspokesperson.wordpress.com/2010/08/25/statistics-womens-service-in-the-idf-for-2010-25-aug-2010/#:~:text=Women%20comprise%2034%25%20of%20all,fly%20a%20F%2D16I%20jet (accessed August 30, 2020).

82   AYALA YARKONEY-SOREK AND NEHEMIA GEVA

the issue of crime.[5] In Israel there is a clear difference between right- and left-wing parties in representation of women. Throughout its history, women have been better represented in the Labor party's organizations (Herzog 1999). In 1986, women comprised 17 percent of the Labor party convention, but only 10 percent of the Likud, the largest right-wing party (Herzog et al. 1989: 7–8). Before 2000 most female MKs were from left parties, though since then more women have been elected from parties on the right. The gender gap in voting shows women tending to vote for center-left parties (Shapira et al. 2016: 42–43; Chazan 2018: 147). Additionally, Israel does not have a national quota law and only three parties have adopted gender quota rules (Labor, Meretz, and National Democratic Assembly), while two parties have minimal reserved seats for women (Likud, Jewish Home) (Quota Project).

Recategorization

What are the processes that do cause people to favor a new form of thinking or a new mental template of a leader? Under what conditions can an Israeli woman candidate be considered as competent? As presented in Chapter 1, social categorization literature theorizes about how members of an out-group can be recategorized as members of the in-group. If a voter shares a prominent attribute with a candidate, the voter may support the candidate as they consider the candidate as an in-group member. Women may be more inclined to recategorize a woman candidate as a leader because they share the same sex. Resistance to women's leadership may be stronger among men than women. In addition, a shared party or coalition may prompt study participants to favorably evaluate a candidate.

Can recategorization take place in Israel? Previous research has demonstrated that women in Israel have organized social movements and groups that gain public support and took significant actions, specifically in fostering social activism and, in particular, articulating a connection between feminism and a peaceful resolution of the Arab-Israeli conflict. These movements provoked opposition especially among other women in Israel claiming that any linkage between feminism and international peace poses a threat to national security (Tessler and Warriner 1997). This line of research suggests that categories such as religiosity, ethnicity, and national identity are as salient as gender in Israeli society. Therefore, a recategorization process may happen based on gender but also based on other salient identity categories (Sorek and Ceobanu 2009) that were not part of the treatments in our study.

---

[5] See Chapter 8 of this volume, about the United States, for further discussion of this topic.

Description of the Israeli Experiment and Dataset

The Israel study, like all the cases in this project, utilized a 2×2×2 factorial design. The three factors are Candidate Gender, Party Platform, and Party Label, presented to participants in a relatively long speech for each of the two largest parties: Avoda on the left and Likud on the right. Each speech discussed seven policy areas. Party Platform was based on campaign speeches given by candidates running in the March 2015 Knesset elections. (See Chapter 2 for a detailed explanation of experiment design and implementation.)

The political atmosphere in Israel in 2015 was affected by early elections for the 20th Knesset. The Likud party, led by incumbent Prime Minister Benjamin Netanyahu, won the most seats in the Knesset (30 out of 120 seats). That was a painful loss for the left that formed an alliance of the two major left-wing parties. This political camp was led by Herzog and Livni, a man and a woman who had agreed to take turns in the role of prime minister. Should they win those elections, Livni would have been Israel's second female prime minister. In the security realm, the situation in Israel was relatively quiet. There were several attacks by terror organizations, but they were considered minor and ended with a low number of casualties.

The experiment was conducted with 564 young adult participants, described in Table 4.1. We conducted the experiment in high school and college classrooms (one university, three junior colleges, two high schools) during normal class times.

How Candidate Gender, Party Platform, and Party Label Influence General Evaluations of Men and Women Candidates

Every participant rated one candidate, with a specific gender (indicated by name and pronoun) and party (either stated or implied) for their suitability. A participant did not compare one candidate to another. We thus avoid using the terms "preferred" and "preferable" as they suggest a direct comparison of candidates by a participant, and instead we refer to which candidate scored higher or lower on average when comparing candidate evaluations across treatment conditions. The notation, H5 through H11, refers to hypotheses and statistical methods outlined in Chapters 1 and 2.

The questionnaire included several questions that we utilize to assess general evaluations of candidates across levels of posts and ability to win votes: In your opinion, how effective would this person be as a (1) member of the Knesset,[6] (2) member of the cabinet,[6] (3) party leader?[6] (4) Would you support this

---

[6] Answers ranged from 1 (outstanding) to 6 (very poor) and have been inverted so that high scores are favorable.

84 AYALA YARKONEY-SOREK AND NEHEMIA GEVA

Table 4.1 Description of Participants in Israel

	Overall	Male only	Female only
Number of participants	564	262	296
Percent of participants	100	47.0	53.0
Average age	22.7	22.3	23.0
Left (1) to Right (10) self-placement	5.43	5.25	5.58
Preferred coalition* (%):			
Coalition with Likud	31.9	33.2	30.6
Coalition with Avoda	33.3	32.4	34.0
Religious parties	23.1	27.0	19.7
No preference stated	11.7	7.3	15.6
Total	100	100	100
Parents' education** (% of participants):			
Fathers w/high level	25.7	29.0	23.3
Mothers w/high level	27.0	25.6	28.4
Fathers w/low level	17.6	17.9	17.6
Mothers w/low level	15.6	18.7	13.2
Parents' occupation (% of participants):			
Fathers w/high status job	54.9	51.8	57.2
Mothers w/high status job	54.1	55.6	52.7
Housewives, as % of participants	10.4	9.3	11.6
Housewives, as the actual number	55	23	32

* Likud coalition included Habaeat Hayehudi & Israel Beytenu; Avoda coalition included Hareshima, Meretz & Yahadut Hatorah; religious parties included Kulanu, Yesh Atid, Ale Yarok and Shas.

** Note: Education levels of participants' parents are divided into "high" (complete university or more) and "low" (complete secondary or less), and the remaining percentage (not shown) is defined as "intermediate" or "don't know."

candidate in the election for the Knesset?[7] (5) Do you think this candidate would be good at winning votes?[8]

To test H8 we conduct a 2×2×2 ANOVA for each general question, using Candidate Gender, Party Platform, and Party Label as factors. This analysis

---

[7] Scored 1 (yes) or 2 (no).
[8] Answers ranged from 1 (very good) to 5 (very poor) and have been inverted so that high scores are favorable.

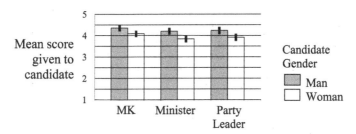

Figure 4.1 Competence as function of Candidate Gender
2×2×2 ANOVA (Candidate Gender, Party Platform, Party Label) 95 percent confidence intervals included.

reveals a significant gender stereotyping effect for evaluations to be an *MK* [F(1,535)=8.967, p=.003], *Cabinet Minister* [F(1,510)=12.300 p=.000], and *Party Leader* [F(1,532)=9.561, p=.002] (see Figure 4.1). For all three posts, across political party associated with the candidate, women candidates were scored lower on average than men candidates. Consistent with H8, it appears that young people's template for leadership is masculine in "general" evaluations.

H9 tests the prediction in the role congruity literature that evaluations of women candidates will be less favorable the higher the level of the post. We explored the proposition of whether the impact of Candidate Gender varies across levels of posts with a repeated measures ANOVA with Post (*MK, Minister, Party Leader*) and Candidate Gender as factors. Here we find that posts are viewed as different, with the most favorable evaluations for *MK* (M=4.223) and least favorable for *Minister* (M=4.019). The main effect of Candidate Gender is significant [F(1,505)=9.633, p=.002], with more favorable evaluations of the man (M=4.266) than of the woman (M=3.946). However, the interaction Post×Candidate Gender is not significant (p=.594 linear, p=.383 quadratic), indicating that the woman candidate is consistently evaluated to be less effective across all levels of posts.

Party Label does not have a significant main effect in the evaluations for these posts (p-values range from p=.158 for *Minister* to p=.659 for *MK*). Party Platform was significant only for evaluations to be a *Party Leader*, with higher scores for the Avoda (M=4.248) than the Likud (M=3.891), and the interaction Candidate Gender×Party Platform is also significant [F(1,532)=4.258, p=.040] (Figure 4.2).[9] Party had an effect only for the Avoda, with more favorable evaluations of the man than of the woman candidate (M=4.55 compared to

---

[9] Candidate Gender and Party Platform have similar sized effects on evaluations as shown with the η_p^2 statistics of .018 for Candidate Gender and .017 for Platform. The interaction has a smaller effect (η_p^2=.008).

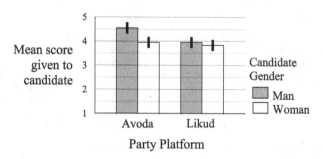

Figure 4.2 Interaction of Candidate Gender and Party Platform for evaluations to be *Party Leader*
2×2×2 ANOVA (Candidate Gender, Party Platform, Party Label) 95 percent confidence intervals included.

M=3.95). The gap against the woman candidates in the Likud is much smaller (M=3.95 compared to M=3.83). This is somewhat surprising given the history of more extensive incorporation of women in the Avoda party over the years (Shapira et al. 2016: 42–43). We interpret those findings in light of the Avoda's political situation in the March 2015 election. Avoda, that had a history and reputation of being the largest and strongest party in Israel, experienced a notable drop in its support in the last two decades (Kenig et al. 2013: 10). In this situation having a woman leader may be considered as too risky. The results of the March 2015 election held two and a half months before we began our study, when a woman was one of two party leaders appears to have marked a female leader as a losing card. Additionally, research shows that females are nominated as leaders following a loss (O'Brien 2015), thus the public recognized that the leader was thrown into the lion's den which signals weakness.

We also find that men candidates are scored more favorably than women for *Support* in Knesset election [F(1,547)=4.783, p=.029]. Party Platform also has a significant main effect (p=.008) for *Support*, with more favorable scores for the Avoda candidate, and the effect of Platform is larger than the effect of Candidate Gender (η_p^2=.013 and .009 respectively). For *Win Votes* none of the factors are significant.

For general evaluations of candidates, most of the evidence appears to indicate that gender is a relevant component of mental templates of leadership, and that traditional leadership templates—leaders are men—are the norm. Yet before we draw that conclusion, we need to examine if participants who share an identity with the candidate are more favorable in their evaluations of women candidates. To explore if there is evidence of a shared sex in-group (H5), we conduct 2×2 ANOVAs for each general question with Candidate Gender and

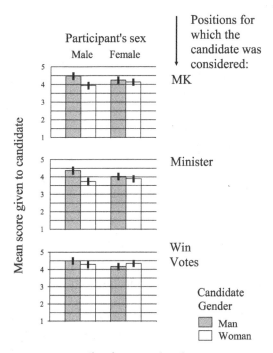

Figure 4.3 Same sex in-group effect for general evaluation questions 2×2 ANOVA (Candidate Gender, Participant Sex) 95 percent confidence intervals included.

Participant Sex as factors, focusing on whether the interaction is significant. For *MK* the main effect of Candidate Gender is still highly significant [$F(1,533)$= 9.788, $p=.002$], but the interaction is also significant [$F(1,533)=4.155$, $p= .042$].[10] While the mean evaluation female participants give men candidates is still more favorable than the mean evaluation they give women candidates ($M=4.25$ compared to $M=4.14$), the gap against the women candidates is much larger for male participants ($M=4.48$ compared to $M=3.94$) (Figure 4.3 top). The same is true for *Minister* (interaction [$F(1,508)=5.321$, $p=.021$]) (Figure 4.3—middle). For *Party Leader* and for *Support* the interaction is not significant (*Party Leader*: [$F(1,530)=.092$, $p=.762$], *Support*: [$F(1,550)=1.228$, $p=.268$]). For those general evaluations both male and female participants give more favorable evaluations to men candidates. For ability to *Win Votes* the interaction approaches significant [$F(1,549)=3.493$, $p=.062$] and supports the shared-sex in-group prediction (Figure 4.3—bottom).

---

[10] The effect size of Candidate Gender is larger than the effect of the interaction ($\eta_p^2=.018$ and .008 respectively).

We also explore if a shared party in-group is related to more favorable evaluations of candidates (H6), conducting 2×2 ANOVAs with Candidate Gender and My Party (yes, no) as factors, again focusing on the interaction. For *MK*, the main effect of Candidate Gender is maintained with men candidates evaluated more favorably than women [F(1,480)=6.462, p=.011], and evaluations are more favorable when the candidate is from the participant's party (M=4.578) than from the opposition (M=3.968) (p=.000). The effect of My Party is larger than the effect of Candidate Gender (η_p^2 scores of .060 and .013 respectively). However, the interaction Candidate Gender×My Party is not significant (p=.242), indicating that there is not a my party in-group effect benefitting women candidates. The findings are substantively the same for *Minister, Party Leader,* and *Support* (though for *Support* the main effect of Candidate Gender is only approaching significant [F(1,488)=3.154, p=.076] though scores are still more favorable for the man than for the woman). For *Win Votes*, as before, Candidate Gender is not significant [F(1,489)=.027, p=.869], but My Party is highly significant (p=.001) with scores more favorable when the candidate is from the participant's party.[11]

In summary, gender matters for candidate evaluations on general questions, and men candidates are scored higher than women candidates. Yet participants also react to party, with more favorable evaluations when the candidate is from their party. In addition, bias against women candidates is tempered by a same sex in-group effect, as female participants often scored men and women candidates as not significantly different.

Evaluations of Men and Women Candidates across Policy Areas

H10 predicts that evaluations of men and women candidates will be contingent on the policy area. The main gap in evaluation of men and women candidates is expected to be in policy areas that are perceived to be masculine, while this gap may decrease or even shift in an opposite direction when the candidates are considered for a stereotypically feminine policy area. Comparisons can be analyzed in our experiment based on whether the policy was discussed in the speech or not, as gender stereotypes are most likely to

---

[11] A 2×3 ANOVA with Candidate Gender and My Party, including participants who did not state a preferred party (N=68), produces substantively similar results for *MK, Minister, Party Leader,* and *Support*, with scores for "no party stated" between the low mean score for "not my party" and the high mean score for "my party." For *Win Votes* evaluations are least favorable from participants who did not state a party (M=3.860), and most favorable for participants whose speech was by a candidate from their party (M=4.607).

COMPETENCE OF WOMEN IN ISRAELI POLITICS   89

influence candidate evaluations when policy information is *not* provided in the speech (H11).

Participants evaluated the candidate's ability in twelve policy areas.[12] For in-depth analysis of policy areas we will focus on *security* (masculine) and *education* (feminine) that were discussed in the speech, and *energy* (masculine) and *women's rights* (feminine) that were not discussed.

Security is a constant threat for Israel. For an open-ended question in a Pew Research Center survey (October 2014 to May 2015), security threats/violence/terrorism and economic problems were most frequently given as the biggest long-term problem faced by the country (38 percent and 39 percent respectively).[13] As mentioned above, no women have held defense or security portfolios in the cabinet, and women are extremely rare in the top officer corps of the IDF, even though Israeli women do mandatory military service, as do men. In the Likud speech security policy focused on external threats and the need to fight to defend our home and not giving up territory, plus increased security on the streets. The Avoda speech focused on improving security on the streets, and also sitting down to negotiate with the Palestinians so that ultimately mandatory military service can be shortened.

Education is a topic of frustration for many parents, even while Israel is lauded for the high level of degree attainment of the population, and its number of internationally recognized institutes of higher education. A 2016 report by the Central Bureau for Statistics, using data from the 2015 social survey,[14] showed, that "[t]he education system ranked first in the report of government services most in need of improvement" (Ziri 2016). Women have held the education portfolio (1992–1993, 2001–2006, 2006–2009).[15] The Likud speech discussed the need for advanced technology in education, including that every student should have a computer, and making more spots available in higher education for military veterans. The Avoda speech addressed education as the need for better performance on international math tests, more teachers, and more investment in education.

Energy is a long term concern for Israel's economy. Hostile relations with Israel's energy producing neighbors make international companies reluctant to open operations in Israel. In 2010 President Shimon Peres stated that "Oil is becoming the greatest problem of our time." Discovery of offshore natural gas fields, particularly since 2009, created new opportunities and new international relations challenges, keeping energy as an important topic for the government

---

[12] Answers scored 1 (very competent) to 5 (incompetent). Scores have been inverted so that high scores are favorable.

[13] Pew Research Center, March 8, 2016, "Israel's Religiously Divided Society" p. 59.

[14] The survey, conducted with 7,100 people between April and December 2015, studied public attitudes toward government institutions and services.

[15] Source: https://guide2womenleaders.com/Israel.htm (accessed August 25, 2020).

90   AYALA YARKONEY-SOREK AND NEHEMIA GEVA

(Bahgat 2011). The ministry in charge of energy policy also covers infrastructure and water. No woman has held the portfolio since it was established in 1977.

Women's rights became a topic of debate even before the state of Israel was created.[16] The debate is fueled by women's organizations demanding gender equality as outlined in the Declaration of Independence, and religious parties objecting to the policies. Like many countries, the Israeli cabinet does not include a ministry of women's affairs. However, in 1998 an Authority for the Advancement of the Status of Women was established within the Prime Minister's Office (Chazan 2018: 145).

We first look at the pair of policies discussed in the speech: *security* (masculine) and *education* (feminine). A 2×2 ANOVA (with Domain as a repeated measure and Candidate Gender as the between group factor) shows the following: Domain is significant [$F(1,556)=41.424$, p=.000] with more favorable evaluations in *education* (M=3.648) than *security* (M=3.275). The between-subjects effect for Candidate Gender is also significant [$F(1,556)=10.150$, p=.002] with more favorable evaluation for the man (M=3.583) than the woman (M=3.341). Of greatest interest for whether gender stereotypes apply in different policy areas, the interaction Domain×Candidate Gender is highly significant [$F(1,556)=64.810$, p=.000] (Figure 4.4—top-left). For *security*, the participants exhibited a traditional, masculine leadership template, with significantly more favorable evaluations of the man candidate. In the feminine policy area (*education*) the woman candidate obtained a higher evaluation than the man. In this comparison the gender stereotype prevailed even though the participants were exposed to the same policy statements by a man and woman candidate from the same party.[17]

Next, we compare policy areas not addressed in the speeches: *energy* (masculine) and *women's rights* (feminine). This 2×2 ANOVA also shows a significant interaction for Domain×Candidate Gender [$F(1,556)=149.392$, p=.000] (Figure 4.4—top-right). Again, we find the pattern of gender stereotypes with men candidates evaluated more favorably in the context of a stereotypically masculine policy, and women candidates are clearly evaluated more favorably than men in the feminine stereotyped policy area.[18] This result is consistent with the

---

[16] Hannah Safran, Jewish Women's Archive, "Suffrage in Palestine" https://jwa.org/encyclopedia/article/suffrage-in-palestine (accessed August 25, 2020).

[17] As a robustness check we replicate this analysis for other masculine and feminine policies discussed in the speech. When Domain is defined as *internal security* and *health*, the interaction Domain×Candidate Gender is highly significant [$F(1,552)=62.128$, p=.000], with the man evaluated more favorably for *internal security*, and the woman more favorably for *health*. Results are similar when Domain is defined as *foreign policy* and *health*, or as *housing* and *health*. The interaction Domain×Candidate Gender is highly significant and the man candidate is evaluated more favorably in the masculine policy area, while the woman candidate is evaluated more favorably for health ([$F(1,555)=19.432$, p=.000] and [$F(1,553)=27.600$, p=.000] respectively).

[18] As a robustness check, we conduct this analysis with the other masculine policy areas not discussed in the speech and we find the same pattern as above. When domain is defined as

COMPETENCE OF WOMEN IN ISRAELI POLITICS 91

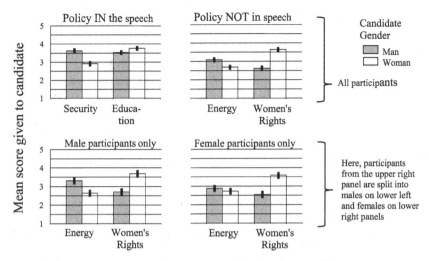

Figure 4.4 Gender stereotypes in stereotypically masculine and feminine policy areas
Top: repeated measures ANOVA (Domain, Candidate Gender); bottom: repeated measures ANOVA (Domain, Candidate Gender, Participant Sex) 95 percent confidence intervals included.

argument made by Shapira et al. (2016: 106) that "the two areas that can be defined unequivocally as belonging to the women's domain are women's issues and children and family issues. In both these categories, there was a significant predominance of women in most forms of parliamentary activity".

Do in-groups affect candidate evaluations in different policy areas? First, to test for a same sex in-group effect (H5), we added Participant Sex as an additional factor in the repeated measure analyses. For *security* and *education* (discussed in the speech), the three-way interaction is not significant [F(1,551)=.107, p=.744], indicating that the more favorable evaluation of men candidates in masculine policy, and women candidates for feminine policy occurs for both female and male participants. For *energy* and *women's rights* (not discussed), the three-way interaction is significant [F(1,551)=4.149, p=.042] (Figure 4.4—bottom). Female participants did not apply the "masculine template" when evaluating the candidate for *energy* (masculine domain), while their male counterparts did apply this template. Both male and female participants, however, applied a gendered template when they evaluated the candidate on *women's rights*.

infrastructure and *women's rights*, as *agriculture* and *women's rights*, or as *treasury* and *women's rights*, the interaction is significant ([F(1,557)=172.446, p=.000], [F(1,556)=131.398, p=.000] and [F(1,556)=182,302, p=.000] respectively).

Second, to test for a same party in-group effect (H6), we included My Party (yes, no) as an additional factor in the repeated measure analyses. For *security* and *education* (discussed in the speech), evaluations are more favorable when the candidate is from the participant's party (M=3.726) than from the opposition (M=3.312). However, the three-way interaction is not significant [F(1,491)= .074, p=.785]. The man candidate is evaluated significantly more favorably than the woman for *security* regardless of whether the candidate is from the participant's party or not, and the woman candidate is evaluated more favorably than the man for *education*.[19] For *energy* and *women's rights* (not discussed in the speech), again the three-way interaction is not significant [F(1,491)=.906, p= .342]. Whether the candidate is from the participant's preferred party or not, the woman candidate is evaluated more favorably on *women's rights*, and the man more favorably on *energy*.[20]

We also explore the impact of party compared to gender in evaluations with 2×2×2 ANOVAs for each policy area with Candidate Gender, Party Platform, and Party Label as factors. Candidate Gender has a significant main effect for all four policy areas, with the man scored higher for *security* [F(1,550)=49.380, p= .000] and *energy* [F(1,551)=19.421, p=.000], and the woman candidate scored higher for *education* [F(1,552)=6.715, p=.010] and *women's rights* [F(1,551)= 105.752, p=.000]. Party Platform also has a significant main effect for *security* (p=.011) with more favorable evaluations for the Likud. *Education* (p=.001) and *women's rights* (p=.000) are both more favorable for the Avoda.[21] These evaluations are consistent with issue ownership of both parties. For *security*, the interaction Candidate Gender×Party Platform is nearing significant [F(1,550)= 3.416, p=.065] and indicates that more favorable evaluations are given to the man candidate with the Likud platform compared to a man candidate with the Avoda platform, while evaluations for women candidates are not significantly different (not shown). Assessing mental templates of leadership, for *security* Candidate Gender has much greater effect than Party Platform, as shown by the η_p^2 values (Candidate Gender=.082, Platform=.012, interaction=.006). The same is true for *women's rights* (Candidate Gender=.161, Platform=.029). For

[19] Though the difference in evaluations favoring the woman candidate for *education* is significant only when she is not from the participant's party.

[20] When we redo these analyses with three categories for My Party (yes, no, no preferred party stated) the results are substantively similar for the comparison of *security* and *education* (discussed in the speech). For the comparison of *energy* and *women's rights* (not in the speech) the three-way interaction is significant [F(1,552)=5.759, p=.003]. Participants who did not state a preferred party score the man and woman candidate as not statistically different for both policy areas.

[21] For *women's rights* the interaction Platform×Label is significant [F(1,551)=3.913, p=.048] with more favorable evaluations of the Avoda when the party name is stated on the speech. The party platforms are not evaluated as significantly different when the party name is not on the speech.

education, in contrast, Party Platform has a larger effect than Candidate Gender (η_p^2 for Platform=.020, Candidate Gender=.012).

In summary, gender stereotypes are applied to both men and women candidates. Participants evaluate the man candidate more favorably in stereotypically masculine policy areas, and the woman candidate more favorably in feminine policy areas, whether or not the policy is discussed in the speech. Party also affects candidate evaluations, as evaluations are more favorable when the candidate is from "my party" and evaluations favor parties on issues where they have issue ownership. Yet Candidate Gender generally has a larger effect on evaluations. This is a particularly important finding for policy areas that were discussed in the speech because it means that even when a candidate states their policy plans, they are still evaluated based on their gender.

Socialization within the Home Environment

This project expects that, along with macro-level factors about one's country, micro-level factors, such as how a person grew up can influence mental templates about leaders. Here we examine whether having a mother with a high level of education or a high-status job is associated with evaluations indicating that women can be leaders in politics (H7). We conduct 2×2 ANOVAs for the general evaluation questions and for the four policy areas examined in the previous sections with Candidate Gender and either variations in Mother Education or Mother Job as factors, both with and without Participant Sex as a factor.

These analyses provide several indications that Mother Education affects when women are viewed as potential leaders.[22] For evaluations of effectiveness to be an *MK, Cabinet Minister* and *Party Leader* average scores for women candidates from participants whose mother has a high level of education are not significantly different from average scores for men candidates. It is participants whose mothers have a lower level of education who do not view the woman candidate as an effective leader (Figure 4.5).[23] For *Support* in Knesset elections the interaction is nearing significant (p=.061) and follows the same pattern. In the stereotypically masculine policy areas, *security* and *energy*, we also find this pattern (Figure 4.5).[24]

---

[22] Low education is coded as complete secondary school or less (N=88) and high education as complete university or greater education (N=152).

[23] The interaction Candidate Gender×Mother Education is significant: *MK* [F(1,221)=6.270, p=.013], *Minister* [F(1,209)=7.995, p=.005], *Party Leader* [F(1,221)=6.059, p=.015].

[24] The interaction Candidate Gender×Mother Education is highly significant: *security* [F(1,234)= 14.764, p=.000], *energy* [F(1,234)=9.128, p=.003].

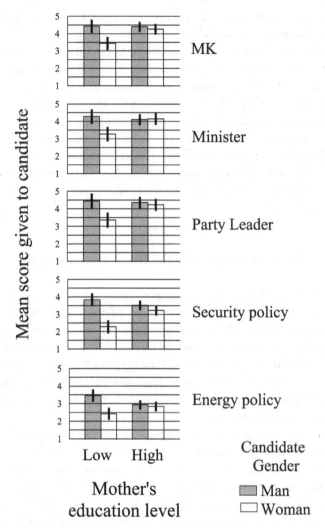

Figure 4.5 Effects of Mother Education on Candidate Evaluations
2×2 ANOVA (Candidate Gender, Mother Education) 95 percent confidence intervals included.

However, for the stereotypically feminine policy areas, Mother Education does not have a significant effect on candidate evaluations. For all questions, results are substantively the same when we add Participant Sex as a factor and the three-way interaction is not significant.[25]

---

[25] The exception is *Support*, where the interaction Candidate Gender×Mother Education is significant at conventional levels [$F(1,229)=3.992$, $p=.047$] when Participant Sex is included as a factor.

Regarding Mother Job,[26] we find a significant interaction only for *education* policy. Contrary to H7, participant's whose mothers have a low status job give more favorable evaluations to the woman candidate than the man [$F(1,520)=$ 7.879, p=.000] (not shown). When Participant Sex is added as a factor, the three-way interaction is not significant [$F(1,512)=.238$, p=.788], indicating that both male and female participants show this pattern.

In summary, with the exception of *education* policy where the impact of the mother is opposite to the prediction, it appears that growing up with a mother who has a higher level of resources is associated with a greater likelihood that gender is not a relevant part of mental templates of leadership. This holds for both male and female participants, even though the in-group analysis presented above indicates that it is male participants who favor men as political leaders.

Discussion of Study Findings in the Israeli Context

Given generalized expectations based on Israel having been one of the first nations in recent history to have a female prime minister and one of few countries where both men and women are obliged to serve in the army one might presume that females would have equal opportunities in politics. Additionally, the Israeli parliamentary system with closed-list proportional representation elections would strengthen this expectation since women are generally more successful in obtaining office in such systems. Yet, we find that for the young Israeli adults in our study gender remains important politically, with women evaluated less favorably than men as political candidates and as less capable in masculine policy areas. These findings reinforce the concern stated in the chapter introduction that in Israel noble intentions to create equality have proven unrealizable without additional legal or cultural changes. There are, however, exceptions that indicate partial recategorization of women as leaders. Female participants, and participants whose mother has a high level of education often give evaluations to women candidates that are not statistically different from their average evaluations of men candidates.

We interpret these findings in view of the low representation of women in the government and the parliament, and the absence of women in the most prestigious and important roles (after prime minster) of defense minister, and treasury minister. In addition, women are over-represented in Knesset committees that

---

[26] Occupations are divided into high status (N=285), low status (N=187), and housewife (N=55) (see Chapter 2 for explanation of occupation coding).

handle stereotypically feminine policy areas (Shapira et al. 2016). The Israeli young adults who took part in this study had not been exposed to women in powerful political positions and it appears they are not yet accustomed to women leaders.

At the same time, the most pressing issue is national security, with Israel in a constant state of security tensions since its establishment, and throughout the lifetimes of our study participants. This situation makes defense, foreign policy, and security the most important policy areas. These issues are masculine in nature, and to a large extent male military leaders have always been at the forefront of society.

Mandatory military service for both men and women could have paved the way for women, however, the Israeli military (the IDF) remains generally similar to other armies in its gendered and masculine nature. Moreover, the military is omnipresent in daily life, soldiers are a commonplace everywhere, and in an atmosphere of constant threat to security, unsurprisingly combat soldiers (93 percent men) are considered the most prestigious segment of society. Thus, the army, instead of granting opportunities for women to integrate, appears to have reinforced traditional gender roles, as reflected in this study's findings.

All the above coupled with the predominant right-leaning politics in the last two decades can only exacerbate bias against women candidates and sustain traditional leadership templates that government leaders are men. Right-wing parties in Israel have been less inclusive of women and are characterized by a militaristic agenda. In our study we find evidence for bias in favor of men candidates at all political levels—parliament, cabinet, party leader. However, as predicted by in-group theory, male participants exhibit stronger bias than female participants, and participants whose mothers have a high level of education do not appear to be biased against women candidates. In addition, while men candidates are clearly scored more favorably in stereotypically masculine policy areas—whether or not the candidate discussed the policy area in the speech, women candidates are scored higher for stereotypically feminine policies. It should be noted that these portfolios have had women as Ministers in the past.

We see Israel as an important case illustrating how context—the potentially powerful impact of external threats and security policy—matters for gender attitudes. The policy agenda of Israel, or policy agenda paired with limited experience observing women in top political posts, shapes mental templates of leaders.

Table A4.1 Factor Analysis of General
Evaluation Questions for Israel

Component matrix component 1	
Q1 MK	.888
Q2 Cabinet Minister	.882
Q3 Party Leader	.843
Q17 Support	−.750
Q18 Win Votes	.537
Variance explained:	62.55%

Extraction method: Principal component analysis.

5

Attitudes Toward Women in Government

Evidence from an Experiment in Canada's Alberta and Quebec Provinces

Melanee Thomas, Valérie-Anne Mahéo, and Guillaume Bogiaris

MACRO-CONTEXT FACTORS: CANADA AND OTHER CASES				
LOW ← Expectation of Strength of Gender Bias → HIGH				
Executive Institutions	**Parliamentary**	**OR**		**Presidential**
	Alberta CA			Chile
	Quebec CA			California US
	England			Texas US
	Israel			Costa Rica
	Sweden			Uruguay
Electoral Institutions	**Party focused ←- - - - - - - - - - - - - - - - - - - -► Candidate focused**			
	Israel	Uruguay	Chile	Alberta CA	California US
	Costa Rica	Sweden		Quebec CA	Texas US
				England	
Policy Agenda Emphasis	**More Social Welfare ←- - - - - - - - - - - -► Less Social Welfare**			
	Sweden	Alberta CA	Uruguay	England	California US
	Costa Rica	Quebec CA	Israel	Chile	Texas US
	Less Defense ←- - - - - - - - - - - - - - - - - - -► More Defense			
	Costa Rica	Alberta CA	Sweden	England	Israel
	Uruguay	Quebec CA	Chile	California US	Texas US
Incorporation of Women in Government	**Greatest ←- -► Least**			
	Sweden	Chile	Alberta CA	Uruguay	Texas US
	Costa Rica	England	Quebec CA	California US	Israel

The history of women's integration into politics in Canada is long and complicated. Louis-Joseph Papineau, an important politician in Lower Canada (later known as Quebec), proudly supported legislation in the 1830s to remove all voting rights from women, even though his mother—a woman with property—had just voted for him (Sangster 2018). Fast-forward to 2015, when Justin Trudeau, Member of Parliament (MP) for the electoral district of Papineau and prime minister of Canada, proudly declared that he had appointed an equal number of women and men to his first cabinet. When asked why, Trudeau shrugged and wryly smiled, "because it's 2015."

Melanee Thomas, Valérie-Anne Mahéo, and Guillaume Bogiaris, *Attitudes Toward Women in Government* In: *The Image of Gender and Political Leadership*. Edited by: Michelle M. Taylor-Robinson and Nehemia Geva, Oxford University Press. © Oxford University Press 2023. DOI: 10.1093/oso/9780197642726.003.0005

Trudeau's parity cabinet aside, women are much less likely to be found in high-profile positions than are men, even if they are not uncommon in Canada's electoral politics. When these experiments were conducted in 2017, women were only 27 percent of federal MPs,[1] and across the country, because parity cabinets are not yet the norm, women remain significantly less likely to be cabinet ministers and party leaders than are men (O'Neill and Stewart 2009; see also Thomas 2018). Worse, evidence from the Canadian Election Study shows that while most Canadians (65 percent in 2011) think the best way to protect women's interests is to elect more women, most Canadians are not bothered by women's low levels of electoral representation. Thus, while it might be reasonable to expect that young Canadians will be familiar with women in government, it is also reasonable to anticipate their leadership frames may be more traditional or masculine.

We begin by outlining how women have been historically integrated into Canada's political institutions, and the national and provincial political contexts in which young adult Canadians participated in the study. We then present results of the two Canadian studies, conducted from March to May 2017 in Alberta (253 participants) and in Quebec (411 participants). We find that, with few exceptions, participants in both cases typically evaluate candidates similarly, regardless of their gender, suggesting that they may not use gender to inform their leadership frames. The clearest exception is with respect to women's rights. In this policy area, young Canadians evaluate women to be the best at protecting women's interests, regardless of the candidate's party affiliation. The presence of this strong gendered leadership frame suggests that politics in Canada is not necessarily gender neutral. Instead, consistent with prior research (Dolan 2014; Schneider and Bos 2014; Bauer 2015), unless young Canadians are explicitly cued to see gender in politics, it is not a salient characteristic they use to evaluate political candidates.

For this study of Canadian young adults' mental templates of leaders, we conducted experiments in two cases: Alberta and Quebec. Like all Canadian provinces, each is an interesting microcosm of attitudes and characteristics that are found across Canada. Both capture the original colonial cleavages surrounding language and religion (French and Catholic in Quebec, English and Protestant in Alberta), but they differ in the industries that structure their economies. Alberta's economy depends on oil and agriculture (ranching and cattle), both strongly masculine industries. Quebec's economy is dominated by agriculture (dairy), mining, and tourism. Most importantly, Alberta and Quebec differ profoundly in their histories of incorporation of women into politics. It is this history that makes these provinces two excellent cases for this project.

---

[1] In the 2015 election eighty-eight women (26 percent) were elected, and four more were elected in 2017 by-elections, soon after we fielded the experiments.

Women in Government in Canada: Past and Present

Formed in 1867, Canada is a decentralized federal constitutional democracy. Its national parliament is bicameral, with an elected House of Commons (338 seats) and an appointed Senate. Unicameral subnational governments exist in ten provinces and three territories, and the responsibilities allocated to each level of government, except territories, are set out in Canada's constitution. The federal government is responsible for policies thought, in the nineteenth century, to be of national interest, such as trade and commerce, defense, fiscal and money systems, criminal law, marriage and divorce, and naturalization. The provinces are responsible for more "local" policies, including the bulk of the modern welfare state (hospitals, schools, charities, social services), as well as municipalities. However, because the provinces' powers of taxation are considerably smaller than the federal government's, it is common for provinces to struggle to fund their welfare state. This creates tensions, as the federal government often seeks to spend in areas of provincial jurisdiction.

Tensions around federalism also structure the history of women's integration into Canadian politics. Federal voting rights were historically devolved to the provinces, so if a person had the right to vote in their province, they also had the right to vote in federal elections. The federal government granted women aged twenty-one or older the federal vote in 1918 if, and only if, they were not excluded from the provincial vote.

Provinces varied widely in their willingness to grant women the vote.[2] Most provinces explicitly restricted the franchise to white men with property over the age of twenty-one. Those campaigning for women's suffrage were also actively engaged in other social movements, including temperance organizations, campaigns for dower rights, and agricultural publications (Sangster 2018). Women were first granted the provincial vote and the right to run for office in the Prairie provinces (Manitoba, Alberta, Saskatchewan) in 1916. White women then won the franchise in British Columbia and Ontario in 1917. Formal restrictions on women's votes in the Atlantic provinces were lifted between 1918 (Nova Scotia) and 1922 (Prince Edward Island), and women could not run for office in New Brunswick until 1934 (Strong-Boag 2016).

Women in Quebec were not granted the provincial vote until 1940. This delay was due to several factors, including that the suffrage movement in English-speaking Canada was focused, at least in part, on the settler colonialism tied to the British Empire, and that the Catholic Church, powerful in Quebec politics at the time, opposed women's suffrage. Though civil society organizations supported women's right to vote as early as 1922, political expediency was

---

[2] The right to run for and hold elected office was typically paired with the right to vote.

required to secure the vote in Quebec. Suffragists within the Liberal Party of Quebec, led by Thérèse Casgrain, agreed to volunteer their labor for the party if the party agreed to endorse women's suffrage (Janovicek and Thomas 2018).[3] This experience in Quebec (and in other provinces, albeit decades earlier) shows how women's integration into electoral politics in Canada is partly tied to some political parties.

Women across Canada were elected as soon as they won the right to stand for election, though in very small numbers. Only one to two women were elected as federal MPs per term between 1921 and 1953; from 1953 to 1968, between two and five women were elected per term, but only one woman was elected (again) in 1968. Women only numbered more than 5 percent of MPs by 1980. The proportion of women elected to the House of Commons then steadily increased to 21 percent by 1997, where it stalled until edging up to 22 percent in 2008, 26 percent in 2015 (calculated from Parliament of Canada 2018), and 29 percent in 2019, a new record.

While women are sometimes more likely to be elected to provincial legislatures, their integration into politics at this level is stalled, too. Quebec typically elects more women than do other provinces—41 percent of Quebec's National Assembly[4] in 2018. Prior to this, though, women's presence there was stalled for at least a decade around 30 to 33 percent (Tremblay 2013). This may seem odd, given women's late enfranchisement in Quebec, but it is consistent with rapid secularization, tied to the Quiet Revolution (The Canadian Encyclopedia 2018). Other provinces are now breaking that 30 percent barrier, though there is no guarantee that these gains will be lasting. Alberta, for example, elected 27 percent women Members of the Legislative Assembly (MLAs) in 1997, only to see this fall precipitously to 16 percent by 2004. Women did not again comprise over 25 percent of Alberta's provincial representatives until 2012 (O'Neill 2013).

At the executive level, women have also been relatively absent. Until recently, women rarely comprised more than 30 percent of any cabinet, federal or provincial, and often comprised far less than that. Notable exceptions include Ontario in 1990 (women were 42 percent of the cabinet), and Canada's first parity cabinet in Quebec in 2007 (Trimble et al. 2013). Recently, the federal government, as well as the provinces of Alberta, British Columbia, and Ontario, all had parity

---

[3] The last restrictions on women's right to vote in Canada are based in racism and xenophobia. Canadians of Asian descent were not permitted to vote in federal elections until 1948. In British Columbia, race-based restrictions on the vote were not removed until 1948 for Japanese and South Asian persons, nor until 1952 for some persons of German descent. Indigenous peoples were not permitted to vote without losing their treaty status until 1960 with the introduction of the federal *Bill of Rights* (Janovicek and Thomas 2018; Sangster 2018).

[4] The elected body of the Canadian Parliament is the House of Commons; most provinces have a Legislative Assembly, but Quebec changed the name to the National Assembly (Assemblée Nationale du Québec) in 1968, motivated in part by nationalism sparked during the Quiet Revolution (Assemblée Nationale du Québec 2009).

cabinets.[5] This suggests that while parity cabinets are not yet the norm, it may be increasingly expected to appoint a concrete floor of women to cabinet (around 30 percent; see Annesley et al. 2019).

Canadian politics appear less open to women as prime minister. To date, no woman has become the prime minister by leading her party to victory in a general election. The one woman to serve as prime minister—Kim Campbell—was selected to that position when she won her party's leadership as it held government in June 1993, and only held the post until her party suffered a dramatic electoral defeat in October 1993. Notably, none of the current leaders of any of the major federal parties are women; given that it is convention that the leader of the largest party in the House forms government and serves as prime minister, this pattern of all-male party leadership means that Canadian prime ministers are, and will likely continue to be, men.

The pattern is similar in the provinces. The chief political executive at the provincial level—the premier—is rarely a woman. By 2017, only eight women had served as provincial premier, and six were selected to that position while their parties held government. The only women made premier *first* through general election did so in Quebec (Pauline Marois in 2012) and Alberta (Rachel Notley in 2015). Some evidence suggests that parties in government in Canada's provinces select women as leaders when they are in crisis or decline (Thomas 2018).

Though Canada's openness to women in government is middling at best, there is good reason to expect young people may be open to it. The Canadian prime minister during data collection, Justin Trudeau, tweeted that he was "proud to be a feminist" during the 2015 election campaign (https://twitter.com/justintrud eau/status/646103864454713344?lang=en). When data were being collected, Canada's parity cabinet included women in several powerful portfolios: foreign affairs, justice, health. Other women were tasked with particularly difficult, though less high-profile, cabinet positions, such as Crown-Indigenous affairs. The first woman to serve as minister of finance, the most powerful cabinet position outside of the prime minister, was appointed in August 2020, well after our data were collected.

The context in the provinces of Alberta and Quebec is, perhaps, more open to women. Because they are responsible for most welfare state programs, provincial politicians are more likely than their federal counterparts to campaign explicitly on women's issues (Thomas 2019). In Alberta's last parity cabinet, in place until 2019, women held reasonably powerful roles based on government priorities, including health, environment and parks, energy, justice.[6] Similarly,

---

[5] Following a change in government, women were only 35 percent of cabinet ministers in Ontario (2018), and 29 percent in Alberta (2019).

[6] After finance, health and education are the most important provincial cabinet posts.

women comprised nearly 40 percent of Quebec's cabinet in 2016, including powerful positions such as justice, and economy. In general, though, many women held less powerful posts, consistent with historical trends about women and cabinet appointments (Trimble et al. 2013).

Government Policy Agendas

Several issues dominated the policy agenda in Canada in the lead-up to our data collection in early 2017. As a result of a decision by the Supreme Court of Canada, the federal government was required to revise the criminal code throughout 2016 to ensure Canadians could access physician-assisted dying. This policy change carried considerable implications for the provinces, as they are responsible for healthcare and, thus, ultimately responsible for regulating those procedures. Climate change featured heavily on the national agenda, as both the federal and some provincial governments moved to regulate greenhouse gas emissions by pricing carbon, and the Alberta and federal governments scrambled to deal with a massive wildfire near several oil sands projects. Yet at the same time, the federal government (with Alberta's support) purchased the Trans-Mountain Pipeline project to move more oil and gas products from Alberta to the western coast. Several provinces, including Quebec, and several Indigenous nations were opposed to this decision.

While the policy agenda in Canada at the time of data collection was not necessarily focused on gender, there were stories about how gender (negatively) affects politics that received considerable media attention. Federally, while breaking up a filibuster designed to delay a vote in the House of Commons, Prime Minister Trudeau physically grabbed the Official Opposition whip (a man); in so doing, he jostled another opposition MP (a woman) in the chest. While the prime minister was criticized for his actions, the woman MP was attacked personally for criticizing the prime minister for elbowing her, because the prime minister is (ostensibly) a feminist (Kirkup 2016). Trudeau subsequently apologized to the MP for elbowing her. More seriously in Alberta, an opposition Member of the Legislative Assembly crossed the floor to the government, citing sexist harassment at the hands of her former party's members (Graney 2016). Alberta also celebrated the hundred-year anniversary of white women first securing the right to vote in provincial elections. Unfortunately, threats to women in Alberta politics spiked at this time (Trynacity 2018).

In Quebec, the government announced a large budget surplus and a reinvestment in healthcare and education, mitigating significant cuts made in previous years. Serious issues arose after a series of sexual assaults on a university campus, leading to several protests about sexual assault and rape culture across the province (Shingler 2016). In addition, several Members of the Quebec National Assembly (MNAs) formally complained about a colleague's lewd behavior to the speaker; the MNA who was the subject of those complaints was later accused of sexual misconduct (Authier 2018).

What Canada's Institutions Predict about Mental Templates of Leadership

The federal and subnational contexts, as well as Canada's political institutions, provide contradictory predictions about how open politics should be to women. However, on balance, Canadian politics should be more open than closed to women. Canada's long standing as a democratic, parliamentary regime suggests politics should be open to women. However, no party has a formal quota for women's inclusion as candidates for election. While the New Democratic Party (NDP) has had an equity statement about candidate nominations in its party constitution since 1984 (Cross 2004), the party never fielded a parity slate of candidates until the Alberta provincial election in 2015. To date, no competitive federal party has nominated an equal number of women and men as candidates in a general election, though a handful of provincial political parties have.

This lack of quotas is perhaps unsurprising given both public opinion and Canada's electoral system. Most Canadians *disagree* that "political parties should be required by law" to run a minimum number of women as candidates (CES 2008), and a super majority does *not* think women's underrepresentation in the House of Commons is a problem (CES 2004). Despite this, most Canadians "agree that the best way to protect women's interests is to have more women in Parliament" (CES 2011). Additionally, Canada's single-member plurality (SMD-P) electoral system is an awkward fit for most gender quotas, which may help explain why no parties consistently apply even a voluntary quota. Because voters are presented with single candidates from each political party in their electoral district, there are few mechanisms for voters to directly intervene to increase the number of women candidates. Candidates are selected by party members, and some evidence suggests that party selectorates show bias against women candidates by nominating them in districts they are unlikely to win (Thomas and Bodet 2013). In general elections, though, evidence shows Canadians are as likely to vote for women candidates as they are for men, regardless of their own gender (Goodyear-Grant and Croskill 2011).

Despite its SMD-P electoral system, during data collection, there were five parties with MPs in both the Canadian House of Commons and Alberta legislature, and four in Quebec's National Assembly. Electoral reform was the subject of contentious debate in 2016, as the Trudeau government promised the 2015 election would be the last held under SMD-P rules. Canadians interested in proportional representation, or in integrations of greater proportionality in the electoral system, argued that one reason to make the change was to increase women's representation. However, experts disagreed, given that there is little evidence to suggest that *changing* the electoral system from a plurality to a proportional formula consistently affects women's election (Roberts et al. 2013; Parliament of Canada 2019).

Status of Women in Canada

Women's relative position to men in Canadian society with respect to education and economic participation also suggests that politics should be more open to women. Women outperform men in terms of grades and degree attainment at most levels of education, including post-secondary, though this varies considerably by field, as women remain underrepresented in fields such as architecture, engineering, and mathematics (Turcotte 2011).

Women comprise about 48 percent of Canada's labor force; and women's participation rate in the labor force is about 80 percent, while men's is 90 percent. Women on average earn only about 87 cents for every dollar men earn. This is exacerbated by race and by parental status. Though this pay gap has improved over time, it persists because traditionally feminine (read: care) work continues to be less compensated than more masculine, male-dominated fields. Women continue to be underrepresented in fields that tend to pay well, including the upper echelons of business (Moyser 2017). This suggests that young Canadians see women in the economy often, though they are arguably less likely to see women in high-profile business positions.

Expectations

Given all of this, we have several expectations about how young Canadians should react to our experimental treatments. Role congruity theory suggests that participants should evaluate women in politics based on what they deem to be their appropriate roles. As young adults see more women in politics, role congruity should matter less to their evaluations. Women's current integration into Canadian politics and society suggests that youth should be comfortable with women in authority positions, so role congruity should produce weak effects or none at all. That said, because men still hold most political positions, we expect that young Canadians will still evaluate men as candidates more favorably than women, especially for more high-profile, powerful posts.

There is good reason to expect that young Canadians should evaluate candidates differently on policy because of that candidate's gender, especially for masculine policy domains. As noted above, it is uncommon for women to serve in finance and economic portfolios in cabinet, and women are not typically found in the upper echelons of Canadian business. This may lead young Canadians to prefer men for these policies over women. Similarly, because women dominate more feminine policy areas, such as healthcare, as workers, we expect young Canadians to score women candidates higher than men on these policies.

With respect to social categorization theory, given that there is no evidence to suggest gender affinity effects are found in Canadian politics, we do not expect female participants to rate women candidates more favorably than men, nor male participants to rate men candidates more favorably (Goodyear-Grant and Croskill 2011). However, because partisanship strongly structures Canadian politics, we expect participants to evaluate women candidates more positively if they are from the participants' preferred party. We also expect that participants whose mothers are highly educated or work in high-status jobs will evaluate women candidates more positively than other participants do.

Canada's parliamentary, party-centered politics further suggest that less gendered leadership templates should be favored here. Government policy is certainly more focused on the welfare state than on stereotypically masculine policies such as defense, but Canada's emphasis on natural resource extraction may temper this.

Description of the Experiment and the Dataset

Like all the cases in this project, we used a 2×2×2 factorial design with Candidate Gender, Party Platform, and Party Label as the three factors presented in a relatively long candidate speech for each of the two largest parties, that each discussed six policy areas. Party Platform was developed from reading the Speech from the Throne for the new Liberal Party government, and Conservative responses, with additional information obtained from each party's 2015 election manifesto. (See Chapter 2 for explanation of the experiment design and implementation.)

All data were collected in March–April 2017. The study was conducted online in three public universities in Calgary (Alberta), and in classrooms (administered by a male or a female member of the research team) during normal class times in one public university and four public Cégeps[7] in Montreal

---

[7] Cégep stands for «Collège d'enseignement général et professionnel.» They are post-secondary education institutions where students complete technical degrees or pre-university degrees, and where all programs share a core curriculum.

ATTITUDES TOWARD WOMEN IN GOVERNMENT IN CANADA 107

Table 5.1 Description of Participants in Alberta and Quebec Cases

	Alberta			Quebec		
	Over-all	Male only	Female only	Over-all	Male only	Female only
Number of participants	253	94	150	419	214	196
Percent of participants	100.0	38.5	61.5	100.0	52.2	47.8
Average age	22.3	22.0	22.5	20.1	20.1	20.2
Left (1) to Right (10) self-placement	4.70	5.12	4.46	4.46	4.40	4.54
Preferred party (%):						
Governing (Liberal)	40.5	37.6	42.7	47.2	44.7	50.5
Largest opposition (Conservative)	30.6	40.9	24.0	3.7	5.3	1.1
NDP	15.5	8.6	19.3	14.1	13.5	15.4
No preference stated*	13.5	12.9	14.0	35.1	36.5	33.0
Total	100	100	100	100	100	100
Parents' education** (%):						
Fathers w/high level	51.0	56.4	48.7	49.6	54.2	44.9
Mothers w/high level	46.6	50.0	45.3	47.0	52.8	41.3
Fathers w/low level	23.3	18.1	25.3	19.8	19.6	20.4
Mothers w/low level	26.1	25.5	24.7	19.3	18.7	20.9
Parents' occupation (%):						
Fathers w/high status job	63.5	66.3	62.5	62.1	62.6	61.0
Mothers w/high status job	40.8	36.8	42.8	48.8	52.8	44.9
Housewives as % of participants	6.0	6.9	5.8	2.1	1.0	2.8
Housewives as the actual number	14	6	8	8	2	5

* Bloc Quebecois, a federal party presenting candidates only in Quebec, was not an option on the questionnaire, so the "no preference" selection in Quebec may signify the absence of their preferred party from the options.

** Note: Education levels of participants' parents are divided into "high" (complete university or more) and "low" (complete secondary or less), and the remaining percentage (not shown) is defined as "intermediate" or "don't know."

(Quebec). Classes varied considerably in size, and they included a variety of topics, from the humanities to the social sciences, vocational training classes, natural sciences, and medicine. Table 5.1 provides descriptions of both the Alberta and Quebec datasets.

108   THOMAS, MAHÉO, AND BOGIARIS

Although the participants likely originated from various regions of both provinces, all participants resided in a major urban area at the time of the study. Therefore, our study does not represent rural populations. However, the occupational and educational backgrounds of participants' families indicate that they come from a variety of socioeconomic backgrounds, enhancing the generalizability of our findings.

Time Period of the Study: Relevant Aspects

The data were collected approximately fifteen months after Canada's 2015 federal election. After that election, the Liberal Party of Canada formed a majority government, winning 184 of 388 seats with 39.5 percent of the popular vote, and Justin Trudeau was appointed as prime minister. He subsequently appointed a parity cabinet. The Official Opposition was the previous incumbent party in government, the Conservative Party of Canada; they won ninety-nine seats and 32 percent of the popular vote. The New Democratic Party of Canada (NDP) won forty-four seats with 20 percent of the popular vote. Two other parties won seats: the Bloc Quebecois (ten seats, 4.7 percent of the popular vote) and the Green Party of Canada (one seat, 3.5 percent of the popular vote).

Table 5.1 shows the party preference of participants in each province. Given that 40–60 percent of Canadians typically report having a party identification (Gidengil et al. 2012), and the 2015 federal election results (Elections Canada, 2018), we are confident the distribution of partisan preferences in our sample fairly represents that of the Canadian population, despite the young age of participants.

How Candidate Gender, Party Platform, and Party Label Influence General Evaluations of Candidates

Each participant scored the suitability of one candidate with a specific gender (indicated by name and pronoun) and party identification (either stated or implied). Participants did not directly compare their candidate to another. We thus avoid using the terms "preferable" or "preferred" that suggest the same participant making a direct comparison. Instead, we present which candidates scored higher or lower when comparing candidate evaluations across treatment conditions. The notation, H5 through H11, refers to hypotheses and statistical methods outlined in Chapters 1 and 2.

ATTITUDES TOWARD WOMEN IN GOVERNMENT IN CANADA   109

To assess how comfortable young Canadians are with women in political roles, we analyzed their answers to five general questions about how effective the candidate would be as 1) a Member of Parliament (MP),[8] 2) a cabinet minister,[8] 3) party leader, [8] and whether 4) they would support the candidate in the election for Parliament,[9] and if 5) the candidate would be good at winning votes.[10] Factor analyses of these general questions for each case are in the Chapter Appendix. Due to the different context of each case, we present the results separately for each province.

To test H8 we conduct ANOVAs with Candidate Gender, Party Platform, and Party Label as factors. Analysis for Alberta indicates that Candidate Gender has no effect on the evaluations of the candidate's effectiveness to be an *MP*, attract *Support* in a federal election, or to *Win Votes*. The only difference for Candidate Gender regards effectiveness as a *Minister*, [F(1,230)=3.05 p=.082] and *Party Leader* [F(1,238)=4.218, p=.041], both showing a more favorable evaluation of the women than the man. The same analyses for Quebec gave generally similar results, except that in Quebec for *Minister* the mean score is higher for the man candidate (M=3.89) than the woman (M=3.66) [F(1,364)=4.150, p=.042]. H9 is based on role congruity theory, which expects that men will be preferred in more prestigious posts. To test H9, we examine the difference in mean scores for men and women candidates for *MP*, *Minister*, and *Party Leader*. As explained above, in Alberta, women candidates are evaluated more favorably than men for all three posts, which contradicts the prediction based on role congruity theory. In Quebec, the man candidate is more favorably evaluated than the woman for *Minister* and *Party Leader*, but the gap is smaller for *Party Leader* (.142) than for *Minister* (.226), again indicating that women are not more incongruous in more prestigious posts.

The next question that we test is whether, in line with the in-group categorization notion, the sex of the participants affects differential preferences for men and women candidates (H5). In Alberta the participants' responses evident in Figure 5.1 (top) illustrate a statistically significant 2×2 interaction (ANOVA (Candidate Gender, Participant Sex) [F(1,230)=3.97, p=.048]) where male participants score the women *MP* candidates higher, while female participants score men and women as equal. The same pattern exists with the question on the candidate's ability to *Win Votes* (bottom) [F(1,237)=6.54, p=.011]. The pattern for *Minister*, *Party Leader*, and *Support* is not significant. In contrast, analysis

---

[8] Answers range from 1 (outstanding) to 6 (very poor). Answers have been inverted so that high scores are favorable.

[9] Answers coded 1 (yes) or 2 (no).

[10] Answers range from 1 (very good) to 5 (very poor). Answers have been inverted so that high scores are favorable.

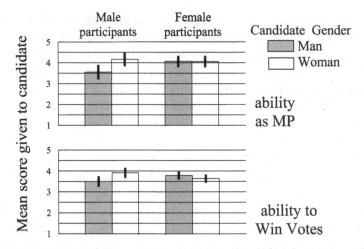

Figure 5.1 Alberta: Differences in evaluations by male and female participants 2×2 ANOVA (Candidate Gender, Participant Sex) 95 percent confidence intervals included.

of Quebec does not portray any interaction of Participant Sex and Candidate Gender for any of the five questions.

As anticipated, Party Platform, not Candidate Gender, is a more powerful predictor of candidate evaluations. In Quebec, the Liberal Party (government) candidate is evaluated more favorably to be an *MP*, *Minister*, *Party Leader*, and for *Support*.[11] A similar though weaker pattern is found in Alberta, especially for evaluations of candidates as *MP*s and for *Support*. Party Label (whether the party name was given on the speech) rarely affected the results.

To test more rigorously the importance of partisanship dynamics in establishing perceived leadership, we generated a variable that indicates whether the participant is affiliated with the same party as the hypothetical candidate. The sense of in-groupness (My Party) should increase the attractiveness of the candidate (H6). We performed 2×2 ANOVAs (My Party, Candidate Gender) on the five general evaluation questions. In both Alberta and Quebec and for four questions (*MP*, *Minister*, *Party Leader*, *Support*), we found strong main effects of My Party that did not interact with Party Label, or Participant Sex.[12]

---

[11] The η_p^2 (effect size) for Party Platform ranges from .043 to .136, while the scores for Candidate Gender range from .000 to .01. Party Label was not significant, either as a main effect, or in interaction with Party Platform, which indicates that the strong effect of Platform is found whether or not the party name is included on the speech.

[12] Some participants did not state a preferred party. We reran these analyses including "no stated party" in a 3×2 ANOVA, and the results are substantively the same for both Alberta and Quebec. Posterior contrasts for the My Party variable with a Scheffe test for the simple contrast among the three categories indicate that the "my party" and "not my party" groups are always significantly different from each other. For most questions "not my party" and "no stated party" are not different. In Alberta for *Party Leader* "my party" and "no stated party" are not different.

The η_p^2 measures of effect size for each factor in these analyses indicate that My Party had a stronger effect than Candidate Gender (My Party ranged from .07 to .15 in Quebec and .01 to .27 in Alberta, Candidate Gender was between .00 and .01).

This stronger effect size for party than candidate gender is in keeping with previous, population-based studies of gender and candidates in Canada. There is no evidence to suggest that voters punish women at the ballot box; instead, voters are motivated by other factors. As explained above, only feminists who explicitly use those beliefs to vote are more likely to vote for women candidates (Goodyear-Grant and Croskill 2011).

The importance of party identification as a social identity can sometimes (though not always) comport with research findings from the United States. There, research shows that partisan effects can be more important than gender to candidate evaluations (Dolan 2014). Given that stereotypes about women candidates can contain partisanship (Huddy and Terkildsen 1993b; Cassese and Holman 2018) and that stereotypes about gender need to be activated for them to meaningfully influence candidate evaluations (Bauer 2015), it is perhaps not surprising that a candidate's party can affect their evaluations more than their gender in this study.

Given that women have not achieved parity in Canadian politics, what might explain these mostly null, sometimes positive findings regarding evaluations of women candidates? Young adult Canadians have seen women occupy high-profile political posts. Though a woman was not premier of Quebec during our data collection, Pauline Marois did serve as the first woman in that role from 2012 to 2014. Similarly, during our data collection, women were premiers in other provinces, notably Ontario (the most populous), Alberta, and British Columbia. This, in combination with the federal parity cabinet, means that young Canadians see more women in powerful positions than did previous generations. For young people, seeing women exercise political power may go a long way in neutralizing more traditional ideas about gender roles.[13] This may also help explain why men are more likely to favor women candidates than they are to favour men: while contrary to expectations of social categorization theory, our findings are congruent with what these participants would have been observing in politics at the time our data were collected.

---

[13] Candidate gender does not have a meaningful effect on candidate evaluations, even when participants report that they think MPs, cabinet ministers, and party leaders have an impact on their lives. Mean evaluations (on a scale from 1=no impact to 5=a lot of impact) in Alberta are 2.96 (MP), 3.01 (cabinet), and 3.32 (party leader), and in Quebec 2.64 (MP), 2.89 (cabinet), and 3.08 (party leader). Thus, these findings cannot be dismissed by suggesting that young people see political representatives as irrelevant to them.

Overall, the results suggest that for young adult Canadians in both provinces with different historical experiences, candidate gender is not a powerful factor in their evaluations of candidates' abilities to win support, or serve as MPs, cabinet ministers, or party leaders. Instead, a candidate's party is a much more powerful factor. This comports with previous research about how party selectorates are more likely to be biased against women as candidates than are voters in Canada, either within their own party's nomination processes, or in perceptions of the quality of their competitors in other parties.

Evaluations in Specific Policy Areas

Policy evaluation in Canada is already strongly structured by federalism and party issue ownership. Recall that while provinces are responsible for policies associated with the welfare state, the federal government has considerably greater spending power. As a result, the federal government can spend more on programming and tries to do so (and thus get political credit for it), sometimes in areas of provincial jurisdiction.

In addition, Canadian parties have established issue ownership that is stable over time and somewhat insulated to government performance (Bélanger 2003; Bélanger and Meguid 2008; Gidengil et al. 2012). The Conservatives "own" the economy, as they are perceived as being better at addressing budget deficits and taxes than the other parties. While the NDP "owns" social programs such as healthcare, education, and childcare, the Liberals are a close second. Thus, young adult Canadians would arguably be able to readily identify which party "owns" which issue.

To this we add gender. Policies and issues are identified as more masculine or feminine based on stereotypes about gender competency. For example, women in general are stereotyped as compassionate and caring; this translates into the idea that women are more competent at handling issues related to care and children than are men (Gilligan 1982; Huddy and Terkildsen 1993b; Schneider and Bos 2014). Similarly, because finance and security are masculine-dominated fields, men are stereotyped as being more competent at handling those issues. This creates a tension in evaluating women candidates in Canada, as voters will be balancing expectations based in federalism and party issue ownership, as well as gender. There is evidence, though, to suggest that Canadians do this, as gender gaps in public opinion in Canada are comparable in size as on other factors, including region (Anderson 2010).

To investigate the influence of candidates' gender and party on evaluation of candidates' ability to deal with policy, we focus on two more traditionally feminine issues (healthcare, women's rights) and two more traditionally masculine policy areas (economy, energy). Health and economics were included in the candidate's speech, while women's rights and energy were not discussed. Discussion of health policy in the Liberal Party speech focused on changing the way healthcare is delivered by investing in home care and long-term care. The Conservative Party speech focused on the aging population and expanded compassionate care benefits so that families can care for a dying loved one or friend. For economic policy, the Liberal Party speech included a tax cut for the middle class, asking the rich to pay more, plus investment in green and social infrastructure to generate quality jobs. The Conservative Party speech emphasized lowering taxes to help business create jobs, rejection of a carbon tax, and maintaining a zero deficit.

Healthcare is one of the largest expenditures for federal and provincial welfare states, totaling over 331 billion CAD in 2022 (Canadian Institutes for Health Information 2022).[14] Women are significantly more likely than men to be employed in healthcare (Moyser 2017).

Many women have held the health and welfare portfolio in national government (1963–1965, 1977–1979, 1980–1983, 1993, 2002–2003, 2008–2013, 2013–2015, 2015–2017). *Economy* is a stereotyped masculine policy area. Complementing men's dominance of corporate Canada, noted earlier, men are more likely than women to prioritize the economy as an issue in Canada. The minister of finance is the most powerful, important position in both provincial and federal cabinets; while women have served as finance minister in some provinces, at the time of the experiment, all federal finance ministers had been men. *Energy* is our second masculine issue, as Canada has a sizeable oil and gas industry, predominantly located in Alberta. Men comprised over 80 percent of employees in this sector when the experiment was conducted. The federal government purchased a contentious pipeline project in the spring of 2018. Though provinces were split in their support (or opposition) to this move, the pipeline purchase highlights the importance of the policy area to Canadian politics at this time. Women served as minister of energy, mines, and resources (later minister of natural resources) in 1984–1986, 1993, 1993–1995, 1995–1997 and 2008–2010. *Women's rights* is by far the least prestigious of these four policy areas. It generally lacks visibility compared to other policy areas and cabinet ministries. However, in the fall of 2016, immediately prior to data being collected, there were multiple allegations of sexual misconduct in Quebec universities and in the National Assembly of Quebec. The *Secrétariat à la condition féminine* piloted a governmental plan to prevent and counter sexual violence. The minister responsible for

---

[14] https://www.cihi.ca/en/national-health-expenditure-trends (accessed November 18, 2022).

114 THOMAS, MAHÉO, AND BOGIARIS

status of women is a junior cabinet position at the federal level, and only women have held this post.

To address the two policies that were part of the speech, *economy* and *health*, we test H10 with a 2×2 ANOVA where Domain is a repeated measure and the between group factor is Candidate Gender. The results show that in both Alberta and Quebec there are no significant effects for Candidate Gender or for the interaction Domain×Candidate Gender. In other words, women candidates are not perceived to be more effective in a feminine policy, nor are men candidates better in the masculine policy. The lack of effects was expected for policies that are covered in the speech, as the participants read the same information attributed to a man and woman candidate from the party. To test H5 we performed an additional analysis to test for in-group preference where we added Participant Sex as another between-groups factor and the three-way interaction Domain×Candidate Gender×Participant Sex was not significant (Alberta p=.948, Quebec p=.432). Essentially, it did not alter the main result, that is, the expected interaction of Domain×Candidate Gender.[15]

The question is reexamined with feminine and masculine policies that were not discussed: *energy* and *women's rights*. H11 is that the lack of information in the speech will lead participants to rely on traditional gender templates to evaluate the candidate's ability in the policy area. If stereotyping matters it is more likely that it will happen here because the participants did not have policy information on which to evaluate the candidate. Again, we conducted the repeated measures ANOVAs. As depicted in Figure 5.2 we obtained a significant interaction of Domain×Candidate Gender in both cases (Alberta $[F(1,250)=8.64, p=.004]$, Quebec $[F(1,400)=15.78, p=.000]$). While both candidates were perceived similarly in the masculine policy area, the participants gave more credit to the woman candidate on the feminine policy.[16] When we added Participant Sex to the analysis to test for same sex

---

[15] For robustness purposes we conducted the analyses with an alternative set of policies that were included in the speech—*security* (masculine) and *education* (feminine). We obtained the same results—no effects for Candidate Gender—in Quebec. In Alberta the woman candidate is scored higher on *security* while there is no difference between men and women candidates in *education*.

[16] For robustness purposes we conducted the analyses with alternative sets of policies that were *not* discussed. First looking at *infrastructure* (masculine) and *childcare* (feminine). We obtained the significant interaction of Domain×Candidate Gender in Quebec, but the interaction was not significant in Alberta. Second, we assessed *agriculture* (masculine) and *childcare* (feminine). The interaction of Domain×Candidate Gender in Quebec is not significant (though the trend was similar, favoring women candidates in *childcare*). In Alberta the new results were comparable to the previous analysis—no interaction, though women candidates were scored higher across the two policies $[F(1,248 = 5.80 p=.017]$.

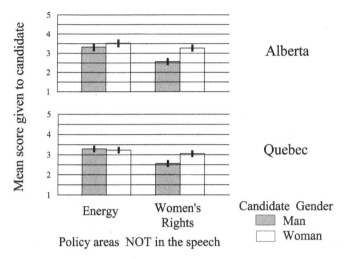

Figure 5.2 Effectiveness of men and women candidates in masculine and feminine policy areas not discussed in the speech
2×2 repeated measures ANOVA (Domain, Candidate Gender) 95 percent confidence intervals included.

in-group effects (H5), the three-way interaction was not significant (Alberta p=.883, Quebec p=.831)

These results imply that for *women's rights*, participants in both provinces always rate women candidates as more competent to deal with that policy than men. Given that, as noted above, nearly two-thirds of Canadians think the best way to protect women's rights is to elect more women, this result with respect to women's rights is not surprising. However, contrary to our expectation that when policy information is lacking gender stereotypes will come to the fore, we do not find evidence that men candidates are more favorably evaluated for *energy* policy.

In keeping with expectations about issue ownership, participants see the Liberal Party as better at handling *women's rights* than are the Conservatives, regardless of Candidate Gender or their own party preferences. In the stereotypically feminine policy area of women's rights, there is also no doubt in young Canadians' mind that women are the leaders. This is illustrated in Figure 5.3 as the 2×2×2 ANOVA (Candidate Gender, Party Platform, Party Label) yields a significant main effect for Party Platform in both Alberta [$F(1,244)=14.60$ p=.000] and Quebec [$F(1,397)=10.16$ p=.002].

The results are much less gendered in the other policy areas, despite the greater prestige and profile associated with those policies. With respect to the

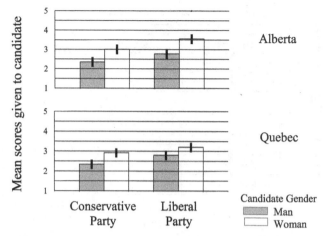

Figure 5.3 Effectiveness of man and woman candidate for *women's rights* policy as a function of Party Platform
2×2×2 ANOVA (Candidate Gender, Party Platform, Party Label) 95 percent confidence intervals included.

other feminine policy, *healthcare*, participants seem to view candidates comparably, regardless of the candidates' gender. While healthcare is a feminine policy area dominated by women, young Canadians do not appear to consistently evaluate women candidates as more competent or able to address health policy. What appears to matter more is issue ownership: 2×2×2 ANOVAs (Candidate Gender, Party Platform, Party Label) for each province show that participants give significantly more favorable evaluations to the Liberal Party candidate on *health* than the Conservative Party candidate, regardless of Candidate Gender (Quebec: [$F(1,401)=36.95$ p=.000], Alberta: [$F(1,240)=24.37$ p=.000]). This is largely in keeping with partisan expectations.

Even though both economy and energy are stereotypically masculine issues, young Canadians do not appear to use a masculine schema to evaluate political candidates on these policies. Party, however, does matter. *Economy*, a "masculine" policy, is owned by the Conservative Party both in Alberta [$F(1,243)=15.65$) p=.000] and Quebec [$F(1,400)=6.83$ p=.009]. The trend is not significant in either province when we analyze *energy*. These findings add to existing work from the United States that suggests that how people feel about political parties matters more to the evaluation of candidates than does that candidate's gender (Dolan 2014).

Overall, the results of policy-based candidate evaluations show that young Canadians believe that both men and women can be policy leaders. And contrary to theoretical expectations, this is the finding for important high-profile

ATTITUDES TOWARD WOMEN IN GOVERNMENT IN CANADA 117

and stereotypically masculine issues, such as the economy and energy. Young Canadians tend to believe that women can be better leaders than men in more stereotypical feminine policy areas, such as women's rights. This suggests that women's underrepresentation in Canada's political institutions is not because Canadian young adults perceive them to be less competent than their male peers.

Socialization within the Home Environment

Up to now, we have seen that candidate gender does not appear to be a relevant dimension of mental templates of leadership for young adult Canadians, or their views are favorable to women in politics, with a few exceptions (i.e., man candidates are evaluated more favorably for the post of minister in Quebec). How generalizable is this? H7 predicts that having a mother who is highly educated or has a high-status job will be associated with leadership templates that include women. The rationale here is straightforward. If young Canadians are used to seeing their mother model powerful behavior in the public sphere, such as working in a high-status job or holding high levels of education, then they would be more favorable to other women exercising power in politics. In this section we examine whether it is this sub-set of the samples who view women as leaders, and whether the effect is the same for both male and female participants.

We conducted additional analysis for each of the "general" and policy questions examined above, with and without controlling for Participant Sex: ANOVAs with Candidate Gender and Mother Job or Mother Education.[17] Though the interaction of Candidate Gender with Mother Job or Mother Education is not significant for many questions, where the interaction is significant the impact generally differs for male and female participants, or is limited to one group. In Alberta Mother Education affects evaluations of the candidate's ability to be an *MP* (three-way interaction [$F_{(1,161)}=3.832$, p$-$.052]) (Figure 5.4 top-left) and approaches significance for *Minister* and *Party Leader* (p-values for the three-way interaction are respectively: p=.077, p=.074), and it is male participants whose mothers have a high level of education who give a more favorable evaluation to the woman candidate. Regarding *energy* policy, the three-way interaction of Candidate Gender×Mother Job×Participant Sex is

---

[17] Lower level of education is coded as complete secondary education or less (N=66 in Alberta, N=81 in Quebec). High level of education is coded as complete university or graduate school (N=118 in Alberta, N=197 in Quebec). For the analysis utilizing Mother Job status we do not include the few participants whose mother was a housewife (N=14 in Alberta, N=8 in Quebec). Chapter 2 explains job categorizations.

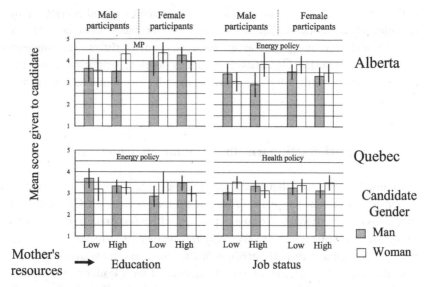

Figure 5.4 Effect of mother's job or education on evaluations
2×2×2 ANOVA (Candidate Gender, Mother Education or Mother Job, Participant Sex) 95 percent confidence intervals included.

significant [F(1,203)=5.325, p=.022].[18] Again, male participants whose mother has a high-status job score the woman candidate higher (Figure 5.4 top-right). In Quebec Mother Job interacts with Participant Sex and Candidate Gender, affecting evaluations for *health* policy [F(1,351)=4.295, p=.039] (Figure 5.4 bottom-right), and approaching significant for being an *MP* [F(1,340)=3.778, p=.053]. However, here it is male participants whose mother has a *low*-status job who score the woman candidate higher. For *energy* policy, regardless of the sex of the participant, it is participants whose mother has a high-status job who score the man candidate higher [F(1,359)=7.013, p=.008]. However, analysis with Mother Education indicates that it is female participants whose mothers have a lower level of education are the ones who score the woman candidate higher [F(1,260)=5.668, p=.018] (Figure 5.4 bottom-left).

In summary, for Alberta, findings conform to predictions about how family background may shape who views women as leaders, though the impact is only found for male participants. In Quebec, where family background is related to which groups view women as leaders, the relationship is contrary to the prediction. However, at least some young Quebecers are open to women's political leadership even if they do not see that being modeled by their own mothers, at

---

[18] For *economics* policy the three-way interaction approaches significance (p=.070).

least through higher levels of education. Perhaps, these participants see their mothers engaging in powerful behavior in ways that are not captured by education levels alone. In addition, while home structure, by serving as a proximate example, may have an impact on young adult's political leadership templates, the impact of family may be modified, or even overridden, by interaction with their peers. The political liberal leaning of their cohort, in particular, may decrease the influence from family.

Discussion of Study Findings in the Context of Alberta and Quebec

These results provide persuasive evidence to show that young Canadians typically do *not* evaluate political candidates differently because of their gender, and that this holds for young Canadian women and men alike, and for diverse family backgrounds. This comports somewhat with our expectations presented in the first half of the chapter, though given men's continued dominance of higher-profile political positions, such as prime minister and minister of finance, as well as masculinized professions and top business management, it is somewhat surprising that candidate gender so rarely matters for young Canadians. When candidate gender does matter, participants often rate women more favorably than men. The most notable exception to this is when participants are evaluating a candidate to serve as *Minister*, where in Quebec the man candidate receives more favorable evaluations. Overall, findings of the Alberta and Quebec experiments add support to research that highlights how bias against women candidates in Canada is found in party selection and not at the ballot box. Similarly, gender does not matter much in terms of policy evaluation either, save for when it comes to *women's rights*. There, young Canadians across the board think that women candidates are better equipped to protect women's rights than are men. Yet, even in some masculine policy areas, such as *energy* or *economy*, some young Canadians appear to be more open to women's political leadership, which is somewhat of a surprise and may indicate new attitudes in the young generation since men still dominate in stereotypically masculine professions like energy and in business top management. Findings from the two Canadian experiments clearly show that party, not candidate gender, dominates candidate evaluations. This comports with our expectations because of the strong way in which partisanship structures Canadian politics.

These results suggest that women's continued, chronic underrepresentation in Canada's electoral politics is not the result of bias, at least from young Canadians, given that young Canadians have already been socialized to think that women would be as good as men in many political roles. But, interpreting these findings as evidence that Canadian young adults do not use gender as a component of leadership templates highlights the limits of that neutrality. It is difficult to escape women's underrepresentation in Canadian politics when women are only 29 percent of MPs and lead no competitive federal parties. This means that representing women in numbers that match their demographic weight—that is, parity—is a long way off in Canada. Given that young Canadians also think that women are much better than men at protecting women's rights, this raises questions about how political Canadian youth think those rights are.

Table A5.1 Factor Analysis of General Evaluation Questions for Canada

Component matrix component 1	Alberta	Quebec
Q1 MP	.918	.817
Q2 Cabinet Minister	.908	.883
Q3 Party Leader	.881	.814
Q17 Support	−.740	−.699
Q18 Win Votes	.575	.436
Variance explained	66.43%	55.76%

Extraction method: Principal component analysis.

6

Young Adults' Attitudes to Women Candidates in Uruguay

No Obstacle to Change

Niki Johnson

MACRO-CONTEXT FACTORS: URUGUAY AND OTHER CASES			
LOW ← Expectation of Strength of Gender Bias → HIGH			
	Parliamentary	**OR**	**Presidential**
Executive Institutions	Alberta CA Quebec CA England Israel Sweden		Chile California US Texas US Costa Rica Uruguay
Electoral Institutions	**Party focused ← – – – – – – – – – – – – – → Candidate focused**		
	Israel Uruguay Chile Costa Rica Sweden		Alberta CA California US Quebec CA Texas US England
Policy Agenda Emphasis	**More Social Welfare ← – – – – – – – – – → Less Social Welfare**		
	Sweden Alberta CA Uruguay England California US Costa Rica Quebec CA Israel Chile Texas US		
	Less Defense ← – – – – – – – – – – – – – → More Defense		
	Costa Rica Alberta CA Sweden England Israel Uruguay Quebec CA Chile California US Texas US		
Incorporation of Women in Government	**Greatest ← – – – – – – – – – – – – – – – – → Least**		
	Sweden Chile Alberta CA Uruguay Texas US Costa Rica England Quebec CA California US Israel		

Introduction

From May to October 2017 this experiment was conducted in Uruguay with 707 participants to test whether there are factors associated with country context, or with characteristics of individuals, that generate responses which categorize women candidates as people who fit the templates of politician and leader

Niki Johnson, *Young Adults' Attitudes to Women Candidates in Uruguay* In: *The Image of Gender and Political Leadership*. Edited by: Michelle M. Taylor-Robinson and Nehemia Geva, Oxford University Press. © Oxford University Press 2023. DOI: 10.1093/oso/9780197642726.003.0006

in comparison to male candidates.[1] Uruguay was chosen for this study because Uruguayan women have high levels of education and participation in the work force, but, even with the application of a gender quota in national elections since 2014, very few women have been elected to Uruguay's parliament, and in only slightly greater numbers have they been designated to the cabinet. On the other hand, the political agenda since the early twentieth century has had an important focus on social welfare issues and in recent years had a strong presence of what may be considered stereotypically feminine policy issues (health, including sexual and reproductive rights; education, including extension of public pre-school care; national system of care for dependents). Uruguay is also interesting because it is the only country in Latin America where public opinion polls regularly show that there is not a significant gender gap in public support for women as political leaders.

To preview the findings, there is broad evidence that leadership templates among young Uruguayan adults do not include gender as an important component. This holds when testing the effect of sex of the participants, with male participants demonstrating egalitarian attitudes to both men and women candidates, while female participants score female candidates more highly. There is also no gender bias evident when participants assess candidates' potential performance in specific policy areas, including those that have been traditionally associated with a masculine template, although on the issue of women's rights female participants again evaluate women candidates slightly more positively. By contrast, in the evaluation of candidates' competence in different policy areas party has a significant effect, with certain policy issues clearly associated with one or other of the two parties, consistent with party issue ownership.

Political System, Country Context, and Gender Politics

Uruguay has a highly institutionalized and stable unitary form of presidential[2] government, and universal suffrage dates back to the 1934 constitution.[3] The democratic regime suffered two authoritarian interludes, from 1933 to 1939 and 1973 to 1984, but apart from experimenting with a collegial executive from 1952 to 1967, and eliminating in the 1996 electoral reform parties' right to field

---

[1] I thank Marcela Schenck and Nicolás Schmidt for their excellent research assistance in fieldwork and data input.

[2] Uruguay has a presidential system, though the legislature is called the parliament.

[3] Male universal suffrage was enshrined in the 1918 constitution, while a law extending suffrage to women was passed in 1932, making Uruguay the first country in Latin America to grant women identical political rights to those enjoyed by men.

multiple presidential candidates, Uruguay's electoral system for national-level posts has remained largely unchanged over time.

The party system is also highly stable, with the origins of the two so-called "foundational" parties—the conservative center-right National Party (Partido Nacional, PN), with links to both Catholic and Evangelical churches, and the liberal, secular, center-right Colorado Party (Partido Colorado, PC)—dating back to the nineteenth century, and a third major party: the center-left Broad Front coalition (Frente Amplio, FA), competing in elections since 1971.[4] Since the re-installment of democratic government in 1985, each of the main parties has been in power at least once, although after winning the presidential elections for the first time in 2004, the FA retained control over national government until 2020, with a small majority in parliament in all three periods.

The national legislative branch is bicameral: the senate has thirty seats elected in a single national constituency, while the chamber of representatives has ninety-nine seats, distributed proportionally among the nineteen departments, with district magnitude ranging from two to forty-one. The department of Montevideo, where the experiment was conducted, is home to around two-fifths of the country's 3.29 million population and has the highest district magnitude. Presidential and legislative elections take place simultaneously every five years with closed and blocked PR lists.

Based on the literature one might expect closed and blocked lists and high district magnitude to favor a focus on parties rather than individual candidates. However, certain particularities of the Uruguayan party and electoral systems mean that this is not necessarily the case. First, ballots are not party lists, but rather faction lists, with voters selecting both party and faction in a "double simultaneous vote." Many factions (especially but not exclusively in the PN and PC) are personalistic, centered around a single figure or a small group of leaders, each of whom have their own electoral base. Legislative competition is therefore high, both among and within parties, and faction leaders are prominent figures in electoral politics, even if their list wins only one seat in the legislature. This, plus no limits on re-election, gives individual candidates more visibility than in most systems using party closed and blocked lists.

Policy Agenda

Social welfare is central in Uruguay's policy agenda, with universal education and social benefits for workers introduced from the early twentieth century. During

---

[4] Minor parties have won seats in the legislature, but none has become a significant electoral force.

the left FA governments (2005–2020), much of the government's agenda centered on social policies including: reinstatement of the tripartite wage councils, creation of an Integrated National Health System to guarantee universal health coverage, introduction of conditional cash transfer welfare benefits, and a national system to provide care services for dependents, whether young children, the disabled or the elderly. In other words, there has been a strong presence in the policy agenda of what may be considered stereotypically feminine issues (see Chapter 1).

This does not mean that more typically masculine policy areas are not important. Economic issues relating to the 2008 crisis, relations within the Mercosur bloc, foreign investments in Uruguay, and new bilateral trade agreements have all in recent years made frontline news. On the domestic front crime and public safety has been a key issue in recent elections and has topped opinion polls as the main problem facing the country.

For the period immediately preceding the application of the experiment, the main policy concerns of Uruguayans can be seen in the Latinobarómetro public opinion survey conducted in mid-2016: crime and public safety (32.5 percent), unemployment (15.4 percent), economy (14.9 percent), and education (7.7 percent). In the same survey, two stereotypically feminine policy issues received the largest share of mentions when respondents were asked which topics were most important for the development of the country: gender equality (61.2 percent), and social inclusion and anti-poverty policies (59.4 percent).

Women in Politics

Very few women have occupied top posts in the legislative or executive branches of national government. Unlike its closest neighbors, Uruguay has never had a female president, and not until 2019 did any of the major parties field women candidates for vice president. Since the 1996 constitutional reform that introduced open primaries to select parties' single presidential candidacies, only three women have contested the presidential nomination within any of the three main parties.

Until 2005, women's presence was also minimal among the top designated executive posts: thirteen ministers and thirteen vice-ministers. A total of twenty-seven female appointments to such posts were made between 1985 and 2018, although these involved only nineteen women, since several held posts more than once (Johnson 2018), while just seven remained in office for the full term. In the FA governments the number of female ministers increased, with four appointed in 2005 (30.8 percent) and five in 2015 (38.5 percent); even so, analysis of ministerial appointments from March 2010 to June 2013 showed that on average women ministers remained in their posts half as long as their male counterparts did (Johnson 2013: 20).

While most female ministerial appointments have been in social welfare portfolios (education, health, social development, housing), in the 2005–2010 administration women also served as ministers or vice-ministers in defense, international relations, and interior, and during the 2015–2020 administration, when we were conducting the experiment, a woman was minister for industry, energy, and mining. However, top posts in the area of the economy and public spending (Ministry for the Economy and Finance, the national Planning and Budget Office) remained steadfastly masculine until a female economy and finance minister was appointed in 2020.

In recent years women have gained access to other more prestigious or visible political positions. In 2010, three women won elections for the first time to the post of *intendente* (head of the departmental executive), including in the country's capital, Montevideo. One of them was re-elected in 2015, and in 2012 a female senator from the Socialist Party won the presidency of the FA in internal elections.

In the legislative arena, following the inauspicious return to democracy for women in 1985, when not a single woman was elected to the national parliament, the percentage of women rose slowly, but remained consistently below 15 percent until 2014. In 2009 a gender quota law was passed requiring parties to field candidates of both sexes every three places on their lists in all elections. Lists that did not comply would not be registered by the electoral authorities. The original law established that for national and departmental elections the quota would only be applied in the 2014/2015 electoral cycle, a reflection of the entrenched resistance among male party leadership to such a measure.[5] Most party factions who won seats applied the quota in a minimalist way, including in each trio of candidates just one woman in the third slot (Johnson 2018).[6] Another tactic that sabotaged the effectiveness of the quota was the duplication of female candidacies in electable positions on faction lists to both the senate and the lower house, which led to them resigning one of their seats to their male alternate. As a result, even with the 33 percent quota in 2014, women only won 20 percent of parliament seats.

---

[5] See Johnson and Pérez (2011) for an in-depth discussion of how quotas were introduced in Uruguay.

[6] Due to low district and party-faction magnitudes, these positions are generally not electable, since very few lists win more than six seats and the majority win just one or two.

126 NIKI JOHNSON

In 2016 the quota law came under review. Bills to introduce parity provisions and/or prevent the use of duplicate candidacies were tabled, but ultimately the only modification to the existing quota law was that it would apply as a permanent measure in national and departmental legislative elections. Parity was again on the political agenda in 2021.

Status of Women in Society

In contrast to women's limited presence in political posts, Uruguayan women achieve high levels of education and participation in the work force. Women have gradually outstripped men in education: by 2012 women accounted for 64 percent of matriculations and 66 percent of graduations at undergraduate level, and 62 percent of postgraduate students at the country's main university (Udelar 2014: 119, 137, 178). Women active in the workforce has risen, with over 75 percent of women aged 18–49 now economically active, and high participation rates (over 60 percent) even when they have three or more children (Inmujeres 2013: 26). In addition, the percentage of women employed as professionals is double that of men (Inmujeres 2013: 30). Nevertheless, gender inequalities persist in the labor market, with women occupying fewer managerial positions than men, and persistent horizontal segregation and wage gaps, with women concentrated in the services sector and with higher levels of informality and under- and unemployment.

The concern for gender equality amongst the Uruguayan public, mentioned above, is also reflected in comparatively open attitudes toward women in politics. The AmericasBarometer survey question asking whether men make better political leaders than women indicates no significant gender difference in support for women as political leaders.[7] As Morgan and Buice (2013: 651) point out, in the 2008 AmericasBarometer survey Uruguay recorded the highest percentage of men supporting female political leadership in the region and was the only country in the region where there was no significant gender difference between men's (70.3 percent) and women's (70.0 percent) views on whether women could make good political leaders. By 2012 the level of support for women as political leaders had increased by almost 14 percentage points. These data are corroborated in the results of the World Values surveys carried out in

---

[7] The question asks: "Some say that in general men are better political leaders than women. Do you strongly agree / agree / disagree / strongly disagree?" Data available for Uruguay in 2008 and 2012 on the Latin American Public Opinion Survey website: https://www.vanderbilt.edu/lapop/raw-data.php.

Uruguay in 2006 (71.7 percent of respondents disagree that men make better politicians than women) and 2011 (82.6 percent). Comparing these results with Argentina and Chile, with whom the country shares many characteristics in terms of political system, culture, and level of human development, but which, unlike Uruguay, had female presidents, we see that Uruguayans' attitudes are far more favorable to women (Chile 2012: 68.7 percent disagree; Argentina 2013: 67.4 percent disagree).

This increasing support for women in politics over 2008–2012 coincided with a period of intermittently intense public debate on the issue of gender electoral quotas. Notably several anti-quota discourses—found in parties across the ideological spectrum—claim to argue from the perspective of the electorate. Male opponents of the quota declared it would violate electors' freedom to vote for the candidates of their choice by obliging them to vote for women,[8] that voters were not concerned about the sex of candidates, and that what did matter was being able to vote for the best candidate for the job (Johnson and Moreni 2009). These arguments reveal the persistence of a traditional masculine leadership template among male party leaders, and their projection of that template on to the electorate.

However, a survey in 2007,[9] when the quota law had not yet been passed, showed that a majority of Uruguayans supported a greater presence of women in politics, including in the cabinet. Only a minority considered that the sex of those holding top elective and designated political positions was irrelevant, the majority evaluated positively women's performance in office and believed that women politicians bring different perspectives and issues to the political agenda. On all of these questions, female respondents' support for women in politics was significantly higher than male respondents', although men also exhibited majority positions favorable to women. Johnson and Pérez (2010: 25) argue—in line with social categorization theory (see Chapter 1)—that the more favorable views held by women would appear to stem at least in part from their identification with women figures in politics.

Of course, public opinion data risks reflecting socially conditioned responses rather than genuine attitudes, especially on social equality questions. The experiment, therefore, provided a unique opportunity to test whether a traditional masculine leadership template persisted behind Uruguayans' apparent support for women in politics.

---

[8] It is worth pointing out the incoherence of the argument concerning violation of voters' liberty, given that in Uruguay electoral lists are closed and blocked.

[9] Survey by the Politics, Gender and Diversity Area of the Institute of Political Science, Universidad de la República with funding from International IDEA.

128 NIKI JOHNSON

Experiment Application and Dataset for Uruguay

Data Collection

Like all the cases in this project, the Uruguay experiment used a 2×2×2 factorial design with Candidate Gender, Party Platform, and Party Label as the three factors presented in a relatively long candidate speech, discussing six policy areas, for each of the two largest parties, the FA and the PN.[10] Party Platform for the FA was developed from the budget review (*Rendición de Cuentas*) debate in the lower house (01/08/2016), President Vázquez's inaugural speech (01/05/2015), and the FA's 2014 electoral platform (*Bases Programáticas Tercer Gobierno Nacional del Frente Amplio 2015–2020*). The PN speech was based on the budget review debate, and the PN's 2014 electoral platform (*Agenda de Gobierno 2015–2020*). While the sources used for writing the speeches dated to up to three years prior to the application of the experiment, the policy issues selected remained prominent on the governmental agenda, in public debate, and in the media.[11]

The experiment was conducted in classrooms during normal class times from May 20 to October 27, 2017. The experiment was completed by 707 participants, including advanced students attending high schools and technical colleges and first- or second-year students at the two main universities. Table 6.1 provides an overview of the participants.

Schools and classes were selected with the aim of ensuring a varied distribution in participants' backgrounds and interests. To increase diversity, we included private-sector educational centers, although public schools include students from a broad range of socioeconomic backgrounds. Diversity among participants was also ensured by including different academic programs and class subjects: engineering, social sciences, communications, and business science, plus a wide range of subject classes in the technical colleges and high schools.[12] All participants reside in the capital, Montevideo,[13] which means that findings are not generalizable to rural populations in the country.

---

[10] Chapter 2 provides a detailed explanation of the experiment design and implementation.

[11] Due to the ruling that materials used in Uruguayan state-run high schools and technical colleges cannot name political parties, the treatments used in those centers substituted ideological position of the party as a proxy for party name (FA=center-left party; PN=center-right party). The stability of the party system and the clearly different ideological profiles of these two parties, evident in the content of the speeches and the short bio of the candidates, meant that it was highly probable that participants would associate the center-right candidate with the PN and the center-left candidate with the FA.

[12] Electronics, electromechanics, automotive mechanics, administration and commerce, physical education, humanities, economics, architecture, medicine, and law.

[13] According to the 2011 census, around 40 percent of the population live in Montevideo.

ATTITUDES TO WOMEN CANDIDATES IN URUGUAY   129

Table 6.1 Description of Participants in Uruguay

	Overall	Male only	Female only
Number of participants	707	323	376
Percent of participants	100.0	46.2	53.8
Average age	20.0	19.8	20.1
Left (1) to Right (10) self-placement	4.47	4.69	4.26
Preferred party* (%):			
Governing (Frente Amplio/center-left)	34.4	30.0	38.4
Largest opposition (National/center-right)	18.6	21.5	16.0
Colorado Party	1.8	2.6	1.1
No preference stated	45.2	45.9	44.4
Total	100	100	100
Parents' education level** (% of participants):			
Fathers w/high level	15.7	18.6	13.6
Mothers w/high level	16.4	19.5	13.8
Fathers w/low level	61.8	59.1	64.9
Mothers w/low level	56.7	52.0	61.7
Parents' occupation (% of participants):			
Fathers w/high status job	39.3	40.8	37.7
Mothers w/high status job	36.6	41.8	32.1
Housewives, as % of participants	7.5	6.9	8.0
Housewives, as the actual number	46	19	27

* In high schools and technical colleges, party names could not be listed on study materials, so "center-left party" and "center-right party" were substituted.

** Note: Education levels of participants' parents are divided into "high" (complete university or more) and "low" (complete secondary or less), and the remaining percentage (not shown) is defined as "intermediate" or "don't know."

Country Context during Experiment Fieldwork

The experiment was carried out midway in the 2015–2020 administration. In the 2014 elections, the left FA won the presidency with 49.5 percent of the vote, taking sixty-five seats (a one-seat majority) in parliament; the conservative PN, won 31.9 percent of votes, or forty-two seats; while the PC received seventeen seats, and five seats were won by two smaller parties. Comparing these vote shares with the distribution of party preferences in the dataset, the most significant difference is that 45.2 percent declared no party preference, while among those who did express a preference, there was a greater inclination towards the left (62.7 percent). During the time the experiment was conducted thirty-one women held seats in parliament (twenty-one in the lower house, ten in the senate), and five women ministers had held office since March 2015 in the following portfolios: social development; education; tourism; housing, territorial planning, and environment; and industry, energy, and mining.

Fieldwork took place at intervals over five months.[14] This situation laid the project open to possible country context changes that might impact on the results of the experiment. However, there were no important political upheavals, although three contextual events are worth mentioning, two of which relate directly to the question of women's political participation. The first was the massive demonstration to mark international women's day on March 8, 2017 (about two months before data collection began). Participation in the march was unprecedented, reaching estimates of over 250,000 people. Although the demands voiced by participants were varied, with much emphasis on the issues of gender-based violence and feminicide, the sheer size of the event and extensive media coverage it received might have impacted public perceptions of women's empowerment and feminist activism, which could in turn influence the gendered nature of leadership templates.

The second was the senate's modification of the gender quota law on March 15, 2017, extending indefinitely its application in national and departmental elections; this was later ratified by the lower house on October 18, 2017. However, since the characteristics of the gender quota did not change (despite parity campaigns in 2016, led by feminist organizations and women politicians), this reform did not attract much media attention nor generate public debate.

The third event was the only important political story that might have impacted on attitudes during the actual fieldwork period: the resignation of the vice-president in early September 2017. However, the series of controversies that eventually led to his resignation first emerged on the political agenda in mid-2015, well before the start of the experiment. Although he was replaced, for the first time in the post of vice-president, by a woman, she was a former first lady and at the time most voted senator, so her nomination did not imply a significant change in either her personal visibility or the more general map of women's

---

[14] The data collection period was extended due to the need to obtain permission to conduct the experiment from five different educational authorities. Once authorization was given for a particular type of school, the experiment was conducted in that educational setting quickly, ranging from five days to three weeks.

political participation. Indeed, the resignation of the vice-president may have had more of an impact on participants' attitudes towards the FA or political parties/politics in general, rather than specifically towards women in politics.

Results

Each participant scored the suitability of one candidate with a specific gender (indicated by name and pronoun) and party identification (either stated or implied). Participants did not directly compare one candidate to another. As a result, we avoid using the terms "preferable" and "preferred" as they suggest a direct comparison by the same participant. Instead, we discuss which candidate scored higher or lower, on average, when comparing candidate evaluations across treatment conditions. The notation, H5 through H11, refers to hypotheses and statistical methods outlined in Chapters 1 and 2.

General Evaluations of Candidates

We begin by exploring whether participants more favorably evaluate the man candidate than the woman candidate in general evaluation questions (H8), as role congruity theory would suggest. We conducted 2×2×2 ANOVAs with Candidate Gender, Party Platform, and Party Label as factors—for four questions: (1) effectiveness of the candidate as a deputy[15] and (2) as a member of the cabinet,[15] (3) whether the participant would vote for the candidate,[16] and (4) how good the candidate would be at winning votes.[17] Factor analysis indicates that all measures load on one dimension (see analysis in Appendix).

The main-effect of Candidate Gender is significant for *Deputy* [$F(1,601)$= 3.851, p=.050] and *Minister* [$F(1,552)$=7.169, p=.008], but not in the direction expected by role congruity theory; rather we observe a more favorable evaluation of the woman candidate than of the man for both posts as shown in Figure 6.1.[18] In addition, contrary to the prediction of H9 that men will be better evaluated than women for more important posts, the gap in mean evaluations of men and

---

[15] Rated on a scale of 1 (excellent) to 6 (very bad) with scores inverted so that high values are more favorable.

[16] Answered 1 (yes) or 2 (no). This is the only question for which low scores are more favorable.

[17] Rated from 1 (very capable) to 5 (not capable) with scores inverted so that high values are more favorable.

[18] We find the more favorable evaluation of women candidates than of men for *Deputy* and *Minister* whether or not the party name (or ideology) is listed on the speech, as indicated by the lack of a significant interaction of Candidate Gender×Label.

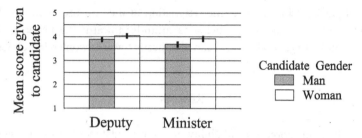

Figure 6.1 Effect of Candidate Gender in general evaluation questions 2×2×2 ANOVA (Candidate Gender, Party Platform, Party Label) 95 percent confidence intervals included.

women candidates is larger (more favorable for women) for *Minister* (-0.238) than *Deputy* (-0.157).

In Uruguay minister is a high visibility and high prestige post, which is more powerful than that of deputy and, along with the posts of senator and departmental governor, considered to be the top ranking post in a political career (Chasquetti 2014).[19] It should be remembered here that while women remain a minority in cabinet posts, their presence as ministers has increased to levels greater than their presence in parliament over the last decade and a half, that is, during the best part of the lifetime of most of the study participants.

These results show that leadership templates among young urban adults in Uruguay do not associate political efficacy with masculinity. In addition, there is no significant main effect of Candidate Gender for *Vote* [$F(1,660)=.376$, $p=.540$] or *Win Votes* [$F(1,682)=.049$, $p=.824$]. This suggests that young people in Uruguay have a positive evaluation of women's capacity to occupy political posts without gender being a factor that will influence whether they will vote for them or not. This is important because, as discussed above, although the voting system in Uruguay is based on closed and blocked lists, which generally implies that voters focus on the party—or in Uruguay's case the party faction—rather than individual candidates, some aspects of the electoral process do give individual candidates more visibility. Our findings do not indicate that candidate gender is a relevant factor in determining voting preferences.

Next we explore whether a shared in-group effect allows the woman candidate to be "recategorized" as a leader, when the candidate and the participant are of the same sex (H5), or they share the same party (H6). In other words, based on

---

[19] This also ties in with participants' responses regarding how much impact deputies and cabinet ministers have on the life of their family (scored 1=no impact, to 5=great impact): the mean for minister (2.89) indicates greater impact than the mean for deputy (2.65).

social categorization theory, do male participants favor men candidates? First, we conduct a 2×2 ANOVA analysis for each general question with Candidate Gender and Participant Sex as factors. For all four general questions the interaction is not significant,[20] indicating that male and female participants evaluate the candidates equivalently. These findings are in line with the results of public opinion surveys discussed above, reconfirming widespread egalitarian attitudes toward women's political activity in Uruguay, with somewhat more support from women citizens.

To test for a shared party in-group effect, for each general question we conduct a 2×3 ANOVA analysis with Candidate Gender and My Party (my party/not my party/no stated party preference) as factors, again focusing on the interaction. We find that, except for *Win Votes*,[21] participants always give a significantly more favorable score to the candidate from their party (p=.000), but the interaction with Candidate Gender is not significant. Especially for the *Deputy* and *Minister* evaluations this is important as it indicates that the higher score for the woman candidate is not dependent on her being from the participant's preferred party.

In sum, with regard to general evaluation questions, we do not find evidence that the young adults who took part in this study have traditional leadership templates. Instead, women are viewed as leaders, and they are even viewed more positively than men candidates to be a deputy or cabinet minister. But are women viewed as capable across diverse policy areas, or only for policies that fit gender stereotypes?

Evaluations of Candidates by Policy Areas

As posited in Chapter 1, role congruity theory and schema theory suggest that certain policy areas tend to be associated with what are considered to be typically masculine or feminine traits. The masculine/feminine categorization of policy areas takes as its starting point the gendered division of labor, which designates activities associated with the public sphere and production as masculine and those linked to the domestic sphere and reproduction as feminine (Skard and Haavio-Mannila et al. 1985; Escobar-Lemmon and Taylor-Robinson 2009). Given the hierarchical nature of the gendered division of labor, it is unsurprising that this distinction between stereotypically masculine and feminine policy areas maps on to Escobar-Lemmon and Taylor-Robinson's (2005) typology of ministries as high-, medium-, or low-prestige, depending on how much power,

---

[20] P-values for the interaction range from p=.101 for *Minister* to p=.904 for *Win Votes*. For both *Deputy* and *Minister* female participants are more favorable than males in their evaluation of the woman candidate, but the difference is not statistically significant.

[21] For *Win Votes*, My Party is not significant (p=.613).

control over resources and visibility they have. Thus masculine policy areas, including, for example, the economy, industry, defense, foreign policy, tend to be high-prestige, while feminine policy areas, such as health, education, social welfare, among others, are generally medium- or low-prestige.

While the definition of which policy areas might be considered stereotypically masculine or feminine may share certain common elements across both time and space, it will also be dependent on contextual factors specific to a country's policy agenda. It is worth remembering here that, with a few notable exceptions, the majority of ministerial posts occupied by women in Uruguay have been in feminine policy areas. Similarly, previous studies on legislative activity in Uruguay (Johnson 2006; Johnson et al. 2015) show that women legislators focus on social welfare issues more than their male colleagues, although this does not mean that they neglect economic policy issues.[22] Male deputies' legislative profiles, on the other hand, tended to be less diversified, with a concentration on economic policy issues, and less attention paid to social welfare issues, even though, as mentioned above, these are prominent on the political agenda.

Based on traditional leadership templates we would expect to find more favorable evaluations of men candidates in stereotypically masculine policy areas, and, conversely, more favorable evaluations of women candidates in stereotypically feminine policy areas. In order to assess whether the lack of a traditional leadership template found in the first part of the analysis holds true across policy areas, we selected four policy areas to study. Two of these were discussed in the candidate speeches and two were not, and within each pair of policies, one can be considered typically masculine and one typically feminine for the case of Uruguay.

The masculine policy areas chosen for this study were agriculture (not in the speech) and the economy (discussed in the speech). The economy is a high prestige policy area and figures among the top four problems facing the country identified by respondents in the Latinobarómetro survey in the last three years before the experiment was conducted. Agricultural production (including livestock and dairy farming) both historically and today accounts for the bulk of Uruguay's gross domestic product and the sector has strong links to the political elite (traditionally stronger with the PN, but also with some sectors of the FA), so is a high-prestige economic policy area. It was not a high-visibility area at the time of the experiment in that it was not mentioned among the major problems facing the country in the Latinobarómetro 2016 survey, but any difficulties or advances in the sector do regularly receive widespread media attention. At the time of the

---

[22] This is similar to what has been found in Sweden (see Sweden chapter, this volume).

experiment no woman had ever been designated to head either the Ministry of the Economy and Finances nor the Government Planning and Budget Office, the two key positions for economic policy; nor has a woman ever been appointed to the Ministry for Livestock, Agriculture, and Fisheries. These two areas, then, can clearly be considered masculine policy areas. In the FA speech discussion of the economy focused on greater control of public finances through progressive taxes rather than social cutbacks, in order to strengthen social policies. In the PN speech economic policy proposals focused on improving the competitivity of the productive sector, tackling the deficit to protect future generations, and the need to reduce government inefficiency and the number of government employees, without cutting social spending.

As for the stereotypically feminine policy areas, we chose education (discussed in the speech) and childcare (not discussed in the speech). Education is the policy area that has most women ministers designated during the post-dictatorship period: 1985–1990, 2008–2010, 2015–2019. Problems with the education system were among the four most mentioned problems facing the country in the last three Latinobarómetro surveys, and as well as frequent strikes by teachers over budget demands, there have been widely reported incidents of violence within educational establishments in recent years, leading to several interpellations of the minister for education, making it a high visibility area. However, the actual running of the education system—including definition of curricula and budget distribution—is under the control of autonomous institutions, not the Ministry of Education, which means that it is not a high prestige institution. In the FA speech the discussion of education policy focused on guaranteeing universal access to education from childcare to university, increased access to technical education, strengthening careers in teaching, and training teachers in human rights and diversity. The PN speech focused on the drop in scores on PISA tests, and how to address the insufficient number of licensed teachers.

Childcare is associated with the Ministry for Social Development (*Ministerio de Desarrollo Social*, MIDES), created by the first FA government in 2005. The MIDES has been a highly feminized portfolio, headed by women from 2005 to 2010, 2010 to 2011, and 2015 to 2019. The ministry is in charge of social welfare programs and presides over the inter-institutional National Care Junta (*Junta Nacional de Cuidado*), which has responsibility for implementing the National Integrated Care System (*Sistema Nacional Integrado de Cuidados*, SNIC) created by law in 2015, which is developing a co-responsible model of care between the state, families, the community, and the market, to provide pre-school childcare and services for the disabled and dependent elderly people.

To examine whether traditional leadership templates (leaders are men) apply in stereotypically masculine policy areas (H10), we use repeated measures

136 NIKI JOHNSON

ANOVA with Domain and Candidate Gender as the factors.[23] We examine policy areas discussed in the speech (*economics* and *education*), then conduct the same analysis for policy areas the candidate did not discuss (*agriculture* and *childcare*) to test our prediction that gender schema will impact candidate evaluations when study participants lacked policy information for making their evaluations (H11). The results of this analysis do not indicate that women candidates are only considered to be capable in stereotypically feminine policy areas as the interaction Domain×Candidate Gender is not significant in either analysis: policy areas discussed in the speech [$F(1,644)=.164$, $p=.686$], not discussed [$(1,607)=.522$, $p=.470$].[24] In both cases Domain is significant ($p=.000$), indicating that the two policy areas are viewed to be different, but Candidate Gender does not significantly affect evaluations, as a main effect or in the interaction. Even without policy information for making their evaluations, participants do not see women as incapable of handling stereotypically masculine policy areas, nor do they see women as advantaged in stereotypically feminine policy areas.[25]

Again, we test for shared in-group effects. First, we add Participant Sex to the above analysis, again to test H5. In both cases (*economics/education* and *agriculture/childcare*) the three-way interaction (Domain×Candidate Gender× Participant Sex) is not significant [$F(1,637)=1.150$, $p=.284$], [$F(1,602)=.205$, $p=.651$] respectively. This indicates that the evaluation that women are able to manage policy in stereotypically masculine areas is not only the assessment of female participants. Next, we test for a shared party in-group effect (H6). As above, the evaluations are more favorable when the candidate is from the participant's party, but the interaction (Domain×Candidate Gender×My Party) is not significant [$F(1,640)=.952$, $p=.387$] and [$F(1,603)=.179$, $p=.836$] respectively. This indicates that the evaluation that a woman candidate is as capable as a man in stereotypically masculine policy areas is not limited to her being from the participant's preferred party.

We also examine each policy area individually in a 2×2×2 ANOVA with Candidate Gender, Party Platform, and Party Label as factors. Candidate Gender is not significant, but Party Platform is highly significant with the PN candidate

---

[23] Participants were asked to "evaluate the ability of the candidate to deal with policy" in twelve policy areas, half of which were discussed in the candidate speeches. Evaluations ranged from 1 (very competent) to 5 (incompetent) and were inverted so that high values are more favorable.

[24] As a robustness check, we examined whether this finding holds when the party name/ideology was not listed on the speech by including Label as a factor in the above analysis, and the three-way interaction is not significant (policies discussed in the speech $p=.345$; not discussed in the speech $p=.803$).

[25] As a robustness check, we replicate these analyses with the other masculine/feminine policy areas. For *security* and *health* (discussed in the speech) the interaction is not significant. For *energy* and *women's rights, infrastructure* and *women's rights,* or *agriculture* and *women's rights* (not discussed) the interaction is highly significant (respectively $p=.001$, $p=.000$, $p=.006$). The man and woman candidates are evaluated as equivalent on the masculine policy, but the woman is scored higher on *women's rights.*

ATTITUDES TO WOMEN CANDIDATES IN URUGUAY   137

receiving a more favorable score on *agriculture* (p=.005), and the FA candidate on *education* (p=.000) and *childcare* (p=.000), which comports with the issue ownership of the parties.

The association of agriculture with the PN is to be expected, as the party was traditionally dominated by the landed elite and continues to enjoy greater electoral support in departments in the interior of the country where agricultural or livestock production is the main source of income.

Similarly, education has figured centrally in FA electoral manifestoes since their rise to power in 2005, with commitments to increasing the budget for education, improvements in infrastructure, and extension of services, which were at least partially met under the three FA administrations. The first FA government also met its electoral promise of giving each child attending a state primary school a personal computer, which is used for teaching purposes, but belongs to the child and is taken home for personal use. This policy, later extended to high school students, was a high-visibility issue and would likely have been a clear trigger for participants' identification of education as an FA policy area.

Until the end of the first decade of the twenty-first century, pre-school childcare had been considered a private question to be resolved either with family members' unpaid labor or by buying childcare services in the market. However, feminist research and pressure from feminist organizations placed the question of childcare on the public agenda during the first FA administration. It was subsequently highlighted as a key policy goal of the FA policy platform in the 2009 and 2014 presidential elections (Johnson and Peréz 2010; Rocha 2015), leading eventually to the creation of the SNIC in 2015.

In short, the Uruguayan case does not produce the results expected by role congruity and schema theories. Overall, young urban adult Uruguayans do not associate specific policy areas with traditional feminine or masculine leadership templates, even when the policy area is not discussed in the speech, but they do associate specific policy areas with specific parties.

Socialization within the Home Environment

In general terms, the findings of the Uruguayan experiment suggest that young adult Uruguayans do not reproduce traditional gender stereotypes about who would make a good politician, and indeed that gender is not a relevant factor in how political competence is evaluated in Uruguay today. In terms of both candidates' ability to occupy top-level elective and designated posts, and their potential performance in specific policy areas, there is no evidence that men candidates are favored. In fact, where a small but significant difference exists in how well the candidate is assessed—*deputy* and *minister*—it is the woman candidate who is evaluated more favorably on average.

138 NIKI JOHNSON

The fact that gender does not appear to be a relevant component of leadership templates in a country where women's presence is still very limited in top political posts suggests that women's presence in such posts is not a necessary condition for the leadership templates to move away from their traditional association with masculinity. It is true that in recent years—those in which the experiment participants were growing up—women have started to gain access to certain high-prestige and high-visibility posts that were previously bastions of male privilege, such as cabinet positions, in party leadership, or in departmental executives. However, in more general terms, women's presence in those posts can only be classed as incipient and still precarious, as other studies have shown (Johnson 2018).

Perhaps what is more relevant in the Uruguayan case for understanding the lack of traditional leadership templates among urban young adults is the fact that women in Uruguay are highly integrated in other sectors of public sphere activity. The fact that women have long outstripped men in terms of attaining higher education levels and that they also have high rates of participation in the paid workforce may influence the leadership templates of the study participants. The closest role models for the students in this sense would be their mothers. Table 6.1 shows that there is little difference between participants' mothers and fathers in terms of university education (16.4 percent vs. 15.7 percent, respectively) and high-status occupation (36.6 percent vs. 39.3 percent), and only 7.5 percent of the sample's mothers are housewives. In other words, in terms of everyday gender role models, many students in our sample have family experiences that show women to have at least equal capabilities and attainments as men.

H7 predicts that participants whose mother is highly educated or has a high-status job will not exhibit traditional leadership templates. To test H7 in the Uruguay sample, for each of the general questions and policy areas examined in this chapter, we conduct 2×2 ANOVAs with Candidate Gender and Mother Education as factors, and 2×3 ANOVAs with Candidate Gender and Mother Job as factors and repeat the same ANOVAs adding Participant Sex as a factor.[26]

Taken together there were thirty-two analyses, and we find a significant interaction between mother resources and Candidate Gender only for *Deputy*, *Minister*, *education*, and *economic* policy; the findings generally contradict the prediction of a high-resource mother serving as a role model. Participants (both male and female) whose mother has a lower level of education evaluate the woman candidate more favorably to be a *Deputy* [$F(1,442)=6.499$, $p=.011$] and to be a *Minister* [$F(1,405)=4.621$, $p=.032$] (Figure 6.2—top). For *education*

---

[26] High education is measured as complete university or graduate school (N=116). A lower level of education is measured as complete secondary or less (N=401). High and low job status are defined in Chapter 2. For mother job we also include a category of "housewife" (N=46).

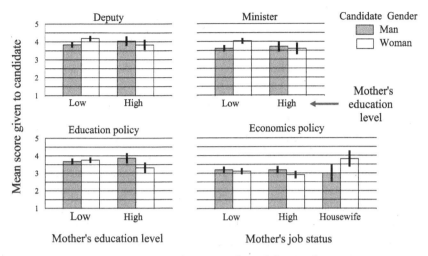

Figure 6.2 Mother Education or Job Status and Candidate Evaluations 2×2 ANOVA (Candidate Gender, Mother Education) or 2×3 ANOVA (Candidate Gender, Mother Job) 95 percent confidence intervals included.

policy, participants whose mother has a high level of education evaluate the man candidate more favorably [F(1,489)=7.021, p=.008] (Figure 6.2—bottom-left). Finally, for *economic* policy, participants whose mother is a housewife evaluate the woman candidate more favorably [F(1,559)=4.331, p=.014] (bottom-right). The family may impact the political leadership templates of young adults, but in ways that are more complex than the predictions about having a high-resource mother. Possibly mothers are role models when their children see them engaging in powerful behavior in ways not related to having a high level of education, such as working to support or help support the home even while raising the family (recall the high level of employment noted above for women with three or more children).

Discussion of Study Findings in the Uruguayan Context

The experiment conducted in Uruguay shows that in general young urban adult Uruguayans do not associate political leadership with men. The analysis offers no evidence of a traditional leadership template, which would associate with masculinity the ability of candidates to occupy top-level political posts or to win votes in elections even though women are still vastly under-represented in Uruguay's government. In addition, women are viewed as leaders across all policy areas. Several aspects of the Uruguayan context may explain this apparent

140 NIKI JOHNSON

"de-gendering" of policy areas that could be classed as masculine or feminine and the acceptance of women as leaders. One is the long-time presence of stereotypically feminine policy issues on the government agenda, as Uruguay established Latin America's first welfare state early in the twentieth century. This is combined with welfare topics regaining prominence on the national agenda during the fifteen years of FA governments (2005–2020), which overlapped with the political development of the study participants. Two is the socio-economic status of women in Uruguayan society, including high rates of workforce participation among women of all classes, including as professionals, which for years has demonstrated the capacity of women. Three, a decade of public opinion polls have shown that there is not a significant gender gap in public support for women as political leaders.

These findings provide interesting new evidence for understanding the barriers to gender parity in politics in Uruguay. For young adults, women fit the mental template of leaders, even though party elites continue to resist greater incorporation of women, or expansion of gender quotas. The data presented here clearly challenge one of the arguments still fielded by male politicians in discussions about why there are fewer women than men in politics in the country, which is that people are not willing to vote for women. This argument does not hold in the case of our sample of young Uruguayans, which while not representative of the population as a whole does include a diversity of socio-economic backgrounds, and clearly indicates acceptance of women's ability to govern in diverse posts and policy areas.

Table A6.1 Factor Analysis of General Evaluation Questions for Uruguay

Component matrix component 1	
Q1 Deputy	.870
Q2 Cabinet Minister	.857
Q17 Support	−.789
Q18 Win Votes	.602
Variance explained:	61.90%

Extraction method: Principal component analysis.

7

England

Young People View Women as Leaders

Claire Annesley, Beatriz Lacerda Ratton, and Jake Watts

MACRO-CONTEXT FACTORS: ENGLAND AND OTHER CASES				
LOW ← Expectation of Strength of Gender Bias → HIGH				

Executive Institutions

Parliamentary		OR		**Presidential**
Alberta CA				Chile
Quebec CA				California US
England				Texas US
Israel				Costa Rica
Sweden				Uruguay

Electoral Institutions

Party focused ←				**→ Candidate focused**
Israel	Uruguay	Chile	Alberta CA	California US
Costa Rica	Sweden		Quebec CA	Texas US
			England	

Policy Agenda Emphasis

More Social Welfare ←			**→ Less Social Welfare**	
Sweden	Alberta CA	Uruguay	England	California US
Costa Rica	Quebec CA	Israel	Chile	Texas US
Less Defense ←			**→ More Defense**	
Costa Rica	Alberta CA	Sweden	England	Israel
Uruguay	Quebec CA	Chile	California US	Texas US

Incorporation of Women in Government

Greatest ←			**→ Least**	
Sweden	Chile	Alberta CA	Uruguay	Texas US
Costa Rica	England	Quebec CA	California US	Israel

Introduction

This chapter presents the findings of the experiment about gender and political leadership in England. The study was conducted with 531 young adults from late October to December of 2017. Overall, the results show that gender is not often relevant in the leadership templates of young adults, and that there is little significant difference in evaluations of men and women candidates' policy competence. Gender bias in favor of a man candidate only kicks in when a participant is assessing the credentials of a candidate s/he does not support politically, and

Claire Annesley, Beatriz Lacerda Ratton, and Jake Watts, *England* In: *The Image of Gender and Political Leadership.* Edited by: Michelle M. Taylor-Robinson and Nehemia Geva, Oxford University Press. © Oxford University Press 2023. DOI: 10.1093/oso/9780197642726.003.0007

then they evaluate men candidates more favorably as MPs and party leaders. We find that gender impacts evaluations of candidates' policy competence minimally, and only when participants do not have specific policy information available on which to make their judgment.

In one sense the absence of traditional leadership templates—that leaders are men—is surprising as gender inequality continues to permeate UK politics and society. Progress toward gender equality in politics has been decidedly incremental rather than fast track, and women remain underrepresented in politics at all levels in the United Kingdom. That said, the United Kingdom is one of few democracies to have been served by three female, Conservative prime ministers—Margaret Thatcher 1979–1990, Theresa May 2016–2019, and Liz Truss in 2022. Note specifically that Theresa May was PM at the time the study was conducted. Also, women's descriptive representation in the UK parliament doubled at the 1997 election when the impact of the Labour Party's all women's short lists kicked in and it has continued to increase since, reaching 32 percent in the 2017 election, conducted just before the study was carried out. Women's representation in cabinet has also increased since 1997 and was at 22.7 percent (five of twenty-two) at the time the study was conducted. The average age of the young people participating in our study is 17.8, meaning that they were born after the 1997 turn in terms of gender equality in politics. For them the norm is of women's presence in parliament and cabinet at around 25 percent, as is a female prime minister.

While these young adults do not judge aspirant political leaders on their gender, they do judge them by party affiliation, making very clear assumptions about their suitability as a leader and policy competence based on traditional political cues. Put most bluntly: Conservatives are good on the economy while Labour are good on welfare and social policy.

Gender Politics in England

For this study, we focus specifically on the attitudes of young English adults. The United Kingdom is a unitary state with some powers devolved to Scotland, Wales, and Northern Ireland assemblies and executives. England does not have its own political representation but is governed by the national parliament and executive in Westminster, hence the focus here is on the profile of the UK political institutions as a whole. The United Kingdom is an example of an old democracy. Women were granted the vote in 1918 and universal suffrage was introduced in 1928—but it has followed an incremental rather than fast-track route to women's inclusion in political life characterized by: women's low levels of descriptive representation, the gendered nature of politics as a workplace, horizontal and vertical gendered segregation in politics, gendered discourses and framing of politicians, and non-gendered public policy (Dahlerup and Leyenaar 2013: 8).

For Lovenduski (2013: 72), responsibility for women's low descriptive representation in the United Kingdom lies squarely with political parties who control the nomination process for all levels of government as well as appointments to the House of Lords, decision-making agencies, commissions, and committees. Sarah Childs (2016) and others have documented the gendered rules and practices of UK Parliament as a workplace and which serve to reinforce the exclusion of incumbent and new women in the institution. UK politics has strong horizontal and vertical gendered segregation. Horizontal segregation refers to the way substantive political roles are allocated, for example, with men taking up finance and defense portfolios and women welfare and education responsibilities, while vertical segregation refers to women being less likely to progress into senior political roles. In the United Kingdom the media focus on female politicians remains squarely on their personal lives, appearance, and gender rather than their policies (Williams 2021), and research has found that generally women are expected to fit into an established male frame of what a political leader looks like (Murray 2014). The United Kingdom has also been slow to apply a gendered lens to policy-making.

The United Kingdom is a Westminster parliamentary democracy. Voters elect MPs to the House of Commons in 650 single member constituencies based on the principle of first past the post. Political systems based on FPTP are less likely than systems using a version of proportional representation to elect high numbers of women to parliament since women are less likely to be selected for winnable seats. Nominations and candidacy for elections are controlled by political parties and there are similarities between the nomination procedures of the three main parties in that they "all maintain an approved list of candidates and each has a selection procedure that involves shortlisting, that is the selection of a small number of applicants [. . .] by local members and activists from the approved list go through to the next round" (Lovenduski 2013: 75). Research into the party nominations demonstrates that it is a strongly gendered process. Culhane and Olchawski's study of gender and candidate selection (2018: 6) found that "the journey to political office, in its current form, is organized such that a number of resources are required at each stage such as money, time, personal credibility, flexibility and party support and networks. These are harder for women to acquire due to the gendered nature of both politics and society." The United Kingdom does not have a system level gender quota law. Instead, at party level, the Labour Party adopted a policy of all women shortlists (AWS), first used in the candidate selection process ahead of the 1997 general election. This new party rule led to a record 101 Labour women being elected to the 1997 parliament, with steady increases since then (Childs 2004).

Governments are formed from the ranks of the largest party in parliament. By convention, cabinet ministers must be members of the UK Parliament, selected predominantly from the government benches of the elected House of Commons, though selection from the appointed House of Lords is also permitted. Compared with many other advanced democracies, women's representation in UK cabinet is historically low and has been slow to increase (Annesley et al. 2019). Between 1929, when the first female cabinet minister was appointed as minister of labour, and 1992, half of all post-election cabinets featured no women, and no cabinet contained more than two women at a time. This is in large part due to the strengths and precedence of affiliation to the prime minister as a criterion for ministerial selection (Annesley et al. 2019). Since 1997, however, multiple women have consistently been appointed to UK cabinets with their presence standing at between four and seven (ranging from 18.2 percent to 33.3 percent of all cabinet posts), and the presence of women in cabinet in their lifetimes might affect the views of the young adults participating in this study. While young voters may not distinguish a preference between men and women candidates, they might hold implicit gendered views about the capacity of aspirant politicians to serve in particular roles or master particular policy briefs based either on perceptions of portfolios being masculine or feminine or based on seniority or prestige. While there is a strong gendered horizontal segregation of ministerial portfolio, since 1997 there has been an increase in the range of ministerial portfolios covered by women. Nevertheless, a number of prominent portfolios are yet to be held by women, including chancellor of the exchequer and defense.[1]

The UK prime minister is the leader of the party of government, elected by MPs and party members. Beckwith (2015) skillfully shows how party leadership campaigns that set up opportunities to be PM are gendered. That said, the UK is one of few democracies to have been served by three female prime ministers: Margaret Thatcher 1979–1990, Theresa May 2016–2019, and Liz Truss in 2022, well after the experiment was conducted—all Conservative. We anticipate that this elite presence of two female PMs could predispose young English voters to not have gender as a central component of their leadership templates.

Beyond politics, women are prominently represented in Higher Education (HE) in the United Kingdom. Women's participation rates in HE caught up with men's by 1992, and by 2005/2006 there was a 7.2 percentage participation gap in favor of women (Broecke and Hamed 2008).[2] This trend has continued.

---

[1] Penny Mordaunt served as secretary of state for defence from May to July 2019, after this study was conducted.

[2] https://dera.ioe.ac.uk/8717/1/DIUS-RR-08-14.pdf.

According to the Office of National Statistics (ONS) (2013) "Over the past 40 years there has been a rise in the percentage of women aged 16 to 64 in employment and a fall in the percentage of men. In April to June 2013 around 67% of women aged 16 to 64 were in work, an increase from 53% in 1971. For men the percentage fell to 76% in 2013 from 92% in 1971." Despite these trends, the UK labor market remains strongly segregated by gender: women are particularly concentrated in occupations related to the welfare state (nursery, primary and secondary education, health, and social care), and women are underrepresented at senior and high-status levels across professions. This is reflected in the fact that in 2018 the gender pay gap[3] in the United Kingdom was 17.9 percent. In sum, young people expect to see women in the labor force, but they are more likely to see them in certain occupational sectors than others, and less likely to see them in senior roles.

Country Context during Experiment Fieldwork

The England study was conducted during the period late October through December 2017, with a few classes added in May 2018. This was shortly after the June 8, 2017 general election, which returned Theresa May as prime minister, albeit with a much-reduced Conservative majority that led to the formation of a minority government. May appointed five female ministers to her cabinet of twenty-two (down from seven of twenty-one in the previous administration). These included prestigious and high-profile appointments such as home secretary, typically considered one of the four great offices of state in the United Kingdom. Women also held the portfolios of education (also minister for women and equalities); international development; digital, culture, media, and sport; and leader of the House of Lords. As such, women were visible and prominent in the UK government at the time the study was conducted.

Two other things are worth noting with respect to women's presence in UK politics in the 2017/2018 timeframe. Nine political parties were represented in House of Commons. Of the seven main parties contesting the 2017 general election, four were, at the time, led by women and were highly visible, not least through televised leader debates.[4] In addition, a new party—the Women's Equality Party—put up candidates in ten seats with manifesto focused on policies to achieve equality. Second, the 2017 General Election saw a record number

---

[3] The gender pay gap is the percentage difference between men's and women's median hourly earnings, across all jobs in the United Kingdom.

[4] At the televised leaders' debate "The Ukip leader addressed two out of three women on the panel as "Natalie." None of them are called Natalie." https://www.newstatesman.com/politics/june2017/2017/05/5-things-we-learned-leaders-debates-smaller-parties.

of women standing for election—30 percent of the 3,300 candidates—and the highest ever number of women elected to the UK Parliament: 208 or 32 percent of all MPs, up from 191 or 29.4 percent in 2015. The presence/absence of women in political campaigns is always a focus of general election commentary, however policy agendas are dominated by other issues.

UK policy agendas are strongly dominated by the economy and public finances (particularly in the context of post-crash austerity), the National Health Service (NHS), and education (Jennings et al. 2010; John et al. 2013). As noted above, no woman has been appointed as chancellor of the exchequer; this portfolio remains a masculine policy domain. In contrast health and education are perceived to be feminized policy domains, and each of these ministerial portfolios has been held by women on multiple occasions: three in health and nine in education. Since 1997 UK policy agendas do pay more attention to issues of gender equality (Annesley and Gains 2013), and gender equality policy features consistently in election campaigns. Since 2010 the gendered impact of economic austerity has been routinely tracked by MPs and think-tanks.

In addition to these routine government agendas, the political and policy context in 2017/2018, when the experiment was conducted was strongly dominated by Brexit, the United Kingdom's decision to end its membership of the European Union (EU). On June 23, 2016, a referendum on the UK's EU membership returned a result of 51.9 percent to Leave and 48.1 percent to Remain. Delivering on Brexit—first negotiating a withdrawal agreement with the EU—was high on the policy agenda for Theresa May's government. A key issue at the time of the referendum was to "take back control" of the UK's political sovereignty as well as of our borders by ending the free movement of people facilitated by membership of the EU's Single Market. To manage Brexit the government created an additional government department and secretary of state for exiting the European Union. The three ministers to have held the Brexit portfolio up to when the study was conducted were men.

Description of the England Experiment and Dataset

The England experiment, like all the cases in this project, used a 2×2×2 factorial design with Candidate Gender, Party Platform, and Party Label as the three factors presented in a relatively long candidate speech for each of the two largest parties, that each discussed six policy areas. Party Platform was developed from reading the Speech from the Throne for the new Conservative Party government, and Labour responses, with additional information obtained from each party's 2017 election manifesto. (Chapter 2 provides a detailed explanation of the experiment design and implementation.)

The research was conducted with 531 predominantly young adults in the south of England. The data were collected by two young researchers: one female and one male. The two researchers visited multiple classes in one university, three colleges, and one school across the region. Study participants therefore included undergraduate university students, students aspiring to university entrance, and students on vocational courses. Participants also represented a range of socio-demographic backgrounds encompassing working-class, middle-class, and upper-middle-class backgrounds attending both state and private schools.

The data were predominantly collected in an urban setting while some students were from a slightly more rural population. Based in the south of England, the study does not capture the ethnic diversity of London and some of the United Kingdom's larger cities in the north of England. Also, by focusing on a region of England, we are not capturing the views of young adults in Scotland, Wales, and Northern Ireland. In the devolved regions of Scotland and Wales gender equality in politics has had a more prominent profile and fast track dynamic than in the older politics of Westminster. Since the first devolved elections in 1999, women's presence in the Welsh Assembly and Scottish Parliament has been consistently higher than in the UK Parliament; and both devolved executives have had parity cabinets on at least one occasion. At the time of the study there was a female leader of the Scottish Nationalist Party, Nicola Sturgeon, who had been First Minister of Scotland since 2014. In Wales and Scotland, therefore, we might anticipate voters' attitudes toward women leaders to differ from those in England.

Implementation of the experiment began about four months after the UK general election, held June 8, 2017. The election returned the governing Conservative Party as the largest single party with 317 seats, though it lost its overall majority (326 required) and, as a minority government, had to enter into a confidence and supply agreement with the Democratic Unionist Party of Northern Ireland. The Labour Party secured 262 seats and retained its position as the official opposition. Based on these election results, the Conservative and Labour Parties were the two parties used in our treatments.

A major constraint to the field research was a national strike called by the University and College Union (UCU) trade union, involving university faculty in sixty-one universities for fourteen specified days over the period February 22 to March 16, 2018. The industrial action reduced the researchers' capacity to access classes and therefore students within those classes. Many classes were cancelled, and, once the strike action was over, there was less scope to take up time in classes to conduct the study before the end of term. The researchers also found that following the strike there was less good will on the part of students to participate in an activity that they did not consider core university business.

148   ANNESLEY, LACERDA RATTON, AND WATTS

Despite this constraint, the study produced 531 participants (see Table 7.1). They were predominantly female (65.8 percent) and they positioned themselves more toward the left on the political scale: 4.08 on a 1–10 Left-Right scale with 1 being Left, with women indicating a more left-leaning ideology than male participants. Women were also more likely than men to declare a preference for parties on the left with 59.8 percent of women stating a preference for Labour compared with 47.1 percent of men and 8.6 percent of women stating a preference for the Greens compared with 7.5 percent of men. Young men were further to the center of the Left-Right scale at 4.49 and declared stronger support than women for the right-wing Conservatives and centrist Liberal Democrats.

The fact that the young adults in our dataset are more left leaning than the population as a whole reflects the pattern of the 2017 general election. At that poll, the Conservatives secured 36.9 percent of vote share, and Labour had 30.4 percent of votes cast at the general election. Ipsos MORI polling after the election suggested that 27 percent of voters aged eighteen to twenty-four cast their ballot for the Conservative Party (compared with just 16 percent of young people's preferences in our dataset) and 62 percent of eighteen to twenty-four-year-old voters supported the Labour Party (compared with 55 percent of young people participating in our study). In the YouGov data 16 percent of eighteen to nineteen-year-olds voted for the Conservatives compared with 66 percent voting for Labour. In short, our experiment participants confirm that young people have more left-leaning preferences than borne out by the general election results as a whole. The reported voting patterns of young people—particularly eighteen to nineteen-year-olds—closely align with the party preferences of our experiment participants (see Table 7.2).

Results: Young People in England Don't Evaluate Politicians by Gender

Each participant scored the suitability of one candidate with a specific gender (indicated by name and pronoun) and party identification (stated or implied), but never directly compared two candidates or parties. Accordingly, when referring to evaluations of candidates we avoid the terms "preferred" and "preferable," which suggest a direct comparison by the same participant. Instead, we present which candidate scored higher or lower when comparing candidate evaluations across treatment conditions. The notation, H5 through H11, refers to hypotheses and statistical methods outlined in Chapters 1 and 2.

Overall, the pattern we observe is not one of traditional leadership templates. There is no evidence that the young people who participated in the study

Table 7.1 Description of Participants in England

	Overall	Male only	Female only
Number of participants	531	179	344
Percent of participants	100	34.2	65.8
Average age	17.8	17.9	17.8
Left (1) to Right (10) self-placement	4.08	4.49	3.86
Preferred party (%):			
Governing (Conservative)	16.4	24.7	11.8
Largest opposition (Labour)	55.3	47.1	59.8
Green	8.1	7.5	8.6
Liberal Democrat	6.6	7.5	5.6
No preference stated	13.5	13.2	13.9
Total	100	100	100
Parents' education* (% of participants):			
Fathers w/high level	44.6	46.9	44.5
Mothers w/high level	49.7	52.0	49.4
Fathers w/low level	31.3	29.1	32.6
Mothers w/low level	33.3	29.6	35.2
Parents' occupation (% of participants):			
Fathers w/high status job	57.3	60.5	55.7
Mothers w/high status job	45.0	48.2	43.4
Housewives, as % of participants	1.0	1.2	0.9
Housewives, as the actual number	5	2	3

* Note: Education levels of participants' parents are divided into "high" (complete university or more) and "low" (complete secondary or less), and the remaining percentage (not shown) is defined as "intermediate" or "don't know"

assess the capacity of candidates to lead according to their gender. This was consistent across level of post, type of political skills, and almost all policy areas. However, these young people do clearly follow traditional cues about the policy competences of the two main political parties: Labour good on social policy; Conservatives good on the economy. This indicates that participants reacted to treatments about party, but not to treatments about gender.

Table 7.2 Comparison of Election Patterns of the England Experiment Sample to Alternative Samples

	Conservatives	Labour
Experiment data (% support)	16	55
Voter share	36.9	30.4
Ipsos MORI 18–24 year olds (% votes cast)	27	62
YouGov 18–19 year olds (% votes cast)	16	66

Part One: General Evaluations of Candidates

Based on literature about role congruity theory, H8 expects that participants will more favorably evaluate the man candidate than the woman candidate in "general" evaluation questions. Participants were asked to evaluate how effective the candidate would be as a (1) member of the House of Commons[5] (which is the post the candidate said he/she was running for), (2) member of the Cabinet,[5] (3) party leader.[5] They were also asked for their assessment of the candidate's political skills, namely (4) if they would support the candidate,[6] and (5) how good the candidate would be at winning votes.[7] Factor analysis of these items indicated that the participants in our sample "located" all these items along one factor (see Chapter Appendix).

We used these five "general" questions as the DVs in 2×2×2 ANOVAs with Candidate Gender, Party Platform, and Party Label as factors. First and foremost, we find no significant difference between the mean evaluations given to man and woman candidates on questions that address the general competence of political leadership capacity.[8] For *Cabinet Minister* the mean evaluation of the woman candidate is slightly more favorable than the mean evaluation of the man candidate, but the difference is not statistically significant. There is no evidence that participants evaluate men more favorably as potential political leaders. There is, however, a significant main effect for Party Platform. Consistent with the partisan leanings of the participants in this study, for all the general evaluation

---

[5] Questions 1–3 asked "In your opinion, how effective would this person be as a member of the House of Commons," member of the government cabinet, party leader? Answers range from 1 (outstanding) to 6 (very poor) and were inverted so that high scores are more favorable.

[6] Question 17 asked "Would you support this candidate in the election for the House of Commons?" (1=yes, 2=no).

[7] Question 18 asked "Do you think this candidate would be good at winning votes?" Answers range from 1 (very good) to 5 (very poor) and were inverted so that high scores are more favorable.

[8] P-values for the main-effect of Candidate Gender range from .293 to .796.

questions the candidate of the Labour Party received a more favorable mean evaluation.

To explore the in-group categorization hypotheses, we examined whether Candidate Gender and Participant Sex interact such that female participants assign higher scores to women candidates and male participants provide men candidates with higher scores (H5). Specifically, 2×2 between groups ANOVAs with Candidate Gender and Participant Sex as factors were performed for each of the five general evaluations of the candidate. In none of these analyses did we find a significant interaction that would support the same-sex shared in-group proposition, though female participants' evaluations of the candidates (in general) are higher than the male participants (analyses available upon request).

We also examined if there is a same party in-group effect (H6) by comparing participants' evaluation when the candidate was described as representing the party they support versus when the candidate is not from their preferred party. For all five general questions, we conducted 2×2 ANOVAs with Candidate Gender and My Party as the two factors. These analyses show that consistently participants favored the candidate of their own party over the candidate who was not affiliated with their party preference (p<.001 for all questions). In addition, for *MP*, *Cabinet Minister*, and *Party Leader* we found a significant interaction (Figure 7.1).[9] Supporting the in-group prediction of H6, participants evaluated the woman candidate as more favorable than the man when she was affiliated with their party. This direction was reversed when participants evaluated the candidate representing the rival party.[10]

Again, building from the literature about role congruity, H9 expects that a gender gap in evaluations will be larger the higher the level of the post. In the United Kingdom, a parliamentary democracy, being party leader is the sole route to becoming prime minister. Also, being a cabinet minister is a high-profile and prestigious position that represents the pinnacle of many a politician's career (Annesley et al. 2019). In this context it would be fair to expect a gap increasing as the level of the post became higher and more prestigious. Despite this, our data reveal no evidence of a growing gap between young people's evaluations of men and women

---

[9] The interaction Candidate Gender×My Party is significant for *MP* [$F(1,429)=6.373$, $p=.012$]; for *Minister* [$F(1,375)=3.998$, $p=.046$], and approaches significant for *Party Leader* [$F(1,433)=3.413$, $p=.065$].

[10] These analyses exclude participants who did not indicate a party identification (N=82). When we include a third level (no declared party), the results of the 2×3 ANOVAs are similar, but the interaction is no longer significant for *Minister* (p=.120) or *Party Leader* (p=.177). We also examined whether the results change if the party name is/is not listed on the candidate speech. When Label is added as a factor, for *MP* the interaction My Party×Label is significant (p=.051), and evaluations are more favorable when the name is given if it is their party, and without the party name when it is not their party. But the three-way interaction is never significant.

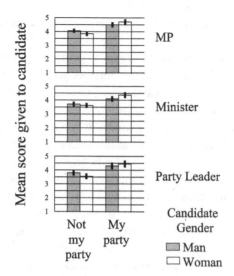

Figure 7.1 Party in-group and Candidate Gender
2×2 ANOVA (Candidate Gender, My Party) 95 percent confidence intervals included.

as the role becomes more senior (the gap moves from +.044 for *MP* to -.023 for *Minister*, favoring the female candidate, to +.080 for *Party Leader*); and this holds for both male and female participants.[11]

We conducted a repeated measures ANOVA, where one factor is Candidate Gender and the other factor is the rating of the candidate on each of the three posts (*MP, Minister, Party Leader*). Participants evaluate the candidates as more competent to be an *MP* (M=4.19) than to be a *Minister* (M=3.87), or *Party Leader* (M=3.95) (p=.000). However, the interaction Government Post×Candidate Gender is not significant (p=.804).[12] Thus, we do not find evidence that study participants exhibit traditional leadership templates, where leaders are men, especially as posts become more important. Recall that two women party leaders—both Conservative—have also served as prime minister, including at the time the study was conducted. Similarly, women's presence in cabinet has been established at around 25 percent since 1997 with women in increasingly high-profile portfolios. This may explain why gender does not appear to be a relevant component in these young people's leadership templates.

---

[11] For male participants the gap moves from +.107 for *MP* to -.008 for *Minister* to +.102 for *Party leader*. For female participants the gap moves from -.004 to -.055 to +.009.

[12] Participants were asked to indicate how much impact each of these positions have on the life of their family, and they rated the party leader (M=3.27) as having the most impact, and cabinet member (M=2.91) as having more impact than the MP (M=2.80).

It is worthwhile to emphasize that in the 2×2×2 ANOVAs (Candidate Gender, Party Platform, Party Label) discussed above, Candidate Gender was also not significant for *Support* or *Win Votes*, which relate to political skills rather than government post, and could be the point that the bias kicks in. Instead, those analyses indicate that a traditional leadership template—that leaders are men—is not used to assess whether the candidate can actually *Win Votes* and whether the participants themselves would *Support* her. This is an important finding given the ballot structure of the United Kingdom, where voters are asked to cast a vote for a single individual named candidate when voting. In this experiment we find no evidence that young people would be less likely to vote for women candidates on a ballot paper than men candidates.

Part Two: Evaluations in Specific Policy Areas

In the United Kingdom we can categorize policy areas as prototypically masculine or feminine as well as high or low prestige and visibility. Through analysis of four policy areas this section explores if traditional leadership templates are associated with gender stereotypes about policy areas. We identify four of the twelve policy areas included in the questionnaire,[13] two of which were addressed in the candidates' speeches. Two are prototypically masculine: national economy and energy; and two are considered feminine: education and women's rights.

	Discussed in speech	Not in speech
Masculine	National economy	Energy
Feminine	Education	Women's rights

The policy area *national economy* (discussed in the speeches) is strongly coded as masculine in the United Kingdom. Economics and business are male dominated subjects and occupations. Economic policy drives other policy making and elections are won or lost on economic competence or perceptions thereof. As a ministerial portfolio HM treasury is considered one of four great offices of state (PM, foreign office and home office, are the others); it is high prestige and high visibility. In UK politics this is the last vestige of male power; there has never been a female chancellor of the exchequer. The candidate speeches emphasized the need to "build an economy that works for everyone," advocating

---

[13] Participants were asked to "evaluate the ability of the candidate to deal with policy in each of the following areas" with scores ranging from 1 (very competent) to 5 (incompetent). Scores were inverted so that high scores reflect a more favorable evaluation.

sound money and fiscal responsibility to reduce the deficit (Conservative) and to "end austerity" for example, by increasing taxation on the 5 percent of highest earners (Labour).

Energy (not in the speeches) is coded masculine in the United Kingdom, covering energy industries, dominated by engineering and STEM, but it is a lower prestige and visibility portfolio than national economy. As a policy area in the United Kingdom, it combined with climate change in 2008 and then was merged into the Department of Business, Energy, and Industrial Strategy in 2016. In terms of ministers, all bar one have been men (May 2015–July 2016).

Education (discussed in the speeches) is coded feminine in the United Kingdom and is high prestige and high visibility. It forms a core component of the UK welfare state and, alongside the National Health Service, remains based on universal principles and is largely immune from spending cuts and retrenchment. Primary and secondary education, as a profession, is dominated by women and, as a feminized policy area, it is one that female voters pay attention to. As a government department, there have been multiple female cabinet ministers with responsibility for education from both governing parties (including Margaret Thatcher), and dating back to the early post-war period: 1945–1947, 1951–1954, 1970–1974, 1976–1979, 1995–1997, 2001–2002, 2004–2006, 2014–2016 and 2016–2018 (thus including the time when we conducted the experiment). The speeches focused on investing in skills and education, shaping the curriculum for technical education, and supporting mental health in schools (Conservatives) and the importance of education for reducing inequalities, support for higher staffing levels, and free school meals in schools (Labour).[14]

Finally, the policy area *women's rights* (not in the speeches) is, unsurprisingly, coded feminine in the United Kingdom, though it enjoys lower visibility and prestige than education. The role of minister for women was established in 1997 though the portfolio has subsequently become minister for women and equality or equalities. This is not a cabinet portfolio and is sometimes unpaid though most incumbents have combined the role alongside another substantive portfolio which does afford cabinet status and visibility as well as bureaucratic and budgetary resources (Annesley and Gains 2010). To date, all ministers for women (and equalities) have been women.

Literature about role congruity and schema theory prompted the expectation of H10 that participants will more favorably evaluate the men than the

---

[14] The Labour speech also referred to the need to "address the cost of education for young people going to university by ending tuition fees." We checked whether the UCU strike may have played into the experiment results, by examining if the findings would be the same if healthcare had been used as the prototypically feminine policy area in the speech. The results are substantively similar to education.

WOMEN AS LEADERS IN ENGLAND   155

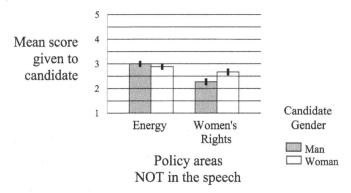

Figure 7.2 Policies not discussed in the speech and effect of Candidate Gender 2×2 repeated measure ANOVA (Policy Domain, Candidate Gender) 95 percent confidence intervals included.

women candidates in the stereotypically masculine policy areas, namely *national economy* and *energy*, and H11 that a gender gap in evaluations will be larger for policy areas not discussed in speech (*energy* and *women's rights*). We also assess whether men candidates are evaluated more favorably in high-visibility and high-prestige policy areas.

When we compare evaluations of men and women candidates along the two "gendered" areas that are discussed in the speech (2×2 ANOVA where policy domain is the repeated measure) we find that there is no main effect for Candidate Gender (p=.974), nor is there a significant interaction of Domain×Candidate Gender [$F(1,519)=2.518$, p=.113].[15] Yet when we move to the two gendered policies that did not appear in the speech, we find a statistically significant interaction that partially conforms to expectations [$F(1,511)=22.87$ p=.000] (Figure 7.2). When the participants evaluate the candidates on *women's rights* policy, the woman candidate is evaluated more positively (M=2.67) than the man candidate (M=2.27). But of greater importance for this study, we see that women are evaluated as competent in the stereotypically masculine policy area, *energy* policy. While the man is evaluated slightly higher (M=3.00) than the woman candidate (M=2.89), the difference is not significant (p=.176).[16]

The strong overall pattern in our findings across twelve policy areas is that men and women candidates are not evaluated differently in policy areas coded

---

[15] As a robustness check, we conduct the same type of analysis using the other stereotypically masculine and feminine policies discussed in the speech: *security* and *health*. Again, the main effect of Candidate Gender is not significant (p=.365), and the interaction is not significant (p=.653).

[16] Again, as a robustness check, we substitute the other stereotypically masculine and feminine policy areas included in the questionnaire: *agriculture, infrastructure, childcare*. For the repeated measure with *agriculture* and *childcare* the interaction is not significant [$F(1,507)=1.202$,

156   ANNESLEY, LACERDA RATTON, AND WATTS

masculine or feminine. We contrast this to the finding that party matters a lot in evaluating the competence of candidates in different policy areas (see discussion below). That said, we do find *some* evidence that men candidates are evaluated more favorably in stereotypically masculine policy areas (e.g., *infrastructure*,[17] but not *energy* or *agriculture*) and that women are evaluated more favorably in feminized policy areas (*women's rights*).

	Discussed in speech		Not discussed in speech	
Masculine	National economy	Gap: +0.10	Energy	Gap: +0.012
Feminine	Education	Gap: –0.07	Women's rights	*Gap:–0.39****

Participants only significantly differentiate in their evaluations of men and women in one of the four policy areas isolated in this analysis: *women's rights* (p<.001). This is not due to a shared sex in-group effect (H5). A 2×2×2 repeated measure analysis with Candidate Gender and Participant Sex as factors indicates that the three-way interaction is not significant for either *economics/education* (p=.472), or *energy/women's rights* (p=.132). The other form of shared in-group effect we hypothesize concerns whether participants got a candidate speech from their preferred party (H6). Again, the findings above still hold. In both analyses (2×2×3 repeated measure ANOVA Domain, Candidate Gender, My Party) the three-way interaction is not significant (policies discussed in the speech p=.581, not discussed p=.461).

What is notable in these findings is that significant differences in evaluations by candidate gender only appear in policies not mentioned in speeches and then only for *women's rights*. When young men and women are presented with information about the candidates' views and experience for *national economy* and *education*, there is no gap in their evaluation of candidates' competence based on gender. National economy and education are also high-visibility and high-prestige portfolios, yet young people in England appear to have no perception

p=.273], indicating that the man and woman candidates are evaluated as not significantly different in both policy areas. For the repeated measure with *infrastructure* and *childcare* the interaction is approaching significance [F(1,499)=3.627, p=.057]. For *infrastructure* the evaluation of the man (M= 3.04) is more favorable than the evaluation of the woman (M=2.92) (p=.083 2-tailed t-test), but for *childcare* the evaluations are statistically not distinguishable (p=.504).

[17] For *infrastructure* a 2×2×2 ANOVA with Candidate Gender, Party Platform, Party Label as factors shows that Candidate Gender approaches significant [F(1,501)=3.682, p=.056] with higher evaluations of the man candidate (M=3.040) than the woman (M=2.898). Party Platform is also significant (p=.000) and as discussed below, evaluations are higher for the Conservative Party (M= 3.181) than for Labour (M=2.757), and the effect size of Party Platform (η_p^2=.062) is greater than the effect of Candidate Gender (η_p^2=.007).

that men would be better qualified to address these high-prestige and high-visibility policy areas.

Part Three: Party, but Not Gender, Affects Evaluations of Candidates

The result that Candidate Gender does not routinely appear to be a relevant component of leadership templates contrasts starkly to our findings in relation to party. In England young people clearly evaluate the credentials of political candidates based on the candidate's party affiliation and these evaluations map on to views about party competence and issue ownership. Across twelve policy areas, there are significant differences in the mean scores given to candidates by party in nine policy areas.

Conducting a 2×2×2 ANOVA (Candidate Gender, Party Platform, Party Label as factors) for each policy area shows that in six policy areas it is the Labour candidate who is evaluated as significantly more competent—*education* (p= .000), *security* (p=.011), *childcare* (p=.020), *healthcare* (p=.001), *unemployment* (p=.000), and *women's rights* (p=.005).[18] The Conservative candidate is evaluated as significantly more competent in three policy areas—*energy* (p=.000), *infrastructure* (p=.000), and *national economy* (p=.000). There are no significant party differences in the mean scores given to candidates in *agriculture* (p=.377), *government reform* (p=.993), and *environment* (p=.180). This fits clearly with traditional views about policy competence and issue ownership of the Labour and Conservative parties. These results are based on a significant main effect for the Party Platform factor, and the results are consistent with party issue ownership, even though there was not partisan-based text in the speech for half of the policy areas, and only half of participants received a speech that stated the candidate's party.

Overall, the data reveal that young people in England are not primed to judge the policy competence of political leaders by their gender: men and women are deemed equally competent. However, they do clearly follow strongly established traditional cues about the policy competences of the two main political parties: Labour good on welfare and social policy; Conservatives good on the economy and infrastructure.

---

[18] It is notable that the three-way interaction Candidate Gender×Party Platform×Party Label is significant for *women's rights* [F(1,517)=5.020, p=.025]. When the party name is not on the speech, the woman candidate is more favorably evaluated for the Labour Party. However, when the party name is included on the speech, the man and woman candidates are evaluated as equivalent when from the Labour Party, but the woman candidate is evaluated more favorable from the Conservative Party.

158 ANNESLEY, LACERDA RATTON, AND WATTS

Part Four: Socialization within the Home Environment

We have seen that English young people in our dataset as a whole generally do not exhibit traditional leadership templates, and when gender is a relevant factor in how candidates are evaluated, it appears to favor women. But do we find traditional leadership templates among young people from families that might be anticipated to hold traditional values about gender roles?

To address these questions about how individual-level context (not country context) impacts leadership templates, we conduct post hoc tests to look at resources of the mother that we predict will provide a role model effect leading to leadership templates that include women: (1) high level of education, compared to a lower level of education,[19] and (2) high-status job, compared to low-status (H7).[20] For this analysis we conduct ANOVAs for each of the general questions and the four policy areas that were the main focus of our analysis above with Candidate Gender and Mother Education or Mother Job as factors. We then redo these analyses controlling for Participant Sex.

With regard to the status of the mother's job, we find a significant three-way interaction (Candidate Gender×Mother Job×Participant Sex) for *Party Leader* [$F(1,461)$=4.534, p=.034], and the interaction Candidate Gender×Mother Job is approaching significant for *Cabinet Minister* [$F(1,407)$=3.386, p=.066]. For *Minister*, conforming to our predictions, participants whose mother has a high-status job are the ones who evaluate the woman candidate more favorably (Figure 7.3—top). For *Party Leader* we see this pattern for male participants, but not for female participants (Figure 7.3—middle). With regard to the education level of participants' mothers, the three-way interaction is significant for *Minister* [$F(1,361)$=4.606, p=.033]. Male participants whose mothers have a lower level of education favor the man candidate, while the rest of participants give evaluations that are not significantly different to men and women candidates (Figure 7.3—bottom). Consistent with the findings presented above, in most cases Candidate Gender is not significant in these analyses,[21] and the interaction is not significant. However, for *Minister* and

---

[19] Complete university or graduate school is coded as high education (N=264). Complete secondary school or less is coded as lower education (N=177).

[20] Low-status occupations generally require manual work, or typically do not place the person in a management position. Examples are day laborer, construction or factory work, transportation jobs, sales, work as an assistant. High-status job (N=220), low-status job (N=264), this analysis does not include participants whose mother was a housewife (N=5).

[21] For *women's rights* policy with Mother Job as a factor or with Mother Education as a factor, the main effect of Candidate Gender is significant (p=.000), and as before the woman candidate is more favorably evaluated. For *economics* policy with Mother Education as a factor, the main-effect of Candidate Gender is significant (p=.050) with a more favorable evaluation of the man candidate.

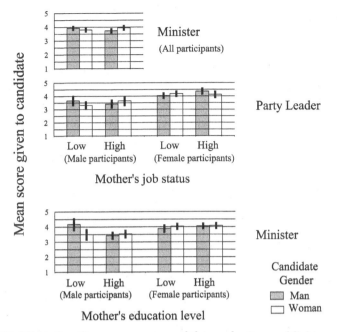

Figure 7.3 Effect of mother resources on candidate evaluations as *Minister* and *Party Leader*
2×2 ANOVA (Candidate Gender, Mother Job), 2×2×2 ANOVA (Candidate Gender, Mother Job, Participant Sex), 2×2×2 ANOVA (Candidate Gender, Mother Education, Participant Sex) 95 percent confidence intervals included.

Party Leader, both prestige posts, we find the anticipated connection between coming from a home with a high resource mother and leadership templates that include women.

Discussion of Study Findings in the English Context

In England gender is not relevant in young people's evaluations of aspirant political leaders. In particular, when it comes to assessing competence as MPs and cabinet ministers, there is no significant difference in how women and men candidates are evaluated. Gender bias in favor of a man candidate only kicks in when a participant is assessing the credentials of a candidate s/he does not support politically, and then they evaluate man candidates more favorably as *MPs* and *Party Leaders*. However, when the candidate is from their preferred party, they evaluate the woman candidate more favorably (as demonstrated in

Figure 7.1 above). Additionally, throughout the analysis party is important to leadership templates. For the general evaluation questions candidates of the Labour Party were evaluated more favorably than Conservatives (regardless of candidate gender), which is consistent with the partisan distribution of the participants who took part in the experiment. For specific policy areas evaluations were more favorable for candidates of the party that "owns" the policy (again, regardless of candidate gender). This is a particularly encouraging finding with regard to women's inclusion in mental templates of leaders given the gendered nature of occupational fields in the UK workforce, and the cabinet portfolios most frequently held by women.

The United Kingdom is an old democracy in which progress toward gender equality has been slow and incremental and gender equality in politics has not been achieved. Young people's lack of traditional leadership templates which equate political leaders to men may derive from women's higher descriptive representation as MPs and cabinet ministers since 1997 (i.e., during the formative years of the study participants) or from the role model effect of the United Kingdom having had two female prime ministers by the time of this study. Future research should explore if young Conservatives are more likely than young Labour supporters to affirm the notion of a female party leader? Are young Labour supporters more likely to support women as MPs?

These findings among young people that leadership templates do not indicate that leaders are expected to be men send a clear message to political parties and parliamentary institutions in the United Kingdom. This young generation does not discriminate by gender when it comes to who stands for election or office and who is more likely to win their vote. They do not appear to care if a candidate is a man or a woman. The onus, then, is on political parties to eradicate the well-documented gender bias that is inherent in their procedures and practices so that men and women candidates have equal opportunities to stand for parliament (Kenny 2014; Childs 2016) and be selected as a cabinet minister (Annesley et al. 2019). In terms of addressing gender bias in parliamentary institutions, continuing to implement the recommendations from Sarah Child's Good Parliament report (Childs 2016) would be an excellent first step.

This research finds that young people in England are still receptive to the traditional ideas about party competence that have tended to dominate British politics in the post-war period. This is a clear sign that young people have a particular set of tools through which they continue to make sense of party politics in a politically unsettled United Kingdom.

Table A7.1 Factor Analysis of General
Evaluation Questions for England

Component matrix component 1	
Q1 MP	.881
Q2 Cabinet Minister	.847
Q3 Party Leader	.823
Q17 Support	−.720
Q18 Win Votes	.599
Variance explained:	60.97%

Extraction method: Principle component analysis.

8

Party over Gender

Young Adults' Evaluations of Political Leaders in California and Texas

Kostanca Dhima and Jennifer M. Piscopo

MACRO-CONTEXT FACTORS: US AND OTHER CASES

LOW ← Expectation of Strength of Gender Bias → HIGH

	Parliamentary	**OR**	**Presidential**
Executive Institutions	Alberta CA		Chile
	Quebec CA		California US
	England		Texas US
	Israel		Costa Rica
	Sweden		Uruguay

	Party focused ◄------------------► **Candidate focused**				
Electoral Institutions	Israel	Uruguay	Chile	Alberta CA	California US
	Costa Rica	Sweden		Quebec CA	Texas US
				England	

	More Social Welfare ◄-----------► **Less Social Welfare**				
Policy Agenda Emphasis	Sweden	Alberta CA	Uruguay	England	California US
	Costa Rica	Quebec CA	Israel	Chile	Texas US
	Less Defense ◄--------------------► **More Defense**				
	Costa Rica	Alberta CA	Sweden	England	Israel
	Uruguay	Quebec CA	Chile	California US	Texas US

	Greatest ◄----------------------------► **Least**				
Incorporation of Women in Government	Sweden	Chile	Alberta CA	Uruguay	Texas US
	Costa Rica	England	Quebec CA	California US	Israel

Introduction

This chapter presents findings from the leadership experiment conducted over January and February 2018 with 734 young adults in California and 1000 in Texas.[1] Fieldwork occurred fourteen months after the defeat of Democratic

---

[1] Jennifer M. Piscopo wishes to thank Alexandra (Allie) Williams and Montana Buss for outstanding research assistance.

Kostanca Dhima and Jennifer M. Piscopo, *Party over Gender* In: *The Image of Gender and Political Leadership.*
Edited by: Michelle M. Taylor-Robinson and Nehemia Geva, Oxford University Press. © Oxford University Press 2023.
DOI: 10.1093/oso/9780197642726.003.0008

presidential candidate Hillary Clinton in the 2016 US presidential election, which ensured that the country's most powerful political office would remain occupied by men. Her loss to Republican candidate Donald Trump had particular symbolism, as Trump won the presidency despite his offensive behavior toward women. Some evidence suggests that voters who favored Trump were motivated by hostile sexism more than other factors (Ratliff et al. 2017). More broadly, Trump's election signaled voters' dissatisfaction with the left-leaning platforms and politics espoused by the Democratic Party, with consequences for women and women's political representation. In the concurrent congressional elections, women lost representation in the House of Representatives (from eighty-four to eighty-three seats) and won just one additional Senate seat (from twenty to twenty-one). The Democratic Party and powerful left-leaning fundraising organizations (such as EMILY's List) long have worked to elect more women, and for those Democrats hoping Clinton's historic candidacy would bring more women into office (including Clinton herself), the 2016 elections were disappointing.

At the same time, Trump's victory motivated an unprecedented number of women, predominantly Democrats, to run for national and state office in the November 2018 midterms. Excluding incumbents, 405 women (302 Democrats and 103 Republicans) ran for the US Congress and 10 for the Senate (6 Democrats and 4 Republicans). Record numbers of women won their races, bringing women's total share of Congress as of January 2019 to 23 percent in the House (102 seats) and 24 percent in the Senate (24 seats). Several of the policy areas tested in the leadership experiment figured prominently in the 2016 and 2018 campaigns, including the stereotypically feminine areas of women's rights and healthcare, and the stereotypically masculine areas of security and infrastructure.

We view the 2016 election results and the 2018 boom of women candidates as a key moment in which to examine whether young adults in the United States hold gendered leadership templates. On the one hand, the failure to elect women at the federal level in 2016 may signal that voters still believe women are not "up to the job." On the other hand, women's presence and victories in the 2018 campaign may signify that such entrenched attitudes are changing. We ask how candidates' gender affects their evaluations by conducing the leadership experiment in two US states: California and Texas. This case selection pairs a classic Democratic ("blue") state with a classic Republican ("red") state, creating variation across party identification, another key variable in the US context.[2]

---

[2] Though we note that the partisan makeup of Texas is changing.

California and Texas differ in their party identification, but have similar proportions of White and Latino/Hispanic voters.[3] Young adults in both states have been exposed to female leaders during their lifetime. (For lifetime exposure, we looked between 2008—when Democrat Barack Obama was elected president for his first term, and our participants would be roughly nine to twelve years old—and 2018, when the experiments were conducted.) At the federal level during the Obama era, women occupied the non-traditional cabinet posts of foreign affairs (secretary of state), justice (attorney general), and homeland security, so US young adults would have matured witnessing women in nontraditional cabinet portfolios, and then watched Hillary Clinton's historic candidacy. Young people in California and Texas also have seen women as lawmakers. Women have held both of California's US Senate seats since 1992 and Kay Bailey Hutchison represented Texas in the US Senate between 1993 and 2013. At the state level, women held about 25 percent of seats in both states' legislatures in 2018, and had occupied some unconventional posts in gubernatorial cabinets in recent years, such as justice (California) and agriculture and infrastructure (Texas). (Table 1.1 in Chapter 1 also compares the two states.)

Our results indicate that neither Californian nor Texan young adults generally evaluate the leadership potential of male candidates more favorably than that of female candidates. We find neither strong nor consistent evidence of gender stereotyped candidate evaluations. We do not find evidence that young adults hold traditional mental templates of leadership. In both states, party cues shape candidate evaluations more than gender cues: Californians prefer Democrats and Texans prefer Republicans, all else equal, and participants give more favorable evaluations of candidates from their preferred party, regardless of whether the candidate is a man or a woman. However, some gender stereotype persists when it comes to policy issues: in the stereotypically feminine policy domain of women's rights, both Texans and Californians evaluate the woman candidate more favorably. Further, Texans evaluate the man candidate more favorably in the stereotypically masculine policies of security and infrastructure.

Taken together, our results show the importance of partisan cues in the US context. Young people in the United States support women's political leadership, no matter whether they reside in red or blue states, but residents of those states largely prefer their own party candidates irrespective of gender. Compared to party, gender has weak effects when evaluating candidates' policy competencies, only in certain policy areas and more in Texas than in California. Women candidates in the United States may win their races, but still encounter some gender stereotypes about policy competencies.

---

[3] https://latino.ucla.edu/wp-content/uploads/2021/08/Election-2020-Report-1.19.pdf.

Electing Women in the United States

US women remain underrepresented in electoral politics, despite their educational attainment and workforce participation. Women's university enrollment outpaces that of men, with women receiving about 57 percent of all undergraduate degrees since the late 1990s.[4] The labor force participation of women with undergraduate degrees and above age twenty-five is 70 percent.[5] Female labor force participation in the United States was 55 percent.[6]

At the time of the experiment, women held 19.3 percent of seats in the House of Representatives and 23 percent of seats in the Senate. These numbers reflect the 2016 election results as well as seat changes in the subsequent months. Women occupied just three of fifteen cabinet posts in January 2018, as Trump nominated fewer women than his predecessor. By comparison, Obama appointed four women to his initial cabinet, and eight women served in cabinet across his two terms. At the time of the experiment, only twenty-eight states had ever elected a woman governor, and nineteen states had fewer than 25 percent women in the lower chamber of their state legislature. Thus, if women's presence in government is a key factor in shaping mental templates of leadership, as would be predicted by role congruity theory, the United States overall is a hard case for aspirant female politicians.

Attitudes toward Women in Leadership

Despite women's low presence in elected and appointed office, the US public overwhelmingly disagrees with the statement, "Men make better political leaders than women." On the 2008 Americans Barometer survey, 70.6 percent of respondents disagreed or strongly disagreed, increasing to 80.1 percent in the 2012 survey. More recently, Pew Research (2015) reported that 76 percent of Americans saw no differences between women and men political leaders overall. Americans also reported no difference between women and men in terms of achieving compromises, being honest and ethical, working to improve the quality of life, standing up for their beliefs, or leading in the executive versus the legislature (Pew Research 2015). During the 2016 election cycle, various polls

---

[4] https://nces.ed.gov/programs/digest/d20/tables/dt20_318.10.asp?current=yes (accessed November 18, 2022).

[5] https://www.pewresearch.org/fact-tank/2022/09/26/women-now-outnumber-men-in-the-u-s-college-educated-labor-force/ (accessed November 18, 2022).

[6] World Bank Databank: https://data.worldbank.org/indicator/SL.TLF.CACT.FE.ZS (accessed February 26, 2019).

showed the majority of Americans responding positively to the possibility of electing a woman chief executive.[7]

These neutral preferences between men and women candidates hold when comparing Americans by age. In the 2008 and 2012 Americas Barometer surveys, there was no statistically significant difference between young respondents (those aged twenty-five and under) and older respondents (those aged twenty-six and above) on the question, "Do men make better political leaders than women" (chi-squared test). Statistically significant differences between men and women did, however, appear within both age cohorts in 2008, with men more likely to agree than women. The gender gap between young respondents disappeared in the 2012 survey, however, suggesting that by the 2010s, young men and young women voters did not differ in their evaluations of women's political leadership.

Differences do appear by party. Democratic and Republican respondents to the Americas Barometer survey both rejected the assertion that men make better political leaders than women. However, Democrats of all ages disagree *more* strongly than Republicans of all ages. In the Americas Barometer 2008, a gap of nearly thirty percentage points appeared among Democrats who strongly disagreed that men make better political leaders than women (42 percent) compared to Republicans of all ages (12.7 percent), and this gap remained constant even as more Democrats and more Republicans strongly disagreed in 2012 (49 percent compared to 21.7 percent). Notably, there was no statistically significant difference when comparing partisans under twenty-five, though the sample sizes were small.

Generally, Democrats see gender differently than Republicans. Democrats believe that acknowledging and overcoming discrimination are important goals, and privileging women candidates for reasons of justice aligns with the party's values. Republicans, by contrast, hold that candidates should be picked on "merit" alone (overlooking how constructions of "merit" are themselves biased toward white men). The uncritical focus on "merit" means that normative arguments about the importance of electing women gain little traction within the Republican party (Och and Shames 2018). Indeed, Democrats are more likely than Republicans to "hope the U.S. elects a female president in their lifetime" (Pew Research 2015). Democrats also evince some pro-women bias, believing that women govern more effectively and more productively than men.[8] Yet women Republicans do favor women's representation more than men Republicans: 44 percent of GOP women compared to 24 percent of GOP men thought there were too few women in office (Pew Research 2018). In the population overall, about seven-in-ten women say there are too few women in high

---

[7] Presidential Gender Watch, 2016: http://presidentialgenderwatch.org/polls/a-woman-president/.

[8] POLITICO/Morning Consult Poll, 2018: https://www.politico.com/story/2018/06/05/women-elections-midterms-partisan-gap-623658. Also, Pew Research (2015).

political offices and in top executive business positions, while just about half of men say the same (Pew Research 2018).

The vast majority of elected women at the federal and state level come from the Democratic Party (CAWP 2018). The gaps in the US Congress are stark: of the eighty-four women in the 2017–2019 US House of Representatives, sixty-one were Democrats and twenty-three were Republicans, and of the twenty-three women in the Senate, seventeen were Democrats and six were Republicans. At the time the leadership experiment was conducted, 61 percent of women serving in the state legislatures were Democrats and 37 percent were Republicans. Differences in the parties' approaches to understanding discrimination and supporting women candidates have shaped which women win elections.

System-Level Explanations for Women in Office

The US electoral system poses significant barriers for women candidates. First, US political parties do not control ballot access. Candidates must step forward and declare their candidacy beneath a party label. Candidates face a party primary, but they compete against other candidates who also self-declare beneath that same party label. The winner-take-all electoral system (technically, single-member district plurality or SMDP), further exacerbates competition. Because parties do not control ballot access, gender quota laws would be difficult to enforce, and so the United States has no gender quotas.

The candidate-centric nature of the US elections means entering the electoral arena depends on individuals' desire. Generally, women appear less likely than men to want to run for office, leading scholars to conceptualize a gender gap in political ambition (Fox and Lawless 2004, 2011, 2014). At the same time, scholars have cautioned against attributing the ambition gap to women's lack of confidence (Dittmar 2015b), but rather to how their candidacy will shape their personal, professional, and political relationships (Carroll and Sanbonmatsu 2013). Women also perceive that men have an advantage in media coverage and fundraising (Shames 2017: 127). Women may thus have equal levels of ambition, but fear electoral competition (Kanthak and Woon 2015). Consequently, women are strategic about their candidate emergence (Fulton et al. 2006): running for office when the expected benefits—such as serving others (Schneider et al. 2016)—outweigh the costs. The 2018 surge in women's candidacies, especially but not exclusively among Democratic women, indicates that ambition is context-dependent, not a fixed character trait.[9]

---

[9] The Center for American Women and Politics media database: http://www.cawp.rutgers.edu/cawp-news (accessed January 29, 2017).

Second, parties still play significant roles in boosting the supply of women candidates—or not. Both parties have been characterized as old-boys' clubs (Sanbonmatsu 2006; Crowder-Meyer 2013), but the Democratic Party devotes resources to recruiting and promoting women within the local and national party structures (Och 2018). For example, the Democratic National Committee in 2016 required gender balance among delegations to the national convention. Countless Democratic-affiliated political action committees (PACs) and non-profit organizations recruit, train, and fund women candidates (Kreitzer and Osborn 2019).

By contrast, Republican PACs, such as The Right Women, face uphill battles in messaging and fundraising due to the party's insistence on finding the "best" candidate, regardless of gender (Och and Shames 2018).[10] Though small nudges about the importance of gender diversity can increase women's nomination as Republican convention delegates (Karpowitz et al. 2017), Republican women are more likely than Democratic women to fear their party will withhold support for their campaigns (Butler and Preece 2016).

Consequently, while public opinion surveys find little difference in Americans' preference for men or women political leaders, the reasons for these seemingly gender-neutral attitudes may vary by party. Democrats may endorse women's leadership because they favor women's inclusion as a normative goal. Republicans may see women as equally capable, but do not actively lobby for more women, thereby preserving the male-dominated character of politics, as evidenced by the fact that most women serving in the US Congress are Democrats.

The leadership experiments allow us to explore how candidates' gender and party shape candidate evaluations among US young adults. Survey evidence suggests that Democrats and Republicans support women candidates, though perhaps for different reasons. However, given the gender stereotypes about personality traits and leadership styles covered in Chapter 1 of this volume, support for women candidates does not mean evaluating women and men candidates the same. Evaluations of women candidates can be conditioned on the congruency between the stereotypes about the candidate herself and her policy competencies, meaning that gendered leadership templates could still apply among US young adults even when overall evaluations of candidates are the same. Alternatively, the intensity of partisan attachments among US voters suggests that, if voters hold leadership templates unaffected by gender, then voters should prefer their party's candidate irrespective of that candidate's sex.

---

[10] https://www.nytimes.com/2018/08/13/us/politics/republican-women-candidates-midterms.html.

Glass Ceilings in California and Texas

Women's representation in California and Texas follows national trends. As expected, California, a solid blue state, elects more women than Texas, a red state. Of California's fifty-three-member delegation to the House of Representatives in the 2017–2019 Congress, seventeen (32 percent) were women, compared to Texas's thirty-six-member delegation, in which three (8.6 percent) were women. At least one Californian woman has run for the Senate in nearly every election since 1992, whereas elections happen in which no Texan women contest the Senate.

Both states also elect more women Democrats than women Republicans. Nancy Pelosi, leader of the Democrats in Congress from 2011 to 2022 (and speaker of the house when the Democrats held the majority), hails from California. Women Democrats occupied both of California's Senate seats from 1993 to 2021, though a woman Republican occupied one of Texas's seats between 1993 and 2013. No woman has governed California, but Texas has elected two women governors, most recently Democrat Ann Richards, who served from 1991 to 1995 (when the participants in our study would have been about five years old or younger).[11]

These patterns—with California electing more women, but both states electing more women Democrats than women Republicans—are reproduced in the state legislatures. At the time of the experiment, women occupied similar proportions of each state's assembly. California's lower house had 25 percent women and Texas's lower house had 19.6 percent women. California's state senate had 22.5 percent women, the Texas senate had 25.8 percent women.[12] In both state legislatures, most women were Democrats, with the exception of the Texas state senate, where most women were Republican.

A record number of women candidates from both states ran for Congress and the state legislatures in 2018, most of whom were Democrats. Women also contested the Democratic primaries for governor in both states; no women won the nomination in California, but Lupe Valdez—an out-lesbian Latina and the former sheriff of Dallas—received her party's nomination in Texas. A Democratic woman, Wendy Davis, contested the previous gubernatorial race after winning fame nationwide for her thirteen-hour filibuster of a state bill that would restrict abortion access. Neither Davis nor Valdez won, but Texas young adults witnessed these races.

---

[11] Miriam "Ma" Ferguson, a Democrat, served from 1925 to 1927 and again from 1933 to 1935.

[12] National Conference of State Legislatures, Women in State Legislatures for 2018, https://www.ncsl.org/legislators-staff/legislators/womens-legislative-network/women-in-state-legislatures-for-2018.aspx (accessed July 24, 2020).

170 KOSTANCA DHIMA AND JENNIFER M. PISCOPO

Young people in Texas and California also would have seen women *and* men occupy state executive office in unconventional roles. Gubernatorial cabinets in both states are elected, not appointed. In 2010, California voters chose women for secretary of state and attorney general and a man for secretary of education, reelecting both officials in 2014. Texans in 2014 elected a woman to oversee oil, natural gas, mining, and utilities, and a man as secretary of education. Though voter knowledge about gubernatorial cabinets is low, young adults participating in the experiment in early 2018 would have some gendered leadership templates challenged by the gendered distribution of state-level office holders.

State level polling data is hard to find, but preliminary evidence supports the idea that voters follow national trends that leadership templates include women. Looking to the 2012 Americas Barometer survey, 76 percent of Texan respondents and 84 percent of Californian respondents disagreed or strongly disagreed that men make better political leaders than women (though the state-level sample sizes are too small to draw definitive conclusions). *Thus, young adults in California and Texas may espouse leadership templates unaffected by gender, the different party identifications of their states notwithstanding.*

At the same time, women candidates and officeholders in both states report prejudice among party leaders, a gender bias that may be reflected among the electorate. Various women stepping forward in California in 2018 were told to "wait their turn" behind prominent men whom the party had previously tapped to run.[13] In Texas, women candidates received more explicit messages: because they do not look the part—meaning, they do not look like men—women have struggled with fundraising and faced harassment on the campaign trail.[14] These stories, reported in the media, indicate that Texas voters, coming from a more conservative state, may evince less egalitarian gender attitudes than California voters. Do young people follow suit? An alternative hypothesis is that *young adults in Texas prefer men candidates over women candidates.*

Studying Young People's Leadership Templates in California and Texas

The two US cases, like all the cases in this project, used a 2×2×2 factorial design with Candidate Gender, Party Platform, and Party Label as the three factors presented in a relatively long candidate speech. Candidates were labeled as

[13] The Los Angeles Times: http://www.latimes.com/politics/la-pol-ca-year-of-the-woman-califor nia-20180528-htmlstory.html#.

[14] https://www.mysanantonio.com/opinion/columnists/bruce_davidson/article/Traditional-Texas-still-lagging-in-women-in-11042107.php.

Democratic or Republican, and their speeches discussed six policy areas. The Party Platform was based on the national, California state, and Texas state party platforms used in the 2016 elections. (See Chapter 2 for a detailed explanation of the experiment design and implementation.)

The experiments in Texas and California were conducted over two weeks in late January and early February 2018, as the proportion of women filing for candidacy in the 2018 midterms increased. The California study was fielded in the southern portion of the state, in four universities across three counties, one coastal and two inland (n=734). The Texas study was fielded in two universities and two high schools in the southeast portion of the state (n=1000). Each school offered distinct populations of students, given their sizes, location, rankings, and status as either public or private. In both states, trained preceptors (one man and one woman of similar age) fielded the experiment in public university and high school classrooms during normal class times. The university classes were large, introductory required government classes with students from across the university. The high school classes were small, required US government courses in most cases. At the private universities, a single trained preceptor (a woman) fielded the experiment in economics and physical science classes. Table 8.1 provides a description of each dataset.

Influence of Candidate Gender, Party Platform, and Party Label on Candidate Evaluations

Each participant scored the suitability of one candidate with a specific gender (indicated by name and pronoun) and party identification (either stated or implied). Participants did not directly compare their candidate to another. Accordingly, we avoid using the terms "preferred" and "preferable," which suggest a direct comparison by the same participant; rather, we talk about which candidates scored higher or lower when comparing candidate evaluations across treatment conditions. The notation, H5 through H11, refers to hypotheses and statistical methods outlined in Chapters 1 and 2.

In this first part of the analysis, we examine how participants in California and Texas rated candidates on four general evaluation questions: How effective would the candidate be as (1) a member of the US House of Representatives[15] and (2) a member of the president's cabinet?[15] (3) Would you vote for the candidate for the US House?[16] and (4) Do you think the candidate would be good

---

[15] Rated from 1 (outstanding) to 6 (very poor). Answer have been inverted so that high scores are favorable.
[16] Scored 1(yes), 2 (no), thus for this question low scores are favorable.

Table 8.1 Description of Participants in California and Texas Cases

	California			Texas		
	Overall	Male only	Female only	Overall	Male only	Female only
Number of participants	734	285	434	1000	502	478
Percent of participants	100	39.6	60.4	100	51.2	48.8
Average age	19.9	20.3	19.7	19.0	19.1	18.8
Left (1) to Right (10) self-placement	4.29	4.41	4.22	5.53	5.93	5.09
Preferred party (%)						
Governing (Republican)	9.9	12.3	8.2	40.2	46.7	32.7
Largest opposition (Democrat)	61.2	56.7	64.6	31.2	25.4	38.2
No preference stated	28.9	31.0	27.2	28.6	27.8	29.0
Total	100	100	100	100	100	100
Parents' education* (% of participants)						
Fathers w/high level	34.3	40.0	31.3	50.2	54.8	46.0
Mothers w/high level	36.1	40.4	33.4	52.0	55.8	49.6
Fathers w/low level	44.0	40.7	45.9	27.9	25.1	31.6
Mothers w/low level	41.7	37.5	44.2	27.5	25.9	29.1
Parents' occupation (% of participants)						
Fathers w/high status job	42.3	44.6	40.9	57.2	59.0	55.5
Mothers w/high status job	38.3	39.2	38.0	43.3	44.7	42.2
Housewives, as % of participants	8.9	6.6	10.0	4.8	3.6	5.6
Housewives, as the actual number	54	15	37	40	15	23
Race/ethnicity**						
White	23.5	23.3	24.2	54.4	56.8	52.1
Hispanic, Latino	47.8	40.7	52.3	34.5	32.7	36.0
African-American	6.3	5.5	6.7	11.9	9.8	13.8
Asian	23.6	24.4	23.0	8.8	8.6	8.9
Other	13.1	18.9	9.5	4.6	4.8	4.2

* Note: Education levels of participants' parents are divided into "high" (complete university or more) and "low" (complete secondary or less), and the remaining percentage (not shown) is defined as "intermediate" or "don't know."

** The race/ethnicity question asked participants to check as many categories as they wished.

at winning votes?[17] Factor analysis of the general evaluation questions for each sample are in the Chapter Appendix.

Overall, this volume examines role congruity theory, which predicts that men will fit people's mental template of leaders in places where women's political representation is low. The United States, Texas, and California all have lower levels of women's representation when compared to other countries, so the US experiments offer a probable instance for finding support for role congruity. Drawing from the role congruity literature, H8 for this volume predicts *participants overall will more favorably evaluate the man candidate than the woman candidate in "general" evaluation questions.* To test H8, we examine whether participants on average score the man candidate higher when considering their effectiveness on the four general questions. Since there are no differences in the speeches by candidates of the same party, any observed differences are due to the manipulation of candidate gender across the treatment conditions.

We examine each case (California and Texas) separately. For each general evaluation question, we conduct a 2×2×2 ANOVA with Candidate Gender, Party Platform, and Party Label as factors, allowing us to measure the strength of the gender effect against our baseline control: the party effect. For both California and Texas, we find no significant differences in the average evaluations of men and women candidates. While across all general evaluation questions, Californians' average scores for the woman candidate are more positive and Texans' average scores for the man candidate are more positive, these differences are not statistically significant at conventional levels. Thus, young adults appear equally willing to think that women are as effective at governing as men and that women are as capable as men in winning votes. The latter finding is particularly interesting given the United States' candidate-centered SMDP electoral system, which the literature argues should elect fewer women than proportional representation.

While the main effect of Candidate Gender is not significant, party—our baseline control—does matter, which indicates that participants reacted to the party treatments. In California, Party Platform is highly significant (p<0.001) for all the general evaluation questions, with Democrats rated more favorably than Republicans. Participants in California score a Democratic candidate higher regardless of that candidate's gender.[18] In Texas, Party Label matters for

---

[17] Scored 1 (very good) to 5 (very poor). Answers have been inverted so that high scores are favorable.

[18] In California, Party Label was not significant, neither as a main effect nor in the interaction with Party Platform, which indicates that the strong effect of Party Platform is found whether or not the party name is included in the speech. However, there is a significant interaction of Candidate Gender×Party Platform×Label for evaluations of the candidate's ability to *Win Votes* [F(1,722)= 3.882, p=.049]. The man Democrat is scored higher when the party name is not on the speech, and the woman Democrat scored higher when the party name is provided.

174   KOSTANCA DHIMA AND JENNIFER M. PISCOPO

all questions except *Vote For Candidate*. Participants in Texas score candidates higher when party name is not included on the speech (p-values range from .020 to .065).[19] Lack of a Party Platform effect in Texas may have resulted from a more balanced set of participant party preferences in Texas than in California (see Table 8.1).

To test H9, which also draws on role congruity theory, we explore whether the gap in scores favoring the man candidate will be larger for higher-ranking posts. In the United States, serving in the president's cabinet is more prestigious than being a member of the House of Representatives.[20] In California, the results were the reverse of the expectation: the woman candidate received higher scores than the man for both posts (mean score difference for man minus woman equals -.125 for *House*, -.116 for *Cabinet Secretary*). In Texas, the man candidate scored higher than the woman as expected, but the gap in the evaluations for *Cabinet Secretary* (+.058) is slightly smaller than for the *House of Representatives* (+.082).[21] In other words, women are accepted for both high- and low-power posts in both states, with Californians even preferring a woman.

To examine the impact of micro-level factors based on in-group theory, first we examine whether participants are more likely to see the candidate as fitting their leadership template when they share the candidate's gender (H5). To test H5, we conduct 2×2 post hoc ANOVA analysis where we define Candidate Gender and Participant Sex as factors. A significant interaction indicates that male and female participants evaluate their in-group candidates differently. We do not find that shared gender produces significant differences in candidate evaluations on the general evaluation questions in either California or Texas (California p-values range from .352 to .985; Texas p-values range from .678 to .899). Contrary to expectations, male participants do not favor the man candidate, nor do female participants favor the woman candidate as a leader.

Next, we test for party in-group effects—whether participants more favorably evaluate candidates from their preferred party (H6). Here, we conduct 2×2 post

---

[19] For *Vote For Candidate*, the three-way interaction is significant [F(1,962)=4.905, p=.027], showing that the woman Democrat is scored higher than the man Democrat when the party name is on the speech. As a robustness check, we examine whether the impact of Candidate Gender differs based on the inclusion of party name on the speech. We only observe an effect for *Win Votes* where the Platform×Label interaction is significant [F(1,977)=4.117, p=.043], indicating the Republican Party candidate scores higher only when the party name is on the speech.

[20] We asked participants how much impact a House member and a cabinet secretary has on the life of their family, from 1 (no impact) to 5 (a lot of impact). In California, cabinet secretaries were more important (mean of 3.25 compared to mean of 3.13). In Texas there was no difference (mean of 3.09 for House and 3.08 for cabinet).

[21] A repeated measures ANOVA using Government Post Prestige (*Representative, Cabinet Secretary*) and Candidate Gender as factors reinforces this assessment. For the California sample and the Texas sample the posts are viewed as different (p=.000), but the interaction Government Post×Candidate Gender is not significant (California: [F(1,657)=.228, p=.633], Texas: [F(1,899)= .604, p=.437]).

hoc ANOVA analyses with Candidate Gender and My Party (yes, no) as factors. For every general evaluation question in both the California and Texas samples, we find that party matters, and participants on average score a candidate from their preferred party higher. However, this party effect does not have a significant interaction with candidate gender. Participants score a candidate from their own party higher, regardless of whether the candidate is a man or a woman. We do note that in Texas, for *Win Votes*, both party and Candidate Gender have a significant main effect (Candidate Gender: $[F(1,679)=4.830, p=.028]$), and the man candidate is scored higher ($M=3.717$) than the woman ($M=3.575$). However, the effect size of My Party is much stronger than the effect size of Candidate Gender (η_p^2 of .062 and .007 respectively).[22]

In summary, for the four general evaluations of candidates, in both California and Texas we find evidence that party plays the dominant role in evaluating leaders. The importance of party is consistent with the strong role that parties play in US politics (see Dolan 2014), reflected in California's strong Democratic leanings and Texas's strong Republican leanings. However, the finding that US young adults do not include gender in their leadership templates calls into question expectations from role congruity theory. Since US women's political representation is lower when compared to other countries, we expected the opposite—that gendered leadership templates persisted because of fewer women role models.

Leadership Templates and Policy Domains

Here, we examine candidate evaluations in relation to stereotypically masculine and stereotypically feminine policy domains. Participants were asked to "evaluate the ability of the candidate to deal with policy" in twelve policy areas.[23] Half of the policy areas were discussed in the speech; the rest were not, allowing us to examine how information affects candidates' evaluations across different policy domains.

Theories focused on gender stereotypes suggest that participants will more favorably evaluate men candidates in stereotypically masculine policy domains, and women candidates in stereotypically feminine policy domains (H10). In

---

[22] We also conduct this analysis as a 2×3 ANOVA including the participants who did not indicate a party preference. The results are substantively the same in both the California and Texas samples, with evaluations by participants who did not state a preferred party falling between the higher scores given to the candidate from "my party" and the lower scores given to the candidate from the opposition. In Texas, when the analysis includes participants who did not state a party preference, for *Win Votes* there is no longer a significant main effect for Candidate Gender $[F(1,979)=1.573, p=.210]$.

[23] Scored 1 (very competent) to 5 (incompetent), scores were then inverted so that high scores are favorable.

176 KOSTANCA DHIMA AND JENNIFER M. PISCOPO

addition, including only some policy areas in the speech allows us to test whether gender stereotypes are used as heuristics to evaluate leaders' competencies over policy areas outside the speech, when compared to in the speech (H11).

The masculine policy areas include security and economy, which were discussed in the speech, and agriculture, energy, and infrastructure, which were not discussed in the speech. For the US analysis, we focus on *security* and *infrastructure*. Concerns about terrorism are perennial in US politics: on the 2018 Americas Barometer survey, 7 percent of Texans and 5 percent of Californians chose terrorism as the most important problem facing the country (these frequencies seem low, but the question was open-ended).[24] Infrastructure is also a perennial concern, with candidates in national elections offering spending plans linked to infrastructure repairs and development. In the Republican speech, security is discussed through a focus on rebuilding the US military into the world's strongest, securing US borders, and enforcing immigration laws. In the Democratic speech, security is tied to working with international allies, strengthening background checks for gun ownership, and a community-based approach to crime fighting that includes ending racial profiling.

The feminine policy areas include education and health, which were in the speech, and childcare and women's rights, which were not. We focus on *health* and *women's rights* given the prominence of these issues in the 2016 and 2018 campaigns. In the Republican speech, health policy appeared as consumer choice for healthcare and replacing the Affordable Care Act with market-based, competitive programs. In the Democratic speech, health policy meant providing healthcare for everyone, ensuring that job loss does not cause loss of health insurance, capping the cost of prescription drugs, and expanding in-home healthcare.

To test H10 and H11, we conducted repeated measures ANOVAs with Domain and Candidate Gender as factors, for the two in-speech policy areas (*security* and *health*) and then for the out-of-speech policy areas (*infrastructure* and *women's rights*). Starting with California, we find that the in-speech policy areas—*security* and *health* policies—are viewed as different (Domain p=.000), but the interaction of Domain×Candidate Gender is not significant [$F(1,718)=.069$, p=.793], which indicates that men and women candidates are evaluated as not significantly different in their competency over each policy. Contrary to expectations based on the theory of gender stereotypes, the woman candidate is viewed as equally capable as the man candidate on *security*. Turning to the out-of-speech policy areas, we find that *infrastructure* and *women's rights* policies are also viewed as different (Domain p=.000), and the interaction Domain×Candidate Gender *is* significant [$F(1,707)=14.048$, p=.000]. The woman candidate is scored

---

[24] "Bad government" was the most common response: national (21 percent), in the California and Texas sub-samples 24 percent and 22 percent, respectively.

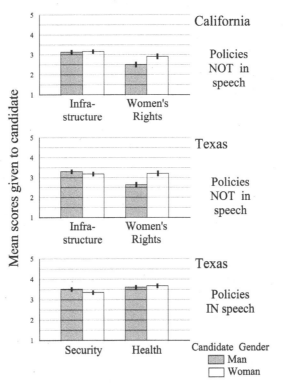

Figure 8.1 Evidence of gender schema in specific policy areas
2×2 repeated measures ANOVA (Domain, Candidate Gender) 95 percent confidence intervals included.

higher than the man candidate for leading on *women's rights*, but both genders are evaluated as not significantly different for *infrastructure* (Figure 8.1—top).[25]

In Texas, gender stereotypes appear more persistent. For the out-of-speech policy areas of *infrastructure* and *women's rights*, the interaction Domain×Candidate Gender is significant [$F(1,968)=59.431$, p=.000]. Participants gave more favorable evaluations to the man for *infrastructure*. Similar to California, they also gave more favorable evaluations to the woman candidate for *women's rights* (Figure 8.1—middle). Unlike in California,

---

[25] For the California sample we conducted robustness checks with the other masculine and feminine policy areas. For *economics* and *education* (discussed in the speech), results are substantively similar. For *energy* and *childcare* (not discussed) the woman candidate is scored higher on *childcare*, while the man and the woman are evaluated as not statistically different on *energy* policy [$F(1,709)=4.084$, p=.044]. For *agriculture* and *childcare* (not discussed) the policy areas are viewed as different (p=.000), but the interaction Domain×Candidate Gender is not significant [$F(1,704)=1.211$, p=.272], indicating that the man and woman candidate are evaluated as not statistically different for either policy.

178   KOSTANCA DHIMA AND JENNIFER M. PISCOPO

however, Texans also expressed gender stereotypes when evaluating the in-speech policy areas, Domain×Candidate Gender [F(1,979)=9.181, p=.003]. The man candidate is scored higher than the woman candidate for *security* policy (Figure 8.1—bottom).[26] This finding especially indicates traditional mental templates of leadership among young adults in Texas: the man and woman candidates' speeches presented the exact same discussion of security policy, but Texas participants favored the man candidate on *security*. In this case, gender stereotypes appear to override policy information provided by the candidate.

We also conduct 2×2×2 ANOVA analysis with Candidate Gender, Party Platform, and Party Label as factors for each policy, to check for the effect of party, our baseline control. In California, while a significant main effect for Candidate Gender is only present for *women's rights* policy (p=.000), we find a highly significant main effect for Party Platform when evaluating candidates' leadership competencies for *infrastructure* (p=.000), *health* (p=.000), and *women's rights* (p=.000). The Democratic Party candidate is scored higher than the Republican candidate for these three policy areas. In addition, the impact of Party Platform is more than double the impact of Candidate Gender for *women's rights* (η_p^2 of .053 compared to .024). In Texas, unlike California, Candidate Gender is significant for *security* (p=.025), *infrastructure* (p=.066), and *women's rights* (p=.000), but like California, Party Platform also is significant.[27] For both *security* and *infrastructure*, the Republican Party candidate is scored significantly higher than the Democratic Party candidate (p=.000 and p=.005 respectively). Additionally, the effect of Party Platform is greater than the effect of Candidate Gender (much greater for *security* [η_p^2 of .028 compared to .005 for Candidate Gender] and larger for *infrastructure* [η_p^2 of .008 for Party Platform and .003 for Candidate Gender]). Party Platform is also significant for *health* (p=.024), with a more favorable evaluation of the Democratic Party. For *women's rights*, the effect for Party Platform is highly significant, with the Democratic Party candidate scoring higher than the Republican Party candidate (p=.000), though for *women's rights* the impact of Candidate Gender is more than twice as large as the impact of Party Platform (η_p^2 of .056 and .019 respectively).

---

[26] With the Texas sample, as robustness checks we also examined the other sets of masculine and feminine policies. For *economics* and *education* (discussed in the speech) the interaction Domain×Candidate Gender is not significant [F(1,980)=2.236, p=.135] indicating that with the policy information provided in the speech, candidate gender is not central to the evaluation. For *energy* and *childcare* and for *agriculture* and *childcare* (not discussed in the speech) the interaction Domain×Candidate Gender is significant (p=.065 for energy/childcare, p=.001 for agriculture/childcare), with the woman candidate scored higher for *childcare*, and the man and woman evaluated as not statistically different for *energy* or *agriculture* policy.

[27] For *health*, the three-way interaction is significant [F(1,978)=4.211, p=.040], showing that the woman Republican candidate is preferred when the speech states the party name; otherwise the man and woman candidates are evaluated as equivalent.

PARTY OVER GENDER IN THE U.S. 179

Again, we explore whether participants' shared sex or party identification creates an in-group that would explain the policy areas in which women candidates are viewed as capable leaders. To test for a shared-sex in-group effect (H5), we add Participant Sex as a factor in the above repeated measures analysis. In California, for *security* and *health* (discussed in the speech) and for *infrastructure* and *women's rights* (not discussed), the three-way interaction Domain×Candidate Gender×Participant Sex is not significant ([F(1,702)=1.138, p=.286] and [F(1,691)=.002, p=.969] respectively). This indicates that both male and female Californians score a woman candidate higher for *women's rights* policy. In Texas, for *security* and *health* (discussed in the speech), with the addition of Participant Sex as a factor the interaction Domain×Candidate Gender is still significant [F(1,958)=8.856, p=.003], but the three-way interaction with Participant Sex is not significant (p=.392). Both male and female Texans score the man candidate higher for *security* policy. For *infrastructure* and *women's rights* (not in the speech), the three-way interaction with Participant Sex is not significant [F(1,947)=.002, p=.961], indicating that both male and female Texans score the man candidate as more capable for *infrastructure* policy, and the woman candidate as more capable for *women's rights*. Overall, we find no evidence of an in-group effect based on shared sex: where gender stereotypes persist for policy areas in California and in Texas, both male and female participants apply them to men and women candidates.

Yet evaluations could be shaped by a party in-group effect, given high levels of partisan polarization in the United States. To test for an in-group effect based on the alignment between the participants' preferred party and the candidate's party (H6), we redo the repeated measures analysis with Candidate Gender and My Party (yes/no/no preferred party) as factors. In California, for policies discussed in the speech, the interaction Domain×My Party is significant [F(1,712)= 25.301, p=.000]. For *health* policy in particular, participants scored candidates from their preferred party higher, as shown in Figure 8.2 (top), but the three-way interaction Domain×Candidate Gender×My party is not significant (p= .582). For the policies not discussed in the speech, the mean evaluation is again more favorable when the candidate is from the participant's party (Domain×My Party [F(1,701)=4.079, p=.017]), for both *infrastructure* and *women's rights* participants score the candidate from their preferred party higher (Figure 8.2, bottom). Domain×Candidate Gender remains significant; however, the three-way interaction is not significant (p=.844).

In Texas, however, for *security* and *health* policy (in the speech), whether the candidate is from participants' preferred party does not have a significant interaction with Domain [F(1,975)=.058, p=.943], and the three-way interaction is not significant (p=.549), but the interaction Domain×Candidate Gender is still significant (p=.003). Texas participants score the man candidate higher for

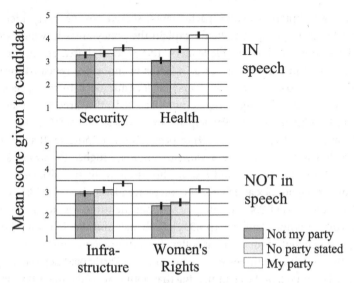

Figure 8.2 California: Interaction of party and candidate evaluations in specific policy areas
2×2×3 repeated measures ANOVA (Domain, Candidate Gender, My Party)
95 percent confidence intervals included.

security policy whether or not he is from their preferred party. For *infrastructure* and *women's rights* (not discussed), Domain×My Party is significant [F(1,964)= 3.502, p=.031] *and* the interaction of Domain×Candidate Gender remains significant. However, the three-way interaction is not significant (p=.156), so the woman candidate is scored higher on *women's rights* regardless of party, and the man candidate is scored higher on *infrastructure*, regardless of party. It is notable here that the effect of Candidate Gender is stronger than the effect of My Party (η_p^2=.055 for Domain×Candidate Gender, η_p^2=.007 for Domain×My Party).

In sum, gender stereotypes hold less traction in California than in Texas. This conclusion holds even when controlling for information, that is, even when looking for stereotypes used as heuristics in high information contexts (policies discussed in speech) and low information contexts (policies not discussed in speech). Californian participants evaluated the men and women candidates as equally capable in stereotypically masculine and feminine policy areas, with the exception of scoring women candidates higher on *women's rights*, which was not discussed in the speech. Generally, party shaped which candidates Californians perceived as better leaders, no matter the policy. Consistent with the Democratic Party preferences of the California sample, participants scored Democrats higher for *security, infrastructure, health,* and *women's rights*, and scored candidates from their preferred party higher regardless of gender.

Overall, Texan participants use gender stereotypes as heuristics more than California participants. Like Californians, Texans scored the woman candidate higher on *women's rights*, but unlike Californians, they also scored the man candidate higher on *security* and *infrastructure*. Here, Texans use gender as a heuristic in both high-information contexts where the man and woman candidates make the same policy statements (security appears in the speech) as well as low-information contexts (infrastructure does not appear in the speech). The strong effect of Candidate Gender regarding *security* is further underscored by the finding that the man candidate receives a higher competency score for *security* regardless of his membership in participants' preferred party. In Texas, some traditional gender stereotypes appear more important than party for how candidates are evaluated, whereas in California, party has a greater effect on candidate evaluations in specific policy areas than does gender.

Socialization within the Home Environment

Another way in which micro-level factors may affect mental templates of leadership could be socialization within the family. A mother with a high-status job or a high educational attainment can serve as a role model, indicating that women are capable actors in the public sphere. Participants with mothers that lack professional employment or high education may be more likely to exhibit traditional leadership templates (H7). To test H7 we conduct 2×3 between groups ANOVA (Candidate Gender, Mother Job) and 2×2 between groups ANOVA (Candidate Gender, Mother Education) for each general evaluation question and each policy area.[28] We also conduct these analyses with Participant Sex as an additional factor.

In both California and Texas, we do not find a significant interaction of Mother Education and Candidate Gender. However, in each state a significant interaction of Mother Job Status and Candidate Gender appears for one question. In California, the three-way interaction Candidate Gender×Mother Job×Participant Sex is significant for *women's rights* [F(1,587)=3.506, p=.031]. While female participants score the woman candidate higher regardless of their mother's job status (as do male participants whose mother has a low-status job), we find that male participants whose mothers have high-status jobs on average score the man and woman candidate as not statistically different for carrying out *women's rights* policy (Figure 8.3—top). In Texas, the three-way interaction is

---

[28] High level of education is defined as complete college or graduate school (California N=265, Texas N=520), a lower level of education is defined as complete high school or less (California N= 306, Texas N=275).

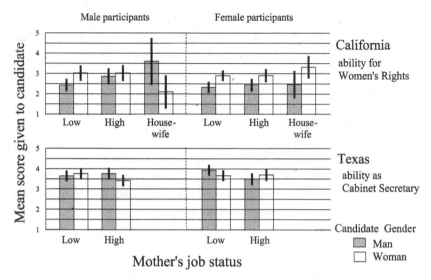

Figure 8.3 How mother job status is related to candidate evaluations
Top: 2×3×2 ANOVA (Candidate Gender, Mother Job, Participant Sex);
bottom: 2×2×2 ANOVA (Candidate Gender, Mother Job, Participant Sex)
95 percent confidence intervals included.

significant for *Cabinet Secretary* [F(1,725)=5.748, p=.017], indicating some difference in evaluations by female and male participants (Figure 8.3—bottom).[29]

Overall, having a high-status mother as a role model does not seem to explain which participants are more likely to view women candidates as more capable leaders. Family relations may have an impact on young adults' political leadership templates, but the impact of family may be modified or overridden by other factors.

One such factor is participants' race and ethnicity. Both Texas and California have large ethnic minority populations, and in the United States, party preferences differ across racial and ethnic groups. Latino voters diverge from White voters in notable ways: they are more likely to be affected by structural inequality and therefore more likely to identify with the Democratic Party, though Latina women are often more conservative in their policy attitudes when compared to Latino men (Donato and Perez 2016). Yet conservative leanings may be gradually loosening, as the election of Donald Trump has prompted

---

[29] For the Texas analysis we do not include the mothers who are housewives (N=40), though the three-way interaction is nearing significance when they are included [F(1,754)=2.919, p=.055]. In the California analysis, if the housewives (N=54) are not included in the analysis, the interaction is not significant [F(1,530)=.481, p=.488].

Latino and Latina young adults to increase their involvement in progressive politics.[30] Both California and Texas have a significant Latino population, with 39 percent of the population identifying as Latino/Hispanic and 40 percent of the population as White/non-Hispanic/non-Latino. For these reasons, we also examine race and ethnicity as a micro-level factor that may influence candidate evaluations.

To evaluate whether White and non-White participants evaluate female candidates differently, we conduct a 2×2×2 ANOVA analysis for general evaluation and policy area questions, with Candidate Gender, Party Platform, and Participant Race/Ethnicity (White or non-White) as factors. While there are statistically significant differences in candidate evaluations depending on participants' ethnicity (White or non-White), the Candidate Gender×Participant Race/Ethnicity interaction is not significant.

Echoing previous results, we find that the significant main effect for both White and non-White respondents is party. In California, Democrats are dominant: both Whites and non-Whites prefer a Democratic candidate (except for *security* policy where Party Platform is not significant [p=.386]). In Texas, party support fractures along racial and ethnic lines. White participants consider the Republican candidate to be more competent while non-White participants rate the Democratic candidate as better. The one exception is *women's rights*: both White and non-White Texans score the Democratic candidate higher. Overall, the patterns in Texas are consistent with national trends, with non-White voters increasingly supporting the Democratic Party, even in classically red states. Candidate Gender is not an influential component of candidate evaluations across racial and ethnic groups, while party once again exerts a strong effect.

California and Texas Findings

For some time, US respondents have manifested little preference for men over women leaders on public opinion surveys. Democrats promote and support women's access to elected office more than Republicans, but when asked whether men and women are equally good political leaders, both Democrats and Republicans respond about the same. These attitudes are largely reflected in the leadership templates observed among young adult participants in California and Texas, where participants from both states viewed women and men as equally capable of serving in the legislature, joining the president's cabinet, and winning votes. Given the candidate-centered nature of SMDP elections and the

---

[30] For Texas, see http://prospect.org/article/turning-southwest-blue-brown-and-beautiful-millennials.

competitive party primaries used in the United States, the positive evaluations of women's ability to win votes is particularly important for increasing women's political representation.

Rather than gender, our results point toward the importance of party, which provides a more relevant cue than gender in candidate evaluations. Participants mostly prefer their own-party candidate no matter whether that candidate is a man or a woman, with implications for increasing polarization. Measured in various ways throughout this chapter, party effects are consistently large, while the effect of candidate gender is either smaller or not significant in candidate evaluations.

At the same time, our results suggest that US political races are not free of gender stereotypes. Security and infrastructure are typed masculine by Texan young adults, and women's rights are typed feminine by Californians *and* Texans. Leadership templates are unaffected by gender when evaluating candidates in general terms, but persistent gender stereotypes when evaluating candidates in certain policy areas also appear. Young adults in the United States have grown up in an era where prominent women have sought and/or held federal and state office—such as Hillary Clinton, Nancy Pelosi, and Wendy Davis. Yet this era is also marked by women's low congressional representation overall. Thus, our results suggest that while US young adults will support women as political leaders, particularly if the woman candidate is from their preferred party, that does not mean their policy-specific evaluations are free of gender stereotypes. Progress remains to be made.

Table A8.1 Factor Analysis of General Evaluation Questions for United States

Component matrix component 1	California	Texas
Q1 House Member	.897	.884
Q2 Cabinet Secretary	.882	.867
Q17 Support	−.804	−.807
Q18 Win Votes	.682	.655
Variance explained	67.34%	65.31%

Extraction method: Principal component analysis.

9

A Generation Without Political Gender Biases?

The Case of Sweden

Elin Bjarnegård, Josefina Erikson, and Pär Zetterberg

MACRO-CONTEXT FACTORS: SWEDEN AND OTHER CASES				
	LOW ← Expectation of Strength of Gender Bias → HIGH			
	Parliamentary	**OR**		**Presidential**
Executive Institutions	Alberta CA			Chile
	Quebec CA			California US
	England			Texas US
	Israel			Costa Rica
	Sweden			Uruguay
Electoral Institutions	**Party focused ←- - - - - - - - - - - - - - - - -→ Candidate focused**			
	Israel	Uruguay	Chile	Alberta CA California US
	Costa Rica	Sweden		Quebec CA Texas US
				England
Policy Agenda Emphasis	**More Social Welfare ←- - - - - - - - - - - -→ Less Social Welfare**			
	Sweden	Alberta CA	Uruguay	England California US
	Costa Rica	Quebec CA	Israel	Chile Texas US
	Less Defense ←- - - - - - - - - - - - - - - -→ More Defense			
	Costa Rica	Alberta CA	Sweden	England Israel
	Uruguay	Quebec CA	Chile	California US Texas US
Incorporation of Women in Government	**Greatest ←- - - - - - - - - - - - - - - - - - - -→ Least**			
	Sweden	Chile	Alberta CA	Uruguay Texas US
	Costa Rica	England	Quebec CA	California US Israel

Introduction

This chapter investigates the political attitudes of young adults in Sweden through an experiment conducted in school classes with 609 participants between March and July 2018.[1] Sweden constitutes an interesting case, where young people have

---

[1] We wish to acknowledge the excellent research assistance provided by Ottilia Eriksson and Johan Bergsten.

Elin Bjarnegård, Josefina Erikson, and Pär Zetterberg, *A Generation Without Political Gender Biases?* In: *The Image of Gender and Political Leadership.* Edited by: Michelle M. Taylor-Robinson and Nehemia Geva, Oxford University Press. © Oxford University Press 2023. DOI: 10.1093/oso/9780197642726.003.0009

186   BJARNEGÅRD, ERIKSON, AND ZETTERBERG

grown up in what is, arguably, one of the most gender-equal political spheres in the world. The young adults who participated in our study are used to seeing as many women as men in politics. They are used to hearing party leaders from across the political spectrum calling themselves feminist. They are accustomed to state policies and laws that are explicitly designed to further gender equality. Their political attitudes have been shaped in an environment where there is a relatively weak masculine political norm. This is not to say that Sweden is a gender equal country in all areas—plenty of gendered norms remain, shaping the behavior and attitudes of men and women alike. However, when assessing the political sphere in particular, we argue that Sweden is as close as we get to gender equal political representation, and that Swedish young adults are among the least likely in today's world to be used to a masculine political norm. An experiment on attitudes to women and men in politics among young adults in Sweden allows us to get closer to answering the question of whether it is possible to shape a less gender-biased generation by ensuring that political gender equality is the norm when they grow up.

Our findings demonstrate that these young adults exhibit very little gender bias. There are few significant differences in their assessments based on the gender of the candidate whose speech they read. The few exceptions that we find mostly work in favor of women: women are perceived as being more competent than men in relation to health issues and gender equality issues. A further finding is that party ideology is important in Swedish politics: we find several significant party effects stronger than any gender effect. Thus, while the left-right ideology is still valid among urban young adults in Sweden, they care very little about whether their representative is a woman or a man. In other words, gender does not appear to be a relevant component of leadership templates.

The Swedish Context

Sweden is often characterized as one of the world's most gender equal countries when it comes to political representation (Inter-parliamentary Union 2011). It has even been stressed that gender equality is an established norm in Swedish politics (Dahlerup and Leyenaar 2013: 233). Although there are studies that display remaining gender inequalities within politics in regard to political debate (Bäck et al. 2014) and demands, expectations, and negative treatment (Erikson and Josefsson 2018), Sweden has in an international comparison made significant progress. Women have taken an important part in politics for at least twenty years. Politics is in many ways rather gender equal, and there is reason to believe that the traditional masculine politician norm has been challenged in its foundation by a more gender equal norm. For the young adults who participated in this study this means that during their entire life, politics have been rather gender equal and they are used to seeing both women and men in politics.

Election Rules

General and equal voting rights were introduced in Sweden when women in 1921 achieved the right to vote. Elections are held every four years, and since the change to unicameralism in the 1970s the Swedish Riksdag consists of 349 legislators who are elected in twenty-nine multi-member constituencies. Sweden uses a flexible-list PR electoral system in which voters can choose to either vote only for a party or also express a preference for a candidate on the party list. The percentage of votes needed to pass the personal vote threshold was lowered from 8 to 5 percent in the 2014 elections (Däubler et al. 2018). However, despite this change the number of MPs elected by a preferential vote continued to be low (only 3.4 percent). Thus, elections in Sweden's multiparty system focus mainly on parties rather than on individual candidates although preferential votes have become more important lately.

The party system has been rather stable over time and divided into left-leaning and right-leaning blocs[2]—the Social Democratic Party, Left Party, and more recently the Green Party to the left, and to the right the Moderate Party, Center Party, Liberal Party, and Christian Democratic Party. Lately there is also a right-wing populist party that, at the time of conducting the experiment, was not part of any bloc: the Sweden Democrats (first elected in 2010).

Women in Government

In contrast to countries where quota reforms have led to a rapid increase of the proportion of women in parliament, the Swedish path is characterized by incremental change that gradually has increased the proportion of women over time. Women's share of legislative seats initially increased slowly but accelerated after the 1970s. The threshold of 20 percent was crossed in the 1970s, 30 percent in the 1980s, and 40 percent in the 1990s. The informal norm of zipped candidate lists (i.e., alternating between men and women) that was introduced in the 1990s in most parties has been important to maintain the level of women above 40 percent (Freidenvall 2006). The Swedish parliament is in fact unique insofar as women

---

[2] Between 2006 and 2018 the left-leaning and the right-leaning blocs were two stable and predictable coalitions. After the outcome of the elections in September 2018 the political scene has somewhat changed. This change was, however, nothing that the participants in this study could have foreseen and it cannot have influenced them.

have held over 40 percent of the seats for more than two decades. After the 2014 elections 44 percent of the legislators were women, and with the 2018 election 47 percent of seats were held by women (Inter-parliamentary Union 2011). In terms of policy content, numerous case studies show that female legislators in Sweden make an actual difference in pursuing gender equality issues (e.g., Esaiasson and Holmberg 1996; Frangeur 1998; Freidenvall 2006; Erikson 2017).

Although the left-right divide has been and still is important in Swedish politics, gender equality issues also have a prominent place on the political agenda. Already in 2002, former prime minister and Social Democrat Göran Persson declared himself a feminist (Aftonbladet 2002, January 24). All of the parties in the left-leaning bloc are proclaimed feminists as well as the Liberal Party and the Center Party (Freidenvall 2006, 2013).

The norm of equal representation has also translated to the government, which since 1994 has been more or less gender equal in numbers (Bergqvist 2015: 27). Women have not only held portfolios in traditionally feminine coded areas but frequently in portfolios such as defense, foreign affairs, justice, and finance. However, it was not until November 2021 (after our data collection was completed) that Sweden had its first woman prime minister: the Social Democrat Magdalena Andersson. Stable and productive minority or coalition governments have been typical for Swedish politics (Arter 2004). The Social Democratic Party has been the largest party in the parliament for almost a century, and from 1932 to 2006 the party was in the government for all but nine years (1976–1982, 1991–1994). Since the 1979 elections, the center-right (liberal-conservative) Moderate Party is the second-largest party in the parliament. They were running coalition governments with other liberal and conservative parties in 1991–1994 and between 2006 and 2014, when the Social Democratic Party returned to power. While the governing power has shifted between coalitions led by the Social Democratic Party and the Moderate Party during the last decades, equal representation of the sexes in the executive has been important regardless of the ideological divide.

Swedish politics is in general not characterized as either extreme or polarized. Most parties tend to move away from the extreme left or right positions toward the middle of the political scale—the Social Democratic Party and the Moderate Party are examples of the traditional right-left divide that structures Swedish political discussion. To put it simply, whereas the Social Democrat Party seeks to further equality between groups in society by advocating a strong presence of the state and a relatively high level of taxes, the Moderate Party favors free choice and market principles as political steering instruments.

The government in place from 2014 to 2018 and at the time this study was conducted was a minority coalition consisting of the Social Democratic and Green Parties with support of the Left Party. The government included twelve women and twelve men. Although Prime Minister Stefan Löfvén was a man, women held several prestigious portfolios—such as finance and foreign affairs. What is more, the government proclaimed itself as the world's first feminist government with an ambitious agenda of including a feminist perspective in all policy areas (Nylund, Håkansson and Bjarnegård 2022).

Government Policy Agenda

The ambition to use policy reforms to improve gender equality in society is not new in Swedish politics. On the contrary, this ambition aligned well with a tradition of using policy tools to improve gender equality in society—for instance, the removal of joint income taxation in the 1970s coupled with the expansion of daycare as a means to encourage women to take part in paid labor. In addition, the introduction of a gender-neutral parental leave in the 1970s and the reserved "daddy months" encouraged more men to fulfill their parental role (Bergqvist et al. 2008; Duvander 2008).

Education and Workforce

With regard to the status of women in society, the equality in political representation is well reflected in educational attainment and in labor market participation although gender gaps in educational and professional choices remain. Turning first to education, 46 percent of the women born in Sweden compared to 35 percent of the men had a higher education in 2012 (Heikkilä 2015: 137). In terms of educational orientations, there seems still to exist "feminine" and "masculine" choices though. While women are overrepresented in education related to the health and social care sector and in pedagogy and teacher education, men are overrepresented in education related to technology and manufacturing (Heikkilä 2015: 161). Turning to the labor market, we discern the same gendered pattern, although women's participation in the labor force over the last decade is almost as high as men's (82–84 percent in comparison to 83–86 percent) (Nyberg 2015: 68). Only three out of the thirty most popular professions in Sweden have a gender balance that meets the criterion for gender equality of at least 40 percent of each sex. The most women-dominated occupations in 2016 were preschool teachers (96 percent women), assistant nurses (92 percent women), childcare workers (90 percent), and nurses (90 percent). Women are thus commonly found in the care sector. For men, the most common professions are wood workers/carpenters (99 percent men), electricians (98 percent), mechanics (97 percent), and truck

190 BJARNEGÅRD, ERIKSON, AND ZETTERBERG

drivers (94 percent). Technology and transport sectors thus largely attract men (Occupational Register, Statistics Sweden 2016).

Designing the Swedish Case Study

Like all the experiments in this volume, the Swedish experiment has a 2×2×2 factorial design. The three factors are Candidate Gender, Party Platform (Social Democratic Party or Moderate Party), and whether or not there is a Party Label in the candidate's speech. Below we present the parties, speeches, and data collection in greater detail.

Parties and Speeches

Selection of political parties was straightforward. The Social Democrats and the Moderate Party represent the two biggest parties, two opposing ideologies, and the two most common government alternatives in modern times.

The speeches were constructed with a general format but were adapted to represent the 2018 political discussion in each party to make them authentic. Each speech text is a composite of party statements found in the written information on each party's webpage: presentation of the party ideology, party platform, and excerpts of real political speeches published at the parties' websites. The candidate names were selected among the most common Swedish names and last names among people born in the 1950s and 1960s: Lars (male) and Lena (female) Lindberg.

In terms of economy, the Moderate Party speech emphasizes the management of public finances, economic growth, and lower taxes. It states that the reliance on welfare benefits needs to decrease while the benefits of making your own money should increase. In contrast, the Social Democrat speech focuses on evening out economic gaps in society: between urban and rural areas, rich and poor, and immigrants and people born in Sweden.

The Moderate Party speech suggests that private healthcare alternatives lead to a more efficient healthcare system, whereas the Social Democrat speech criticizes the possibility of profit among private actors. Likewise, in education, the Moderate Party stands for free choice and private alternatives while the Social Democrats point to the segregation caused by increasing market mechanisms in the school system.

Regarding the environment, the Moderate Party emphasizes technological development, while the Social Democrats want to introduce stricter regulations to affect behavior in a climate-friendly direction. Considering security, the speeches also point to different approaches. The Moderate Party speech suggests that Sweden should become a member of NATO, and that the Swedish security service in general needs increased resources. The Social Democrat Party speech points to the need to battle the causes of crime, and a belief in international collaboration, even when it means a transfer of power to organizations such as the EU and the UN.

Despite the fact that Swedish politics is not known for being highly polarized, the two constructed speeches clearly communicate two common and well-developed approaches to Swedish politics. Although they are not exact copies of real speeches, we deem them to be valid indicators of the parties' standing on a variety of issues and thus to cue party as a treatment.

Data Collection and Study Participants

Data collection took place from March to July, 2018, with about 90 percent of the data collected during March to May. While the data collection took place the election campaign of the September 2018 parliamentary elections had not yet started. Usually, campaigns are quite short in Sweden: about four to five weeks. In 2018, the campaign was even shorter (about three to four weeks); as a consequence, we have no reason to believe that events taking place in relation to the election have affected the results of the study. It is also important for our study that there were no major political events taking place in Sweden during the time of data collection. The parties prepared themselves for the election campaign, but it was very much a period of political stability. Looking at opinion polls from the time period of data collection, there were no major shifts in party attitudes. The only notable change in party attitudes was from April to May 2018 for the populist radical-right party—the Sweden Democrats—that had a three percentage-point (20 percent) increase in support. This increase was most likely a result of a renewed focus on migration issues in the public debate during that time of 2018. However, in general we have few reasons to believe that political events during the time of data collection have affected the results of our study.

Data collection was nevertheless surrounded by several challenges. In Sweden, the teachers in high school and university have substantial autonomy; whether to participate in studies such as the present one is basically up to the individual teacher. This factor complicated our data collection in that we had to contact individual teachers to get their permission in order to run the experiment in class, sometimes many different teachers in the same school. Another challenge was that high school schedules are very tight, and several teachers decided not to participate for that reason. Many teachers wanted to integrate the survey into their regular classes and felt that this was a "social science related topic." We thus had some difficulties reaching students from orientations including less social science. Most high school programs also do not offer social science during the final and third year, the target year for our survey. At the university it was easier to reach students from different orientations and most teachers were helpful and supportive. However, many of them scheduled our visits after mandatory lectures to underscore the voluntariness of the survey.

School visits were scheduled by a research coordinator, and the data was collected primarily by two research assistants, one woman and one man, both in their twenties and former political science students. In total we contacted over forty high schools and university programs, which included in total 1,500 students from both academic and vocational programs of different orientations. Twenty-seven classes/programs at twelve institutions responded (nine high schools, two universities, one college), which resulted in 609 students who accepted to be part of the study. While most universities are public in Sweden and we therefore did not include the few private ones, we did contact both public and private high schools although mostly public ones participated.

All schools are in Uppsala or Stockholm. The majority of the students from high schools were from different social science programs for the reason described above, but a few were from a vocational program. Most were seventeen to nineteen years old. The university students came from social sciences, law, and natural sciences programs. Most participants were from the first year of their studies and were below the age of twenty-five.

Like many countries, Sweden has an urban/rural divide. This applies to socio-economic status but also to political opinion. A few participants stated that they are originally from villages and small towns, and some may commute, but even so the rural parts of Sweden are still largely unrepresented in this dataset. In terms of gender there is an overweight of women (64.6 percent).

The dropout rate was rather high and especially so for the university, for the reasons mentioned above. It should be noted that the students who decided to leave did so as soon as they heard that the study was voluntary, and thus before they saw the study materials. In some cases, as much as 75 percent of the class left before we could present the study. In high school classes, on the other hand, it was not very common for people to leave before or during the experiment. In a few cases the teachers had told the students beforehand that participation was voluntary, which resulted in less attendance. If the dropout has skewed the sample in any direction, it is likely that ambitious students with high political interest are overrepresented among those who participated, in other words students who might be particularly receptive to political gender equality norms.

For several reasons this is not a truly representative sample of the country's population—women from social science programs in urban areas are overrepresented—but we still consider it useful to study norms and attitudes towards gender within these groups of young adults. The sample can be seen as a most likely case for gender equal attitudes toward political candidates: if we are to see evaluations of candidates that are not based on sex stereotypes, it should be within this kind of sample. If, on the contrary, not even this group displays leadership templates in which gender is not a relevant component, other groups are unlikely to do so. The dataset is described in Table 9.1.

Table 9.1 Description of Participants in Sweden

	Overall	Male only	Female only
Number of participants	609	208	380
Percent of participants	100	35.4	64.6
Average age	20.7	21.5	20.3
Left (1) to Right (10) self-placement	4.66	5.35	4.25
Preferred party (%):			
Governing (Social Democratic)	20.9	16.7	23.2
Largest opposition (Moderate)	15.4	24.1	10.7
Left Party	16.2	11.8	18.9
Swedish Green Party	11.2	5.9	14.1
Center Party	11.7	6.4	15.0
Liberal Party	7.7	12.3	5.1
Sweden Democrats	3.3	7.4	0.8
Christian Democratic Party	0.9	1.0	0.6
No preference stated	12.6	14.3	11.3
Total	100	100	100
Parents' education* (% of participants):			
Fathers w/high level	55.5	50.5	58.7
Mothers w/high level	63.2	61.5	65.8
Fathers w/low level	25.9	30.8	24.2
Mothers w/low level	23.2	22.6	23.9
Parents' occupation (% of participants):			
Fathers w/high status job	63.1	60.8	63.8
Mothers w/high status job	58.6	53.1	61.8
Housewives, as % of participants	0.7	1.0	0.3
Housewives, as the actual number	4	2	1

* Note: Education levels of participants' parents are divided into "high" (complete university or more) and "low" (complete secondary or less), and the remaining percentage (not shown) is defined as "intermediate" and "don't know."

Results

Each study participant scored the suitability of one candidate with a specific gender (indicated by name and pronoun) and party identification (either stated or implied). Participants did not directly compare their candidate to another candidate. We thus avoid using the terms "preferred" and "preferable," which suggest a direct comparison by the same participant. We instead observe which candidate scored higher or lower when comparing candidate evaluations across treatment conditions. The notation, H5 through H11, refers to hypotheses and statistical methods outlined in Chapters 1 and 2.

The overall finding of the Swedish experiment is that the participants do not seem to hold traditional stereotypes about men and women in politics. In general, the differences between the men and women candidate are small. And in almost all cases in which there is a significant difference in evaluations, the woman candidate is evaluated more positively than the man.

General Evaluations of Candidates

Participants were asked to evaluate the candidate on seven general questions: How effective this person would be as a (1) member of the parliament,[3] (2) member of the cabinet,[3] and (3) party leader.[3] Would they (4) use their preference vote for the candidate,[4] and (5) vote for the candidate's party list,[4] and whether the candidate would be good at winning (6) preference votes,[5] and (7) votes for their party.[5] Principal components factor analysis on the general questions is provided in the Chapter Appendix.

In the "general" evaluations of the candidates, there are no significant differences with regard to Candidate Gender, regardless of the level of the post, or in willingness to support or vote for the candidate.[6] For *Member of Parliament, Minister,* and *Party Leader,* the woman candidate has a higher mean score than the man candidate; however, the differences are far from significant (*MP* [$F_{(1,557)}=.464$, $p=.496$], *Minister* [$F_{(1,526)}=.580$, $p=.447$], *Party Leader* [$F_{(1,531)}=1.121$, $p=.290$]). Similarly, for *Win Preference Votes* or *Win Party Votes,* the man candidate is scored higher, but again the difference is not significant ([$F_{(1,589)}=2.471$, $p=.116$] and [$F_{(1,588)}=.877$, $p=.349$]

---

[3] Answers range from 1 (outstanding) to 6 (very poor) and were inverted so that high scores are favorable.

[4] Answered 1 (yes), 2 (no). These are the only questions for which a lower score is more favorable.

[5] Answers range from 1 (very good) to 5 (very poor) and were inverted so that high scores are favorable.

[6] Analyses are 2×2×2 ANOVAS with Candidate Gender, Party Platform, Party Label as factors.

WITHOUT POLITICAL GENDER BIASES IN SWEDEN   195

respectively). That men and women candidates are evaluated as equivalent for ability to win preference votes is important in light of expectations that electoral rules that allow voters to focus on individual candidates are unfavorable to women (because they allow voters to apply gender stereotypes). The findings in this study in Sweden comport with Valdini (2013), who argues that whether a personal-vote system is prejudicial to women candidates depends on the level of bias in the society against women being leaders. When it comes to party differences, on the other hand, the Social Democratic Party candidate receives more positive evaluations than the candidate of the Moderate Party. These differences are significant for: *MP* (p=.021), *Use Preference Vote* (p=.030), and *Vote For Party List* (p=.000).

Literature about role congruity prompted H8 and H9 that men would be favored in "general" evaluation questions and for higher level posts. However, the Sweden findings do not indicate that women are viewed as incongruous,[7] which fits with the macro-predictions of the study that leadership templates will be less likely to include gender when a country has extensive experience with women in government and where the government's policy agenda emphasizes social welfare policy, as is the case in Sweden. Next, we look at whether leadership templates are influenced by the candidate being from the participant's in-group.

Theory of in-groups predicts that male participants will give men candidates more favorable evaluations, whereas female participants will give women candidates more favorable evaluations (H5). For this analysis we conduct 2×2 ANOVAs with Candidate Gender and Participant Sex as factors for each general evaluation question. The interaction is not significant for any of the general questions; thus, the results show that participants do not assess candidates of their own sex more favorably.

In-group theory also predicts that participants will evaluate women candidates more favorably if they are from the participant's party (H6). For this test we conduct 2×2 ANOVAs with Candidate Gender and My Party (yes, no) as factors for each general evaluation question. Our results generally do not point in that direction as the interaction is not significant. However, the impact of party is clear, as participants always give a more favorable evaluation of a candidate from their own party (p=.000 for all questions except *Win Preference Votes* p=.053 and *Win Party Votes* p=.109).[8]

---

[7] Regarding H9, repeated measures ANOVA with Post (*MP, Minister, Party Leader*) and Candidate Gender as factors shows the interaction is not significant (p=.536 linear, p=.748 quadratic).

[8] As a robustness check we also ran this analysis including Party Label. Interactions with Party Label are not significant, indicating that these findings do not depend on the party name being listed on the speech. However, for *Vote For Party List* and *Win Party Votes* the interaction My Party×Label is significant ([F(1,561)=4.818, p=.008] and [F(1,583)=4.549, p=.011] respectively). For participants who read a speech by a candidate from their preferred party or who did not state a preferred party,

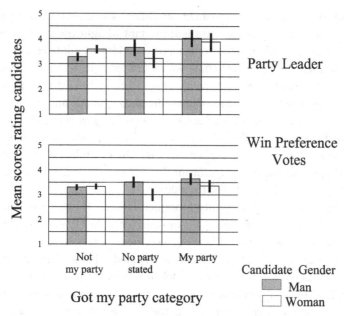

Figure 9.1 Party in-group
2×3 ANOVA (Candidate Gender, My Party) 95 percent confidence intervals included.

In relation to this set of analysis of general evaluations, participants seem to evaluate men and women candidates differently in two additional cases. When we examine participants who did not state a preferred party (3×2 ANOVA with My Party and Candidate Gender as factors), the interaction is significant for *Party Leader* [F(1,533)=4.109, p=.017] and for *Win Preference Votes* [F(1,590)= 4.809, p=.008][9] shown in Figure 9.1. For both we observe that participants who did not state a preferred party give a more favorable evaluation to the man candidate than to the woman. This could mean that people who lack a party affiliation still partly rely on traditional gender schema to make their vote decision.[10]

---

their evaluations are more favorable when the party name was provided. For participants whose speech was from the opposition, evaluations are more favorable when the party name was not on the speech. We also ran 3×2 ANOVAs substituting My Coalition for My Party. The results are substantively the same, and participants give a more favorable evaluation to the candidate who is from their preferred coalition, except for *Win Preference Votes*, for which My Coalition is not significant [F(1,586)=1.871, p=.155].

[9] For *Win Preference Votes* the main-effect of Candidate Gender is also significant (p=.003) and the mean evaluation of the man candidate (M=3.483) is more favorable than the mean evaluation of the woman candidate (M=3.227).

[10] We also conducted this analysis with My Coalition and the results are substantively the same.

Competence across Policy Areas

Next, we examine candidate evaluations in relation to policy areas. We explore if there are gendered patterns in that women or men are perceived as more competent in certain policy areas and whether such differences are related to gender stereotypes of "feminine" and "masculine" issue areas. Previous research from the Swedish parliament (Wängnerud 1998, 2000; Bäck et al. 2014; Erikson and Josefsson 2016) shows that some policy areas stand out as "masculine" or "feminine." Analyzing the Swedish MP surveys (conducted in 1985, 1988, 1994), Wängnerud (2000) finds that women legislators to a greater extent than men have engaged with gender equality issues and social welfare policy issues including social policy, family policy, elder care, and healthcare in their campaigning. In much the same vein Bäck et al. (2014) find that women legislators are more active in the chamber debate in typically female issues while men to a greater extent dominate the debate in male coded issues. In studies of preferred committees, Wängnerud (1998) identifies the following committees as "male": macroeconomics, energy, transportation, banking, finance and domestic commerce— whereas communications; health; labor, employment, and immigration; education; and social welfare are identified as "female." A similar pattern is found in a survey presented in a report by Erikson and Josefsson (2016), where the Committee on Health and Social Welfare stands out as a typically female committee and the Committees on Finance and Defense stand out as typically male committees. What is more, while women's and men's preferred committees differ, men's top preferences coincide with the preferred committees of all MPs (regardless of sex) to a higher extent than women's. In fact, the Committees on Industry and Trade and on Foreign Affairs, which are men's two favorite committees, are the top committees on the preference list of all MPs as well and on the top five of the women's list. In contrast, women's first choice, the Committee on Health and Social Welfare, is not even on men's top-ten list. In short, there are still typical "female-" and "male-" coded issues, and there is a tendency that while women seem to like men's first choices as well, men are not to the same extent attracted by women's first choices.

Drawing on the issues and committees pointed out as either "feminine" or "masculine" in these studies, we have coded security and energy as masculine policy areas and healthcare and gender issues as feminine. Security and healthcare were both discussed in the candidate speeches (speech content for each party was described above in the "Parties and Speeches" section of the chapter). Gender patterns in the ministers' portfolios show that while the portfolios of health and welfare, energy, and defense have been rather equally shared between women and men since 2000 (3/2, 3/4, 5/4), the portfolio of

198 BJARNEGÅRD, ERIKSON, AND ZETTERBERG

gender equality has been assigned to eight women and only one man during the last two decades.

To explore whether men and women candidates are evaluated differently based on the gendered stereotypes of the policy area (H10), we conducted repeated measures ANOVAs with Domain and Candidate Gender as factors for the pair of policies that were discussed in the speech, and the pair of policies that were not discussed. For *security* and *health* (discussed in the speech), the interaction is not significant [F(1,584)=2.124, p=.146] indicating that evaluations of the man and woman are not statistically different in either policy area. However, if we examine policy areas individually (ANOVA with Candidate Gender, Party Platform, Party Label as factors), we observe that Candidate Gender has a significant main-effect for *health* policy, with the woman candidate favored (woman candidate M=3.472, man candidate M=3.316, [F(1,585)=3.669, p=.056]).[11] For *security* policy there is a significant interaction of Candidate Gender×Party Platform [F(1,581)=3.962, p= .047], indicating that the woman candidate is evaluated more favorably when she is from the Moderate Party than when she is from the Social Democratic Party (Figure 9.2—top). When policy information is not provided in the speech, for *energy* and *gender equality* the interaction is highly significant [F(1,553)=8.698, p=.003] and indicates that, while the man and woman candidates are evaluated to be equivalent in the masculine policy area, the woman candidate is evaluated significantly more favorably on *gender equality* (Figure 9.2—bottom).[12] These findings remain the same if we add Participant Sex as a factor.[13]

The results of our analysis on policy areas confirm the picture from the general evaluations: men candidates are not assessed more favorably than women candidates. However, our findings indicate that women candidates are scored higher than men in stereotypically feminine policy areas, regardless

[11] The three-way interaction is also significant [F(1,585)=4.369, p=.037] indicating that the woman candidate is evaluated more favorably than the man when she is from the Social Democratic Party but the party name is not on the speech.

[12] As robustness checks, we replicate the repeated measures analysis with the other stereotypically masculine and feminine policy areas: *education* and *economy* (discussed in the speech), and *childcare, agriculture,* and *infrastructure* (not discussed). For the *economy* and *education* repeated measure ANOVA the interaction Domain×Candidate Gender is again not significant (p=.611). Regarding policies not discussed in the speech, for *agriculture* and *childcare* and for *infrastructure* and *childcare* repeated measures the interaction Domain×Candidate Gender is significant ([F(1,543)=4.03, p=.045] and [F(1,543)=5.078, p=.025] respectively). Party effects are visible with *education* and *childcare*. Social Democratic candidates are perceived as more competent to deal with these issues than their Moderate colleagues. Importantly, however, we see no effects for Candidate Gender when we look at these policy areas. We also note that Party Platform matters for *economics* policy as the Moderate Party is more favorably evaluated.

[13] Three-way interaction Domain×Candidate Gender×Participant Sex for policy areas discussed in the speech [F(1,565)=.000, p=.992], and for policies not discussed [F(1,535)=2.761, p=.097].

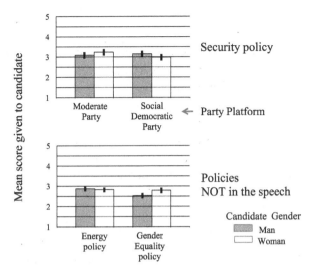

Figure 9.2 Policy areas and Candidate Gender
Top: 2×2×2 ANOVA (Candidate Gender, Party Platform, Party Label);
bottom: repeated measures ANOVA (Candidate Gender, Domain not discussed in the speech) 95 percent confidence intervals included.

of whether the policy was discussed in the speech (*health*) or not discussed (*gender equality*), which is interesting since the literature predicts that gender is more likely to be used as a heuristic if policy information is not available (H11). For *gender equality* the results are mainly driven by female participants. Male participants perceive men candidates to be as competent as women candidates to deal with *gender equality* policies (M=2.77, M=2.84 respectively p=.616, 2-tailed), whereas there is a large sex difference among female participants (M=2.79 for the woman candidate, M=2.40 for the man candidate, p=.001, 2-tailed).

A closer look at party differences, however, shows that *health* and *gender equality* are also clearly party-related issues. In the entire sample and among male and female participants separately, the Social Democratic candidates are perceived as more competent to deal with these issues than their Moderate counterparts. For both policy areas η_p^2 statistics indicate that Party Platform has a greater impact on evaluations than Candidate Gender (η_p^2 *health* = .062 for Platform, .006 for Candidate Gender; for *gender equality* η_p^2 = .045 for Platform, .015 for Candidate Gender). Thus, while candidate gender matters for evaluations in these two stereotypically feminine policy areas, and women candidates are favored, on average party (being a Social Democrat) matters more.

Socialization within Home Environment

The somewhat skewed sample raises an important question: how likely are these findings to travel to young Swedish adults at large? It could be argued that gender stereotypes are more common within other sub-groups. For instance, survey data on a national sample of adolescents has shown that individuals with immigrant background or with low-educated parents are more likely to have gender unequal political attitudes (Ekman and Zetterberg 2010). Our data allow us to explore the latter aspect, which also engages H7 that having a mother who has a high level of education, or a high-status job is when leadership templates will include women, as those mothers could serve as role models that women can work in the public sphere.

To test this, for each of the general evaluation questions, and for the four policy areas that were our focus above, we conduct ANOVAs with Candidate Gender and Mother Education or Mother Job as factors, both with and without Participant Sex as a factor to see if the interaction is significant.[14] For most general and policy evaluations we continue to find that Candidate Gender is not significant, even when controlling for the mother's background. In two questions, *Win Preference Votes* and *security* policy, we find support for the prediction of a mother role model effect, though only for male participants. The three-way interaction (Candidate Gender×Mother Education×Participant Sex) is significant ([$F(1,504)=4.377$, $p=.037$] and [$F(1,494)=5.555$, $p=.019$] respectively) and indicates that male participants whose mothers have a lower level of education give the man candidate a more favorable evaluation, and the reverse for female participants (see Figure 9.3—right). However, in three cases what we observe is contrary to expectations. For *Member of Parliament* and *Party Leader* ([$F(1,486)=4.286$, $p=.039$] and [$F(1,465)=4.005$, $p=.046$] respectively), participants whose mother has a lower level of education give a more favorable evaluation to the woman candidate (Figure 9.3—left). Similarly, for *health* policy when we control for Sex of Participant the participants whose mothers have a low-status job give a more favorable evaluation to the woman candidate [$F(1,538)=4.519$, $p=.034$] (not shown).

In sum, while home structure, by serving as a proximate example, may affect the political leadership template of young adults, other factors, such as interaction with peers, might have a greater effect. In particular, in the case of this sample of Swedish young adults, it is possible that the political liberal leaning of the cohort may decrease the influence of the home-based example.

---

[14] Low education is coded as complete secondary school or less (N=141), and high education is complete university or more (N=385). For analysis using Mother Job participants whose mother is a housewife are not included (N=4). Chapter 2 explains coding of high and low job status.

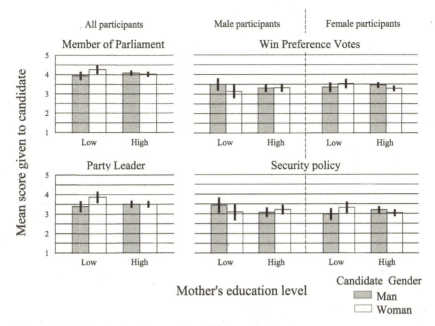

Figure 9.3 Mother's education and candidate evaluations
Right: cases supporting the mother role model prediction 2×2×2 ANOVA (Candidate Gender, Mother Education, Participant Sex); left: cases that contradict the prediction 2×2 ANOVA (Candidate Gender, Mother Education) 95 percent confidence intervals included.

Discussion

Is it possible to reduce gender stereotypes in politics and thereby shape a generation without gender biases toward women politicians? While we know that Sweden—just like any other country in the world—has historically not been exempted from political gender stereotypes, our main results suggest that these stereotypes indeed can be largely absent. At least in our young-adult sample, gender seems to have little to do with how political competence in general is perceived in Sweden today—that is, with mental templates of leadership. We do not find evidence of traditional leadership templates in that men would automatically be perceived as better leaders. Our respondents seem to have fairly equal perceptions of men and women candidates' competences and chances to be elected. If anything, women are seen as slightly more competent than men in certain issue areas.

In light of Sweden's tradition of gender equality in politics with over two decades of gender equal representation in parliament and gender balanced governments, the findings are somewhat expected. At the same time the findings are encouraging in so far as gendered norms, practices and stereotypes have proven to be resistant to change in many contexts. While Sweden has made progress in terms of gender balanced political representation, recent studies show that there are still hurdles within politics related to more subtle norms and practices with gendered implications; women pay a higher price for their political engagement. For instance, studies from the Swedish Riksdag show that women MPs experience higher demands and more anxiety and are more exposed to negative treatment (Erikson and Josefsson 2018, 2021), and that debate participation still is gendered (Bäck et al. 2014). Although not the only factor of importance, it is an important step toward political gender equality that urban young adults hold unbiased attitudes toward men and women politicians—it might be an indication of, and a stepping-stone for, further changes.

To qualify our main findings, politicians' gender cannot be deemed entirely irrelevant—it still seems to matter for how competence is perceived in certain issue areas. Our findings show that women politicians are seen as slightly more competent than men in gender equality and health policy, issues traditionally seen as "feminine" policy areas. To understand these findings, we should consider the very much present horizontal division of labor between men and women in different societal sectors. The educational sector and the labor market are highly gender segregated in feminine and masculine domains in Sweden, which is a sign that certain domains and issues are still coded as masculine or feminine. The gendered division is partly reflected in our findings, but contrary to what we would expect, men are not perceived as more competent in traditionally male issues such as security and energy. A possible explanation for our findings is that women have struggled to prove themselves to fit with the masculine politician role and to be competent in traditionally masculine policy areas, whereas men have not felt a similar need to prove themselves competent in traditionally female areas. Erikson and Josefsson's (2016) study of MPs' preferred committees supports such an interpretation. They find that while men's favorite committees are seen as attractive by women MPs as well, women's preferred committees are not seen as desirable by men MPs. Looking at ministerial portfolios, there is also a clear trend that women have made it into traditionally male areas, whereas at least gender equality is still a post that has been highly dominated by women.

With respect to gender equality issues, our findings show that especially female participants tend to see women candidates as more competent. This finding might reflect the fact that men until now have been less engaged with gender equality issues in politics. Bergqvist et al. (2018) have suggested that men politicians' lack of engagement is largely a result of low expectations: whereas women politicians often perceive that they are mandated to engage with gender equality issues, their male colleagues rarely perceive such an obligation. As a consequence, citizens are used to seeing women working with these issues. However, an alternative interpretation is that women—due to their common experiences of being from the disadvantaged group—perceive of gender equality issues as somewhat equivalent with women's issues. They thereby value women's competence as higher in this area. Regardless of interpretation, our findings point to the fact that Swedish women have in different sectors of society made inroads to the traditionally male domains, but that the next step for gender equality is to make men step into women's domains as well. The need for such a shift in men's behavior can clearly be noted in family life but should also hold true in politics (see also Bergqvist et al. 2018).

A further finding is that party ideology is important in Swedish politics: we find a significant party effect on several items that is stronger than the gender effect.[15] For instance, regardless of participants' own party preferences or gender, we find that Social Democratic candidates are perceived as more competent to deal with health issues and gender equality issues. Accordingly, these issues are not only perceived of as "women's" issues; they are also perceived of as Social Democratic areas of expertise. Against the background of a strong Social Democratic welfare state that has promoted gender equality and Social Democratic prime ministers who proclaim themselves feminists, this finding is maybe not surprising. The importance of party ideologies in the Swedish context is further indicated by a tendency of gender biases favoring men when looking at participants who did not state a preferred party. Although we only find evidence of traditional leadership templates on a few items, our findings suggest that gender is not completely irrelevant. These findings emphasize the importance of including both gender and party when studying gender biases towards political candidates.

Conclusion

This chapter has shown that, in general, young and urban Swedish adults do not seem to hold traditional stereotypes about men and women in politics. The few exceptions that we find to the main pattern mostly work in favor of women: they are perceived as being more competent than men in relation to health and gender equality policies.

To understand this general lack of political gender stereotypes, we should consider the society that young Swedish adults have grown up in. As described above, Sweden has had an almost equal number of men and women in parliament and cabinet during these people's entire life. Although gender inequalities of course still exist, the gender equality norm has been strong for the last two decades—not only in politics but in the Swedish society at large. The young, urban, and educated individuals that are represented in our specific sample are

---

[15] The η_p^2 statistic for Party Platform is more than twice as large as for Candidate Gender for *health* policy and for *gender equality*.

likely to be among the first ones to adhere to that gender equality norm. Having that in mind, the findings are not surprising.

Future work on gender stereotypes in Sweden could preferably look closer at different sub-groups. As Swedish society has become more gender equal, there are also pockets of resistance—among those who believe that Swedish feminism has gone too far. And these ideas, which travel easily through social media, are more widespread among low-educated men in rural areas than among the highly educated women in urban areas that are over-represented in our sample. Thus, although our study confirms the picture of Sweden as a frontrunner in political gender equality, there are reasons to pay close attention to the potential impact of the conservative trends—with increased focus on traditional family values—that sweep over Europe. As radical right-wing populism gains importance in European politics (Swedish politics included), it is likely that there will be less of a consensus on progressive gender equality policies. In the long run, such an increased polarization over policy may also challenge women's role as political actors.

Table A9.1 Factor Analysis of General Evaluation Questions for Sweden

Component matrix

	Component	
	1	2
Q1 Member of Parliament	.740	.352
Q2 Cabinet Minister	.760	.345
Q3 Party Leader	.671	.438
Q17 Use Preference Vote	−.780	−.130
Q17b Vote Party List	−.717	.175
Q18 Win Preference Votes	.140	.836
Q18b Win Votes for Party	.118	.828
Variance explained:	48.51%	17.19%

Extraction method: Principal component analysis.
Rotation: Varimax.

10

Chile's Shift to the Left and
the Rise of Women

Alejandra Ramm, José Manuel Gaete, and Milena Morales Bonich

MACRO-CONTEXT FACTORS: CHILE AND OTHER CASES

LOW ← Expectation of Strength of Gender Bias → HIGH

	Parliamentary	OR			Presidential
Executive Institutions	Alberta CA				Chile
	Quebec CA				California US
	England				Texas US
	Israel				Costa Rica
	Sweden				Uruguay

	Party focused ← - - - - - - - - - - - - - - → Candidate focused				
Electoral Institutions	Israel	Uruguay	Chile	Alberta CA	California US
	Costa Rica	Sweden		Quebec CA	Texas US
				England	

	More Social Welfare ← - - - - - - - - - - - → Less Social Welfare				
Policy Agenda Emphasis	Sweden	Alberta CA	Uruguay	England	California US
	Costa Rica	Quebec CA	Israel	Chile	Texas US
	Less Defense ← - - - - - - - - - - - - - - → **More Defense**				
	Costa Rica	Alberta CA	Sweden	England	Israel
	Uruguay	Quebec CA	Chile	California US	Texas US

	Greatest ← - → Least				
Incorporation of Women in Government	Sweden	Chile	Alberta CA	Uruguay	Texas US
	Costa Rica	England	Quebec CA	California US	Israel

Introduction

This chapter presents findings about Chilean young adults' attitudes about gender and political leadership based on an experiment conducted with 811 students from September to November of 2018. Analysis of the political attitudes of Chilean university students is confounded by sociological and political factors unique to contemporary Chile. Pinochet's right-wing military dictatorship (1973–1989) encouraged neoliberalization of the educational system, through

Alejandra Ramm, José Manuel Gaete, and Milena Morales Bonich, *Chile's Shift to the Left and the Rise of Women*
In: *The Image of Gender and Political Leadership.* Edited by: Michelle M. Taylor-Robinson and Nehemia Geva,
Oxford University Press. © Oxford University Press 2023. DOI: 10.1093/oso/9780197642726.003.0010

expanding private universities, but also endorsed neoconservatism, reinforcing conventional gender roles. In fact, the first article of Pinochet's 1980 Constitution establishes "the family," that is, patriarchal and heterosexual, as the fundamental nucleus of society. Only in 2011, and thanks to student mobilizations, post-authoritarian governments started to challenge neoliberalism and later gender inequality in education (Simbüerger and Neary 2015). From May to July 2018, there were massive student protests across the country, led by young feminists who demanded an end to "sexist education" (Zerán 2018; De Fina Gonzalez and Figueroa Vidal 2019). Afterward some of these young women were elected to congress. Thus, in today's Chile students are at the forefront of educational reform and attitudinal change of conventional gender roles.

Women's Long Struggle to Enter Politics

Women's efforts to become incorporated into Chilean politics began in a context of strong masculine domination. Political emancipation of women began with their struggle to obtain the right to attend university, which was achieved in 1877 (Landaeta Sepúlveda 2019). In the early twentieth century, middle-class and working-class women became politically active, demanding better working conditions, social protection, and the right to vote, which they obtained in 1949. Nonetheless, it should be noted that the female vote was supported by conservative parties, because women were expected to be more conservative, which has frequently been borne out in women's votes for right-wing political parties (Power 2002). Women gaining the right to vote did not eliminate male dominance of the political system, as men still controlled political parties, parliamentary seats, and executive positions.

A general hostility toward the struggle for women's rights in Chile is rooted in deep-seated beliefs that assimilate womanhood to motherhood and normative ideals about "the family," which permeate politics and social policies (Ramm 2020a). For example, Thomas found that both supporters and opponents of Pinochet's Dictatorship "consistently referenced similar beliefs about the importance of family, familial identities, and the relationship of the family to the state" (2011: 2). More recently, Thomas analyzed twenty-four years of post-dictatorship government by center-left coalitions, concluding that persistence of inequities in Chile, with regard to feminism and women's rights, "reflects the role played by heteropatriarchal norms, particularly an idealized vision of the family" (2018: 117).

The return to democratic rule in 1990, included few women in government despite women's leading role in pressuring for regime change (Baldez 2002). Unexpectedly, in 2006, Chile became the third Latin American country to elect

CHILE'S RISE OF WOMEN 207

a woman president, Michelle Bachelet (2006–2010 and 2014–2018). Bachelet's second term in office ended six months before our study began. Bachelet, an agnostic and divorced mother of three children, of the Socialist Party, had been minister of health and then defense for President Ricardo Lagos (2000–2006), who was also from the Socialist Party within the center-left *Concertación* coalition. Bachelet was trained as a physician and lived in exile in East Germany, after being tortured and her father—an air force general—assassinated by the dictatorship. As president she pursued several pro-woman policies, such as the creation of the Ministry of Women and Gender Equity, housing subsidies for single mothers, expanded preschool programs for poor families, a gender quota law, and abortion rights (under limited circumstances) (Waylen 2016; Reyes-Housholder 2018; Thomas 2018; Ramm 2020b). Between her two terms (2010–2013) Bachelet served as director of UN-Women, and Chile was led by the first post-dictatorship president from a right-wing coalition, Sebastian Piñera. Piñera was then elected for a second term (2018–2022), with the support of a similar right-wing coalition (*Chile Vamos*).

Even though Chile is one of the few countries to have elected a woman president, women's representation in national government has been steadily low. The cabinet of the first administration after the return to democracy (Aylwin 1990–1994, *Concertación*) included only one woman. The Frei administration (1994–2000, *Concertación*) included three women. In the administration of President Lagos (2000–2006, *Concertación*) women made up 25 percent of the people who over time held cabinet posts. During Bachelet's first administration her initial cabinet fulfilled her campaign promise to establish a parity cabinet, and over time women made up 46 percent of total people holding cabinet posts (González-Bustamante and Olivares 2016).

In Piñera's first administration, 26 percent of cabinet posts were held by women. Bachelet's second term did not have a parity cabinet, although 37 percent of cabinet posts were held by women. In Piñera's second term, his initial cabinet included seven (29 percent) women. Thus, there is no clear trend showing a steady increase in women holding cabinet posts. In addition, women entered the cabinet in stereotypically feminine policy domains, such as education, health, women's issues (ECLAC 2017), reflecting the transfer of gender roles within society to government. However, over time women have held more diverse posts, including defense, energy, foreign relations, and transportation. The appointments in 2006, and again in 2015, of a woman chief of staff (*Secretaria General de la Presidencia*, SEGPRES) were milestones for women's inclusion in leadership roles.

Concertación cabinets were dominated by *technopols*, people with technical *and* political background, who typically were male economists (Joignant 2011). In contrast, most of Piñera's ministers were from the private sector, with "technocratic" but little to no political experience (Avendaño and Dávila 2018: 103–4). Bachelet, in her first presidential campaign, criticized post-dictatorial politicians (mostly male) for being authoritarian, exclusionary, and technocratic. By contrast, she appealed to her maternal qualities, presenting herself as more humane, caring, and inclusive (Christie 2016). Nonetheless, some women politicians presented themselves as "technocratic caretakers" emphasizing their policy credentials, but also allowing them "to draw on experiences that emerge from the gendered division of labor" (Franceschet et al. 2015: 24). In other words, technocratic discourses do not necessarily challenge conventional gender roles (Montecinos 2001).

It is notable that public opinion polls in 2018 showed the highest approval ratings for cabinet members to be those for women in the women and gender equity post (66 percent) and transportation and telecommunication (65 percent), while the lowest ratings were for male ministers of interior and public security (43 percent), justice (42 percent), and labor (42 percent) (CADEM 2018). Furthermore, cabinet restructurings during data collection for this study included the transfer of the woman minister of environment to education to replace a man removed from office for mismanagement. Press coverage of this cabinet change increased the public visibility of the new female appointee.

The percentage of women in the congress remains below the regional average. In the first democratic elections, only 5 percent of seats in the lower chamber and 6 percent in the senate were held by women. In the congress that took office in 2014, 16 percent of seats were held by women, compared to 26 percent in the Latin American region (Reyes-Housholder 2018). Elections held on November 19, 2017, for the 2018 term, included a gender quota for the first time, requiring parties to nominate at least 40 percent women candidates.[1] Parties nominated the required numbers of women, but gave less funding to female candidates and more women than men candidates received no funding at all. Women won only 23 percent of seats as the quota paired with open-list elections did not directly apportion seats or financial support from parties (UNDP 2018).

Despite low representation, in January 2018 women deputies from the left and center formed the Julieta Kirkwood Feminist Caucus, with a primary aim to create a Committee of Women's Affairs and Gender Equity.[2] In June 2018 the permanent committee was created "to serve as a policy analysis center addressing discrimination and violence affecting women and sexual diversity; as well as a

---

[1] Other election rule changes implemented in 2017 are outlined below.

[2] One right-wing female deputy also joined this Caucus, but in doing so she challenged her own political party and coalition (*Chile Vamos*).

CHILE'S RISE OF WOMEN   209

place where specific measures for correcting human rights infringements can be adopted" (Chilean Chamber of Deputies 2018). So far, all committee members have been women. Against this backdrop, it is truly noteworthy that gender parity was achieved in the Constituent Assembly, elected in 2021.

In August 2018, just a few weeks before this study began, debate on abortion resurfaced in response to a bill proposed by deputies from leftist parties that would legalize free abortion through the fourteenth week of pregnancy and expand abortion access. However, later that year the Constitutional Court further facilitated claiming institutional conscientious objection for private health facilities, which highlights how contentious abortion is for Chilean society. The topic of gender again gained attention in September 2018 when, after five years of discussion, the Senate approved the Law of Gender Identity allowing persons over fourteen years of age to change their gender in the Civil Registry. Opposition from a woman senator and leader of the Independent Democratic Union Party (UDI) provoked policy differences between the ultra-conservative right and the center-right of the governing coalition. Approval of the law was the most important news of the week (33 percent) according to public opinion polls (CADEM 2018).

In recent years, the education level of women has surpassed men (10.03 years for women, 10.01 for men, with 0.8 percent of both women and men enrolled in masters and doctoral programs, and 12.8 percent women, compared to 11.9 percent men enrolled in professional programs [2017 census]). Yet a sizeable gender gap in employment remained in 2018 with 70.6 percent of men versus 49.1 percent of women employed, albeit the smallest gender gap since 2010. Women remain under-represented in management positions, particularly in the largest firms. In 2015, women held 28.4 percent of general management positions, though only 12.8 percent in the largest firms, and 20.3 percent in medium-sized firms. Women are also paid less than men.[3] The most recent data, from 2015, showed women with below upper secondary education, earn on average 78 percent of what men earn; women with post-secondary (non-tertiary) education earn 73 percent; and those with a tertiary education 65 percent, which is the largest pay gap in the OECD.[4]

---

[3] Chilean National Statistics Institute (INE), "Evolución de la tasa de participación en la fuerza laboral y brecha por sexo según año" and "Distribución porcentual y brecha entre las gerencias generales, por sexo y por año (2007, 2009, 2013, 2015)"; Enfoque Estadístico: Género y Empleo, INE, May 2017.

[4] OECD. 2018. "Education at a Glance 2018: OECD Indicators" OECD Publishing, Paris http://dx.doi.org/10.1787/eag-2018-en (p. 100); "Chile has highest gender pay gap in OECD: fingers point at education system," Frances Jenner, *Chile Herald* September 12, 2018 https://chileherald.com/gender-pay-gap-chile-oecd/1433/ (accessed May 24, 2020).

Institutions and Policy Agenda of the Main Coalitions

Prior to 1973, Chile was Latin America's oldest democracy. Nevertheless, the military staged a harsh coup on September 11, 1973, and General Augusto Pinochet led a military dictatorship until 1989. A constitution was approved in 1980 by a plebiscite of questioned legitimacy, which laid the foundations for the political, economic, and social institutions of the current democratic system. The military regime developed with the support of social and economic conservatives on the political right, and of business elites that stood to profit from privatization and economic deregulation (Nogueira 2008: 327). These groups could be characterized as strongly free market, right leaning and religious, adhering to conservative Catholicism (e.g., Opus Dei and Legionarios de Cristo) (Thumala Olave 2007; Undurraga 2014). Chile has been described as an "incomplete democracy" due to the authoritarian enclaves inherited from the dictatorship that have endured, regardless of reforms to the 1980 constitution (Garretón and Garretón 2010: 1).

Despite these authoritarian legacies, Chile shows consistent Polity scores of 10 since 2006 (systemicpeace.org), and scores of 1 from Freedom House for political rights and civil liberties since 2003 (freedomhouse.org).[5] However, ongoing legacies of the dictatorship and perceived inadequate responses by post-authoritarian governments help to explain the student protests that began in 2006. In 2018, when this experiment was conducted, student protests were still going on, that year with a focus on ending sexist education. Similarly, Chile is facing a "representation crisis" wherein many people "perceive themselves to have little influence in decision making, feel unrepresented by politicians, and have very low levels of confidence in institutions" (de Tezanos-Pinto et al. 2016: 5).

Chile has a presidential democracy with a unitary government and very strong presidency (Siavelis 2000; Mardones 2007). The Chamber of Deputies and Senate are elected by open-lists presented by coalitions or individual parties, with votes cast for an individual candidate on the voter's preferred list. Until 2017, the electoral system was a legacy of the Pinochet regime (Valenzuela 1992). Districts sent two representatives to each chamber, and a coalition had to receive at least 67 percent of the vote to gain both seats, which advantaged the conservative coalition. The 2015 electoral reform retained open-lists but increased the number of seats in the lower chamber, decreased the number of districts from sixty to twenty-eight, and increased district magnitude (range 3–8, average 5.5), making it possible for more parties to win seats (Gamboa and Morales 2016).[6]

---

[5] The civil liberties dimension score was lowered to 2 in the 2020 Freedom House report.
[6] Similar changes were made to the Senate.

As explained above, the new election law also included a 40 percent gender quota. The change in electoral rules happened during a time when Chileans "were tired of infrequent replacement of representatives and open to supporting new candidates" (Reyes-Housholder 2018: 4). People began seeing more candidates with women's faces in a country historically over-represented by men. The outcome of the 2017 election was a more diverse congress with twenty parties (many within the three largest coalitions) winning seats, including expansion of the left-wing *Frente Amplio* coalition to 13 percent of seats, compared to the two largest coalitions winning 96.7 percent of the seats in the previous term (Toro Maureira and Valenzuela Beltrán 2018). However, seats won by women only increased to 23 percent in both chambers (UNDP 2018).

Yet there were still two main coalitions, which serve as the Coalition Label and Platform treatments in our experiment. These coalitions are *Chile Vamos* (right leaning), led by the victorious presidential candidate, Sebastián Piñera, and *Nueva Mayoría* (center-left), which built on the *Concertación* coalition that had won all but two terms since the restoration of democracy.

The *Chile Vamos* policy agenda was developed in agreement with the coalition's parties: Renovación Nacional [RN], Unión Demócrata Independiente [UDI], and Evopoli. It covers, in order of descending priority: public safety, pensions and the elderly, dignified quality healthcare, quality education, economic growth and employment, childhood, infrastructure, protecting the middle class, urban transportation, life quality, social policy, inclusion, animal protection, agriculture, the Araucanía Plan, and sports.

On May 23, 2018 (three months before we began our study), the Piñera government released its "Women's Agenda" to "achieve full equality of rights, duties and recognition of equal dignity for all men and women" (https://www.gob.cl/noticias/agenda-mujer-gobierno-presento-12-medidas-para-promover-la-equi dad-de-genero/) with initiatives about: violence, abuse, and nondiscrimination; maternity; marriage; employment; and health. The agenda's focus on protecting women in situations of violence, abuse, and discrimination matches international social and cultural perspectives denouncing those forms of violence. The agenda also focuses on protection of mothers and unborn children, which is a component of maternity that historically and still holds a central place in public policies for women in Chile. Employment is not emphasized, except to work to improve conditions that may help solve employment problems in the future and encourage " 'modern' women . . . to be both mothers and workers" (Ramm 2020a: 30). Except for support for assisted reproduction therapies, no sexual or reproductive right is included, but safeguarding the institution of matrimony is included. This agenda indicates a conservative turn in the second Piñera government compared to his first administration (Godoy and Raposo 2020), also signaled by appointment of a conservative woman from the UDI to head the Ministry of Women and Gender Equity.

Implementation of the Study

The Chile experiment used a 2×2×2 factorial design with Candidate Gender, Coalition Platform, and Coalition Label as the three factors presented in a relatively long candidate speech for each of the two largest coalitions. Coalitions have long been the major actors in Chilean politics, and these are pre-electoral coalitions composed of relatively stable groups of independent parties. Each speech discussed six policy areas developed from campaign materials of each coalition's presidential candidate from the 2017 election[7] (*Programa de Gobierno 2018–2022 Construyamos Tiempos Mejores Para Chile, Sebastián Piñera Echeñique; Programa de Gobierno Alejandro Guillier Alvarez, Nuestras Ideas Para Chile*). (See Chapter 2 for detailed explanation of the experiment design and implementation.) Beyond the use of a coalition, rather than a party, all aspects of the treatment were the same in Chile as in the other cases.

We conducted the experiment in Santiago and Valparaíso from September to early November of 2018 with 811 young adults from eleven institutions of higher education. Two research teams, each comprised of a male and a female senior or graduate student, implemented the study. The study took place in classrooms during normal class meetings with classes on topics such as engineering, nursing, photography, sociology, teaching. Table 10.1 describes the participants.

General Evaluations of Candidates: What Is the Impact of Candidate Gender and Coalition?

Each participant scored the suitability of one candidate with a specific gender (indicated by name and pronoun) and coalition (either stated or implied). Participants did not directly compare their candidate to another. For this reason, we avoid using the terms "preferable" or "preferred" as they suggest the same participant making a direct comparison. Instead, we present which candidates scored higher or lower when comparing average candidate evaluations across treatment conditions. The notation, H5 through H11, refers to hypotheses and statistical methods outlined in Chapters 1 and 2.

To assess young adults' views of women as political leaders we analyze their answers to six general questions: How effective would this candidate be as a

---

[7] The first round of the election was held on November 19, 2017, and the run-off on December 17.

CHILE'S RISE OF WOMEN 213

Table 10.1 Description of Participants in Chile

	Overall	Male only	Female only
Number of participants	811	376	415
Percent of participants	100	47.5	52.5
Average age	21.5	21.4	21.7
Left (1) to Right (10) self-placement	3.91	4.04	3.77
Preferred coalition (%):			
Governing (Chile Vamos)	8.5	9.6	7.6
Largest opposition (Nueva Mayoria)	3.0	2.7	3.3
Frente Amplio	28.3	25.1	31.5
Other or no preference stated	60.3	62.6	57.7
Total	100	100	100
Parents' education* (% of participants):			
Fathers w/high level	36.3	34.6	39.0
Mothers w/high level	28.9	27.7	30.1
Fathers w/low level	33.4	30.9	35.7
Mothers w/low level	37.9	37.5	38.6
Parents' occupation (% of participants):			
Fathers w/high status job	53.3	53.3	53.6
Mothers w/high status job	37.3	37.8	36.5
Housewives, as % of participants	16.0	14.8	17.6
Housewives, as the actual number	120	51	69

* Note: Education levels of participants' parents are divided into "high" (complete university or more) and "low" (complete secondary or less), and the remaining percentage (not shown) is defined as "intermediate" or "don't know."

(1) *Deputy* in the Congress,[8] (2) Cabinet *Minister*,[8] would you (3) *Vote for this Candidate*,[9] (4) *Vote for this Coalition*,[9] do you think this Candidate would be good at (5) *Attracting Votes*,[10] and (6) *Winning Votes for their Party*?[10] Factor analysis of these questions is presented in the Chapter Appendix.

[8] Scored from 1 (excellent) to 6 (very bad). Scores have been inverted so that high scores are positive.

[9] Answered 1 (yes), 2 (no). Note that for these questions a low score is positive.

[10] Scored from 1 (very good) to 5 (very bad). Scores have been inverted so that high scores are positive.

To test the expectation based on the literature of role congruity that men will be more favorably evaluated than women on "general" evaluation questions (H8), we conduct 2×2×2 between groups ANOVAs with Candidate Gender, Coalition Platform, and Coalition Label as factors. Candidate Gender has a significant main effect only for effectiveness as a *Deputy* (the post the candidate was running for), and contrary to the prediction that men would be favored, women candidates are scored higher (M=3.358) than men (M=3.207) [F(1,753)=4.340, p=.038].[11] Label is also significant (p=.044), with higher scores when the speech does not contain the coalition name. The three-way interaction is significant (p= .006) indicating that the highest scores are for a woman candidate with the *Chile Vamos* platform, without the coalition name on the speech. When the coalition name is on the speech, the man and woman candidates are not significantly different (Figure 10.1—top). The effect size of the interaction (η_p^2=.010) is larger than the effect of Candidate Gender (.006) or Label (.005).

Candidate Gender was significant for one, whereas Coalition Platform or Coalition Label were significant for five of the six general questions, indicating that participants reacted to the treatments. For *Minister*, the main effect of Platform is highly significant (p=.002) with higher scores for *Nueva Mayoría* candidates. Candidate Gender×Platform is also highly significant (p=.008) (Figure 10.1—bottom), showing that scores of the woman candidate are not significantly different regardless of her Platform, but the man is scored lower when his platform is *Chile Vamos*. The effect size of Platform (η_p^2=.014) is larger than the effect of the interaction (η_p^2=.010). Platform is also highly significant for *Vote for the Candidate* (p=.004) and *Vote for the Coalition* (p=.000), with more favorable scores for *Nueva Mayoría*. Label as well has a highly significant main effect for *Vote for the Candidate* (p=.009), and for *Candidate Attract Votes* (p=.003), with better scores when the speech does not state the coalition name. For *Candidate Attract Votes* the three-way interaction is significant (p=.042) (Figure 10.1—middle), indicating that men and women candidates differed when the speech is not labeled. Given Chilean's lack of confidence in established parties where most established politicians are men, and open-list elections where people vote for a specific candidate, it is noteworthy that the man candidate, but not the woman, benefits from the lack of a label on the coalition that governed for most years since the return of democracy (*Nueva Mayoria*). Still, the effect of Label (η_p^2=.011) is larger than the effect of the interaction (η_p^2=.005).

Typically, Candidate Gender is not, while coalition is a strong component of leadership templates. Consistent with the frustration in Chile with the major

---

[11] For the other general questions Candidate Gender is not significant (p-values range from .126 for *Minister* to .727 for *Win Votes for their Party*).

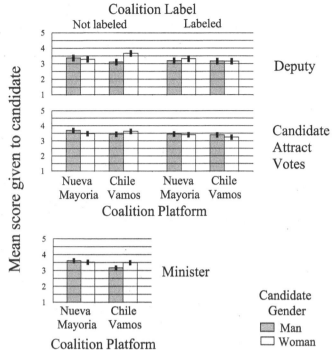

Figure 10.1 Effects of Candidate Gender and Coalition in general evaluations of the candidate
2×2×2 ANOVA (Candidate Gender, Coalition Platform, Coalition Label) 95 percent confidence intervals included.

coalitions—a frustration that is particularly relevant among young people—candidate evaluations are more favorable when the speech does not state a coalition name. Given the left-leaning preferences of most study participants, it makes sense that scores are higher for the center-left coalition (*Nueva Mayoría*). This analysis does not indicate that men are evaluated more favorably than women candidates in general evaluation questions (H8). Instead, women are viewed as capable in government posts and ability to win votes.

H9 also builds on role congruity literature, with the expectation that traditional leadership templates (that leaders are men) will be more common for higher posts. To test H9, first we look at the difference in the mean scores of the man and woman candidates for *Deputy* and for *Minister*. For both posts, scores for the woman candidate are higher. Second, we conducted a repeated measures ANOVA with Government Post (*Deputy* and *Minister*) and Candidate Gender as factors. The posts are viewed as different [F(1,698)=25.259, p=.000] with more favorable evaluations for *Minister* (M=3.444) than *Deputy* (M=3.264). However, the interaction Government Post×Candidate Gender is not significant (p=.728). Neither test indicates that women are only viewed as leaders in lower-ranking/-prestige posts.

Theory about in-groups predicts that a shared-group identity may influence evaluations. Female participants may view the woman candidate as a leader, while male participants may view just the man candidate as a leader. A shared coalition may be another case where women candidates are evaluated as capable to be leaders.

To explore if there is evidence of a shared sex in-group effect (H5), we conduct 2×2 post hoc ANOVAs for each general question with Candidate Gender and Participant Sex as factors, focusing on if the interaction is significant. The interaction is significant only for *Win Votes for the Party* [F(1,777)=5.803, p=.016] and shows the man candidate receives higher scores from male participants (Figure 10.2—top). Overall, however, these analyses reveal that it is not only female participants that evaluate women candidates as leaders. Nonetheless, with Chile's open-list elections, the higher score from male participants for the man candidate could affect candidate's chances of winning election, and it is consistent with findings in other countries that open-list elections can be challenging for women candidates (Valdini 2013).

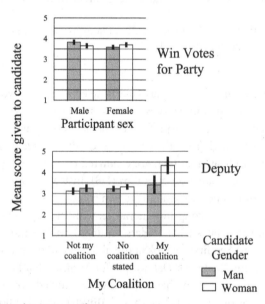

Figure 10.2 Shared in-group effects
Top: 2×2 ANOVA (Candidate Gender, Participant Sex); bottom: 2×3 ANOVA (Candidate Gender, My Coalition) 95 percent confidence intervals included.

To test for a shared coalition in-group effect (H6), we conduct 2×3 ANOVAs with Candidate Gender and My Coalition (yes, no, no preferred coalition stated) as factors, again focusing on the interaction. This analysis also provides another measure of how coalition affects candidate evaluations. Note however that, due to young adults' lack of support for the traditional coalitions (see Table 10.1) plus the great increase in the number of parties that won seats in 2018, only 45 participants (5.5 percent) received a speech from a candidate affiliated with their preferred coalition, 264 got a candidate from a rival coalition, and 502 participants did not report a preferred coalition. Nonetheless, coalition impacts candidate evaluations. For four of six general questions, the main effect of My Coalition is highly significant, with higher scores when the candidate is from the participant's coalition (p-values from .000 to .009), nearly significant (p=.074) for *Candidate Attracts Votes*, not significant (p=.195) only for *Winning Votes for the Party*. As a robustness check, we examined whether My Coalition's effect depends on whether the coalition name is stated on the speech. Findings are substantively the same when we control for Label, and the three-way interaction is not significant.[12] This pattern corresponds to the coalition in-group hypothesis, but more favorable scores for a candidate from your preferred coalition are not gendered—the in-group effect benefits women and men candidates. Regarding the finding above for *Deputy*, that scores are higher for the woman than the man candidate, the main effect of Candidate Gender is again significant in an ANOVA including My Coalition and Label [F(1,749)= 11.357, p=.001], and the interaction Candidate Gender×My Coalition is significant (p=.033) with higher scores for a woman candidate from the participant's preferred coalition (Figure 10.2—bottom).

With respect to general evaluations, these young adults evaluate candidates based on their coalition, but Candidate Gender rarely appears to be a key part of leadership templates. Yet when Candidate Gender is significant, scores are higher for the woman candidate. In general evaluations we find no evidence that women do not fit templates of leaders.

Evaluations across Policy Areas

To investigate whether women candidates are considered to be competent to manage diverse policy areas or only viewed as leaders for stereotypically feminine policies, we examine a pair of policies discussed in the speech, and a pair

---

[12] The main effect of Label is significant (except for *Vote for Coalition*), with more favorable scores when the coalition name is not on the speech. For *Minister*, when the analysis includes Label, Candidate Gender is significant [F(1,705)=4.411, p=.036] with higher scores for the woman candidate.

that were not discussed. Theory about heuristics and gender stereotypes leads to the expectation that Candidate Gender will affect evaluations more for policies not discussed in the speech (H11).

Participants evaluated the candidate's ability to handle twelve policy areas, half of which were discussed in the speech.[13] Here we examine *economics* and *education*, which were discussed in the speech, and *infrastructure* and *women's rights*, which were not discussed.

Education is a stereotypically feminine policy and several women have been education minister (1982–1983, 2002–2003, 2005–2006, 2006–2008, 2008–2010, 2013–2014).[14] Education was the fifth most listed problem facing Chile in the 2018 Latinobarometer survey. The *Chile Vamos* speech focused on state-run low-interest loans to pay for college, giving parents options to choose schools, modernizing technical-professional education, and decreasing the dropout rate. The *Nueva Mayoría* speech focused on public education as the backbone of the education system, free access to technical professional education, expanding access to the free universal higher education benefit, and expanding the apprenticeship program.

Economics is stereotypically masculine, and no woman has been minister of treasury. President Piñera leads a business-oriented coalition, the business community has a marked political position on the right, and Piñera's background is in business. In the 2018 Latinobarometer survey unemployment was the second most listed problem. The *Chile Vamos* speech focused on opening the economy, simplifying regulations, flexible work schedules and telecommuting, improving small-business access to financing, and regional investment. The *Nueva Mayoría* speech focused on growth with good jobs to replace jobs without work contracts, freedom for unions, worker retraining during crisis times, and progressive tax reform.

Infrastructure is stereotyped masculine. Piñera's campaign emphasized new methods to produce energy, developing new water resources for irrigation and human needs, and expanding roads, airports, and ports to create more economic opportunities (*Plan de Gobierno* pp. 58, 63, 67). Guillier and *Nueva Mayoría* discussed infrastructure as it relates to providing education and healthcare, expanding the metro in the largest cities, road construction, and corruption problems in infrastructure contracts (*Plan de Gobierno* pp. 23, 25, 40, 49).

Women's rights were a key issue when the study was conducted, particularly for students who demanded an end to sexism in education. The National Women's Service (SERNAM), established in 1991, was raised to full

---

[13] Scored from 1 (very capable) to 5 (incapable), and scores have been inverted.
[14] Source: https://guide2womenleaders.com/Chile.htm (accessed August 13, 2020).

ministerial rank by President Bachelet in 2016. SERNAM has always been led by a woman.

To explore whether acceptance of women as leaders is limited to stereotypically feminine policies (H10), we conducted repeated measures ANOVAs where Domain is the repeated measure and Candidate Gender is a between-group factor. For policy areas discussed in the speech Domain evaluates *economics* and *education*. The interaction Domain×Candidate Gender is not significant (p=.520), indicating that scores of men and women candidates are not significantly different. The woman and man candidate of the same coalition said the exact same thing about each policy. When information is provided about the policy, gender schema do not appear significant for how candidates are evaluated.[15]

For policy areas not discussed in the speech, Domain evaluates *infrastructure* and *women's rights*. Here the interaction Domain×Candidate Gender is highly significant [F(1,773)=31.910, p=.000]. Most importantly for assessing whether women are viewed as capable outside of stereotypically feminine policies, the man and woman candidates are not significantly different in their scores for ability to manage *infrastructure*. The woman candidate, however, is scored significantly higher for *women's rights* policy (Figure 10.3—top).[16] In sum, women are viewed as capable in policy areas that do not fit gender stereotypes, whether or not policy information was provided in the speech.

For each policy area we performed 2×2×2 ANOVAs with Candidate Gender, Coalition Platform, Coalition Label as factors to investigate the relative effect of coalition and gender on candidate evaluations. For all four policy areas Platform is significant (p=.000 for *economics*, *education*, and *women's rights*, p=.066 for *infrastructure*). Scores are higher for candidates with the *Chile Vamos* platform for *economics* and *infrastructure*, and the *Nueva Mayoría* platform for *education* and *women's rights*, which is consistent with right parties dominating economics issues and left-leaning parties dominating social welfare issues. For *women's rights* the main effect of Candidate Gender is also significant [F(1,782)=25.860, p=.000] with higher scores for the woman candidate (M=2.397) than the man (M= 1.964), and the effect size of Candidate Gender (η_p^2 =.032) is greater than the

---

[15] As a robustness check we conducted the same analysis for the other stereotypically masculine and feminine policy areas discussed in the speech: *security* and *health*. Here the interaction is significant [F(1,791)=4.636, p=.032]. Importantly for acceptance of women outside of stereotypically feminine policies, the man and woman candidates are not scored as significantly different on *security*. They are also not scored as significantly different for *health* policy.

[16] As a robustness check we conducted the same analysis for the other masculine and feminine policy areas not discussed in the speech. For *agriculture* and *childcare* and for *energy* and *childcare* the interaction is significant ([F(1,773)=4.707, p=.030] and [F(1,776)=5.054, p=.025] respectively), but the man and women candidates are not scored as significantly different in the masculine policy area. The woman, however, is scored higher on *childcare* policy, but not significantly higher.

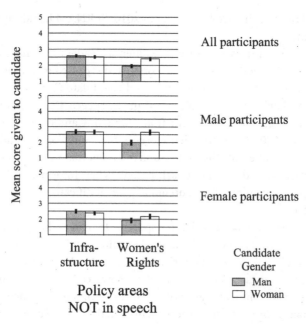

Figure 10.3 Policy areas not in the speech and gender stereotypes
Top: 2×2 repeated measures ANOVA (Domain, Candidate Gender); middle and bottom: 2×2×2 repeated measures ANOVA (Domain, Candidate Gender, Participant Sex) 95 percent confidence intervals included.

effect of Platform (η_p^2=.017), which is expected as women's rights are viewed as women's issues in Chile.[17]

To explore if a shared sex in-group explains when women candidates are evaluated positively (H5), we add Participant Sex to the repeated measure ANOVAs with Domain and Candidate Gender. For *economics* and *education* (discussed in the speech) the three-way interaction is not significant [F(1,770)= .267, p=.606], indicating that women and men candidates are scored as not significantly different for both the masculine and feminine policy areas regardless of whether the participant is male or female. For policy areas not discussed in the speech (*infrastructure* and *women's rights*), the three-way interaction is weakly significant (p=.079) and shows that the gap (higher score for the woman candidate on *women's rights*) is greater for male participants than for female participants (Figure 10.3—middle and bottom). This might reflect frustration by women with the lack of success of women politicians at accomplishing more on

---

[17] In all cases the Platform×Label interaction is not significant, indicating that a coalition is favored regardless of whether its name is on the speech.

CHILE'S RISE OF WOMEN   221

women's rights topics (though that is not something we can access with this experiment); however, it does *not* indicate a shared-sex in-group effect.

To explore if there is a shared coalition in-group effect (H6), we add My Coalition to the repeated measure ANOVAs with Domain and Candidate Gender. For policies discussed in the speech (*economics* and *education*), and for policies not discussed in the speech (*infrastructure* and *women's rights*), the three-way interaction Domain×Candidate Gender×My Coalition is not significant ([F(1,786)=1.056, p=.348] and [F(1,769)=1.252, p=.286] respectively). Evaluations that women are not significantly different from men in masculine policy areas are not dependent on the woman candidate being from the participant's preferred coalition.

In summary, these young adults clearly view women candidates as leaders in both stereotypically masculine and feminine policy areas, even when the masculine policy is not discussed in the speech, which is when we predicated that gender stereotypes would be most likely to influence evaluations. Women candidates are, however, evaluated higher than men for feminine policy areas that are not discussed in the speech, and sometimes even when the policy area was discussed (health policy). Additionally, participants view women as leaders even when there is no shared in-group.

Socialization within the Home Environment

A micro-level factor that may produce variance within a country in how candidates are evaluated is the participant's family experience. In particular, a mother's possession of higher education or a high-status job may make her a role model showing that women can hold public leadership positions.

To examine if there is evidence of such a micro-level influence (H7) we conduct 2×2 post hoc ANOVAs (Candidate Gender, Mother Education) and 2×3 post hoc ANOVAs (Candidate Gender, Mother Job) for the general questions and the four policy areas.[18] We also conduct these analyses adding Participant Sex as a factor.

The Mother Job×Candidate Gender interaction is significant for *Minister* [F(1,657)=4.118, p=.017] and for *Candidate Attract Votes* [F(1,741)=3.164, p=.043]. The three-way interaction (including Participant Sex) is significant for *education* policy [F(1,715)=3.215, p=.041]. Findings, however, are mixed. For *Minister*, participants whose mothers have low-status jobs give higher scores

---

[18] Mother education is coded as low (complete secondary education or less, N=307) or high (complete university or more, N=234). Mothers' jobs are divided into low status (N=349), high status (N=279) (described in Chapter 2), and housewife (N=120).

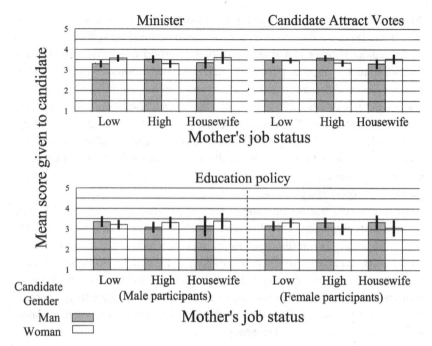

Figure 10.4 Mother job status and candidate evaluations
Top: 2×3 ANOVA (Candidate Gender, Mother's Job); bottom: 2×3×2 ANOVA (Candidate Gender, Mother's Job, Participant Sex) 95 percent confidence intervals included.

to the woman candidate (Figure 10.4—top-left). For *Candidate Attract Votes*, participants whose mothers have high-status jobs give higher scores to the man candidate (Figure 10.4—top-right). For *education* policy, it is only for male participants that a high-status mother appears to fit a role model expectation (Figure 10.4—bottom).

For *women's rights* policy, when Participant Sex is included as a factor, the Candidate Gender×Mother Education interaction [$F(1,509)=4.109$, $p=.043$] indicates that participants (male *and* female) with highly educated mothers give higher scores to the woman candidate (Figure 10.5—top). For *Minister*, and for *Win Votes for the Party*, it is male participants whose mothers have a high level of education who give higher scores to the man candidate (*Minister* [$F(1,457)=6.542$, $p=.011$], *Win Votes for the Party* [$F(1,515)=4.303$, $p=.039$]) (Figure 10.5—middle and bottom).

In Chile it appears that influence of mothers as a role model is complex. Mothers may be the center of family, but maternal level of education or employment status does not follow current theoretical models. For example, Michelle

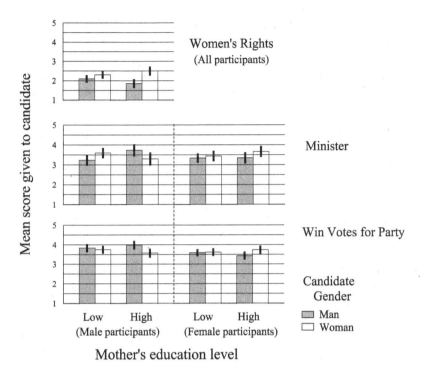

Figure 10.5 Mother education and candidate evaluations
2×2×2 ANOVA (Candidate Gender, Mother's Education, Participant Sex) 95 percent confidence intervals included.

Bachelet received much support from low-income women, and in particular women heads of households, in her 2006 election (Morales Quiroga 2008). Possibly that support for a woman president was transmitted to children. Further research is needed to explore how family, and the maternal figure in particular, influences leadership templates.

Discussion of Study Findings in the Chilean Context

This study shows that mental templates of leadership for urban young adults in Chile include women, across levels of posts, as able to win votes, and in diverse policy areas. However, young adults' carrying women in their mental templates of leaders is only one factor. Coalition, not gender, is most influential for young adults' candidate evaluations in Chile. These findings are somewhat unexpected given the low level of election of women to the congress, and the continuing strength of traditional gender roles in Chile. Entrenched social inequalities and a social welfare system, which perpetuated, rather than diminished, them, was a major topic of public debate in the lead up to the experiment and precipitated massive protests across the country in 2019. These protests led to a political agreement for electing a Constituent Assembly. That women are considered able political leaders was confirmed by those elections. In 2021 Chile became the first country in the world to hold a constitutional convention with gender parity. Furthermore, an indigenous (Mapuche) woman was elected as convention president. Gender parity was achieved thanks to strong lobbying from feminist political scientists in collaboration with congresswomen, which introduced a "best loser" system (Piscopo 2021).

For eight of the twelve years preceding this experiment—the formative years for the political views of the young adult participants in the experiment—Michelle Bachelet was the country's president. President Bachelet, further, appointed more women to cabinet, including more diverse posts. Drawing on the terminology and conclusions of Annesley, Beckwith and Franceschet (2019: Chapter 1), whose research included Chile, inclusion of women in top executive posts in Chile appears to have achieved a quite high "concrete floor." In addition to these top-down changes, there have been bottom-up transformations. The student protests in 2018 were one of the biggest feminism mobilizations in Chile, a year later, during the October 2019 social uprising, the feminist chant "A rapist in your path" was performed by thousands of women in Chile and later, across the world.[19] Thus, Chilean young adults have seen women as leaders both in top executive posts, and as "on the street" leaders. With the persistent "crisis of representation" in Chile (de Tizanos-Pinto et al. 2016: 5), young adults appear to be open to supporting new candidates (Reyes-Housholder 2018: 4), and women, with their still low numbers in the congress, may be beneficiaries of this attitude.

Likewise of relevance for gender politics in Chile, female participants are not clearly aligned with right-wing political leaders, as was the case for almost sixty years after women were allowed to vote, and until Michelle Bachelet's first election. Female participants view women candidates as capable to hold office and able to win votes. In addition, when their evaluations are more favorable for one coalition than the other, they favor the *Nueva Mayoría*.[20] In Chile, another important finding is that urban young adult women who are pursuing higher education have mental templates of leaders that include women, and also include the left-leaning coalition.

---

[19] https://www.theguardian.com/society/2020/feb/03/the-rapist-is-you-chilean-protest-song-chanted-around-the-world-un-iolador-en-tu-camino.

[20] For *Deputy*, female participants give significantly more favorable evaluations to candidates with the *Nueva Mayoría* platform than *Chile Vamos* when the speech is labeled with the coalition name, while for male participants scores favor *Chile Vamos* [F(1,729)=4.029, p=.045].

Yet, there are still challenges faced by women politicians. Women's campaigns are still underfinanced by parties, and men still dominate party leadership. In addition, elections for several posts do not include a gender quota. For example, in 2021 in addition to elections for the constituent assembly, there were elections for regional governor and for mayor. Only three women were elected as regional governors, compared with thirteen men;[21] and only 17 percent of the elected mayors were women.[22] On the whole, it seems that the real barrier in Chile for women being elected is not the voters (at least not young adults), but a political system, traditional political parties in particular, that act as strongholds of male domination: opposing introduction of gender quotas as an in-built feature of the Chilean electoral system.

Table A10.1 Factor Analysis of General Evaluation Questions for Chile

Component matrix

	Component	
	1	2
Q1 Deputy	.704	.246
Q2 Cabinet Minister	.782	.239
Q17 Vote for Candidate	−.813	−.062
Q17b Vote for Coalition	−.690	.088
Q18 Attract Votes	.146	.860
Q18b Win Votes for Party	.056	.886
Variance explained:	42.83%	22.55%

Extraction method: Principal component analysis.
Rotation: Varimax with Kaiser Normalization.

[21] https://www.pauta.cl/politica/resultados-eleccion-2021-gobernadores-regionales.
[22] https://www.emol.com/noticias/Nacional/2021/05/19/1021290/alcaldesas-concejalas-electas-sin-paridad.html.

PART III
CROSS-NATIONAL FINDINGS AND CONCLUSIONS

11

Meta-Analysis Assessment of Candidate Gender as an Attribute of Young Adult Leadership Templates

Michelle M. Taylor-Robinson and Nehemia Geva

A multi-country experiment enables us to empirically test predictions based on diverse literatures that underpin key assumptions about how people assess women's competence to govern. As we show below, the experiment worked as planned, in the sense that it always provided robust statistically valid quantitative contrasts between Party and Gender effect sizes. The results, however, call into question many assumptions about gender stereotypes, role congruity, and the importance of extensive representation of women in government for acceptance of women as leaders. The central conclusion is that Party, not Gender, is the primary driver of young adults' attitudes toward political candidates. Across diverse policy areas and over different levels of post, in fact, women are viewed as leaders.

In this chapter we assess the eleven hypotheses developed from various literatures presented in Chapter 1, holistically with all ten cases. We begin with hypotheses 1–4 that examine context factors that vary across cases, and which were therefore not testable earlier in the volume. We also examine findings for hypotheses 5–11 that were explored in each case. Here we examine those hypotheses with an eye toward drawing more extensive assessments of the literature's predictions.

Context Factors That Vary *across* Cases

The literature points to several explanatory factors that vary across countries that are thought to influence the differing extent of women in government. As outlined in Chapter 1, from these literatures we extrapolated four general expectations about case-level context that would make candidate gender a more or less important attribute in leadership templates. To test hypotheses 1–4, we analyze participant responses to several general questions, assessing their candidate in

Michelle M. Taylor-Robinson and Nehemia Geva, *Meta-Analysis Assessment of Candidate Gender as an Attribute of Young Adult Leadership Templates* In: *The Image of Gender and Political Leadership.* Edited by: Michelle M. Taylor-Robinson and Nehemia Geva, Oxford University Press. © Oxford University Press 2023. DOI: 10.1093/oso/9780197642726.003.0011

230 MICHELLE M. TAYLOR-ROBINSON AND NEHEMIA GEVA

relation to different posts and electability (4–7 questions depending on country electoral rules and government type). Participants also evaluated the candidate's ability in twelve total policy areas, which included policy areas stereotyped as masculine, feminine or neutral, where six policy areas were and six were not discussed in the speech (see Figure 2.1, Chapter 2). To simplify interpretations of each case, country chapter authors selected one feminine and one masculine policy area both in and not in the speech that they as country experts considered of greatest relevance to country context for in-depth analysis and interpretation. These 4–7 general + 4 policy area questions generated, for each case 8–11 two-way contrasts each for Candidate Gender (man vs. woman candidate), Party Platform (governing vs. major opposition party), and Party Label (party name stated vs. not stated on the speech). Across our ten cases, that produces eighty-nine comparisons each for Candidate Gender, Party Platform, and Party Label.

In Chapters 3–10, results for each case are presented typically by giving the mean for each treatment factor level (e.g., man candidate and woman candidate for the Candidate Gender treatment), along with the probability that the two levels are statistically different (p-value), sometimes also with the partial eta squared (η_p^2) to utilize the effect size to assess the relative impact of multiple significant factors. Here in Table 11.1 we present the η_p^2 value from the ANOVAs as the more reliable and transportable measure of the differential Effect Size across factors, that is, the effect's importance as opposed to its statistical significance, as the latter is a necessary but insufficient prerequisite of real-world impact. We present the η_p^2 value in Table 11.1 only for effects that are statistically significant and otherwise enter "ns" into the cell. The relative magnitude of the η_p^2 values can be interpreted as our best gauge of the relative importance of effects within and across cases.

Role congruity theory predicts that mental templates of who "fits" the image to do a job are influenced by the type of people seen doing the job. Politics has always been a male domain, and throughout history almost all leaders have been men. With this history, plus predominant stereotypes about feminine traits, women are not expected to "have what it takes for important leadership roles" (Koenig et al. 2011: 616). But the literature also indicates that roles can change, especially with recent experience with women as leaders (Koenig et al. 2011). Based on this literature H1 is that *leadership templates will be less traditional (leaders are men) as representation of women in government increases.*

We expected greatest acceptance of women candidates in the Sweden and Costa Rica cases. Sweden, since the 1970s, has been a world leader in incorporation of women into parliament, cabinet, and local governments, and has a norm of parity cabinets. Costa Rica's extensive inclusion of women in government is more recent, but since the late 1990s women have consistently held 30–40 percent of seats in the legislature and cabinet, and the country's first woman

Table 11.1 Comparison of Effect Size of Candidate Gender and Party on Candidate Evaluations

Presidential systems	Texas, US (1)*			California, US (1)			Chile (3)			Uruguay (4)			Costa Rica (5)		
	Gender	Party Platform	Party Label	Gender	Party Platform	Party Label	Gender	Party Platform	Party Label	Gender	Party Platform	Party Label	Gender	Party Platform	Party Label
Deputy	ns	ns	.004	ns	.174	ns	.006W	ns	.005	.006W	ns	ns	ns	.010	.011
Cabinet Minister	ns	ns	.005	ns	.157	ns	ns	.014	ns	.013W	ns	ns	.005W	ns	.012
Vote for Candidate	ns	ns	ns	ns	.240	ns	ns	.010	.009	ns	ns	.005	.011W	.008	.012
Vote for List	–	–	–	–	–	–	ns	.025	ns	–	–	–	–	–	–
Candidate Win Votes	ns	ns	.006	ns	.067	ns	ns	ns	.011	ns	ns	ns	ns	.016	.005
Win Votes for List	–	–	–	–	–	–	ns	ns	.009	–	–	–	–	–	–
MASC1	.005M	.028	ns	ns	ns	ns	ns	.026	ns	ns	ns	ns	ns	ns	.010
MASC2	.003M	.008	ns	ns	.022	ns	ns	.004	ns	ns	.013	ns	ns	.017	ns
FEM1	ns	.005	ns	ns	.118	ns	ns	.075	ns	ns	.027	ns	ns	ns	.011
FEM2	.056W	.019	ns	.024W	.053	ns	.032W	.017	ns	ns	.033	ns	.007W	.009	ns

(*continued*)

Table 11.1 Continued

Parliamentary systems	Alberta, CA (2)			Quebec, CA (2)			England (2)			Sweden (4)			Israel (5)		
	Gender	Party Platform	Party Label	Gender	Party Platform	Party Label	Gender	Party Platform	Party Label	Gender	Party Platform	Party Label	Gender	Party Platform	Party Label
MP	ns	.014	ns	ns	.048	ns	ns	.030	ns	ns	.010	ns	.016M	ns	ns
Cabinet Minister	.013W	ns	ns	.011M	.043	ns	ns	.010	ns	ns	ns	ns	.024M	ns	ns
Party Leader	.017W	ns	ns	ns	.050	ns	ns	.018	ns	ns	ns	ns	.018M	.017	ns
Vote for Candidate	ns	.081	ns	ns	.136	ns	ns	.032	.009	ns	.008	ns	.009M	.013	ns
Vote for List	–	–	–	–	–	–	–	–	–	ns	.031	ns	–	–	–
Candidate Win Votes	ns	ns	ns	ns	ns	ns	ns	.009	ns	ns	ns	ns	ns	ns	ns
Win Votes for List	–	–	–	–	–	–	–	–	–	ns	ns	ns	–	–	–
MASC1	ns	.060	ns	ns	.017	ns	ns	.027	ns	ns	ns	.009	.082M	.012	ns
MASC2	ns	ns	ns	ns	ns	ns	ns	.051	ns	ns	ns	ns	.034M	ns	ns
FEM1	ns	.092	ns	ns	.084	ns	ns	.056	ns	.006W	.062	ns	.012W	.020	ns
FEM2	.116W	.056	ns	.040W	.025	ns	.030W	.015	ns	.015W	.045	ns	.161W	.029	ns

Notes: Values are Partial Eta Square statistics from 2×2×2 ANOVA (Candidate Gender, Party Platform, Party Label). MASC1 and FEM1 are policies discussed in the candidate's speech; MASC2 and FEM2 were not discussed. "W" indicates more favorable evaluation of the woman candidate, "M" the man candidate. "ns" means factor not statistically significant. Policy areas are those selected for analysis in the country chapter. *Party Leader* is only utilized in the parliamentary systems because party leaders are the contenders for the post of Prime Minister. *Vote for List* and *Win Votes for List* questions were asked only in Chile and Sweden because they use open-list or preferential votes.

*Number in parentheses beside case indicates ranking on personal-partisan vote dimension.

META-ANALYSIS ASSESSMENT OF CANDIDATE GENDER   233

president completed her term two months before we conducted the experiment there. That time-period is when the Costa Rican participants were growing up. In both Sweden and Costa Rica, when Candidate Gender was a significant factor in evaluations, the woman candidate's mean score was more favorable than the man's (as indicated by "W" next to the η_p^2 values in Table 11.1).

In Alberta, Chile, and England our data again showed that women are accepted as leaders—when Candidate Gender was significant, again the women's mean score was more favorable than the man's. These cases have experienced less extensive incorporation of women into government, but in all three cases a woman was president/PM/provincial premier during or right before the experiment. This pattern, that women fit leader templates, continues in Uruguay and California, two cases where women's representation is still quite limited. Plausibly, young adults' leadership templates have been modified by observing women leaders in other professions, countries, or high-profile political roles (e.g., Angela Merkel as Germany's Chancellor [2005–2021]; Michelle Bachelet [2006–2010, 2014–2018], Cristina Fernández [2007–2015], and Dilma Rousseff [2011–2016] simultaneously serving as presidents in Chile, Argentina, and Brazil; Nancy Pelosi as Speaker of the US House [2007–2011, 2019–2022]).[1]

In Israel, Texas, and Quebec we detected a significant main effect for Candidate Gender in evaluations for some questions, with a more favorable evaluation of the man candidate on 6, 2, or 1 questions respectively (as indicated by "M" next to the η_p^2 value in Table 11.1). Israel and Texas are both cases where representation of women in government is notably limited (see Table 1.1 and the country chapters). Those cases might be viewed as fitting traditional role congruity predictions. But in Quebec a woman had recently been provincial premier (Pauline Marois' term ended three years before our experiment) and the Quebec participants, like participants in Alberta, came of age in politics during the time of PM Trudeau's gender parity cabinet. In sum, our findings overall are generally consistent with Hypothesis 1, but the degree of acceptance of women as fitting leader templates is far more advanced in several cases than expected simply based on numbers of women in the national legislature or cabinet.

Preferences for men candidates in Israel and Texas provide support for the expectation of our H2 regarding the national policy agenda: *leadership templates will be less traditional as the government policy agenda focuses more on social welfare policy and less on defense* (see Table 11.1). In Israel, defense and security perpetually dominate the government's agenda and are major concerns for the electorate. Israel, further, is the only case where Candidate Gender frequently has a stronger effect than party. In Texas the man also is evaluated more

---

[1] We thank Zachary Greene for the suggestion that young people's mental templates of leaders may be influenced by seeing women leaders in neighboring countries.

234 MICHELLE M. TAYLOR-ROBINSON AND NEHEMIA GEVA

favorably than the woman candidate though only on stereotypically masculine policies (security, infrastructure). Texas is a US state with an apparent need to preserve a "wild west" mentality where open-carry of guns is legal (Texas has 725,000 privately owned firearms, more than in any other US state [ATF 2019], for hunting and livestock predators but also self-defense), while state-sponsored social welfare programs in Texas are minimal.[2] Additional support for the policy agenda prediction also comes from Canada and Uruguay where defense is of relatively low importance and incorporation of women in government is still relatively low, but government has long played a key role in social welfare provision. In those cases, women do appear to fit our young adults' mental templates of leadership.

The literature also led us to anticipate that institutions influence leadership templates. It has been more common for women to become head of government in parliamentary systems where leaders can be removed by parliament or their party, than in presidential systems where the president serves a fixed term (Jalalzai and Krook 2010). Electoral rules that create incentives to seek a personal vote (versus a party vote) are predicted to disadvantage women, though Valdini (2013) shows that the extent to which personal-vote systems create barriers for women depends on bias in the society. Based on the institutions literature, we expected that: *Across countries leadership templates will be less traditional* (H3) *in parliamentary compared to presidential democracies*, and (H4) *where electoral rules are party-centered instead of candidate-centered.*

To examine our evidence relating to H3, Table 11.1 divides the cases into presidential systems (top panel) and parliamentary systems (bottom panel). We gauge bias against women leaders by the number of ANOVA's in which Candidate Gender has a significant main effect and the mean evaluation of men candidates is more favorable (cells with M) than the mean evaluation of women candidates (cells with W). Comparisons between the two panels do not indicate bias against women is more common in presidential systems, or that more favorable evaluations of women candidates are more common in parliamentary systems.

Cases are also arrayed within each panel of Table 11.1 from strongest personal vote incentive (left) to strongest party vote incentive (right).[3] Overall, regarding H4 there is no clear pattern of greater acceptance of women in party-centered electoral systems than in candidate-centered systems, and findings reflect broad acceptance of women as leaders by participants across seven countries (Israel excepted). This supports Valdini's (2013) conclusion that it is bias in the *society*

---

[2] In 2017 Texas had the highest percentage of residents lacking health insurance across the fifty US states (Quinn 2017; Conway 2019).

[3] See Carey and Shugart (1995) for a systematic means of classifying voting systems.

META-ANALYSIS ASSESSMENT OF CANDIDATE GENDER   235

against women leaders, more so than electoral rules, that obstructs women's inclusion in politics.[4] Opportunities for women in government are still restricted by other factors that are beyond the scope of our study, which we discuss in Chapter 12.

Party Is More Important Than Gender
in Leadership Evaluations

Party (expressed operationally as Party Platform and Party Label) serves as this experiment's baseline control against which we can assess the impact of Candidate Gender. Several aspects of our analysis indicate that party is more important than gender in candidate evaluations. The η_p^2 statistic from ANOVA in Table 11.1 shows that Candidate Gender often does not have a significant main effect on evaluations (the gender main effect is significant for twenty-seven of eighty-nine questions [30.3 percent] across our ten cases). In contrast, Party Platform or Party Label are significant, for sixty-eight of eighty-nine questions (76.4 percent). In addition, where Candidate Gender is significant, the main effect of Party Platform or Party Label is equal to or greater than the effect of Candidate Gender for eleven of the twenty-seven questions, as indicated by the η_p^2 statistic. To paraphrase an adage from US President Bill Clinton's 1992 campaign, "It's the party, stupid!" not gender. Perhaps party selectorates who remain reluctant to nominate and appoint women or to encourage, recruit, and finance women candidates should heed this advice, robustly supported by our results.

We also find that party is important in candidate evaluations when we measure party by whether the candidate and the participant share the same party affiliation. Shared traits are predicted to enable an outsider to be *re*categorized as part of the in-group (Gaertner et al. 1989; Cutler 2002; Holman et al. 2011). We explored two ways that women candidates might become part of the in-group and fit mental templates of leadership, even though political leaders have historically been men: where the participant and the candidate are from the same party (Hypothesis 6), or when they are of the same sex (Hypotheses 5).

Shared gender and shared party in-group effects vary within cases and were presented in the country chapters. Here we assess their effects across all of our cases. This meta-analysis shows that the main effect of My Party is significant

---

[4] Gender quota laws can increase the numbers of women elected, and debate continues about whether increased incorporation of women via quota laws will aid women's acceptance as leaders. Costa Rica, Chile, and Uruguay have gender quota laws, with Costa Rica's quota being both older and more effective. Candidate evaluations by participants in these three cases indicate that women are viewed as leaders, but that is also what we find in countries without quota laws, thus we cannot say if gender quota laws affect leadership templates.

236 MICHELLE M. TAYLOR-ROBINSON AND NEHEMIA GEVA

in sixty-two of sixty-nine post-hoc ANOVAs (89.9 percent) (see Table 11.2),[5] as participants give better evaluations to candidates of the party they prefer. But the My Party×Candidate Gender interaction is rarely significant (six of sixty-nine ANOVAs).[6] This refutes H6 that predicted a party in-group connection would help women to be accepted as leaders. Instead, evaluations of both men and women candidates are more favorable when they are from the participant's party. Figure 11.1 illustrates the effect of same-party in-group for *Deputy* (my party, not my party, no preferred party stated)[7] in the 2×3×10 ANOVA.[8] The interaction Candidate Gender×My Party is not significant: p=.912.

We find little support for the shared sex in-group prediction (H5). The interaction Candidate Gender×Participant Sex is significant for only eight of sixty-nine post-hoc ANOVAs (see Table 11.2), and for three of these it is the male participants who give the woman candidate higher mean scores. Figure 11.2 shows that for ability as a *Deputy* significant interaction of Candidate Gender×Participant Sex is detected for only two of ten cases (Alberta and Israel).[9] In Israel male participants give higher scores to the candidate of their sex, but for female participants the mean evaluations for men and women candidates do not statistically differ. In Alberta, contrary to a same sex in-group effect, male participants give higher scores to the woman candidate. We conclude that this study's finding that young adults view women as leaders is *not* driven only by female participants seeking to incorporate more women into government.[10]

We also conduct 2×2 ANOVAs for each dependent variable in each case with My Sex and My Party as factors. This permits direct comparison of the effect size of participant and candidate being of the same sex with participant and candidate being of the same party (coalition in Chile). For seventy-six of eighty-nine

[5] The number of post hoc ANOVA's is smaller than in Table 11.1 because here the policy areas analysis utilizes repeated measures comparing two policy areas discussed or not discussed in the speech.

[6] For three post-hoc ANOVAs in England, the mean score of the woman candidate is higher when she is from the participant's party, while the mean score of the man candidate is higher when he is from the opposing party.

[7] Theoretically participants coded as both 0 (not my party) or 2 (no preferred party stated) do not share a political affinity with the candidate. We assumed that these two groups will not be that different in that both should lead to lower evaluations than group 1 (candidate from my party). However, if participants coded 2 have no party ID, then they differ from participants coded 0 as they were not faced with a candidate from a party they actively oppose.

[8] Figure 11.1 also shows that in some cases the "rift" between the parties is less extreme than in others (see Costa Rica), which accounts for the significant interaction of My Party×Case (p=.000).

[9] For the 2×2×10 ANOVA graphed in Figure 11.2 the interaction Candidate Gender×Case is significant [F(1,5831)=3.420, p=.000], but the three-way interaction Candidate Gender×Participant Sex×Case is not significant (p=.098).

[10] It is noteworthy that in Israel, the case where Candidate Gender is most often a significant component of the leadership template, for four measures (*MK, Minister, Win Votes, energy* policy), only male participants have a more favorable mean score for men candidates. Female participants in Israel view women as capable leaders, as mean evaluations of men and women candidates are not statistically different (see Chapter 4).

Table 11.2 Summary of Findings for Social Categorization Theory: Shared Sex and Shared Party In-Groups

Presidential systems	Texas, US (1)*			California, US (1)			Chile (3)			Uruguay (4)			Costa Rica (5)		
	Shared sex	Shared party	My party	Shared sex	Shared party	My party	Shared sex	Shared party	My party	Shared sex	Shared party	My party	Shared sex	Shared party	My party
Deputy	no	no	yes	no	no	yes	no	no	yes	no	no	yes	no	no	yes
Cabinet Minister	no	no	yes	no	no	yes	no	no	yes	no	no	yes	no	no	yes
Vote for Candidate	no	no	yes	no	no	yes	no	no	yes	no	no	yes	no	no	yes
Vote for List	–	–	–	–	–	–	no	no	yes	–	–	–	–	–	–
Candidate Win Votes	no	no	yes	no	no	yes	no	no	yes	no	no	no	no	no	yes
Win Votes for List	–	–	–	–	–	–	yesW	no	no	–	–	–	–	–	–
Policies IN speech	no	no	yes	no	no	yes	no	no	yes	no	no	yes	no	no	no
Policies NOT disc	no	no	yes	no	no	yes	yesM	no	no	no	no	yes	no	no	yes

(*continued*)

Table 11.2 Continued

Parliamentary systems	Alberta, CA (2)			Quebec, CA (2)			England (2)			Sweden (4)			Israel (5)		
	Shared sex	Shared party	My party	Shared sex	Shared party	My party	Shared sex	Shared party	My party	Shared sex	Shared party	My party	Shared sex	Shared party	My party
MP	yesM	no	yes	no	no	yes	no	yes	yes	no	no	yes	yesW	no	yes
Cabinet Minister	no	no	yes	no	no	yes	no	yes	yes	no	no	yes	yesW	no	yes
Party Leader	no	no	yes	no	no	yes	no	yes	yes	no	yes	yes	no	no	yes
Vote for Candidate	no	no	yes	no	no	yes	no	no	yes	no	no	yes	no	no	yes
Vote for List	–	–	–	–	–	–	–	–	–	no	no	yes	–	–	–
Candidate Win Votes	yesM	yes	no	no	no	no	no	no	yes	no	yes	yes	yesW	no	yes
Win Votes for List	–	–	–	–	–	–	–	–	–	no	no	no	–	–	–
Policies IN speech	no	no	yes	no	no	yes	no	no	yes	no	no	yes	no	no	yes
Policies NOT disc	no	no	yes	no	no	yes	no	no	yes	no	no	yes	yesW	no	yes

Notes: Results of post-hoc factorial ANOVAs examining candidate × participant shared sex and shared party effects, contrasted with the main effect of My Party measured when participants did or did not receive a candidate of their preferred party. A "yes" or "no" indicates statistical significance presence or absence. "M" or "W" next to "yes" means male (M) or female (F) participants gave highest average score to a woman candidate. Policy areas are results from repeated measures ANOVAs with a masculine and a feminine policy area discussed in the speech, or not discussed in the speech. Number in parentheses beside case indicates rank on personal-partisan vote dimension.

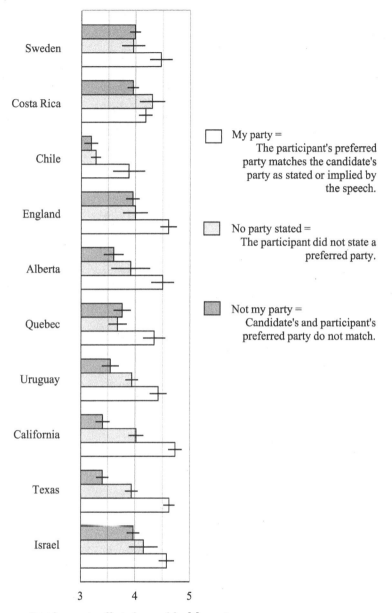

Post-hoc party effect observed for My party based on mean score (1-6) Given to candidate for competence as *Deputy* (the office for which the candidate was running)

Figure 11.1 Party in-group and evaluation of candidates as a Deputy 2×3×10 ANOVA (Candidate Gender, My Party, Case). Cases ordered from greatest to least incorporation of women in government. 95 percent confidence intervals included.

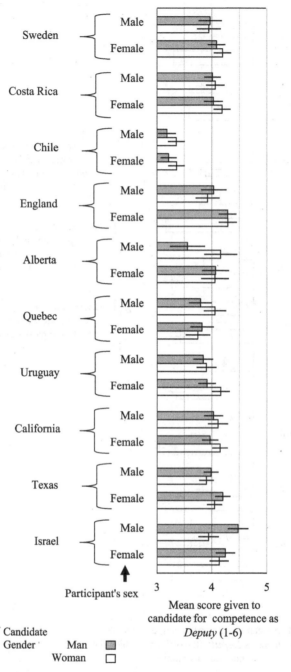

Figure 11.2 Illustration of (lack of) shared sex in-group effect in evaluations of candidates to be a Deputy
2×2×10 ANOVA (Candidate Gender, Participant Sex, Case). Cases ordered from greatest to least incorporation of women into government. 95 percent confidence intervals included.

ANOVAS the effect size of My Party is larger (often much larger) than the effect size of My Sex (bold numbers in Table 11.3).

In sum, this project's findings indicate in multiple ways that party is a major attribute of leadership templates. By comparison, the candidate's gender is of far less importance.

Family background is another individual-level factor that varies within cases that could affect leadership templates. H7 predicted that *participants with a mother who is highly educated or has a high-status job will not exhibit traditional leadership templates.* The high work status/educated mother could serve as a role model of an empowered woman. Family background was examined in the country chapters, but again we want to assess family background effects across all our cases. Post hoc tests with sub-groups of participants based on mother education or job-status indicate that Candidate Gender is not a central component of leadership templates (see Table 11.4). For fifty-six (63 percent) of the eighty-nine total study-wide dependent variables examined (eighty-nine is the sum of general + policy area questions analyzed across the ten cases), there is no significant interaction of mother status with Candidate Gender. Mean evaluations by participants whose families could be expected to foster traditional leadership templates are not statistically different from mean evaluations by participants whose mothers have superior education or job resources: women are accepted as capable leaders across diverse family settings.

However, for thirty-three questions analyzed within specific cases there are significant interactions between Mother Education or Job and Candidate Gender (see Table 11.4). Many fit the mother resources role-model prediction. For example, in Israel participants (male and female) whose mothers have a low level of education gave a more favorable evaluation of the man candidate on six questions. In Alberta, male participants with high resource mothers give more favorable evaluations to women candidates on four questions. But for twelve questions analyzed within specific cases, participants with low-resource mothers gave a more favorable evaluation of the woman candidate, and results for five questions strongly contradicted the mother resources role-model prediction because participants (though sometimes only male participants) with high-resource mothers have a more favourable mean evaluation for the man.

While there are some analyses in each case that indicate a significant effect of mother's resources, as would be expected with the number of analyses conducted, they are rare. The primary finding of the tests of H7 is that participants from diverse family backgrounds score both women and men candidates as capable to govern, win votes, and manage diverse policy topics. Future studies should explore how family socialization experience molds leadership templates, as this analysis only begins to scratch the surface of this topic.

Table 11.3 Comparison of Effect Size for Candidate Evaluations of Getting a Candidate of the Same Sex or Same Party as the Participant

Presidential systems:	Texas, US (1)*			California, US (1)			Chile (3)			Uruguay (4)			Costa Rica (5)		
	My Sex	My Party	Inter-action	My Sex	My Party	Inter-action	My Sex	My Party	Inter-action	My Sex	My Party	Inter-action	My Sex	My Party	Intera-ction
Deputy	.000	.256	ns	.001	.290	ns	.003	.052	ns	.014	.175	ns	.000	.016	ns
Cabinet Minister	.000	.208	ns	.001	.250	ns	.002	.025	ns	.007	.140	ns	.000	.015	ns
Vote for Candidate	.000	.350	ns	.001	.431	ns	.014	.067	.018	.005	.244	ns	.001	.037	ns
Vote for List	–	–	–	–	–	–	.000	.118	ns	–	–	–	–	–	–
Candidate Win Votes	.000	.068	ns	.001	.098	ns	.011	.010	.016	.000	.001	ns	.005	.011	ns
Win Votes for List	–	–	–	–	–	–	.002	.004	.010	–	–	–	–	–	–
Fem (in speech)	.001	.153	ns	.006	.192	ns	.000	.012	ns	.000	.027	ns	.002	.003	ns
Masc (in speech)	.002	.139	ns	.000	.018	ns	.020	.004	.013	.008	.014	ns	.000	.003	.006
Fem (not in speech)	.001	.015	ns	.004	.081	ns	.011	.010	ns	.006	.013	ns	.005	.017	ns
Masc (not in speech	.000	.072	.007	.003	.053	.009	.004	.002	ns	.001	.008	ns	.001	.034	ns

Parliamentary systems:	Alberta, CA (2)			Quebec, CA (2)			England (2)			Sweden (4)			Israel (5)		
MP	.010	**.161**	ns	.003	**.077**	ns	.000	**.120**	ns	.000	**.041**	.010	.011	**.064**	ns
Cabinet Minister	.000	**.169**	ns	.008	**.081**	ns	.000	**.088**	ns	.000	**.041**	ns	.008	**.059**	ns
Party Leader	.002	**.129**	ns	.006	**.062**	ns	.000	**.087**	ns	.000	**.027**	ns	.000	**.049**	ns
Vote for Candidate	.000	**.270**	ns	.005	**.145**	ns	.001	**.149**	ns	.000	**.113**	ns	.003	**.108**	ns
Vote for List	–	–	–	–	–	–	–	–	–	.000	**.168**	ns	–	–	–
Candidate Win Votes	**.035**	.010	.016	**.023**	.011	ns	.002	**.032**	ns	.000	**.007**	ns	.007	**.022**	.007
Win Votes for List	–	–	–	–	–	–	–	–	–	.000	**.005**	ns	–	–	–
Fem (in speech)	.015	**.101**	ns	.006	**.132**	ns	.004	**.064**	ns	.001	**.025**	ns	.003	**.028**	ns
Masc (in speech)	.002	**.039**	ns	**.015**	.002	ns	.000	**.018**	ns	.000	**.006**	ns	.001	**.038**	ns
Fem (not in speech)	.004	**.080**	ns	.003	**.052**	ns	.002	**.028**	ns	.012	**.022**	ns	.002	**.015**	ns
Masc (not in speech	.003	**.102**	ns	.003	**.035**	ns	**.004**	.000	ns	.002	.004	**.006**	.013	.010	ns

Notes: Partial Eta Square statistics for main effects of My Sex, My Party, and the interaction from 2×2 ANOVAs (My Sex, My Party). Bold face type indicates the greater effect size for each DV and country case. "ns" indicates not statistically significant. Policies are the stereotypically masculine and feminine policy areas selected for analysis in each country chapter. *Party Leader* is utilized in the parliamentary systems because party leaders are the contenders for the post of prime minister.

*Number in parentheses beside case indicates ranking on personal-partisan vote dimension

Table 11.4 Participants' Mother's Resources and Candidate Evaluations* (H7)

Case	Questions with significant interactions	Instances where the impact of mother's resources is linked to Participant's Sex	The Primary Hypothesis: Participants with a high-resource mother score a woman candidate high (H7)	Counter to Hypothesis: Participants with a low-resource mother score a woman candidate high	Participants with a high-resource mother score a man candidate high
Sweden	5 of 11	2	1. Preference Vote† 2. Security†	3. MP 4. Party Leader 5. Health†	
Costa Rica	1 of 8	0		1. Minister	
Chile	5 of 10	2	1. Education† 2. Women's Rights	3. Minister	4. Candidate Win Votes 5. Win Votes for Party†
England	2 of 9	1	1. Minister 2. Party Leader†		
Alberta	4 of 9	4	1. MP† 2. Minister† 3. Party Leader† 4. Energy†		
Quebec	3 of 9	3		1. MP† 2. Health† 3. Energy**	

Uruguay	4 of 8	0		1. Deputy 2. Minister 3. Economics	4. Education
California	1 of 8	1			1. Women's Rights†
Texas	1 of 8	1	1. Cabinet Secretary**		1. Cabinet Secretary†
Israel	7 of 9	0	1. MK 2. Minister 3. Party Leader 4. Support 5. Security 6. Energy	7. Education	

*ANOVAs with Candidate Gender, Mother Job or Mother Education, with and without Participant Sex as a covariate were conducted for each general evaluation question and policy area used in each country chapter.

**Female participants only. †Male participants only.

Note: Regarding California for women's rights policy, male participants whose mothers have a high-status job give equivalent mean scores to the man and woman candidate. Regarding England for Minister, whereas participants (male and female) whose mothers have high-status jobs favor the woman candidate, male participants whose mothers have low education favor the man candidate.

Role Congruity and Level of Post

Literature about role congruity prompted H8 that *participants overall will more favorably evaluate the man candidate than the woman candidate on the "general" evaluation questions*. However, for thirty-seven of forty-nine "general" questions (75.5 percent), Candidate Gender did not have a significant main effect (see Table 11.1). Only in Israel (four questions) and Quebec (one question) was the man candidate scored higher than the woman in responses to certain general questions. In Costa Rica, Uruguay, Alberta (two questions each) and Chile (one question), we obtained data rejecting Hypothesis 8 with a significantly more favorable evaluation of the woman on general questions. These findings resemble Matland's results from his 1991 experiment in Norway, which provided the conceptual seed of our study (Matland 1994).

Role congruity theory also prompted H9 that *a gender gap in evaluations will be larger the higher the level of the post*. As a first approach to test this prediction across our ten cases we conduct a repeated measures ANOVA where *MP* and *Minister* are the components of the repeated measure, and Candidate Gender and Case are the other factors in the analysis. The three-way interaction (Post×Candidate Gender×Case) is nearing significant [$F(1,5565)=1.795$, $p=.064$]. However, of greatest relevance for our study of the role of candidate gender in candidate evaluations, the interaction of Post×Candidate Gender is not significant ($p=.441$).

As a second approach to test H9, we examine the gap in mean evaluations for men and women candidates across levels of posts. Support for the role congruity prediction would require the difference in the mean score (man candidate minus woman candidate) to increase from *MP* to *Minister* and in parliamentary systems to increase further for *Party Leader*.[11] Instead, in six of ten cases (California, Chile, Uruguay, Costa Rica, Alberta, Sweden) young adults give more favorable evaluations to women candidates for all levels of posts (as seen by negative values in Table 11.5). In Uruguay, Costa Rica, Alberta, and Sweden, the gap favoring women candidates increases as post level increases.[12] In England, Israel, Quebec, and Texas, the mean evaluation of the man candidate is more favorable than the

---

[11] We do not include *Party Leader* in this analysis for the presidential systems because party leader is not a prominent post in presidential systems, and it is not the typical route to becoming president.

[12] Greater perceived importance and power of cabinet minister than MP posts is not just theoretical but confirmed by our data. For the 8 cases included in the NSF grant we asked at the end of the questionnaire: When you consider (1) members of the (name of legislature), (2) members of the government cabinet, and (3) a leader of a major political party—how much impact does she or he have on the life of your family? Each question scored 1 (no impact) to 5 (a lot of impact). In each of the parliamentary cases the mean "impact" score increased across the three questions. In the presidential cases the mean "impact" score increased from legislator to minister in Chile, Uruguay, and California. In Texas the mean "impact" score was 3.09 for Representative and 3.08 for cabinet secretary.

META-ANALYSIS ASSESSMENT OF CANDIDATE GENDER 247

Table 11.5 Differences between Mean Evaluations by Participants of Either a Woman or a Man Candidate Across Levels of Posts of Increasing Prestige, Where a Positive Value Indicates That Men Received Higher Mean Scores than Women Candidates, and a Negative Value That Women Were Scored Higher than Men* (H9).

Type of government	Case**	Deputy	Cabinet Minister	Party Leader
Presidential system:	Texas (1)	+ .082	+.058	***
	California (1)	− .125	− .116	***
	Chile (3)	− .151	− .120	***
	Uruguay (4)	− .157	− .238	***
	Costa Rica (5)	− .109	− .121	***
Parliamentary system:	Alberta (2)	− .229	− .271	− .355
	Quebec (2)	− .086	+ .226	+ .142
	England (2)	+ .044	− .023	+ .080
	Sweden (4)	− .051	− .070	− .107
	Israel (5)	+ .311	+ .387	+ .360

*Evaluations are based on ANOVAs with Candidate Gender, Party Platform and Party Label as factors.

**Numbers in parentheses beside cases denote case ranking on personal-partisan vote dimension.

***The Party Leader post is only included for parliamentary systems because party leaders are the contenders for the post of Prime Minister.

mean evaluation of the woman candidate for some or all posts, but the gap does not increase consistently for more powerful posts. We conclude that, for these young adults, leadership templates include women in high-ranking as well as in less prestigious posts.

Women Are Viewed as Capable Leaders across Diverse Policy Areas

Gender stereotypes and personality traits are expected to increase acceptance of women politicians in stereotypically feminine policy areas. Conversely, policy areas requiring hard-nosed negotiations, or linked to male-dominated occupations are expected to favor acceptance of men politicians (see, e.g., McDermott 1998; Herrnson et al. 2003; Lee and James 2007; Lammers et al. 2009). In addition, experiments typically find that gender stereotypes are most exhibited when a policy topic is not discussed in the treatment text.[13] Thus we have H10: *Participants will more favorably evaluate the man candidate than the woman candidate in stereotypically masculine policy areas*, and H11: *a gender gap in evaluations will be larger for policy areas not covered in the candidate's speech.*

In all ten cases the mean evaluation for policy areas discussed by the candidate is more favorable than for policies the candidate did not discuss, and all such differences are large and statistically highly significant (see Table 11.6). Our next question is whether lack of policy information produces gendered evaluations of candidates. When people lack information about a candidate's stance on a policy, they are expected to rely on other information that is available, such as gender stereotypes, as a heuristic and Candidate Gender is always stated in our experiment.

We examine all the cases by conducting a repeated-measures ANOVA where the average for all feminine policies and the average for all masculine policies are the components of the repeated measure, and Candidate Gender is the other factor in the analysis. We do this analysis twice for each of our ten cases, first looking at policy areas discussed in the candidates' speeches,[14] then examining policy areas that were not discussed in the speeches.[15]

Men and women candidates of the same party made identical policy statements, so we do not expect to see differences in evaluations associated with Candidate Gender unless gender stereotypes override policy information, which would be strong evidence that women do not fit mental templates of leadership. In most of our cases, gender stereotypes do not appear to dominate candidate evaluation regarding policy areas discussed in the speech as the interaction Policy Domain×Candidate Gender is not significant (Figure 11.3—left). However, in Israel and Texas, even though men and women candidates said the same things in their speech, men are evaluated more favorably on masculine policy areas (in Texas only for defense). In Israel, in addition, women candidates are evaluated more favorably than men on feminine policy areas.

[13] Even recent experiments (e.g., Holman et al. 2016; Ono and Yamada 2020) find evidence of gender stereotypes, particularly when information is lacking.

[14] In all cases except Costa Rica and Israel, masculine policy areas in the speech are *economics* and *security*; in Costa Rica: *security, economics*, and *energy*; in Israel: *defense, foreign relations, internal security*, and *housing*. In Costa Rica the only feminine policy area discussed in the speech is *education*, and in all other cases the feminine policy areas are *education* and *health*.

[15] Masculine policies not discussed in the speech, in all cases except Costa Rica and Israel, are *agriculture, energy, infrastructure* and *unemployment*. In Costa Rica they are *agriculture, foreign relations*, and *unemployment*. In Israel they are *agriculture, energy, infrastructure*, and *treasury*. In Israel *women's rights* was the only feminine policy area not discussed in the speech. In all the other cases *women's rights* and *childcare* were the feminine policy areas not discussed in the speech, and in Costa Rica, *health* as well.

META-ANALYSIS ASSESSMENT OF CANDIDATE GENDER   249

Table 11.6 Evaluation of Policy Areas Discussed in the Speech vs. Not Discussed

Case	In Speech	Not in Speech	Paired 2-tailed t-test	N
Sweden	3.25	2.75	.000	492
Costa Rica	3.44	2.98	.000	696
Chile	3.11	2.53	.000	743
England	3.55	2.94	.000	467
Alberta, CA	3.30	3.04	.000	241
Quebec, CA	3.36	3.03	.000	370
Uruguay	3.29	2.81	.000	554
California, US	3.41	3.03	.000	663
Texas, US	3.47	3.09	.000	927
Israel	3.39	2.93	.000	546
Across Cases	3.35	2.91	.000	10

In Speech is the average of all policy areas discussed in the speech. Not in Speech is the average of all policy areas not discussed in the speech. High scores more favorable.

Cases ordered from greatest incorporation of women into government to least incorporation.

Regarding policy areas *not* in the speech, in all ten cases women candidates are evaluated more favorably than men in stereotypically feminine policy areas. But what is most important for our study of whether women are viewed as political leaders, and for evaluation of H10, is that in stereotypically masculine policy areas men and women candidates receive similar evaluations (i.e., evaluations do not differ at the conventional minimum level of statistical significance, p= .05) (Figure 11.3—right). The exceptions are Israel, where the man candidate is perceived as more competent than the woman, and Alberta where the woman candidate is evaluated more favorably for masculine policy areas. In sum, in almost all cases women are viewed as capable leaders in stereotypically masculine policy areas even when the candidate provided no information on the policy topic.

In summary, our findings indicate that gender stereotypes do not restrict women politicians to stereotypically feminine policy areas. In addition, lack of information about a policy does not typically trigger gender schema usage to judge the ability of candidates. Party, however, consistently affects candidate evaluations for specific policy areas. As shown in the country chapters, young adults know which party "owns" key policy areas in their country's politics, and those parties' candidates score higher on owned policies.

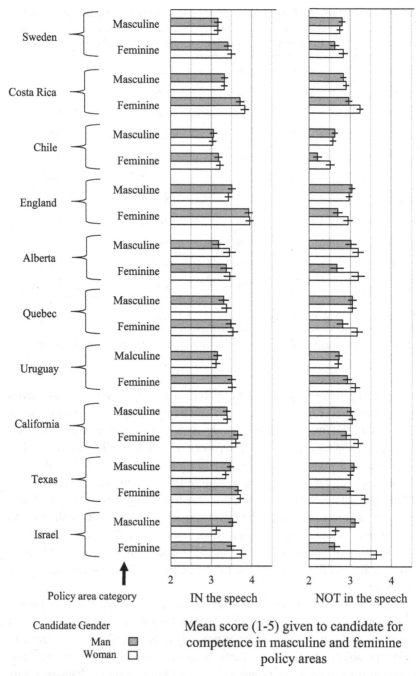

Figure 11.3 Evaluation of women and men candidates' capacity for masculine and feminine policy areas
Repeated measures ANOVAS (Domain, Candidate Gender) 95 percent confidence intervals included.

Conclusions from the Multi-Country Analysis

Across eight countries (ten cases) that provide diverse contexts with respect to women's incorporation into government, national policy agenda, and institutions, we find that the impact of Candidate Gender on evaluations was small or undetectable compared to the impact of Party, which was the baseline control in our experiments. These results call into question the breadth of applicability of key assumptions in the existing literature outlined in Chapter 1, highlighting the importance of rigorous and systematic multi-country research, such as realized with this parallel experiment.

The young adult participants in the experiments consistently weighted party heavily in their assessments of candidates' ability to hold different posts, win votes, and manage diverse policy areas. Candidate Gender rarely had a consistent significant effect, except for *Women's Rights* policy, where women were evaluated more favorably. Women candidates were often scored better than men when Candidate Gender was significant. These results hold for both male and female participants—hence it is not only women who view women candidates as leaders. The results also hold for policy topics that were not included in the candidate speech. The major exception to these findings is that Candidate Gender has a strong impact on evaluations in contexts where defense dominates the policy agenda. In Israel, and to a lesser extent in Texas, we find evidence of traditional—leaders are men—leadership templates. In Chapter 12 we discuss implications of these findings and offer suggestions for further research.

12

Do Women Fit the Leadership Image? Yes!

Michelle M. Taylor-Robinson and Nehemia Geva

In politics, gender is important, but views differ wildly regarding *how* important and *when*. The primary objective of this study was to rigorously measure the magnitude of importance of Candidate Gender when directly, quantitatively compared with a political variable, Party, that is universally viewed as one of the most important factors in democratic politics. To measure the importance of Candidate Gender, we implemented a strategically designed experiment conducted in eight countries (ten cases) offering different contexts regarding incorporation of women in government, national policy agenda, and institutions. The results indicate broad acceptance of women as leaders among urban young adults; women fit young adults' mental templates of leaders. Women are scored by our participants as capable members of the legislature, and for more powerful and prestigious posts—cabinet minister, party leader—where women are still less commonly seen. Women are broadly accepted as capable in stereotypically masculine policy areas where women's representation in the workforce and in key government posts remains limited (e.g., economics, energy, agriculture, infrastructure, and in some cases security), as well as in feminine policy areas. Even in the case of Israel, where we found the least evidence of acceptance of women as leaders, and where security concerns dominate the policy agenda, female study participants view women and men candidates as equivalent on many questions. These findings have important implications that party elites should consider when recruiting future politicians.

In all ten cases, party matters for whom is viewed as a capable leader. The impact of the candidate being from the participant's preferred party is larger than the impact of participant and candidate being of the same sex. Our finding that party is more important than gender in young adult's mental templates of leaders agrees with Dolan's (2014) US survey-based results for candidates for the US House of Representatives, Senate, and state governors. Though Dolan's study included all age groups in the US case, our data reveal a similar phenomenon for young adults across a broader range of country contexts, including variance in the history and extent of women's incorporation in government. Women fit the leadership image of young adults across different types of electoral systems, not just where closed-list PR draws voter attention to the party instead of individual

Michelle M. Taylor-Robinson and Nehemia Geva, *Do Women Fit the Leadership Image? Yes!* In: *The Image of Gender and Political Leadership.* Edited by: Michelle M. Taylor-Robinson and Nehemia Geva, Oxford University Press. © Oxford University Press 2023. DOI: 10.1093/oso/9780197642726.003.0012

DO WOMEN FIT THE LEADERSHIP IMAGE? YES! 253

candidates, and in both presidential and parliamentary systems. Women fit the image of a leader where social welfare policies are important components of the national government's policy agenda. However, when defense is a major focus, that is where traditional leadership templates (leaders are men) appear. Overall, this study finds that women are accepted by young adults as capable leaders in a broader set of conditions than expected based on predictions in literatures about exposure to women in government, role congruity theory, and theory of in-groups. This is a very positive finding that may bode well for future incorporation of women into government.

Valdini (2019) in *The Inclusion Calculation* theorizes that male party elites may decide it is worthwhile to put more women on their candidate lists as a strategy to repair the party's image. Yet for that to occur Valdini theorizes that the benefits of including women must outweigh various costs, including an "incongruity cost" that women do not look like leaders "due to their association with stereotypically feminine personality traits" (p. 19). Brooks (2013: 165) concluded in her study about the United States that "it is important that political power brokers understand that a choice to support a promising female candidate is not an inherently risky move." The strong findings of this study that women are viewed as capable leaders show that the incongruity cost, or riskiness of women candidates appears low, at least for young adults.

Our treatment—the candidate's quite lengthy speech—presented party stance on six policy topics, not personality traits of the candidate. Our findings are thus comparable with Bauer (2020a) whose experiment conducted with US adults found that women candidates are not penalized for highlighting stereotypically feminine issues (education, healthcare), though they can be penalized for exhibiting feminine traits. Our findings differ in interesting ways from Matland's findings from the experiment he conducted with young adults in Norway in 1991, which formed the basis for this study. Matland (1994: 279) hypothesized that "Gender distinctions will not exist for those policy areas that are discussed in the speech." He found that women candidates were evaluated equally as favorably as men candidates to be an MP or prime minister.[1] However, the man candidate received more favorable evaluations for foreign policy (Conservative Party) and economy (Labour Party) and the woman for childcare (Conservative Party), and those policy areas were discussed in the speech.[2] He concluded that, because gender differences still occur even when the man and woman candidate said the same thing about a policy topic, is "a compelling indication that broad representation of women does not eliminate the use of gender schemata"

---

[1] For the Norwegian Labour Party the woman candidate was evaluated more favorably to be an MP.

[2] Matland also uncovered gendered stereotypes in evaluations for policy areas not discussed in the speech.

(Matland 1994: 287). Twenty-five years later, it appears that young adults' leadership templates are broadly inclusive of women as leaders in stereotypically masculine policy areas, even where incorporation of women has been less extensive than it was in Norway in 1991. Except in the most defense-oriented cases (Israel and Texas), young adults evaluate women candidates favorably for diverse policy areas that are stereotypically masculine, whether or not the policy is discussed in the candidate's speech.

In this study young adults exhibit mental templates that include women as leaders in government in a wide range of settings: where many women are in the legislature, or occupy numerous cabinet posts, or where a woman recently led the country, and in cases where women are still not common in government. This challenges the literature that implies that extensive experience with women in government is needed to change attitudes about the appropriateness of women in politics. Yet it echoes Campbell and Wolbrecht's (2006) findings about socialization of adolescent girls to participation in politics. They found that it is the *visibility* of female politicians and women running for high-profile posts that predict girls' interest in politics, not the *number* of women candidates, many of whom are not known to the general population, and that coverage of women as "firsts," unique, or unusual can increase their visibility.[3] Acceptance of women as leaders, even where women are still not common as national government officials, may come from young adults growing up in an era when more women are candidates (McDonald and Deckman 2021), and where more women play prominent roles in global politics, such as Angela Merkel, who, over the many years of her chancellorship in Germany, came to be viewed as the de facto leader of Europe. As another example, while Uruguay has had few women in its national government, the young adults in the Uruguay study came of age when women held the presidency in three neighboring countries: Argentina, Brazil, and Chile.[4] As young people get much of their news from the internet and social media, they could be aware of politicians outside their own country as easily as domestic politicians.

Policy context also matters for women's acceptance as leaders. Women are viewed as leaders where social welfare topics hold a prominent place in the national policy agenda even when women are not very common in government (Canada, Uruguay). Where security dominates the agenda, women face tough challenges across all types of posts and particularly in stereotypically masculine

---

[3] "Simply being a female in a prominent political position, however, does not necessarily attract women's attention" as few in Gidengil et al.'s (2010: 342) study of Canadian women could name the female Governor-General.

[4] This possible international influence is supported by Lay et al.'s (2021) study of coverage of women leaders in TIME for Kids, which is a common teaching tool in US schools. They show that women leaders (in the US and globally) received more coverage in this magazine than their numbers in office.

policy areas (e.g., Israel, Texas).[5] More research is needed on relationships between government policy agenda, policy concerns of individual voters, and mental templates of leaders, because socio-political contexts in which women are seen as leaders appear far more nuanced than predicted by incorporation of women in government, and can go beyond women still being questioned as leaders on defense topics. Women playing leadership roles on security policy may be key for changing images.

Another aspect of this nuanced relationship could be that, particularly where women in government are still rare, people may view women politicians as more qualified than men because it is harder for women to get elected unless they have extraordinary credentials, and they may hold women candidates to higher standards (Fulton 2012; Bauer 2020b: chapter 5). As Bauer (2020b: 101) predicts in her US study, "The gender-role congruity between being male and serving in leadership roles creates a baseline advantage for male candidates" so a woman candidate must be better qualified than a man to win.[6] Bauer goes on to write that "Gender-typicality standards can create a false sense of security for female candidates because the use of these standards creates the appearance of favorable attitudes among voters," leading women to not feel the urgency of highlighting their credentials (p. 116). Such a danger, however, would be less likely to exist in systems with closed-list PR elections where voters cannot vote for, or against, a particular candidate.

Avenues for Future Research

Our study benefits from participant groups in each country that are made up of diverse young urban adults: students enrolled in high schools, technical schools, junior colleges, or universities, studying a wide range of topics (from philosophy to medicine to air conditioning systems repair). Participants' families span the full socioeconomic spectrum based on parent occupations (see Table 2.3, Chapter 2).

---

[5] Deckman and Cassese (2021) find that "gendered nationalism," which is their label for a belief that US society has become "too soft and feminine," explains votes for Donald Trump and against Hillary Clinton in 2016. They conclude that, "It seems plausible that gendered nationalism is bound up not only in preferences for male candidates who emphasize their masculine traits, as we find here, but also in policy preferences associated with strong nationalist postures in areas like immigration and national security" (p. 296). Also see Yarkoney Sorek (2018) for an MTurk experiment that found in international conflict Americans feel safer when the rival is led by a woman than by a man.

[6] Bauer's (2020b: 103) theory also predicts that a female incumbent will not be assessed against a gender-typicality standard because she has already won a seat, say, in Congress. She will be judged, instead, by a "female politician" standard. We note that in our US experiment, both the man and the woman candidate were incumbents.

256 MICHELLE M. TAYLOR-ROBINSON AND NEHEMIA GEVA

Our study centered on a political candidate that was in fact hypothetical, but the candidate was described to the participant in a very realistic context in a lengthy candidate speech, carefully constructed to include six current policy areas with relevant stances stated using the jargon and buzz words of a real party within the participant's country. Different participants received different speeches, representing different parties and candidate genders, and participants often could identify the party based on the stances and jargon even if the party's name was omitted. Thus, while the setting facilitated replication and random assignment of treatment along with highly relevant experimental control treatments, to enable conclusive findings regarding the primary hypotheses, it simultaneously resolved shortcomings commonly attributed to experiments in the social sciences. Conducting the experiment with 6,324 students in 212 classrooms in 69 schools, across eight countries (ten cases) expanded the study's external validity.

The findings demonstrate the experiment's reliability and feasibility of adaptation to address many additional questions. Given that we studied mental templates of leaders held by young adults, it would be illuminating to use this same method to study older generations' attitudes toward women leaders, as well as urban/rural comparative studies. Our cases are established democracies, and attitudes may differ in countries with recent regime change. The accelerated global nature of exchange of ideas and values across populations via internet and social media means that the impact on mental templates of leadership of women leaders in a cross-country context should be studied.

There are many ways that the speech (treatment) could be modified in further studies. The speech could signal a feminist bent for the candidate, or the candidate's race/ethnicity, as an experimental manipulation. The treatment could include a speech plus a resumé, with elements of a conjoint experiment comparing effects of candidate background and policy views. Future research could include elements of gendered personality traits for the candidate and partisan policy stances, to study the impact of traits alongside policy. The treatment could remind participants about a gender quota or include party policy statements about gender quotas as part of the manipulation. Political party was our baseline for comparing the effect of candidate gender. Future studies could manipulate emphasis on party polarization to explore if candidate gender may be even more overshadowed by party when parties are highly polarized.

Our results indicate that women are evaluated as competent in stereotypically masculine policy areas. Future work could manipulate a man or woman minister's success in implementing policy, or in handling a crisis on their watch. Such a study could explore whether participants evaluate policy success of men and women equally, and whether women—as relative newcomers to top policy roles—are punished more harshly for policy failures. Another salient unanswered question is how long a prominent woman leader (president, prime minister, speaker of the house) might influence mental templates of leadership after her term, if she is not followed by other prominent women in leadership posts transmitting the signal that women can run government. The converse question, also important, regards negatively viewed women leaders and their impact on mental templates. Former presidents Laura Chinchilla in Costa Rica and Michelle Bachelet in Chile, for example, were not viewed very positively by the end of their terms, and Prime Minister Theresa May struggled to find a way for Britain to exit the EU after the Brexit vote. Interestingly, young adults who "came of age" during their terms evaluated women candidates favorably in our study, which differs from findings that women leaders are particularly badly punished in the court of public opinion by corruption scandals and policy failures (Carlin et al. 2020). Future research should also explore female voter anger against women candidates when voters consider progress on women's rights under a woman leader to be inadequate.

This study examined leadership templates of young adults, not whether the participants actually vote for women candidates, and we do not know whether the leadership templates young adults exhibited in this study will carry forward into their middle age. Our findings indicate that party selectorates do not need to worry that women candidates and political appointees will not "fit the image" of political leaders within the younger generation. But can party selectorates expect young people to vote? We conducted this experiment in a diverse set of countries, and voter turnout, overall and across age cohorts, is another way the cases vary as illustrated in a national election close in time to implementation of our experiments (see Figure 12.1). In some of our cases turnout is quite consistent across age groups, although overall turnout varies from very high (Sweden) to relatively high (Alberta Canada, Costa Rica). In other cases, newly eligible voters *and* people in their twenties and thirties are less likely than people of middle age to vote (Chile, England, Quebec Canada, United States). In still other cases newly eligible voters participate at lower rates than people in their mid-twenties (Israel, Uruguay). Key events can motivate young adults to vote, as occurred in Chile in the 2020 elections for the constituent assembly where young voters were most prominent at the polls. Thus, concerns that young people do not vote, and therefore will not take leadership templates that include women to the polls, are unsupported across our cases. Future research should explore whether young adults who exhibit the most inclusive leadership templates (e.g., including women, race/ethnic, and other minorities) are more likely to vote than young adults with traditional leadership templates.

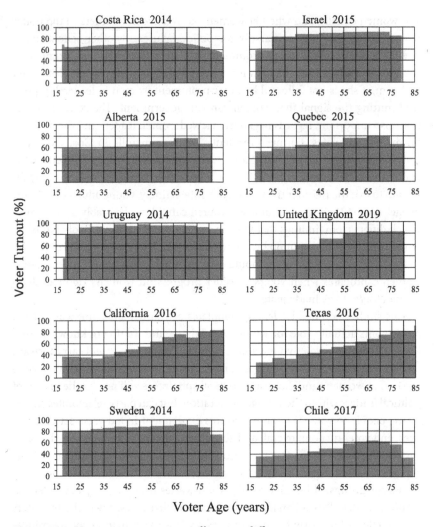

Figure 12.1 Voting across age groups illustrates differences across cases

Sources: Costa Rica Tribunal Supremo de Elecciones (2014a). Estadísticas del sufragio. February 2014 https://www.tse.go.cr/estadisticas_elecciones.htm; Israel European Social Survey (ESS8-2016) filtered to remove survey participants not eligible to vote https://www.europeansocialsurvey.org/data/download.html?r=8; Alberta and Quebec Elections Canada https://www.elections.ca/content.aspx?section=res&dir=rec/eval/pes2019/vtsa&document=index&lang=e; Uruguay Latinobarometer 2015 survey filtered to only include citizens and people old enough to vote; UK British Election Study https://www.britishelectionstudy.com/bes-findings/age-and-voting-behaviour-at-the-2019-general-election/#.YPS5VehKiUl; California and Texas 2016 Cooperative Election Study using the validated vote https://cces.gov.harvard.edu/; Sweden Statistics Sweden https://www.scb.se/en/finding-statistics/statistics-by-subject-area/democracy/general-elections/general-elections-participation-survey/; Chile Servício Electoral de Chile https://www.servel.cl/estadistica-de-participacion-por-rango-de-edad-y-sexo-elecciones-2017/.

Implications for Expanding Incorporation
of Women into Politics

Our question is not whether gender is a component of voters' leadership templates, but rather whether it is an *important* component. Our findings, across general evaluation questions and diverse policy areas, in eight countries, strongly support that it is party, not candidate gender, that typically dominates candidate evaluations by young adults. These are encouraging findings predicting a future with increased gender equality throughout government.

Even so, women who aspire to be political leaders still face challenges. Transition of women into full and equal players in government will require many changes. Campaign finance resources from parties and donors still are less available to women than men (see, e.g., Chapter 10 about Chile; Wylie and dos Santos 2016), and "strategic discrimination" prompts donors to not back women candidates because donors often believe many voters will not support women (Bateson 2020). Party leaders also still avoid selecting women as candidates. When faced with a gender quota, parties often act as if the quota is the maximum number of women they need to nominate, or find creative ways to circumvent the quota (see, e.g., Chapter 6 about Uruguay; Paxton et al. 2020: 185–93; Gatto and Wylie 2022). Party selectorates still often avoid nominating women in competitive districts, actively discourage women candidates, or express fears that voters will not vote for women (see Chapter 6 about Uruguay; Chapter 8 about the United States). Women in government and women candidates are targets of violence and threats, ranging from psychological abuse (see Chapter 9 about Sweden) to physical violence (Krook 2020; Bjarnegård and Zetterberg 2023).

These barriers are strong impediments to women running for office, getting elected, and rising through the ranks to top government posts. That young adults in these diverse democracies view women as leaders—across levels of posts and in stereotypically masculine and feminine policy areas—is certainly encouraging and should send a clear signal to party selectorates that women are strong potential candidates and government officials, eliminating pretexts for strategic discrimination. It should also signal party leaders that campaign funds can successfully promote women candidates, and that their parties should aggressively suppress threats and violence in all their forms.

In addition, our finding that young adults' mental templates of leaders include women even in countries where incorporation of women into government is not extensive does not diminish the importance of greater incorporation of women into government. Increased descriptive representation of women in government is important for policy. Women legislators are more likely than men to propose bills on topics of concern for women. Women in the executive branch bring different perspectives to policy development and implementation. Women in all

260 MICHELLE M. TAYLOR-ROBINSON AND NEHEMIA GEVA

branches of government signal to men, who have always controlled government power, that women are political people, and more women in government amplifies that signal. As explained in Chapter 1, women in government signals that women are citizens, acknowledging that women's opinions and expertise benefit government.

Parties' elites should pay attention as they encourage candidates and appoint officials. This study clearly shows that urban young adults in diverse democratic settings view women and men as potential political leaders. Both male and female young adults in our cases see women as leaders, and sex in-group effects are not critical. Women candidates do not appear to be risky for parties seeking to attract young voters, and they may well be the route to victory.

With the exceptions of Israel and Texas, our findings indicate that women are broadly accepted as leaders. Overall, party matters more than gender, and the policy emphasis of government would appear to be a more important factor influencing women's future incorporation into government in a given country than is extensive prior experience with women in that country's government. Our findings reveal a future need for research on cognitive balance of party in-group and gender in-group effects within leadership templates. Young adults who participated in our study clearly understood party issue ownership, and the My Party in-group favored evaluations of both men and women candidates. Our findings suggest that when provided with policy information on some policy areas, participants extrapolated from what they read or from the party label to assume the candidate's party-based stances in other policy areas. This could elucidate why both female and male participants usually evaluated women candidates as capable leaders even when information about a policy topic was not provided in the speech, and why female participants were often not more favorable than male participants in their evaluations of women candidates.

In conclusion, key findings are robustly supported and consistent that party not gender is the primary shaper of mental templates of leaders in the minds of young adults in the cases included in this study. With notable exceptions in Israel and Texas, where government policy is dominated by defense concerns, the findings show young adults view women as leaders over a very wide range of posts, policy areas, and levels of current and historic participation of women in government and in a wide range of political systems and electoral rules.

But is the struggle for women over? No! This research shows progress that is encouraging for the future of gender parity in government. Parties should consider the implications of these findings and incorporate more women into their ranks. Yet the struggle goes on.

References

Aftonbladet 2002, January 24, interview with Prime Minister Göran Persson.

Agassi, Judith Buber. 1989. Theories of gender equality: Lessons from the Israeli Kibbutz. *Gender & Society* 3(2):160–86.

Aguilar, Rosario, Saul Cunow, and Scott Desposato. 2015. Choice sets, gender, and candidate choice in Brazil. *Electoral Studies* 39: 230–42.

Ahroneim, Anna. 2019. IDF Manpower Head: Not All Combat Positions Suitable for Women. *The Jerusalem Post.* https://www.jpost.com/Israel-News/IDF-Manpower-head-Not-all-combat-positions-suitable-for-women-579179.

Alexander, Amy. 2012. Changes in women's descriptive representation and the belief in women's ability to govern: A virtuous cycle. *Politics & Gender* 8(4): 437–64.

Alexander, Amy C., and Farida Jalalzai. 2016. The symbolic effects of female heads of state and government. In *The gendered executive: A comparative analysis of presidents, prime ministers, and chief executives.* Edited by Janet M. Martin and MaryAnne Borrelli, 25–43. Philadelphia, PA: Temple University Press.

Alexander, Deborah, and Kristi Andersen. 1993. Gender as a factor in the attribution of leadership traits. *Political Research Quarterly* 46(3): 527–45.

Alfaro-Redondo, Ronald. 2010. Elecciones nacionales 2010 en Costa Rica. Una mujer al mando 60 años después. *Revista de Ciencias Sociales* 130: 101–15.

Alfaro-Redondo, Ronald, and Steffan Gómez-Campos. 2012. Costa Rica: Reconfiguración política en un contexto de gobierno dividido. *Revista de Ciencia Política* 32(1): 109–28.

Alfaro-Redondo, Ronald, and Steffan Gómez-Campos. 2014. Costa Rica: Elecciones en el contexto político más adverso arrojan la mayor fragmentación partidaria en 60 años. *Revista de Ciencia Política* 34(1): 125–44.

Amnå, Erik, and Pär Zetterberg. 2010. A political science perspective on socialization research: Young Nordic citizens in a comparative light. In *Handbook of research on civic engagement in youth.* Edited by Lonnie R. Sherrod, Judith Torney-Purta and Constance A. Flanagan, 43–65. John Wiley & Sons.

Anderson, Cameron. 2010. Regional heterogeneity and policy preferences in Canada: 1979 2006. *Regional and Federal Studies* 20(4–5): 447–68.

Annesley, Claire, Karen Beckwith, and Susan Franceschet. 2019. *Cabinets, ministers, and gender.* New York: Oxford University Press.

Annesley, Claire, and Francesca Gains. 2010. Gender, politics and policy change: The case of welfare reform under new Labour. *Government and Opposition* 45(1): 50–72.

Annesley, Claire, and Francesca Gains. 2013. Investigating the economic determinants of the UK gender equality policy agenda. *British Journal of Politics and International Relations* 15(1): 125–46.

Arter, David. 2004. Parliamentary Democracy in Scandinavia. *Parliamentary Affairs* 57(3): 581–600.

Assemblée Nationale du Québec. 2009. Traditions and symbols. http://www.assnat.qc.ca/en/abc-assemblee/organisation-travaux-assemblee/symboles.html.

262 REFERENCES

ATF 2019. Firearms commerce in the United States, annual statistical update, 2019, United States Department of Justice, Bureau of Alcohol, Tobacco, Firearms and Explosives. https://www.atf.gov/firearms/docs/report/2019-firearms-commerce-rep ort/download (accessed October 21, 2020).

Authier, Phillip. 2018. Liberal MNA facing sexual misconduct allegations leaves party caucus. *Montreal Gazette* https://montrealgazette.com/news/quebec/facing-miscond uct-allegations-liberal-mna-withdraws-from-caucus.

Avendaño, Octavio, and Mireya Dávila. 2018. Together we govern: Portfolio allocation in Chile (1990–2014). In *Government formation and minister turnover in presidential cabinets: Comparative analysis in the Americas.* Edited by Marcelo Camerlo and Cecilia Martínez-Gallardo, 90–110. London: Routledge.

Bahgat, Gawdat. 2011. Israel's energy security: Regional implications. *Middle East Policy Council* 18 (Fall, 3): 25–34. https://mepc.org/israels-energy-security-regional-impli cations (accessed August 26, 2020).

Baldez, Lisa. 2002. *Why women protest: Women's movements in Chile.* New York: Cambridge University Press.

Baldez, Lisa. 2003. Women's movements and democratic transition in Chile, Brazil, East Germany, and Poland. *Comparative Politics* 35(3): 253–73.

Banwart, Mary Christine. 2010. Gender and candidate communication: Effects of stereotypes in the 2008 election. *American Behavioral Scientist* 54(3): 265–83.

Barnes, Tiffany D. 2016. *Gendering legislative behavior: Institutional constraints and collaboration.* New York: Cambridge University Press.

Barnes, Tiffany D., and Stephanie M. Burchard. 2013. 'Engendering' politics: The impact of descriptive representation on women's political engagement in Sub-Saharan Africa. *Comparative Political Studies* 46(7): 767–90.

Barnes, Tiffany, and Michelle M. Taylor-Robinson. 2018. Women cabinet ministers in highly visible posts and empowerment of women: Are the two related? In *Measuring women's political empowerment across the globe.* Edited by Amy C. Alexander, Catherine Bolzendahl, and Farida Jalalzai, 229–55. Palgrave MacMillan.

Bateson, Regina. 2020. Strategic discrimination. *Perspectives on Politics* 18(4): 1068–87.

Bauer, Nicole M. 2015. Who stereotypes female candidates? Identifying individual differences in feminine stereotype reliance. *Politics, Groups, and Identities* 3(1): 94–110.

Bauer, Nicole M. 2020a. A feminine advantage? Delineating the effects of feminine trait and feminine issue messages on evaluations of female candidates. *Politics & Gender* 16(3) 660–80.

Bauer, Nicole M. 2020b. *The qualifications gap: Why women must be better than men to win political office.* New York: Cambridge University Press.

Beaman, Lori, Reghabendra Chattopadhyay, Esther Duflo, Rohini Pande and Petia Topalova. 2009. Powerful women: Does exposure reduce bias? *The Quarterly Journal of Economics* 124(4): 1497–1540.

Beckwith, Karen. 2015. Before prime minister: Margaret Thatcher, Angela Merkel, and gendered leadership contests. *Politics & Gender* 11(4): 718–45.

Bélanger, Éric. 2003. Issue ownership by Canadian political parties, 1953–2001. *Canadian Journal of Political Science* 36(3): 539–58.

Bélanger, Éric, and Bonnie M. Meguid. 2008. Issue salience, issue ownership, and issue-based vote choice. *Electoral Studies* 27(3): 477–91.

Bergqvist, Christina. 2015. Delmål 1: En jämn fördelning av makt och inflytande. In *SOU 2015:86 Forskarrapporter till jämställdhetsutredningen.* Stockholm: Statens offentliga utredningar.

REFERENCES 263

Bergqvist, Christina, Per Adman, and Ann-Christine Jungar. 2008. *Kön och politik*. Stockholm: SNS.

Bergqvist, Christina, Elin Bjarnegård, and Pär Zetterberg. 2018. The gendered leeway: Male privilege, internal and external mandates, and gender-equality policy change. *Politics, Groups, and Identities* 6(4): 576–92.

Bjarnegård, Elin, and Pär Zetterberg (ed.). 2023. *Gender and violence against political actors*. Philadelphia, PA: Temple University Press.

Boldry, Jennifer, Wendy Wood, and Deborah A. Kashy. 2001. Gender stereotypes and the evaluation of men and women in military training. *Journal of Social Issues* 57(4): 689–705.

Bolzendahl, Catherine I., and Daniel J. Myers. 2004. Feminist attitudes and support for gender equality: Opinion change in women and men, 1974–1998. *Social Forces* 83(2): 759–89.

Borrelli, MaryAnne. 2010. Gender desegregation and gender integration in the president's cabinet, 1933–2010. *Presidential Studies Quarterly* 40(4): 734–49.

Branton, Regina, Ashley English, Samantha Petty, and Tiffany D. Barnes. 2018 The impact of gender and quality opposition on the relative assessment of candidate competency. *Electoral Studies* 54: 35–43.

Brescoll, Victoria L., Erica Dawson, and Eric Luis Uhlmann. 2010. Hard won and easily lost: The fragile status of leaders in gender-stereotype-incongruent occupations. *Psychological Science* 21(11): 1640–42.

Broecke, Stijn, and Joseph Hamed. 2008. Gender gaps in higher education participation. DIUS Research Report 08 14 https://dera.ioe.ac.uk/8717/1/DIUS-RR-08-14.pdf.

Brooks, Deborah J. 2013. *He runs, she runs: Why gender stereotypes do not harm women candidates*. Princeton, NJ: Princeton University Press.

Brown, Michael J., and Nancy Gladstone. 2012. Development of a short version of the gender role beliefs scale. *International Journal of Psychology and Behavioral Sciences* 2(5): 154–58.

Burden, Barry, Yoshikuni Ono, and Masahiro Yamada. 2017. Reassessing public support for a female president. *Journal of Politics* 79(3): 1073–78.

Butler, Daniel M., and Jessica Robinson Preece. 2016. Recruitment and perceptions of gender bias in party leader support. *Political Research Quarterly* 69(4): 842–51.

Bystrom, Dianne. 2006. Advertising, web sites, and media coverage: Gender and communication along the campaign trail. In *Gender and Elections: Shaping the Future of American Politics*. Edited by Susan J. Carroll and Richard J. Fox, 169–88. Cambridge: Cambridge University Press.

Bäck, Hanna, Marc Debus, and Jochen Müller. 2014. Who takes the parliamentary floor? The role of gender in speech-making in the Swedish Riksdag. *Political Research Quarterly* 67(3): 504–18.

CADEM. 2018. *Encuesta Plaza Pública, tercera semana de diciembre*. Santiago de Chile: CADEM.

Campbell, David E., and Christina Wolbrecht. 2006. See Jane run: Women politicians as role models for adolescents. *Journal of Politics* 68(2): 233–47.

Carey, John M., and Matthew Soberg Shugart. 1995. Incentives to cultivate a personal vote: A rank ordering of electoral formulas. *Electoral Studies* 14(4): 417–39.

Carli, Linda L. 2001. Gender and social influence. *Journal of Social Issues* 57(4): 725–41.

Carli, Linda L., and Alice H. Eagly. 2007. Overcoming resistance to women leaders: The importance of leadership style. In *Women and leadership: The state of play and strategies for change*. Edited by Barbara Kellerman and Deborah L. Rhode, 127–48. San Francisco: Jossey-Bass.

264 REFERENCES

Carlin, Ryan E., Miguel Carreras, and Gregory J. Love. 2020. President's sex and popularity: Baselines, dynamics and policy competence. *British Journal of Political Science* 50(4): 1359–79.

Carroll, Susan J., and Richard L. Fox. 2006. Introduction: Gender and electoral politics into the twenty-first century. In *Gender and elections: Shaping the future of American politics*. Edited by Susan J. Carroll and Richard J. Fox, 1–11. Cambridge: Cambridge University Press.

Carroll, Susan J., and Kira Sanbonmatsu. 2013. *More women can run: Gender and pathways to the state legislatures*. New York: Oxford University Press.

Cassese, Erin C., and Mirya R. Holman. 2018. Playing the woman card: Ambivalent sexism in the 2016 US presidential race. *Political Psychology* 40(1): 55–74.

CAWP. 2018. Center for American Women in Politics. 2018. "Current Numbers." http://www.cawp.rutgers.edu/current-numbers (accessed August 22, 2018).

CES. 2004. Blais, André, Elisabeth Gidengil, Neil Nevitte, Patrick Fournier, and Joanna Everitt. The 2004 Canadian Election Study. [dataset]

CES. 2008. Gidengil, Elisabeth, Joanna Everitt, Patrick Fournier, and Neil Nevitte. The 2008 Canadian Election Study. [dataset]

CES. 2011. Fournier, Patrick, Fred Cutler, Stuart Soroka and Dietlind Stolle. The 2011 Canadian Election Study. [dataset]

Chang, Chingching, and Jacqueline C. Bush Hitchon. 2004. When does gender count? Further insights into gender schematic processing of female candidate's political advertisements. *Sex Roles* 51(3–4): 197–208.

Chappell, Louise, and Georgina Waylen. 2013. Gender and the hidden life of institutions. *Public Administration* 91(3): 599–615.

Chasquetti, Daniel. 2014. *Parlamento y carreras legislativas en Uruguay. Un estudio sobre reglas, partidos y legisladores en las cámaras*. Montevideo: Cuace-FCS.

Chattopadhyay, Prithviraj, Malgorzata Tluchowska, and Elizabeth George. 2004. Identifying the ingroup: A closer look at the influence of demographic dissimilarity on employee social identity. *The Academy of Management Review* 29(2): 180–202.

Chazan, Naomi. 2018. Israel at 70: A gender perspective. *Israel Studies* 23(3): 141–51.

Childs, Sarah. 2004. *New Labour's women MPs: Women representing women*. Routledge.

Childs, Sarah. 2016. *The Good Parliament*. Bristol: University of Bristol. www.bristol.ac.uk/media-library/sites/news/2016/july/20%20Jul%20Prof%20Sarah%20Childs%20The%20Good%20Parliament%20report.pdf.

Chilean Chamber of Deputies. June 12, 2018, debates. https://www.camara.cl/prensa/noticias_detalle.aspx?prmid=134252 (accessed March 20, 2019).

Chin, Michelle L., and Michelle M. Taylor-Robinson. 2005. The rules matter: An experimental study of the effects of electoral systems on shifts in voters' attention. *Electoral Studies* 24(3): 465–83.

Christie, Jane L. 2016. *Negotiating gendered discourses: Michelle Bachelet and Cristina Fernández de Kirchner*. Lanham: Lexington Books.

Clayton, Amanda, Diana Z. O'Brien, and Jennifer M. Piscopo. 2019. All male panels erode citizens' perceptions of democratic legitimacy. *American Journal of Political Science* 63(1): 113–29.

Clayton, Amanda, Amanda Lea Robinson, Martha C. Johnson, and Regnhild Muriaas. 2020. (How) do voters discriminate against women candidates? Experimental and qualitative evidence from Malawi. *Comparative Political Studies* 53(3–4): 601–30.

REFERENCES   265

Conway, Douglas. 2019. Percentage of people with public health insurance up in 11 states, down in two. November 7, 2019. https://www.census.gov/library/stories/2019/11/state-by-state-health-insurance-coverage-2018.html (accessed September 28, 2020).

Cross, William. 2004. *Political parties.* Vancouver: UBC Press.

Crowder-Meyer, Melody. 2013. Gendered recruitment without trying: How local party recruiters affect women's representation. *Politics & Gender* 9(4): 390–413.

Culhane, Leah, and Jemima Olchawski. 2018. Strategies for success: Women's experiences of selection and election in UK Parliament. Fawcett Society. https://www.fawcettsoci ety.org.uk/Handlers/Download.ashx?IDMF=b8a66d72-32a4-4d9d-91e7-33ad1ef4a 785 (accessed September 9, 2020).

Cutler, Fred. 2002. The simplest shortcut of all: Sociodemographic characteristics and electoral choice. *Journal of Politics* 64(2): 466–90.

Dahlerup, Drude, and Monique Leyenaar, eds. 2013. *Breaking male dominance in old democracies.* Oxford: Oxford University Press.

Davis, Shannon N., and Jeremiah B. Wills. 2010. Adolescent gender ideology socialization: Direct and moderating effects of fathers' beliefs. *Sociological Spectrum* 30: 580–604.

Deckman, Melissa, and Erin Cassese. 2021. Gendered nationalism and the 2016 US presidential elections: How party, class, and beliefs about masculinity shaped voting behavior. *Politics & Gender* 17(2): 277–300.

De Fina Gonzalez, Débora, and Francisca Figueroa Vidal. 2019. Nuevos 'campos de acción política' feminista: Una mirada a las recientes movilizaciones en Chile. *Revista Punto Género* 11: 51–72. doi:10.5354/0719-0417.2019.53880.

DePaola, Maria, Vincenzo Scoppa, and Rosetta Lombardo. 2010. Can gender quotas break down negative stereotypes? Evidence from changes in electoral rules. *Journal of Public Economics* 94(5–6): 344–53.

De Tezanos-Pinto, Pablo, Flavio Cortés, and Mariella Concha. 2016. *Participación política y descontento en Chile: Una tensión entre el interés en los temas políticos y la desafección generalizada.* Santiago de Chile: MIDEvidencias UC No.6.

Devroe, Robin, and Bram Wauters. 2018. Political gender stereotypes in a list-PR system with a high share of women MPs: Competent men versus leftist women? *Political Research Quarterly* 71(4): 788–800.

Diekman, Amanda B., Wind Goodfriend, and Stephanie Goodwin. 2004. Dynamic stereotypes of power: Perceived change and stability in gender hierarchies. *Sex Roles* 50(3 4): 201–15.

Ditonto, Tessa M., Allison J. Hamilton and David P. Redlawsk. 2014. Gender stereotypes, information search, and voting behavior in political campaigns. *Political Behavior* 36(2): 335–58.

Dittmar, Kelly E. 2015a. *Navigating gendered terrain: Stereotypes and strategy in political campaigns.* Philadelphia, PA: Temple University Press.

Dittmar, Kelly. 2015b. Encouragement is not enough: Addressing social and structural barriers to female recruitment. *Politics & Gender* 11(4): 759–65.

Dolan, Kathleen A. 2010. The impact of gender stereotyped evaluations on support for women candidates. *Political Behavior* 32(1): 69–88.

Dolan, Kathleen. 2014. *When does gender matter? Women candidates and gender stereotypes in American elections.* New York: Oxford University Press.

266 REFERENCES

Donato, Katharine M., and Samantha L. Perez. 2016. A different hue of the gender gap: Latino immigrants and political conservatism in the United States. *The Russell Sage Foundation Journal of the Social Sciences* 2(3): 98–124.

Dotti Sani, Guilia M., and Mario Quaranta. 2017. The best is yet to come? Attitudes toward gender roles among adolescents in 36 countries. *Sex Roles* 77: 30–45.

Dovidio, John F., Samuel L. Gaertner, Ana Validzic, Kimberly Matoka, Brenda Johnson, and Stacy Frazier. 1997. Extending the benefits of recategorization: Evaluations, self-disclosure, and helping. *Journal of Experimental Social Psychology* 33(4): 401–20.

Duerst-Lahti, Georgina. 2005. Institutional gendering: Theoretical insights into the environment of women officeholders. In *Women and Elective Office*. Edited by Sue Thomas and Clyde Wilcox, 230–43. New York: Oxford University Press.

Duvander, Ann-Zofie. 2008. *Family policy in Sweden: An overview*. Vol. 15, *Social insurance report, working paper 2008:5*. Stockholm: Stockholm University Linnaeus Center on Social Policy and Family Dynamics in Europe, SPaDE.

Däubler, Thomas, Love Christensen, and Lukáš Linek. 2018. Parliamentary activity, re-selection and the personal vote. Evidence from flexible-list systems. *Parliamentary Affairs* 71(4): 930–49.

Eagly, Alice H. 2007. Female leadership advantage and disadvantage: Resolving the contradictions. *Psychology of Women Quarterly* 31(1): 1–12.

Eagly, Alice H., and Steven J. Karau. 2002. Role congruity theory of prejudice toward female leaders. *Psychological Review* 109(3): 573–98.

Eagly, Alice H., Mona G. Makhijani, and Bruce G. Klonsky. 1992. Gender and the evaluation of leaders: A meta-analysis. *Psychological Bulletin* 111(1): 3–22.

Eagly, Alice H., Steven J. Karau, and Mona G. Makhijani. 1995. Gender and the effectiveness of leaders: A meta-analysis. *Psychological Bulletin* 117(1): 125–45.

Eagly, Alice H., and Sabine Sczesny. 2009. Stereotypes about women, men, and leaders: Have times changed? In *The Glass Ceiling in the 21st Century: Understanding Barriers to Gender Equality*. Edited by Manuela Barreto, Michelle K. Ryan, and Michael T. Schmitt, 21–47. Washington, DC: American Psychological Association.

ECLAC. 2017. Observatorio de Igualdad de Género de América Latina y el Caribe. https://oig.cepal.org/es (accessed November 18, 2022).

Ekman, Joakim, and Pär Zetterberg. 2010. *Vad förklarar skillnaderna mellan 14-åringars medborgarkompetens: En tvånivåanalys av den svenska delen av ICCS-undersökningen. Skolverkets Analysrapport till 345, Skolor som politiska arenor: Medborgarkompetens och kontrovershantering*. Stockholm: Fritzes.

Elections Canada Online. 2018. Official Results, 42nd General Election (October 19, 2015). http://www.elections.ca/content.aspx?section=res&dir=rep/off/sta_2015&document=p2&lang=e#24 (accessed February 14, 2019).

Erikson, Josefina. 2017. *Criminalising the client. Institutional change, gendered ideas, and feminist strategies*. New York: Rowman and Littlefield International.

Erikson, Josefina, and Cecilia Josefsson. 2016. Jämställdheten i riksdagen-en enkätstudie. Rapport till riksdagens arbetsgrupp för jämställdhet.

Erikson, Josefina, and Cecilia Josefsson. 2018. The legislature as a gendered workplace: Exploring members of parliament's experiences of working in the Swedish parliament. *International Political Science Review* 40(2): 197–214.

Erikson, Josefina, and Cecilia Josefsson. 2021. Equal playing field? On the intersection between gender and being young in the Swedish Parliament. *Politics, Groups, and Identities* 9(1): 81–100.

REFERENCES 267

Esaiasson, Peter, and Sören Holmberg. 1996. *Representation from above*. Hants: Dartmouth Publishing Company Limited.

Escobar-Lemmon, Maria C., and Michelle M. Taylor-Robinson. 2005. Women ministers in Latin American government: When, where, and why? *American Journal of Political Science* 49(4): 829–44.

Escobar-Lemmon, Maria C., and Michelle M. Taylor-Robinson. 2009. Getting to the top: Career paths of women in Latin American cabinets. *Political Research Quarterly* 62(4): 685–99.

Escobar-Lemmon, Maria, and Michelle M. Taylor-Robinson. 2016. *Women in presidential cabinets: Power players or abundant tokens?* New York: Oxford University Press.

Falk, Erika, and Kate Kenski. 2006. Issue saliency and gender stereotypes: Support for women as presidents in times of war and terrorism. *Social Science Quarterly* 87(1): 1–18.

Florez-Estrada, María. 2010. La campaña de Laura Chinchilla y las mujeres. Oportunismo o compromiso con un nuevo pacto sexual? *Revista de Ciencias Sociales* 130: 85–99.

Forsyth, Donelson R., Michele M. Heiney, and Sandra S. Wright. 1997. Biases in appraisals of women leaders. *Group Dynamics: Theory, Research, and Practice* 1(1): 98–103.

Fox, Richard L., and Jennifer L. Lawless. 2004. Entering the arena? Gender and the decision to run for office. *American Journal of Political Science* 48(2): 264–80.

Fox, Richard L., and Jennifer L. Lawless. 2011. Gendered perceptions and political candidacies: A central barrier to women's equality in electoral politics. *American Journal of Political Science* 55(1): 59–73.

Fox, Richard L., and Jennifer L. Lawless. 2014. Uncovering the origins of the gender gap in political ambition. *American Political Science Review* 108(3): 499–519.

Frajman, Eduardo. 2014. The general election in Costa Rica, February/April 2014. *Electoral Studies* 35: 61–66.

Franceschet, Susan. 2005. *Women and politics in Chile*. Boulder, CO: Lynne Rienner.

Franceschet, Susan, Mona Lena Krook, and Jennifer M. Piscopo. 2012. Conceptualizing the impact of gender quotas. In *The Impact of Gender Quotas*. Edited by Susan Franceschet, Mona Lena Krook, and Jennifer M. Piscopo, 3–24. New York: Oxford University Press.

Franceschet, Susan. 2018. Informal institutions and women's political representation in Chile (1990–2015). In *Gender and Representation in Latin America*. Edited by Leslie A. Schwindt-Bayer, 140–55. New York: Oxford University Press.

Franceschet, Susan, Jennifer M. Piscopo, and Gwynn Thomas. 2015. Supermadres, maternal legacies and women's political participation in contemporary Latin America. *Journal of Latin American Studies* 48(1): 1–32.

Frangeur, Renée. 1998. *Yrkeskvinna eller makens tjänarinna? Striden om yrkesrätten för gifta kvinnor i mellankrigstidens Sverige*. Eslöv: Arkiv förlag.

Freidenvall, Lenita. 2006. *Vägen till Varannan damernas: Om kvinnorepresentation, kvotering och kandidaturval i svensk politik 1970–2002*. Stockholm: Stockholm University.

Freidenvall, Lenita. 2013. Sweden: Step by step—women's inroads into parliamentary politics. In *Breaking male dominance in old democracies*. Edited by Drude Dahlerup and Monique Leyenaar, 97–123. Oxford: Oxford University Press.

Fridkin Kahn, Kim. 1992. Does being male help? An investigation of the effects of candidate gender and campaign coverage on evaluations of U.S. Senate candidates. *Journal of Politics* 54(2): 497–517.

268 REFERENCES

Fridkin Kahn, Kim. 1994. Does gender make a difference? An experimental examination of sex stereotypes and press patterns in statewide campaigns. *American Journal of Political Science* 38(1): 162–95.

Fridkin, Kim L., and Patrick J. Kenney. 2007. Examining the gender gap in children's attitudes toward politics. *Sex Roles* 56(3–4): 133–40.

Fridkin, Kim L., and Patrick J. Kenney. 2009. The role of gender stereotypes in U.S. Senate campaigns. *Politics & Gender* 5(3): 301–24.

Fridkin, Kim L., and Patrick J. Kenney. 2015. *The changing face of representation: The gender of U.S. Senators and constituent communications*. Ann Arbor: University of Michigan Press.

Fulton, Sarah A., Cherie D. Maestas, L. Sandy Maisel, and Walter J. Stone. 2006. The sense of a woman: Gender, ambition, and the decision to run for Congress. *Political Research Quarterly* 59(2): 235–48.

Fulton, Sarah A. 2012. Running backwards and in high heels: The gendered quality gap and incumbent electoral success. *Political Research Quarterly* 65(2): 303–14.

Gaertner, Samuel L., Jeffrey Mann, Andrey Murrell, and John F. Dovidio. 1989. Reducing intergroup bias: The benefits of recategorization. *Journal of Personality and Social Psychology* 57(2): 239–49.

Gamboa, Ricardo, and Mauricio Morales. 2016. Country note: Chile's 2015 electoral reform: Changing the rules of the game. *Latin American Politics and Society* 58(4): 126–44.

Garretón, Manuel Antonio, and Roberto Garretón. 2010. La democracia incompleta en Chile: La realidad tras las rankings internacionales. *Revista de Ciencia Política* 30(1): 115–48.

Gatto, Malu A. C., and Kristin N. Wylie. 2022. Informal institutions and gendered candidate selection in Brazilian parties. *Party Politics* 28(4): 727–38.

Gidengil, Elisabeth, Brenda O'Neill, and Lisa Young. 2010. Her mother's daughter? The influence of childhood socialization on women's political engagement. *Journal of Women, Politics & Policy* 31(4): 334–55.

Gidengil, Elisabeth, Neil Nevitte, André Blais, Joanna Everitt, and Patrick Fournier. 2012. *Dominance and decline: Making sense of recent Canadian elections*. Toronto: University of Toronto Press.

Gilligan, Carol. 1982. *In a different voice*. Cambridge, MA: Harvard University Press.

Godoy, Carmen Gloria, and Paula Raposo. 2020. Economic modernization and redefining womanhood: Women, family and work in a center right-wing government. In *Motherhood, social policies and women's activism in Latin America*. Edited by Alejandra Ramm and Jasmine Gideon, 267–90. Switzerland: Palgrave Macmillan.

Golan, Galia. 1997. Militarization and gender: The Israeli experience. *Women's Studies International Forum* 20(5–6): 581–86.

González-Bustamante, Bastián, and Alejandro Olivares. 2016. Cambios de gabinete y supervivencia de los ministros en Chile durante los gobiernos de la Concertación (1990–2010). *Colombia Internacional* 87(May–August): 81–108. DOI: http://dx.doi.org/10.7440/colombiaint87.2016.04.

Gonzalez-Suarez, Mirta. 1994. With patience and without blood: The political struggles of Costa Rican women. In *Women and politics worldwide*. Edited by Barbara J. Nelson and Najma Chowdhury, 174–88. New Haven, CT: Yale University Press.

Goodyear-Grant, Elizabeth, and Julie Croskill. 2011. Gender affinity effects in vote choice in Westminster systems: Assessing "flexible" voters in Canada. *Politics & Gender* 7(2): 233–50.

REFERENCES 269

Graney, Emma. 2016. Watch: Ex-Tory MLA Sandra Jansen slams sexism, harassment, abuse in first statement since crossing floor. *Edmonton Journal* November 22. https://edmontonjournal.com/news/politics/watch-ex-tory-mla-sandra-jansen-slams-sexism-harassment-abuse-in-first-statement-since-crossing-floor (accessed November 18, 2022).

Hasson, Yael, and Noga Dagan Buzaglo. 2019. The care deficit in Israel: What it means and how it can be reduced. Adva Center: January 2019.

Hauser, Orlee. 2010. Women in the Israeli army. *Jewish Journal of Sociology* 52: 33–55.

Hayes, Danny. 2011. When gender and party collide: Stereotyping in candidate trait attribution. *Politics & Gender* 7(2): 133–65.

Hayes, Danny, and Jennifer L. Lawless. 2015. A non-gendered lens? Media, voters, and female candidates in contemporary Congressional elections. *Perspectives on Politics* 13(1): 95–118.

Heath, Roseanna, Leslie Schwindt-Bayer, and Michelle M. Taylor-Robinson. 2005. Women on the sidelines: The rationality of isolating tokens. *American Journal of Political Science* 49(2): 420–36.

Heikkilä, Mia. 2015. Delmål 2: Ekonomisk jämställdhet (Utbildning). In *SOU 2015:86 Forskarrapporter till Jämställdhetsutredningen*. Stockholm: Statens offentliga utredningar.

Heilman, Madeline E. 2001. Description and prescription: How gender stereotypes prevent women's ascent up the organizational ladder. *Journal of Social Issues* 57(4): 657–74.

Hernández Naranjo, Gerardo, and Jesús Guzmán Castillo. 2018. Diverse profiles within single-party cabinets: Portfolios allocation in Costa Rica (1978–2014). In *Government Formation and minister turnover in presidential cabinets: Comparative analysis in the Americas*. Edited by Marcelo Camerlo and Cecilia Martínez-Gallardo, 48–66. London: Routledge.

Herrick, Rebekah, and Almira Sapieva. 1997. Perceptions of women politicians in Kazakhstan. *Women & Politics* 18(4): 27–40.

Herrnson, Paul S., J. Celeste Lay, and Atiya Kai Stokes. 2003. Women running "as women": Candidate gender, campaign issues, and voter-targeting strategies. *Journal of Politics* 65(1): 244–55.

Herzog, Hanna, Michal Shamir, and Alan S. Zuckerman. 1989. The Israeli politician: The social and political bases of Israeli Labor and Herut parties' activists. [In Hebrew.] Jerusalem: Jerusalem Institute for Israel Studies.

Herzog, Hanna. 1999. *Gendering politics: Women in Israel*. Ann Arbor: University of Michigan Press.

Hinojosa, Magda, and Miki Caul Kittilson. 2020. *Seeing women, strengthening democracy: How women in politics foster connected citizens*. New York: Oxford University Press.

Holman, Mirya R., Jennifer L. Merolla, and Elizabeth J. Zechmeister. 2011. Sex, stereotypes, and security: A study of the effects of terrorist threat on assessments of female leadership. *Journal of Women, Politics & Policy* 32(3): 173–92.

Holman, Mirya R., Jennifer L. Merolla, and Elizabeth J. Zechmeister. 2016. Terrorist threat, male stereotypes, and candidate evaluations. *Political Research Quarterly* 69(1): 134–47.

Horowitz, Leonard M., and Bulent Turan. 2008. Prototypes and personal templates: Collective wisdom and individual differences. *Psychological Review* 115(4): 1054–68.

Huddy, Leonie, and Theresa Capelos. 2002. Gender stereotyping and candidate evaluation: Good news and bad news for women politicians. In *The social psychology of politics*. Edited by Victor C. Ottati, R. Scott Tindale, John Edwards, Fred B. Bryant, Linda

270 REFERENCES

Health, Daniel C. O'Connell, and Yolanda Suarez-Balzacar, 29–53. New York: Kluwer Academic/Plenum Publisher.

Huddy, Leonie, and Nadya Terkildsen. 1993a. The consequences of gender stereotypes for women candidates at different levels and types of offices. *Political Research Quarterly* 46(3): 503–25.

Huddy, Leonie, and Nayda Terkildsen. 1993b. Gender stereotypes and the perception of male and female candidates. *American Journal of Political Science* 37(1): 119–47.

INEC. 2015. Encuesta Nacional de Hogares 2015. San José (http://ww.inec.go.cr/educacion).

Inglehart, Ronald, and Pippa Norris. 2003. *Rising tide: Gender equality and cultural change around the world*. Cambridge: Cambridge University Press.

Inmujeres. 2013. *Estadísticas de género 2013. Evolución de los indicadores de género en el período 2009–2013*. Montevideo: MIDES-Instituto Nacional de las Mujeres.

Inter-Parliamentary Union. 2011. Gender-sensitive parliament: A global review of good practice. Report and Document 65. Geneva: IPU.

Inter-Parliamentary Union. 2018. Women in national parliaments: World classification. http://archive.ipu.org/wmn-e/classif-arc.htm (accessed November 18, 2022).

Jacob, Suraj, John A. Scherpereel, and Melinda Adams. 2014. Gender norms and women's political representation: A global analysis of cabinets, 1979–2009. *Governance* 27(2): 321–45.

Jalalzai, Farida. 2013. *Shattered, cracked, or firmly intact? Woman and the executive glass ceiling worldwide*. Oxford: Oxford University Press.

Jalalzai, Farida, and Mona Lena Krook. 2010. Beyond Hillary and Benazir: Women's political leadership worldwide. *International Political Science Review* 31(1): 5–21.

Janovicek, Nancy, and Melanee Thomas. 2018. Canada: Uneven paths to suffrage and women's electoral participation. In *Global handbook of women's political rights*. Edited by Susan Franceschet, Mona Lena Krook, and Netina Tan, 169–84. London: Palgrave.

Jennings, M. Kent. 2006. The gender gap in attitudes and beliefs about the place of women in American political life: A longitudinal, cross-generational analysis. *Politics & Gender* 2(2): 193–219.

Jennings, M. Kent, Laura Stoker, and Jake Bowers. 2009. Politics across generations: Family transmission reexamined. *Journal of Politics* 71(3): 782–99.

Jennings, Will, Shaun Bevan, and Peter John. 2010. The agenda of British government: The speech from the throne, 1911–2008. *Political Studies* 59(1): 74–98.

JNS (Jewish News Syndicate). 2014. IDF Welcomes First Female Combat Doctor in Elite Counterterror Unit. January 9, 2014. https://www.algemeiner.com/2014/01/09/idf-welcomes-first-female-combat-doctor-in-elite-counterterror-unit.

Joignant, Alfredo. 2011. Tecnócratas, technopols y dirigentes de partido: Tipos de agentes y especies de capital en las élites gubernamentales de la Concertación (1990–2010). In *Notables, tecnócratas y mandarines: Elementos de sociología de las élites en Chile (1990–2010)*. Edited by Alfredo Joignant and Pedro Güell, 49–76. Santiago de Chile: Ediciones Universidad Diego Portales.

John, Peter, Anthony Bertelli, Will Jennings, and Shaun Bevan. 2013. *Policy agendas in British politics*. Palgrave Macmillan.

Johnson, Niki. 2006. Actuación parlamentaria y diferencias de género en Uruguay, 2000–2005. *Revista de Ciencia Política de la Universidad de Chile* 46: 173–98.

Johnson, Niki. 2013. *Mujeres en cifras: El acceso de las mujeres a espacios de poder en Uruguay*. Montevideo: Cotidiano Mujer.

REFERENCES 271

Johnson, Niki. 2018. Marginalization of women and male privilege in political representation in Uruguay. In *Gender and representation in Latin America*. Edited by Leslie Schwindt-Bayer, 175–95. New York: Oxford University Press.

Johnson, Niki, and Alejandra Moreni. 2009. *Representación política de las mujeres y la cuota en Uruguay*. Montevideo: Parlamento del Uruguay. Documento elaborado para el I Encuentro Nacional de Mujeres Convencionales, organizado por la Bancada Bicameral Femenina, setiembre 2009.

Johnson, Niki, and Veronica Pérez. 2011. From vanguard to straggler: Women's political representation and gender quotas in Uruguay. In *Diffusion of gender quotas in Latin America and beyond. Advances and setbacks in the last two decades*. Edited by Adriana Piatti-Crocker, 151–72. New York: Peter Lang.

Johnson, Niki, and Veronica Pérez. 2010. *Representación (s)electiva. Una mirada feminista a las elecciones Uruguayas 2009*. Montevideo: Cotidiano Mujer, ICP-FCS-Udelar, UNIFEM.

Johnson, Niki, Veronica Pérez, and Cecilia Rocha. 2015. *Carreras políticas y actuación parlamentaria en Uruguay. Un análisis desde la representación política y de género*. Unpublished research report, ANII Fondo Clemente Estable.

Jones, Mark P. 2004. Quota legislation and the election of women: Learning from the Costa Rican experience. *Journal of Politics* 66(4): 1203–23.

Kahneman, Daniel. 2011. *Thinking fast and slow*. Canada: Doubleday.

Kanter, Rosabeth Moss. 1977. Some effects of proportions on group life. In *The gender gap in psychotherapy*. Edited by Patricia Perri Rieker and Elaine Hilberman Carmen, 53–78. Boston, MA: Springer.

Kanthak, Kristin, and Jonathan Woon. 2015. Women don't run? Election aversion and candidate entry. *American Journal of Political Science* 59(3): 595–612.

Karpowitz, Christopher F., and Tali Mendelberg. 2014. *The silent sex: Gender, deliberation and institutions*. Princeton, NJ: Princeton University Press.

Karpowitz, Christopher F., J. Quin Monson, and Jessica Robinson Preece. 2017. How to elect more women: Gender and candidate success in a field experiment. *American Journal of Political Science* 61(4): 927–43.

Kenig, Ofer, Michael Philippov, and Gideon Rahat. 2013. Party membership in Israel: An overview. *Israel Studies Review* 28(1): 8–32.

Kenny, Meryl. 2014. Gender and political recruitment. In *Deeds and Words: Gendering Politics*. Edited by Rosie Campbell and Sarah Childs, 167–82. Colchester: ECPR Press.

Kereval, Yann P., and Lonna Rae Atkenson. 2013. Explaining the marginalization of women in legislative institutions. *Journal of Politics* 75(4): 980–92.

Kerevel, Yann P., and Lonna Rae Atkeson. 2015. Reducing stereotypes of female political leaders in Mexico. *Political Research Quarterly* 68(4): 732–44.

Kirkland, Patricia A., and Alexander Coppock. 2018. Candidate choice without party labels: New insights from conjoint survey experiments. *Political Behavior* 40(3): 571–91.

Kirkup, Kristy. 2016. Ruth Ellen Brosseau target of personal attacks since being elbowed by Trudeau. *The Canadian Press* May 20, 2016. https://www.cbc.ca/news/politics/brosseau-trudeau-elbowing-attacks-1.3590066.

Kittilson, Miki Caul, and Leslie A. Schwindt-Bayer. 2012. *The gendered effects of electoral institutions: Political engagement and participation*. Oxford: Oxford University Press.

Klein, Uta. 1999. "Our best boys": The gendered nature of civil-military relations in Israel. *Men and Masculinities* 2(1): 47–65.

272 REFERENCES

Koenig, Anne M., Alice H. Eagly, Abigail A. Mitchell, and Riina Ristikari. 2011. Are leader stereotypes masculine? A meta-analysis of three research paradigms. *Psychological Bulletin* 137(4): 616–42.

Kottasová, Ivana. 2021. Angela Merkel endured as others came and went. Now world's crisis manager steps down. CNN January 17, 2021. https://www.cnn.com/2021/01/17/europe/angela-merkel-retirement-germany-analysis-grm-intl/index.html (accessed July 9, 2021).

Kreitzer, Rebecca, and Tracy Osborn. 2019. Women candidate recruitment groups in the States. In *Good reasons to run: Women and political candidacy*. Edited by Shauna Shames, Rachel Bernhard, Mirya Holman, and Dawn Langan Teele, 183–92. Philadelphia: Temple University Press.

Krook, Mona Lena. 2020. *Violence against women in politics*. New York: Oxford University Press.

Krook, Mona Lena, and Diana Z. O'Brien. 2012. All the president's men? The appointment of female cabinet ministers worldwide. *Journal of Politics* 74(3): 840–55.

Kruglanski, Arie W., and Moshe Kroy. 1976. Outcome validity in experimental research: A re-conceptualization. *Representative Research in Social Psychology* 7(2): 166–78.

Lammers, Joris, Ernestine H. Gordijn, and Sabine Otten. 2009. Iron ladies, men of steel: The effects of gender stereotyping on the perception of male and female candidates are moderated by prototypicality. *European Journal of Social Psychology* 39(2): 186–95.

Landaeta Sepúlveda, Romané V. 2019. Women and science: Reflections on female access to university studies in Chile in the 20th century. *Culture and History Digital Journal* 8(1): e003. https://doi.org/10.3989/chdj.2019.003.

LAPOP. 2014. Datos del Barómetro de las Américas. Capítulo Costa Rica. San José, Costa Rica.

Lawless, Jennifer L. 2004. Women, war, and winning elections: Gender stereotyping in the post-September 11th era. *Political Research Quarterly* 57(3): 479–90.

Lay, J. Celeste, Mirya R. Holman, Angela L. Bos, Jill S. Greenlee, Zoe M. Oxley, and Allison Buffett. 2021. TIME for Kids to learn gender stereotypes: Analysis of gender and political leadership in a common social studies resource for children. *Politics & Gender* 17(1): 1–22.

Lee, Peggy M. and Erika Hayes James. 2007. She'-E-OS: Gender effects and investor reactions to the announcements of top executive appointments. *Strategic Management Journal* 28(3): 227–41.

Leeper, Mark Stephen. 1991. The impact of prejudice on female candidates: An experimental look at voter inference. *American Politics Quarterly* 19(2): 248–61.

Levin, Dana S. 2011. "You're always first a girl": Emerging adult women, gender, and sexuality in the Israeli army. *Journal of Adolescent Research* 26(1): 3–29.

Lord, Robert, G., and Jessica E. Dinh. 2014. What have we learned that is critical in understanding leadership perceptions and leader-performance relations? *Industrial and Organizational Psychology* 7(2): 158–77.

Lord, Robert G., Roseanne J. Foti, and Christy L. De Vader. 1984. A test of leadership categorization theory: Internal structure, information processing, and leadership perceptions. *Organizational Behavior and Human Performance* 34(3): 343–78.

Lovenduski, Joni. 2013. United Kingdom. Male dominance unbroken? In *Breaking Male Dominance in Old Democracies*. Edited by Drude Dahlerup and Monique Leyenaar, 72–96. Oxford University Press.

REFERENCES 273

Luna, Elba, Vivian Roza, and Gabriela Vega. 2008. El camino hacia el poder: Ministras Latinoamericanas 1950–2007. Interamerican Development Bank, Programa de Apoyo al Liderazgo y la Representación de la Mujer (PROLID). http://www.iadb.org/docum ent.cfm?id=1415084 (accessed March 17, 2014).

Mansbridge, Jane. 1999. Should blacks represent blacks and women represent women? *Journal of Politics* 61(3): 628–57.

Mardones, Rodrigo. 2007. Chile: Todas íbamos a ser reinas. *Revista de Ciencia Política* 27: 79–96.

Matland, Richard E. 1993. Institutional variables affecting female representation in national legislatures: The case of Norway. *Journal of Politics* 55(3): 737–55.

Matland, Richard E. 1994. Putting Scandinavian equality to the test: An experimental evaluation of gender stereotyping of political candidates in a sample of Norwegian voters. *British Journal of Political Science* 24(2): 273–92.

Matland, Richard E., and Güneş Murat Tezcür. 2011. Women as candidates: An experimental study in Turkey. *Politics & Gender* 7(3): 365–90.

McDermott, Monika L. 1997. Voting cues in low-information elections: Candidate gender as a social information variable in contemporary United States elections. *American Journal of Political Science* 41(1): 270–83.

McDermott, Monika L. 1998. Race and gender cues in low-information elections. *Political Research Quarterly* 51(4): 895–918.

McDermott, Monika L. 2005. Candidate occupations and voter information shortcuts. *Journal of Politics* 67(1): 201–19.

McDermott, Rose. 2011. Internal and external validity. In *Cambridge Handbook of Experimental Political Science*. Edited by James N. Druckman, Donald P. Green, James H. Kuklinski and Arthur Lupia, 27–40. Cambridge University Press.

McDonald, Jared and Melissa Deckman. 2021. New voters, new attitudes: How gen Z Americans rate candidates with respect to generation, gender and race. *Politics, Groups, and Identities*. doi.org/10.1080/21565503.2021.1962372.

MEP. 2009. Ministerio de Educación Pública. Programas de estudios de educación cívica. Tercer ciclo de la educación general básica y educación diversificada. San Jose: MEP.

Mo, Cecilia Hyunjung. 2015. The consequences of explicit and implicit gender attitudes and candidate quality in the calculations of voters. *Political Behavior* 37(2): 357–95.

Montecinos, Verónica. 2001. Feminists and technocrats in the democratization of Latin America: A prolegomenon. *International Journal of Politics, Culture, and Society* 15(1): 175–99.

Mook, Douglas G. 1983. In defense of external invalidity. *American Psychologist* 38(4): 379–87.

Morales Quiroga, Mauricio. 2008. La primera mujer presidenta de Chile: ¿Qué explicó el triunfo de Michelle Bachelet en las elecciones de 2005–2006? *Latin American Research Review* 43(1): 7–32.

Morgan, Jana, and Melissa Buice. 2013. Latin American attitudes toward women in politics: The influence of elite cues, female advancement and individual characteristics. *American Political Science Review* 107(4): 644–62.

Morton, Rebecca B., and Kenneth C. Williams. 2010. *Experimental political science and the study of causality: From nature to the lab*. Cambridge: Cambridge University Press.

Moyser. 2017. https://www150.statcan.gc.ca/n1/pub/89-503-x/2015001/article/14694-eng.htm.

274 REFERENCES

Murphy, Heather. 2018. Picture a leader. Is she a woman? *The New York Times* (online version) March 16, 2018.

Murray, Rainbow. 2014. Quotas for men: Reframing gender quotas as a means of improving representation for all. *American Political Science Review* 108(3): 520–32.

Nogueira Alcalá, Humberto. 2008. La evolución político-constitucional de Chile 1976–2005. *Estudios Constitucionales* 6(2): 325–70.

Norouzian, Reza and Luke Plonsky. 2018. Eta- and partial eta-squared in L2 research: A cautionary review and guide to more appropriate usage. *Second Language Research* 34(2): 257–71.

Nyberg, Anita. 2015. Delmål 2: Ekonomisk jämställdhet (exklusive utbildning). In *SOU 2015:86 Forskarrapporter till Jämställdhetsutredningen*. Stockholm: Statens offentliga utredningar.

Nylund, Mia-Lie, Sandra Håkansson, and Elin Bjarnegård. 2022. The transformative potential of feminist foreign policy: The case of Sweden. *Journal of Women, Politics & Policy*. doi.org/10.1080/1554477X.2022.2113662.

O'Brien, Diana Z. 2015. Rising to the top: Gender, political performance, and party leadership in parliamentary democracies. *American Journal of Political Science* 59(4): 1022–39.

Och, Malliga. 2018. The grand old party of 2016: No longer a party of white men? In *The right women, republican party activists, candidates, and legislators*. Edited by Malliga Och and Shauna L. Shames, 3–24. New York: Praeger.

Och, Malliga, and Shauna L. Shames, eds. 2018. *The right women: Republican party activists, candidates, and legislators*. New York: Praeger.

O'Neill, Brenda. 2013. The Alberta advantage? Women in Alberta politics. In *Stalled: The representation of women in Canadian governments*. Edited by Linda Trimble, Jane Arscott, and Manon Tremblay, 36–54. Vancouver: UBC Press.

O'Neill, Brenda and David Stewart. 2009. Gender and political party leadership in Canada. *Party Politics* 15(6): 737–57.

Ono, Yoskijuni, and Masahiro Yamada. 2020. Do voters prefer gender stereotypic candidates? Evidence from a conjoint survey experiment in Japan. *Political Science Research and Methods* 8: 477–92.

Pacheco, Julianna Sandell. 2008. Political socialization in context: The effect of political competition on youth voter turnout. *Political Behavior* 30(4): 415–36.

Parliament of Canada. 2018. Women Candidates in General Elections—1921 to 2015. https://lop.parl.ca/About/Parliament/FederalRidingsHistory/hfer.asp?Language=E&Search=WomenElection.

Parliament of Canada. 2019. http://www.ourcommons.ca/Committees/en/ERRE.

Paxton, Pamela, Melanie M. Hughes, and Tiffany D. Barnes. 2020. *Women, politics and power: A global perspective*. Lanham, MD: Roman and Littlefield.

Peterson, Erik. 2017. The role of the information environment in partisan voting. *Journal of Politics* 79(4): 1191–1204.

Pew Research. 2018. Gender and leadership. Washington, DC: Pew Research Center. http://www.pewsocialtrends.org/2018/09/20/women-and-leadership-2018/gender-and-leadership-full-report/ (accessed February 26, 2019).

Pew Research. 2015. Women and leadership: Public says women are equally qualified, but barriers persist. Washington, DC: Pew Research Center. http://assets.pewresearch.org/wp-content/uploads/sites/3/2015/01/2015-01-14_women-and-leadership.pdf.

Phillips, Anne. 1995. *The politics of presence*. New York: Oxford University Press.

REFERENCES 275

Pignataro, Adrián. 2017. Lealtad y castigo: Comportamiento electoral en Costa Rica. *Revista Uruguaya de Ciencia Política* 26(2): 7–25.

Pignataro, Adrián, and María José Cascante. 2018. *Los electorados de la democracia costarricense. Percepciones y participación en torno a las elecciones nacionales de 2014.* San José: IFED.

Piscopo, Jennifer. 2018. Parity without equality: Women's political representation in Costa Rica. In *Gender and Representation in Latin America.* Edited by Leslie A. Schwindt-Bayer, 156–74. New York: Oxford University Press.

Piscopo, Jennifer M. 2021. Electing Chile's constitutional convention: "Nothing about us without us." NACLA May 12, 2021 https://nacla.org/news/2021/05/10/chile-constitutional-convention-election-women.

Power, Margaret. 2002. *Right-wing women in Chile: Feminine power and the struggle against Allende, 1964–1973.* University Park: Pennsylvania State University Press.

Programa Estado de la Nación, 2017. Compendio Estadístico. San José, Costa Rica. (https://www.estadonacion.or.cr/estadisticas-index#social).

Quinn, Mattie. 2017. States with the highest and lowest uninsured rates. September 13, 2017. https://www.governing.com/topics/health-human-services/gov-uninsured-rate-census-2016-states.html.

Ragauskas, Rimvydas. 2021. Party-determined viability and gender bias in open-list proportional representation systems. *Politics & Gender* 17(2): 250–76.

Ramm, Alejandra. 2020a. Latin America: A fertile ground for maternalism. In *Motherhood, social policies and women's activism in Latin America.* Edited by Alejandra Ramm and Jasmine Gideon, 13–37. Switzerland: Palgrave Macmillan.

Ramm, Alejandra. 2020b. Technocracy and strategic maternalism: Housing policies, 1990–2014. In *Motherhood, social policies and women's activism in Latin America.* Edited by Alejandra Ramm and Jasmine Gideon, 167–94. Switzerland: Palgrave Macmillan.

Ratliff, Kate A., Liz Redford, John Conway, and Colin Tucker Smith. 2017. Engendering support: Hostile sexism predicts voting for Donald Trump over Hillary Clinton in the 2016 U.S. presidential election. *Group Processes & Intergroup Relations* 22(4): 578–93.

Raventós Vorst, Ciska, Marco Vinicio Fournier, Diego Fernández y Ronald Alfaro. 2012. *Respuestas ciudadanas ante el malestar con la política: Salida, voz y lealtad.* San José: UCR, TSE.

Reingold, Beth, and Jessica Harrell. 2010. The impact of descriptive representation on women's political engagement: Does party matter? *Political Research Quarterly* 63(2): 280–94.

Reyes-Housholder, Catherine. 2018. *Notas COES de política pública: Cuotas de género, repensando la representación política.* Santiago de Chile: Centro de Estudios de Conflicto y Cohesión Social.

Reyes-Housholder, Catherine. 2019. A theory of gender's role on presidential approval ratings in corrupt times. *Political Research Quarterly* 73(3): 540–55.

Rhode, Deborah L. and Barbara Kellerman. 2007. Women and leadership: The state of play. In *Women and Leadership: The State of Play and Strategies for Change.* Edited by Barbara Kellerman and Deborah L. Rhode, 1–62. San Francisco, CA: Jossey-Bass.

Richardson, John T. E. 2011. Eta squared and partial eta squared as measures of effect size in educational research. *Educational Research Review* 6: 135–47.

Ridgeway, Cecilia L. 2001. Gender, status, and leadership. *Journal of Social Issues* 57(4): 637–55.

276   REFERENCES

Roberts, Andrew, Jason Seawright, and Jennifer Cyr. 2013. Do electoral laws affect women's representation? *Comparative Political Studies* 46(12): 1555–81.

Rocha, Cecilia. 2015. La representación sustantiva de género y diversidad sexual en los programas partidarios. In *Renovación, paridad: Horizontes aún lejanos para la representación política de las mujeres en las elecciones Uruguayas 2014*. Edited by Niki Johnson, 177–230. Montevideo: Cotidiano Mujer, ICP-FCS-Udelar.

Rosenbluth, Frances, Joshua Kalla, and Dawn Teele. 2015. The female political career. The World Bank.

Rosenwasser, Shirley M., Robyn R. Rogers, Sheila Fling, Kayla Silvers-Pickens and John Butemeyer. 1987. Attitudes toward women and men in politics: Perceived male and female candidate competencies and participant personality characteristics. *Political Psychology* 8(2): 191–200.

Rosenwasser, Shirley M., and Jana Seale. 1988. Attitudes toward a hypothetical male or female presidential candidate: A research note. *Political Psychology* 9(4): 591–98.

Rosenwasser, Shirley, and Norma Dean. 1989. Gender role and political office: Effects of perceived masculinity/femininity of candidate and political office. *Psychology of Women Quarterly* 13: 77–85.

Sagot Rodríguez, Montserrat. 2010. Demandas desde la exclusión: Representatividad democrática y cuotas de participación política en Costa Rica. *Revista de Ciencias Sociales* 130: 29–43.

Saint-Germain, Michelle A., and Martha I. Morgan. 1991. Equality: Costa Rican women demand "the real thing." *Women and Politics* 11(3): 23–75.

Sanbonmatsu, Kira. 2002. Gender stereotypes and vote choice. *American Journal of Political Science* 46(1): 20–34.

Sanbonmatsu, Kira. 2006. Do parties know that "women win"? Party leader beliefs about women's electoral chances. *Politics & Gender* 2(4): 431–50.

Sanbonmatsu, Kira, and Kathleen Dolan. 2009. Do gender stereotypes transcend party? *Political Research Quarterly* 62(3): 485–94.

Sangster, Joan. 2018. *One hundred years of struggle: The history of women and the vote in Canada*. Vancouver: UBC Press.

Sapiro, Virginia. 1981–82. If US Senator Baker were a woman: An experimental study of candidate images. *Political Psychology* 3(1–2): 61–83.

Sasson-Levy, Orna. 2003. Feminism and military gender practices: Israeli women soldiers in "masculine" roles. *Sociological Inquiry* 73(3): 440–65.

Schneider, Monica C., and Angela L. Bos. 2014. Measuring stereotypes of female politicians. *Political Psychology* 35(2): 245–66.

Schneider, Monica C., Mirya R. Holman, Amanda B. Diekman, and Thomas McAndrew. 2016. Power, conflict, and community: How gendered views of political power influence women's political ambition. *Political Psychology* 37(4): 515–31.

Schwindt-Bayer, Leslie A. 2010. *Political power and women's representation in Latin America*. New York: Oxford University Press.

Schwindt-Bayer, Leslie A. 2018. An introduction to gender and representation in Latin America. In *Gender and representation in Latin America*. Edited by Leslie A. Schwindt-Bayer, 2–16. New York: Oxford University Press.

Sczesny, Sabine, Janine Bosak, Daniel Neff, and Birgit Schyns. 2004. Gender stereotypes and the attribution of leadership traits: A cross-cultural comparison. *Sex Roles* 51(11–12): 631–45.

Shames, Shauna L. 2017. *Out of the running: Why millennials reject political careers and why it matters*. New York: New York University Press.

Shapira, Assaf, Ofer Kenig, Chen Friedberg, and Reut Itzkovitch-Malka. 2016. The Representation of Women in Israeli Politics: A Comparative Perspective. Policy Paper 10E. The Israel Democracy Institute. https://en.idi.org.il/media/4123/the-representation-of-women-in-israeli-politics.pdf (accessed November 18, 2022).

Shingler, Benjamin. 2016. How recent campus controversies forced a debate about rape culture in Quebec. *CBC News* October 24, 2016. http://www.cbc.ca/news/canada/montreal/quebec-university-sexual-assault-rape-culture-1.3817841.

Siavelis, Peter M. 2000. *The president and congress in post-authoritarian Chile: Institutional constraints to democratic consolidation*. University Park: Pennsylvania State University Press.

Sigelman, Lee, and Carol K. Sigelman. 1982. Sexism, racism, and ageism in voting behavior: An experimental analysis. *Social Psychology Quarterly* 45(4): 263–69.

Simbüerger, Elisabeth, and Mike Neary. 2015. Free education! A "live" report from the Chilean student movement, 2011–2014—reform or revolution? [A political sociology for action]. *Journal for Critical Education Policy Studies* 13(2): 150–96.

Skard, Torild, Elina Haavio-Mannila, et al. 1985. Women in parliament. In *Unfinished Democracy: Women in Nordic Politics*. Edited by Elina Haavio-Mannila et al., 51–80. Oxford: Pergamon Press.

Sorek, Tamir, and Alin M. Ceobanu. 2009. Religiosity, national identity and legitimacy: Israel as an extreme case. *Sociology* 43(3): 477–96.

Statistics Sweden. 2016. SCB yrkesstatistik.

Stauffer, Katelyn E. 2021. Public perceptions of women's inclusion and feelings of political efficacy. *American Political Science Review* 115(4): 1226–41.

Strong-Boag, Veronica. 2016. Women suffrage in Canada. *The Canadian Encyclopedia* June 21, 2016. https://www.thecanadianencyclopedia.ca/en/article/suffrage.

Sweet-Cushman, Jennie. 2022. Legislative vs. executive political offices: How gender stereotypes can disadvantage women in either office. *Political Behavior* 44(1): 411–34.

Swirski, Shlomo, Etty Konor-Attias, Barbara Swirski, and Yaron Yecheskel. 2001. Women in the labor force of the Israeli welfare state. *Adva Center: Information on Equality and Social Justice in Israel*, Tel-Aviv July 2001. https://adva.org/wp-content/uploads/2014/09/Women-in-the-Labor-Force.pdf (accessed November 18, 2022).

Tavares, Gustavo M., Filipe Sobral, Rafael Goldszmidt, and Felipe Araújo. 2018. Opening the implicit leadership theories' black box: An experimental approach with conjoint analysis. *Frontiers in Psychology* 9:100 doi:10.3389/fpsyg.2018.00100.

Teele, Dawn Langan, Joshua Kalla, and Frances Rosenbluth. 2018. The ties that double bind: Social roles and women's underrepresentation in politics. *American Political Science Review* 112(3): 525–41.

Tessler, Mark, and Ina Warriner. 1997. Gender, feminism, and attitudes toward international conflict: Exploring relationships with survey data from the Middle East. *World Politics* 49(2): 250–81.

Thames, Frank C., and Margaret S Williams. 2010. Incentives for personal votes and women's representation in legislatures. *Comparative Political Studies* 43(12): 1575–1600.

The Canadian Encyclopedia. 2018. Women and the quiet revolution. October 11, 2018. https://www.thecanadianencyclopedia.ca/en/article/women-and-quiet-revolution (accessed November 18, 2022).

278 REFERENCES

Thomas, Gwynn. 2011. *Contesting legitimacy in Chile: Familial ideals, citizenship, and political struggle, 1970–1990*. University Park: Pennsylvania State University Press.

Thomas, Gwynn. 2014. Women presidents and troubled coalitions: How party crisis shapes presidential agendas and government capacity. Paper presented at the ECPR Joint Sessions Workshops, Salamanca, Spain, April 10–15, 2014.

Thomas, Gwynn. 2018. Working within a gendered political consensus: Uneven progress on gender and sexuality rights in Chile. In *Seeking rights from the left: Gender, sexuality, and the Latin American pink tide*. Edited by Elisabeth Jay Friedman, 115–43. Duke University Press.

Thomas, Melanee. 2018. In crisis or decline? Selecting women to lead provincial parties in government. *Canadian Journal of Political Science* 51(2): 379–403.

Thomas, Melanee. 2019. Governing as if women mattered: Rachel Notley as Alberta premier. In *Doing politics differently? Women premiers in Canada's provinces and territories*. Edited by Sylvia Bashevkin, 250–74. Vancouver: UBC Press.

Thomas, Melanee, and Marc André Bodet. 2013. Sacrificial lambs, women candidates, and district competitiveness in Canada. *Electoral Studies* 32(1): 153–66.

Thomsen, Danielle M. 2020. Ideology and gender in U.S. House elections. *Political Behavior* 42: 415–42.

Thumala Olave, María Angélica. 2007. *Riqueza y piedad: El Catolicismo de la elite económica Chilena*. Santiago de Chile: Random House Mondadori.

Toro Maureira, Sergio, and Macarena Valenzuela Beltrán. 2018. Chile 2017: Ambiciones, estrategias y expectativas en el estreno de las nuevas reglas electorales. *Revista de Ciencia Política* 38(2): 207–32.

Tremblay, Manon. 2013. Hitting a glass ceiling? Women in Quebec politics. In *Stalled: The representation of women in Canadian governments*. Edited by Linda Trimble, Jane Arscott, and Manon Tremblay, 192–213. Vancouver: UBC Press.

Tremblay, Manon, and Daniel Stockemer. 2013. Women's ministerial careers in cabinet, 1921–2010: A look at socio-demographic traits and career experiences. *Canadian Public Administration* 56(4): 523–41.

Trimble, Linda, Jane Arscott, and Manon Tremblay, eds. 2013. *Stalled: The representation of women in Canadian governments*. Vancouver: UBC Press.

Trynacity, Kim. 2018. "A wake-up call": Documents detail litany of threats against Premier Rachel Notley. *CBC News* May 4, 2018. https://www.cbc.ca/news/canada/edmonton/notley-premier-threats-security-1.4644989.

TSE-IFED. 2010. Tribunal Supremo de Elecciones-Instituto de Formación y Estudios en Democracia. Procesos Electorales Estudiantiles. San José: TSE.

Turcotte, Martin. 2011. Women and education. In *Women in Canada: A gender-based statistical report*. Statistics Canada. https://www150.statcan.gc.ca/n1/en/pub/89-503-x/2010001/article/11542-eng.pdf?st=LDNYn08l.

Udelar. 2014. *Estadísticas básicas 2013 de la Universidad de la República*. Montevideo: Dirección General de Planeamiento-Universidad de la República.

Ulrich, Bernd. 2017. How Angela Merkel has redefined leadership. Carnegie Europe. September 22, 2017. https://carnegieeurope.eu/strategiceurope/73195 (accessed July 9, 2021).

UNDP. 2018. *Representación política de mujeres en el legislativo: Análisis de las cuotas de género en las elecciones parlamentarias de 2017*. Santiago de Chile: UNDP Chile.

Undurraga, Tomás. 2014. *Divergencias: Trayectorias del neoliberalismo en Chile y Argentina*. Santiago de Chile: Ediciones Universidad Diego Portales.

Valdini, Melody Ellis. 2013. Electoral institutions and the manifestation of bias: The effect of the personal vote on the representation of women. *Politics & Gender* 9(1): 76–92.

Valdini, Melody E. 2019. *The inclusion calculation: Why men appropriate women's representation*. New York: Oxford University Press.

Valenzuela, J. Samuel. 1992. Democratic consolidation in post-transitional settings: Notion, process and facilitating conditions. In *Issues in Democratic Consolidation*. Edited by Scott Mainwaring, Guillermo O'Donnell and J. Samuel Valenzuela, 57–104. Notre Dame, IN: University of Notre Dame Press.

Valitutti Chavarría, Gina, Saskia Salas Calderón, Ziomara Castro Chaves, Erika Rojas Calderón, and Marianela Vargas Acuna. 2015. Segundo estado de los derechos humanos de las mujeres en Costa Rica. Instituto Nacional de las Mujeres en Costa Rica (INAMU).

Verge, Tània, Ana Espírito-Santo, and Nina Wiesehomeier. 2015. The symbolic impact of women's representation on citizens' political attitudes: Measuring the effect through survey experiments. Paper presented at the 4th European Conference on Politics and Gender, Uppsala, Sweden, June 11–14.

Wängnerud, Lena. 1998. *Politikens andra sida. Om kvinnorepresentation i Sveriges riksdag*. Göteborg: Statsvetenskapliga institutionen.

Wängnerud, Lena. 2000. Testing the politics of presence: Women's representation in the Swedish Riksdag. *Scandinavian Political Studies* 23(1): 67–91.

Watson, Robert P., Alicia Jencik, and Judith A. Selzer. 2005. Women world leaders: Comparative analysis and gender experiences. *Journal of International Women's Studies* 7(2): 53–76.

Waylen, Georgina. 2000. Gender and democratic politics: A comparative analysis of consolidation in Argentina and Chile. *Journal of Latin American Studies* 32(3): 765–93.

Waylen, Georgina. 2016. *Gender, institutions, and change in Bachelet's Chile*. Palgrave Macmillan.

Williams, Blair. 2021. A tale of two women: A comparative media analysis of UK Prime Ministers Margaret Thatcher and Theresa May. *Parliamentary Affairs* 74(2): 398–420.

Wylie, Kristin N., and Pedro dos Santos. 2016. A law on paper only: Electoral rules, parties, and the persistent underrepresentation of women in Brazilian legislatures. *Politics & Gender* 12(3): 415–42.

Yarkoney Sorek, Ayala. 2018. Leaders' gender and state conflict. PhD dissertation, Texas A&M University.

Young, Iris Marion. 2000. *Inclusion and democracy*. Oxford: Oxford University Press.

Yuval-Davis, Nira. 1987. Front and rear: The sexual division of labour in the Israeli Army. In *Women, state and ideology: Studies from Africa and Asia*. Edited by Haleh Afshar, 186–204. London: Palgrave Macmillan UK. https://doi.org/10.1007/978-1-349-18650-1_11 (accessed May 14, 2020).

Zerán, Faride (ed.). 2018. *Mayo feminista. La rebelión contra el patriarcado*. Santiago de Chile: Lom.

Zhang, Yan, and Hongyan Qu. 2016. The impact of CEO succession with gender change on firm performance and successor early departure: Evidence from China's publicly listed companies in 1997–2010. *Academy of Management Journal* 59(5): 1945–68.

280 REFERENCES

Zhu, David H., Wei Shen, and Amy J. Hillman. 2014. Recategorization into the in-group: The appointment of demographically different new directors and their subsequent positions on corporate boards. *Administrative Science Quarterly* 59(2): 240–70.

Ziri, Danielle. 2016. 48% of parents unhappy with education system. *Jerusalem Post* August 28, 2016. https://www.jpost.com/Israel-News/48-percent-of-parents-unha ppy-with-education-system-466278 (accessed August 25, 2020).

נשים בכנסת". 2020. "בכנסת ישראל". https:// main.knes set.gov.il/ about/ hist ory/ pages/ womeninknesset.aspx.

Index

For the benefit of digital users, indexed terms that span two pages (e.g., 52–53) may, on occasion, appear on only one of those pages.

Note: Tables and figures are indicated by *t* and *f* following the page number

Alberta, 15*t*, 236, 241, 246–47, 249. *See also* Canada
  incorporation of women in government, 100, 101–2, 233
  Notley, Rachel, 102
  parity cabinet, 101–3
analytical strategy, 28, 39–40, 41*t*, 230, 235–41, 246–47, 248

baseline control, 5, 22, 23–24, 27, 38, 39, 40, 57–58, 65–66, 70–71, 235, 251, 256
  Candidate Gender, larger effect than party, 92–93, 178, 179–80, 219–20, 231*t*, 233–34, 235, 251
  My Party, effect of, 20, 235–41, 237*t*, 243*t*, 252–53, 260 (*see also* California; Canada; Chile (My Coalition); Costa Rica; England; Israel; Sweden; Texas; United States; Uruguay)
  Party Label, effect of, 231*t*, 235 (*see also* California; Chile (Coalition Label); Costa Rica; Sweden; Texas United States)
  Party, larger effect than Candidate Gender, 20, 21, 68, 72–73, 86, 88, 92–93, 110–11, 115–16, 136–37, 150–51, 157, 164, 173–74, 178, 186, 194–95, 199, 214–15, 229, 231*t*, 235–41, 249–51, 252–53, 259, 260
  Party Platform, effect of, 20, 231*t*, 235, 249 (*see also* California; Canada; Chile (Coalition Platform); Costa Rica; England; Israel; Sweden; Texas; United States; Uruguay)

California, 15*t*, 19–20, 246–47. *See also* United States
  incorporation of women in government, 164, 169–70, 233
  My Party, significance of, 174–75, 179
  Party Label, significance of, 173n.18
  Party Platform, significance of, 173–74, 178
  traditional leadership templates, lack of, 164, 180

campaign finance, 7, 167–68, 208, 259
Canada, 15*t*, 18–20, 233–34, 254–55. *See also* Alberta; Quebec
  Candidate Gender, effect of, 99, 109, 114, 115–16, 117, 119
  economic policy, 112–14, 116, 119
  electoral rules, 104–5
  energy policy, 103, 113–15, 116, 117–18, 119
  environment policy, 103
  gender quotas, 104
  health policy, 103, 112–14, 115–16, 117–18
  incorporation of women in government, 98–99, 100, 101–2, 113–14
  in-group effects of party, 106, 110–11
  in-group effects of sex, 106, 109–10, 114–15
  mother's education and job, effect of, 117–18
  My Party, significance of, 110–11
  parity cabinet, 98, 101–2, 108, 111, 233
  party issue ownership, 112, 115–16
  Party Platform, significance of, 110, 115–16
  social welfare policy, 100, 102–3, 112, 233–34
  traditional leadership templates, lack of, 111, 115, 116, 119, 233–34
  women's education and employment, 105
  women's rights policy, 99, 113–15, 119
Candidate Gender, effect of as driver of attitudes toward candidate. *See* baseline control
Chile, 15*t*, 18–20, 233, 246–47
  Candidate Gender, effect of, 214–16, 217, 219–20, 223–24
  coalition issue ownership, 219–20
  Coalition Label, significance of, 214–15, 217n.12
  Coalition Platform, significance of, 214–15, 219–20
  economic policy, 218, 219–21
  education policy, 205–6, 218, 219–22
  electoral rules, 208, 210, 214, 216
  feminism in, 205–6, 224
  gender quota law, 206–7, 208, 211, 223–24, 225

282 INDEX

Chile (*cont.*)
 incorporation of women in government, 205–9, 211, 224, 233
 infrastructure policy, 218, 219–21
 in-group effects of party, 217, 221
 in-group effects of sex, 216, 220–21
 mother's education and job, effect of, 221–23
 My Coalition, significance of, 217
 parity cabinet, 207
 party system fragmentation, 210–11, 217
 student protests in, 205–6, 210, 224
 traditional leadership templates, lack of, 214–16, 217, 219, 221, 223–24
 women's education and employment, 209
 women's rights policy, 206–7, 211–12, 218–21, 222
Clinton, Hillary, 162–63, 184, 255n.5
coalition government, 28
Costa Rica, 15t, 18–20, 24, 28, 246–47
 Candidate Gender, effect of, 57–58, 66–67, 69–71, 72–73, 74
 childcare policy, 69–71, 72
 economic policy, 60, 69–70n.26
 education policy, 60, 68–71, 72–73
 electoral rules, 59
 gender quota law, 58–59
 incorporation of women in government, 57–60, 68–69, 230–33
 in-group effects of party, 67–68, 71–72
 in-group effects of sex, 67, 71
 military, lack of, 60, 69
 mother's education, effect of, 73–74
 My Party, significance of, 67–68, 71–72
 party identification, lack of, 65–66
 Party Label, significance of, 57–58, 65–67, 68, 70–71, 73n.32
 Party Platform, significance of, 57–58, 65–67, 68, 70–71, 73n.32
 party system fragmentation, 59, 63
 security/crime policy, 60, 68, 69, 70–71
 social welfare policy, 57–58, 60, 68
 traditional leadership templates, lack of, 57–58, 65–67, 68, 72, 73–74
 unemployment policy, 69–71
 women's education and employment, 62
 women's rights policy, 63, 70n.27

dataset, 29

electoral rules, 11, 13, 19, 23–24, 29, 40, 234–35, 252–53. *See also* Canada; Chile; Costa Rica; England; Israel; Sweden; United States; Uruguay

England, 15t, 18–20, 233, 246–47
 Brexit, 146
 Candidate Gender, effect of, 141–42, 148–49, 150–51, 153, 155–56, 159–60
 economic policy, 153–54, 155, 156–57
 education policy, 134, 154, 156–57, 158n.21
 electoral rules and nomination procedures, 143, 153
 energy policy, 154, 155–56, 157
 gender equality policy, 146
 gender quotas, 143
 incorporation of women in government, 142–43, 144, 145–46, 147, 153–54, 233
 infrastructure policy, 155–56, 156n.17, 157
 in-group effects of party, 151, 156
 in-group effects of sex, 151, 156
 mother's education and job, effect of, 158–59
 My Party, significance of, 151, 159–60, 236n.6
 parity cabinets (Scotland, Wales), 147
 party issue ownership, 142, 148–49, 157, 159–60
 Party Platform, significance of, 150–51, 157, 159–60
 traditional leadership templates, evidence of, 141–42, 159–60
 traditional leadership templates, lack of, 142, 152–53, 160
 women party leaders, 145–46, 147, 152
 women Prime Ministers, 142, 144, 145, 152
 women's education and employment, 144–45
 women's rights policy, 154, 155, 156–57, 158n.21
ethics approval, 37, 37n.9
experimental control. *See* baseline control
experiment implementation, 4–5, 23–25, 37–39, 62, 83, 106–7, 128–31, 145, 147, 171, 191–92, 209, 212
 debriefing in, 37–38
 randomized blocks in, 24–25
exposure to women in government, 4–5, 8, 230–33, 254, 255, 260. *See also* incorporation of women in government
external validity, 23–24, 27–28, 31, 256

family background, 4, 12, 14, 20, 32t, 39–40, 241, 244t
 effect of mother's education
  in Canada, 106, 117–19
  in Chile, 222
  in Costa Rica, 73–74
  in England, 158–59
  in Israel, 93–94, 95, 96
  in Sweden, 200

in the United States, 181–82
in Uruguay, 138–39
effect of mother's employment
in Canada, 106, 117–19
in Chile, 221–22
in Costa Rica, 73–74
in England, 158–59
in Israel, 95
in Sweden, 200
in the United States, 181–82
in Uruguay, 138–39

gendered policy competence stereotypes, 4–5,
9–10, 18–19, 247–49
in Canada, 112
in Costa Rica, 72
in Israel, 90–91, 93, 248
in Sweden, 202
in the United States, 164, 180–81
gender issue ownership, 9
gender quotas, 8, 18, 235n.4, 256, 259. See also
Canada; Chile; Costa Rica; England;
United States; Uruguay
gender stereotypes, 4–5, 10, 14, 248–49, 248n.13

Implicit Leadership Theory, 6
incongruity cost of women candidates, 253
incorporation of women in government, 13, 18,
19–20, 22–23, 31, 40, 230–33, 252–53,
254, 255, 259–60. See also Alberta;
California; Canada; Chile; Costa
Rica; England; exposure to women in
government; Israel; Quebec; Sweden;
Texas; United States; Uruguay
in-group effects of party, 4, 11, 14, 20, 39–40,
235–41, 237t, 243t, 252–53. See also
Canada; Chile; Costa Rica; England;
Israel; Sweden; United States; Uruguay
in-group effects of sex, 4, 14, 20, 39–40, 236,
237t, 243t, 251, 252–53, 260. See also
Canada; Chile; Costa Rica; England;
Israel; Sweden; United States; Uruguay
Israel, 15t, 20, 24, 26, 28, 233–34, 246–47, 249,
252, 253–55, 260
Candidate Gender, effect of, 77–78, 84–86,
90–93, 95
childcare policy, 79
education policy, 89, 90, 91–93, 95
electoral rules, 77–78
energy policy, 89–94
gender gap in partisan voting, 81–82
incorporation of women in government, 77–79,
81–82, 85–86, 95–96, 233

in-group effects of party, 88, 92
in-group effects of sex, 82, 86–87, 91, 95, 236
military service for men, 80–81, 96
military service for women, 77–78, 80–81, 96
mother's education, effect of, 93–94, 95, 241
My Party, significance of, 88, 92, 93
party issue ownership, 92–93
Party Platform, significance of, 85–86, 92–93
security policy, 89, 90, 91–94
security threat, 77–78, 80, 89, 96, 233–34, 252
traditional leadership templates, evidence of,
77–78, 84–85, 86–87, 90–91, 93, 96, 233,
248, 251, 260
women's employment, 79
women's equal rights law, 78
women's rights policy, 90–93

low information context. See policy
information, effect of

Matland, Richard, 22–23, 31–37, 246, 253–54
mental templates of leadership, 3–5, 7
change in, 4, 6, 8
context and, 4, 13, 13f, 14–19
exposure to women in government and, 4–5,
8, 13, 18, 19–20 (see also incorporation
of women in government)
family background and, 4, 12, 14, 20 (see also
family background)
government's policy agenda and, 4, 9, 13, 20
(see also national government policy
agenda)
heuristics, 6–7, 10, 11, 26n.3, 28, 181, 198–99,
248–49
in-groups and, 4, 11, 14, 20 (see also in-group
effects of parties; in-groups effects of sex)
institutions and, 10–11, 13, 19 (see also
electoral rules; parliamentary systems;
presidential systems)
role congruity and, 12, 14, 20 (see also role
congruity)
specificity, 6
Merkel, Chancellor Angela, 3, 233, 254

national government policy agenda, 4, 9, 13,
18–19, 20, 40, 233–34, 251, 252–53,
254–55, 256–60
in Canada, 103–4, 106
in Chile, 205–6, 208–9, 210, 211–12
in Costa Rica, 57–58, 60–61
defense policy, role in, 4, 9, 10, 13, 18–19, 20,
40, 60, 80–81, 106, 233–34, 251, 252–53,
254–55, 260

284 INDEX

national government policy agenda (*cont.*)
 in England, 146
 in Israel, 80–81, 96
 social welfare policy, role in, 4, 9, 13, 18–19,
   40, 57–58, 60, 68, 74–75, 106, 139–40,
   203, 233–34, 252–53, 254–55
 in Sweden, 188–89
 in the United States, 176, 233–34
 in Uruguay, 121–22, 123–24, 139–40
Norway, 22–23, 246, 253–54

parliamentary systems, 10–11, 13, 40, 234,
   252–53
partial eta squared (η_p^2), 39, 230, 231*t*
party effects. *See* baseline control
party issue ownership, 20, 249, 260
party leader gender bias, 104, 112, 119, 127,
   140, 143, 160, 168, 170, 225, 235, 253,
   257, 259
party selectorates. *See* party leader gender bias
polarization, 27–28, 179, 184, 188, 191, 204, 256
policy domains, 14. *See also* stereotypically
   feminine policy; stereotypically
   masculine policy
policy information, effect of, 9–10, 14, 20, 22–23,
   247–49, 249*t*, 253–54, 260
 in Canada, 114–15, 249
 in Chile, 219, 221
 in Costa Rica, 69–70
 in England, 141–42, 154–55, 156–57
 in Israel, 90–91, 93, 248–49
 in Sweden, 198–99
 in the United States, 176–78, 181, 248
 in Uruguay, 135–36
political socialization, 31, 61
presidential systems, 10–11, 13, 40, 234, 252–53

Quebec, 15*t*, 246–47. *See also* Canada
 incorporation of women in government,
   100–3, 233
 Marois, Pauline, 102, 111, 233
 parity cabinet, 101–2
questionnaire, 5, 23, 29–30, 40
 background questions about participant, 29
 manipulation checks, 29, 30*t*
 policy evaluation questions, 29–30

recategorization theory, 11, 82, 106, 111, 127,
   132–33, 235–41, 237*t*
role congruity, 12, 14, 230, 231*t*, 246–47, 247*t*
 in Canada, 105, 109, 246–47
 in Chile, 214–16, 246–47
 in Costa Rica, 65–67, 72, 246–47

in England, 150, 151–52, 154–55, 246–47
in Israel, 85, 246–47
levels of posts, 12, 14, 20, 29, 246–47, 247*t*,
   252, 259, 260
in Sweden, 195, 246–47
in the United States, 165, 168, 173, 174, 175,
   246–47
in Uruguay, 131–32, 133–34, 137, 246–47

schema, 5–6, 23, 72, 116, 133–34, 135–36, 196,
   219, 248–49, 253–54
social categorization theory. *See*
   recategorization theory
social desirability bias, 22, 38, 131–32
socialization within the home. *See* family
   background
speeches of candidates. *See* treatments
   (speeches)
stereotypically feminine policy, 9–10, 14, 20,
   22–23, 27–28, 247–49, 259
 in Canada, 106, 114, 115–17
 in Chile, 219, 220–21
 in Costa Rica, 60, 72–73
 in England, 146, 154
 in Israel, 78–79, 81, 93–94, 96, 248
 in Sweden, 198, 202
 in the United States, 164, 176–77, 184
 in Uruguay, 121–22, 123–24, 133–34, 135–36
stereotypically masculine policy, 9–10, 14, 20,
   22–23, 27–28, 247–49, 252, 253–54,
   256–57, 259
 in Canada, 106, 114, 116–17, 119, 249
 in Chile, 219, 220–21
 in Costa Rica, 61, 69–70, 72–73
 in England, 146, 153–54
 in Israel, 81, 93–94, 95, 96, 248–49
 in Sweden, 198
 in the United States, 164, 176–78, 184, 248
 in Uruguay, 124, 133–36
study participants, 30–37, 32*t*, 41*t*, 255
 Canada, 107*t*, 108
 Chile, 213*t*, 217
 Costa Rica, 62–63, 64*t*
 England, 142, 147, 148, 149*t*
 Israel, 83, 84*t*
 socioeconomic background of, 31–37, 32*t*
 Sweden, 192–93, 193*t*
 United States, 171, 172*t*
 Uruguay, 128, 129*t*, 138
 young adults as, rationale for, 22–23, 31
Sweden, 15*t*, 19–20, 246–47
 Candidate Gender, effect of, 186, 194–95,
   196, 198, 199, 200, 201, 203

coalition governments, 188–89
economic policy, 190
education policy, 190, 198n.12
electoral rules, 187, 194–95
energy policy, 198, 202
environment policy, 190–91
feminist party leaders, 185–86, 188, 203
feminist perspective in policy, 188–89
gender equality policy, 186, 198–99, 202–3, 203n.15
health policy, 186, 190, 198, 199, 200, 203n.15
incorporation of women in government, 186–89, 197–98, 201, 203–4, 230–33
in-group effects of party, 195–96
in-group effects of sex, 195, 198–99
masculine and feminine policy areas, 197, 202
mother's education, effect of, 200
My Party, significance of, 195–96
party ideology, 186, 203
party issue expertise, 203
Party Label, significance of, 195–96n.8
Party Platform, significance of, 194–95, 198, 199, 203n.15
party system, 187
security policy, 190–91, 198, 200, 202
social welfare policy, 195
traditional leadership templates, evidence of, 196, 203
traditional leadership templates, lack of, 194, 201, 203
women's education and employment, 189–90, 202

Texas, 15*t*, 233–34, 246–47, 253–55, 260. *See also* United States
incorporation of women in government, 164, 169–70, 233
infrastructure policy, 164, 177–80, 184
My Party, significance of, 174–75, 179
Party Label, significance of, 173–74
Party Platform, significance of, 178
security policy, 164, 177–80, 184, 248
traditional leadership templates, evidence of, 20, 164, 177–78, 181, 233, 248, 251, 260
traditional leadership templates, 13–14. *See also* California; Canada; Chile; Costa Rica; England; Israel; Sweden; Texas; United States; Uruguay
evidence of, 20, 233–34, 248–49, 251, 252–53
lack of, 19–20, 21, 233–35, 241, 246–47, 249, 252–54, 257
treatments (speeches), 5, 23, 24–25, 25*f*, 28

basis of formulating, 23, 27–28, 64–65, 83, 106, 128, 146, 170–71, 190, 212, 256
candidate bio, 23, 24–27
Candidate Gender treatment, 26–27
example speeches, 29, 40
Party Label treatment, 23, 28
Party Platform treatment, 27–28

United States, 15*t*, 19. *See also* California; Texas
Candidate Gender, effect of, 164, 173, 174–75, 176–78, 179–80, 183–84
electoral rules and primaries, 167, 173, 183–84
gender differences in attitudes about women in politics, 166–67
gender quotas, lack of, 167
health policy, 176–77, 178–79
incorporation of women in government, 164, 165–68, 169–70
infrastructure policy, 164, 176, 177–80, 184
in-group effects of party, 174–75, 179–80
in-group effects of sex, 174, 179
My Party, significance of, 164, 174–75, 179–80, 184
Obama, Barack, 164, 165
party differences, about promoting women, 163, 166–67, 168, 183–84
party differences, in attitudes about women in politics, 166–67, 168
party differences, in election of women, 167, 169
Party Label, significance of, 173–74
Party Platform, significance of, 173–74, 178, 183
Pelosi, Nancy, Speaker of the House, 169, 184, 233
race and ethnicity, 29, 172*t*, 182–83
security policy, 164, 176–80, 183, 184
traditional leadership templates, evidence of, 164, 177–78, 181
traditional leadership templates, lack of, 164, 173–74, 175, 180
Trump, Donald, election of, 162–63, 165, 255n.5
women's education and employment, 165
women's rights policy, 164, 176–80, 181–82, 183, 184
Uruguay, 15*t*, 19–20, 233–34, 246–47, 254–55
agriculture policy, 134–37
Candidate Gender, effect of, 122, 131–32, 135–37, 138–39
childcare policy, 135–37
economic policy, 134–36, 138–39
education policy, 135–37, 138–39
electoral rules, 122–23, 124, 132

286 INDEX

Uruguay (*cont.*)
gender differences in attitudes about women in politics, 126–27
gender quota law, 121–22, 125–26, 127, 130
incorporation of women in government, 121–22, 124–26, 129–30, 132, 134, 233
in-group effects of party, 133, 136
in-group effects of sex, 132–33, 136
My Party, significance of, 133, 136
party elites, traditional leadership templates in, 127, 140
party issue ownership, 122, 137
Party Platform, significance of, 136–37
social welfare programs, 121–22, 123–24, 139–40, 233–34
traditional leadership templates, lack of, 122, 132, 133, 135–36, 137–38, 139–40, 233–34
women's education and employment, 121–22, 127, 138, 139–40
women's rights policy, 136n.25

violence against women in politics, 259
voter turnout, 257, 258*f*

women presidents, 9–11
Bachelet, Michelle, 206–7, 218–19, 222–23, 224, 233, 256–57
Chinchilla, Laura, 58, 59–60, 75, 256–57
Fernández, Cristina, 233
Rousseff, Dilma, 233
women prime ministers, 10–11
Andersson, Magdalena, 188
Campbell, Kim, 102
May, Theresa, 142, 144, 145, 256–57
Meir, Golda, 79
Thatcher, Margaret, 142, 144, 154
Truss, Liz, 142, 144
women's rights policy, 251, 256–57. *See also* Canada; Chile; Costa Rica; England; Israel; Sweden (gender equality policy); United States; Uruguay